THE AMERICAN PEOPLE

A HISTORY

THE
AMERICAN PEOPLE

A HISTORY

BY

THOMAS JEFFERSON WERTENBAKER

EDWARDS PROFESSOR OF AMERICAN HISTORY
PRINCETON UNIVERSITY

NEW YORK
CHARLES SCRIBNER'S SONS
1928

TO MY WIFE

REFACE

es ago English-speaking America con-
le colonies stretching out at intervals
disunited, fearing the Indians, striving
less. To-day it has become a great nation,
tlantic to the Pacific, filled with populous
farms, united, prosperous, powerful. The
kable change is fascinating. That American
t interest and romance is about as far from
g can be. This misconception has so widely
use we have just been passing through that
e when, in order to establish new facts, it was necessary to
manuscripts, to publish valuable documents, and to
onographs on innumerable topics.

students and writers of history are becoming aware of
the futility of writing history which only historians read.
They are making a conscious and determined effort to reinvest
the story of America with the charm which naturally and right-
fully belongs to it. They do not intend to do this with a sacrifice of truth or historical perspective. They are not committed
to any form of propaganda. Their sole desire is to tell the story
with as much of the interest and glamour as may be possible
to the imagination of the writer. With the purpose of con-
tributing ever so slightly to this important work this book
has been written.

To compress American history into one volume has required
a very rigid selection and a definite plan. Facts of secondary
importance have often been passed over to make room for
more essential matters. It is hoped that sufficient space has

been devoted to fundamental developments to mak
the reconstruction of some of the crucial scenes of o
and the depiction of the men who built the nation.

To Professor Charles G. Osgood, Professor Clifton
and Professor Edward S. Corwin, all of Princeton Un
who have rendered invaluable assistance in the making
book, the author offers his sincere and grateful thank

THOMAS J. WERTENBA

CONTENTS

CHAPTER   PAGE

I. ACROSS THE ATLANTIC 1

II. THE SCHEME OF EMPIRE 16

III. THE STRUGGLE FOR SELF-GOVERNMENT 25

IV. THE BATTLE FOR A CONTINENT 36

V. THE ASSAULT ON AMERICAN LIBERTY 50

VI. THE REVOLUTION 63

VII. UNDER THE ARTICLES 96

VIII. THE CONVENTION 11

IX. LAUNCHING THE GOVERNMENT . . . .

X. DEMOCRACY TRIUMPHANT . . . .

XI. WORLD TRADE 18

XII. WAR OF 1812 197

XIII. THE NEW ENGLAND REVOLUTION 214

XIV. RISE OF THE NEW WEST 229

XV. THE DIVIDING LINE 241

XVI. PASSING OF THE VIRGINIA DYNASTY 251

XVII. THE REIGN OF ANDREW JACKSON 272

XVIII. MANIFEST DESTINY 292

XIX. CONFLICT IRREPRESSIBLE 314

XX. CIVIL WAR 340

XXI. RECONSTRUCTION 366

CONTENTS

CHAPTER		PAGE
XXII.	The Changing Order	382
XXIII.	A Nation Moving West	396
XXIV.	Dominion over Palm and Pine	415
XXV.	The New Freedom	433
XXVI.	The European Maelstrom	440
XXVII.	Problems—Solved and Unsolved	463
	Index	473

THE AMERICAN PEOPLE

A HISTORY

CHAPTER I

ACROSS THE ATLANTIC

ABORIGINAL America was a land of wild beauty—forests stretching out interminably, like green blankets; great prairies, mile upon mile of yellow grass over which wandered herds of buffaloes; deserts, dotted with sage-brush and chaparral and inhabited only by rattlesnakes and coyotes; wide plateaus topped by mountain ranges; rivers, tumbling down mountain defiles or flowing through the plains to the ocean.

Here lived a savage race of men, with reddish skin, high cheek-bones, black eyes, and straight black hair. So meagre were the returns of their crude agriculture, their hunting and fishing, that a region which now sustains 115,000,000 people, then sustained less than 500,000. The Indians were divided into great families, differing widely in language, customs, stature and dress, and each family was subdivided into numerous nations or tribes.

The village, with its collection of wigwams, was the centre of Indian life. Here could be seen the warrior engaged in fashioning his bow and arrow, or laboriously making his war-club and tomahawk, or stripping the bark from the birch-tree for his canoe, or bending the pliant bough into the snow-shoe; here the squaw cultivated the soil with shells and sticks, ground the corn in the wooden mortars, dried the meat brought back from the hunt, made the skins into moccasins or other clothing, gathered wood for the fire, chiselled out the crude wooden household utensils.

The wigwams were very simple. Poles were planted in a circle, the small ends fastened together and the whole covered with skins or bark. At the top an opening was left for ventilation and to permit the smoke to escape. The villages were often surrounded by palisades or closely planted beams. The Iroquois, a powerful confederation of central New York, had more pretentious dwellings, made of strips of bark laid over

1

a framework of poles or saplings. Some of these structures were one hundred feet in length.

The Western tribes depended largely for their food upon the buffalo, and life and industry were almost wholly related to this animal. It furnished not only meat for food, but hides for clothing. The Indians moved from place to place, following the herds, and so made little advance in agriculture. In the woodlands the Western Indians dwelt in cone-shaped wigwams, in the plains in earth lodges and light teepees.

Far to the southwest were the Pueblo Indians of Arizona and New Mexico. Here the natives brought down water from the mountains to the arid plains in artificial ways. By this means they raised corn, pumpkins, beans, and other vegetables. The Pueblo dwellings, built of clay baked in the sun, were made like apartment-houses. Some were several stories high, each story set back a little from the one below. To enter one had to climb to the top by a ladder and let oneself down through the roof.

The civilization of northern and central North America, crude though it was, unquestionably had required many centuries for its development, just how many no one knows. Had the Indians been left to work out alone their own destiny, it would probably have been many centuries more before they learned the use of metals and emerged from barbarity. But fate willed it that, while they were still in the Stone Age, the discoveries of a great explorer should throw them into conflict with the highly developed civilization of Europe.

As darkness fell over the western Atlantic on the evening of October 11, 1492, three little vessels, their sails spread, at their mastheads the pennant of Spain, ploughed through the waste of water. On board the sailors went about their tasks sullenly, or met in groups to converse in subdued tones. This man Columbus, they said, this lunatic, is leading us on to destruction. Now that we have passed through the sea of weeds, who can tell what new perils will open before us? May we not be devoured by some sea-monster, or scorched by the burning waters of the equator, or sail over the edge of the earth into nothingness? Suddenly the admiral, standing on the tower-like poop of his vessel, cried out: "A light, a light ahead!" But this beacon of hope instantly disappeared, and, as anxious eyes strained through the night, hope again sank. Soon, however, the familiar roar of the surf was heard, and with the first streaks of dawn there stretched out before them the long, low lines of the coast.

With cries of joy the men lowered the boats and rowed ashore. Clad in a full suit of armor and holding the flag of Ferdinand and Isabella, Columbus stepped out, gave thanks to God, and christened the land San Salvador. The officers embraced Columbus, the sailors threw themselves at his feet, and implored his future favors. Thus did the *Santa Maria*, the *Pinta*, and the *Niña* bear the great explorer across the Atlantic, and open two continents to European civilization.

Columbus had set out on this all-important voyage in quest of a new route to Asia. For centuries the spices, silks, dyes, and precious stones of the East had found their way to Europe through the Red Sea, or Persia and Syria, or the Black Sea. In the fifteenth century the gradual development of the Turkish power proved a serious menace to this trade. The Turks burdened the merchants with restrictions and placed high custom duties on their goods. So the mercantile peoples of Europe bestirred themselves to find new routes to China and India— around the coast of Africa, or westward across the Atlantic. The activity in exploration, coinciding with advances in navigation and geography, were in large measure responsible for the discovery of America.

Throughout the sixteenth century Spain and Portugal, alone of European powers, made conquests and settlements in the New World. In 1519 the Spaniard Hernando Cortez led an expedition to Mexico, and after many battles and hairbreadth escapes subdued that country. The Mexicans had little in common with the savage tribes to the north. Their great temples, walled cities, agriculture, and vessels of gold and silver bespoke a fairly advanced civilization. So rich was the booty that the conquerors sent out at once new expeditions to south and north. By 1600 Spain held all South America save Brazil, all Central America, Florida, and California, while her explorers had pushed far up the Atlantic coast and Mississippi valley, and her missions extended from the Santee to Santa Fé. The Gulf of Mexico and the Caribbean Sea were Spanish lakes.

At first other European powers seemed disinclined to dispute with Spain the great prize. France was diverted from all thought of colonial enterprises by her fratricidal religious wars. England advanced a claim to North America, based on the voyage of John Cabot, in 1497, but she dared not press it so long as the Spanish fleet held the mastery of the sea. It seemed that Spain would be permitted to extend her civilization in the New World without interruption, until it extended from the St. Lawrence to the Strait of Magellan. But the Spanish power, both in America and in Europe, had already passed the zenith. The wars of Philip II wasted Spanish resources, paralyzed Spanish industry, and checked emigration to the colonies. In 1588 Spanish sea power received a fatal blow when the English defeated the Invincible Armada. Dread of Spain gradually waned, and the way was open for other European peoples to try their fortunes in North America. The English were the first to avail themselves of this opportunity, for conditions in England at the end of the sixteenth century were ripe for colonization.

We may imagine some of the far-seeing economists and explorers of the day gathered in Sir Thomas Smythe's house in Philpot Lane, discussing the promise which America held forth for England. Here was Edmund Hakluyt, famous for his *Voyages;* Sir George Somers, who had served under Sir Walter Raleigh and commanded several successful expeditions to the West Indies; Thomas Harriot, historian of the Raleigh expedition of 1585; Captain Edward-Maria Wingfield, veteran of the wars in the Netherlands; Raleigh Gilbert, William Parker, George Popham, sea dogs who had breasted many a storm in the western Atlantic.

"The safety and prosperity of England is threatened by the dwindling of our forest areas," says Hakluyt. "In former days, when our woodlands covered the country, there was no need to look abroad for staple commodities. Then we had timber and masts for our ships, fuel for our glass and iron furnaces, wood for our potashes. Now the dwindling groves of England and Ireland are not sufficient, and we are dependent upon the precarious Baltic trade."

"Yes," adds Smythe, "and the King of Denmark, who controls the entrance to the Baltic, can cut us off from this traffic at his will. The northern voyage is long and costly, the ports are closed by ice during the winter months, and wars often interrupt. The merchants know that the eternal quarrels of Poland and Muscovy endanger all their traffic for masts, pitch, tar, cordage, iron, and potashes. Would that we could free ourselves from this dependency."

"It grieves me to see how English shipping wanes," joins in Sir George Somers. "You know how many ships are daily sold to foreigners, how many sailors, for want of employment, leave for Tunis, Spain, and Florence. There are scarce two vessels of one hundred tons burden belonging to the whole city of Bristol, and few or none along the Severn from Gloucester to Land's End. This explains why English industry declines, why our cities swarm with idle men, our highways with sturdy beggars and our jails with thieves."

"Is not the remedy within our grasp?" asks Hakluyt. "England must secure colonies to supply the products for which her forests are no longer adequate. Most of us in this room have already crossed the Atlantic, and have seen the forests of America spreading back from the shore as far as the eye can see. Why should we make the hazardous journey to the Baltic, when the New World invites us? Now that the overthrow of the Spanish Armada has opened the way, why not avail ourselves of the timber of America to free ourselves from economic bondage?"

Such conferences bore rich fruit. Many of the great lords, knights, and merchants of the kingdom formed a corporation which they called the Virginia Company of London, and set about the business of colonization. In this movement these patriotic men had the enthusiastic support of the nation. It was understood that the company was but the instrument of England to gain a foothold on the continent of America.

In May, 1607, three little ships—the *Sarah Constant*, the *Discovery*, and the *Goodspeed*—the new Union Jack flying at the maintops, the cross of St. George at the fore, sailed boldly into the Chesapeake Bay between the low-lying coasts of Cape Henry and Cape Charles. They cast anchor and sent a boat ashore. There a beautiful scene opened before the Englishmen, who for many weeks had battled the waves of the Atlantic—meadows sweet with the smell of spring; bits of woodland, resounding to the song of the mocking-bird and the cardinal; clear rivulets beneath the trees and in the sunlight of the fields. They had been warned not to settle near the coast, so they returned to their ships, entered the mouth of a river which they called the James and made their way cautiously into the country.

They came to a peninsula which thrust itself into the middle of the channel, where Captain Newport sounded his trumpet, lowered his sails, and the little fleet came to anchor. The men clambered ashore, bringing the clothing, food, arms, hoes, seed and ammunition so necessary for the first planting of a colony, and there, amid the enchantment of a Virginia spring, they set to work to build their town. Axes swung against oak and pine, hammer and saw were busy, and soon there arose at the water's edge a triangular fort, enclosing a cluster of cabins covered with clapboards and thatched with reeds.

Such was the beginning of the British colonial empire in America. Prosperity was long in coming, and for years the whole enterprise hung by a thread. At one time the settlers abandoned Jamestown, and started down the river on their way to England, but were turned back by a large fleet coming in with new settlers and fresh supplies.

The hostility of the savages proved an unending source of annoyance. One day, a few weeks after the landing, a number of English were at work near the fort, putting out their crop of grain. Suddenly the war-whoop of the Indians sounded, and a shower of arrows fell among the workers. In dismay the men dropped their hoes and rushed to the fort. Muskets flashed from within the palisades, and the cannon of the ships burst forth, while the Indians shot their arrows into the fort. But they could not stand before the superior weapons of the white men, and as their warriors began to fall, picked up the dead and wounded and disappeared in the forest.

The long-drawn-out struggle with the natives thus begun pales beside the overwhelming disaster of the Virginia sickness. Hardly had Captain Newport left on his return to England before this terrible spectre brought suffering and death. "If there were any conscience in men, it would make their hearts to bleed to hear the pitiful murmurings and outcries of our sick men without relief, every night for the space of six weeks," says Captain George Percy; "in the morning their bodies trailed out of their cabins like dogs to be buried." So deadly was the epidemic that when relief came with the approach of cold weather, only thirty-eight of the colonists were alive. Year after year this scourge swept the infant settlement, until it seemed that not one Englishman would be left.

The patriotic men of the London Company refused to be daunted by these misfortunes. They contributed anew to the enterprise, continued to send ship after ship with stores and settlers. Of the newcomers, as of their predecessors, the larger part died, but those who survived the epidemics, the tomahawk, and starvation remained to form the entering wedge of English civilization in America.

When James I, in 1603, went south through shouting crowds to assume the throne of England, he found the kingdom rent with religious dissension. On the one hand was the Puritan, clinging to the tenets of Calvin, demanding simplicity in worship, holding the most rigid standards of morality; on the other hand the high Anglicans, insisting upon the use of the prayer-book and defending the church government by bishops. The Puritans were divided into two groups, those who wished to remain within the Anglican Church to make it accord with their own views, and those who wished to separate by forming independent congregations.

James hated Calvinism. He had not forgotten the day when a Puritan preacher had plucked him by the sleeve and called him "God's silly vassal." "Are the English Puritans at one with the Presbyterians of Scotland?" he asked. "Then I will make them conform, or I will harry them out of the land." In the days of persecution which followed, certain members of a Separatist congregation at Scrooby, in Nottinghamshire, sought relief by fleeing to Holland. Here they remained for twelve years, under the leadership of the gentle and learned John Robinson, worshipping God according to their consciences.

But they were not satisfied to remain permanently in a foreign land. The strange jungle of heresies surrounding them made them tremble for the souls of their children. Moreover, they were compelled to work early and late to earn a living, and it seemed certain that they would be swallowed up in the Dutch population. Soon we find them seeking permission to found a colony in America within the territory of the Virginia Company. Sir Edwin Sandys pleaded for them with the king, and in the end James's interest in colonial expansion got the better of his dislike for the Puritans. He would not grant them liberty of conscience under the broad seal, but he gave his word that they should not be molested, provided they carried themselves peaceably.

The Pilgrims sailed from Delftshaven in the *Speedwell* in the latter part of July, 1620, and four days later arrived at Southampton, where they found the *Mayflower* awaiting them. Early in August both vessels cleared for America. But the *Speedwell* proved so unseaworthy that it stopped for repairs, first at Dartmouth and then at Plymouth. Finally some of the company were left behind, and the others went on in the *Mayflower*.

On September 16 the *Mayflower* weighed anchor, and amid the prayers of her passengers sailed out of Plymouth harbor. She was a stanch little vessel with broad beam, square rig and high forecastle and poop. On board were the Pilgrims, 102 in all, besides the master and his rough crew. Below decks were the stores necessary for making the long voyage and for planting the colony; live stock—goats, swine, poultry—penned in the spar-deck forward; food—bread, butter, cheese, eggs, fish, meat, vegetables, vinegar, beer; clothing —shirts, jerkins, doublets, stockings, shoes; books, cooking-utensils, farm implements, muskets, armor, cannon, ammunition, and articles for trade with the Indians. So heavy was the burden that the little vessel rode low in the seas, and now and again the waves washed over the leaky decks, sprinkling those below with icy water.

After nine weeks on the seas, the Pilgrims began to encounter signs of land—wild fowl, floating branches of trees, the smell of the woods. At daybreak on November 9 they made out the sandy shores and high bluffs of Cape Cod. As they designed to settle in the territory of the Virginia Company, they tacked about and stood for the south. But soon they fell among the dangerous shoals and foaming breakers off Monomoy, which forced them to return to Cape Cod Bay. Now the Pilgrims gathered in the main cabin to make out and sign a compact, in which they agreed to obey such laws as were necessary for the interests of all. A few weeks later the little band landed at Plymouth, on the western shore of the bay, took off their tools and stores and began to build their town.

As the Jamestown settlement heartened the Pilgrims to cross the Atlantic, so the establishing of the Pilgrims at Plymouth led thousands to follow into the Massachusetts wilderness. From 1620 to 1630 Puritan leaders in England became deeply discouraged. Not only did they see little prospect of controlling the Anglican Church, but they were subjected to persecution by the over-zealous Archbishop Laud. At the same time the Protestants of the continent of Europe were suffering repeated disasters in the Thirty Years' War. It seemed that Calvinism might be expelled from Europe, and pious men began to think of establishing in America a refuge to which all of like mind could flee.

In the latter part of July, 1629, a conference took place in the residence of the Earl of Lincoln, at Sempringham, which was to be of vital importance to America. In the group were John Winthrop, distinguished by his long beard, prominent nose, and curly hair; Isaac Johnson, the brother-in-law of the Earl of Lincoln; Thomas Dudley, who had served his time as a volunteer under Henry IV of France; the pious, learned John Humphrey, and several others. The stern faces of the little group indicated the gloomy thoughts in the minds of all.

"The Lord hath admonished us," says Winthrop, "yet we grow worse and worse. We have provoked Him more than all the nations round about us, therefore He is turning the cup toward us. I am persuaded that He will bring some heavy affliction on this land, and that speedily."

"Truly the times are dark," adds Johnson. "The high priests of Baal rule in the church of God. Our presses, formerly open to truth and piety, are now closed to all save error, superstition, and profaneness; the prelates are determined to remove from us the comfortable light of God's word, so that we must walk in darkness. Until we hang some of these bishops as the Gibeonites did the seven sons of Saul, we can never gain for this land the blessings of God."

"But we cannot purge the church so long as the King defies the people, crushes Parliament and rules by his own will alone," adds Humphrey. "We are robbed of our Parliament, the godly Eliot is imprisoned in the Tower and liberty is at an end."

"But if the Lord seeth it will be good for us. He will provide a shelter, as did Zoar for Lot," says Winthrop. "May it not be His will that we depart this land and erect in the wilderness of America a reformed church? There we can be free from the persecution of the bishops and the interference of the King, there we can make a government of our own which will serve as the handmaiden of the church. Who knows but that God hath provided this place as a refuge for many whom he means to save out of the general calamity?"

"True, we may have to leave dear England," adds Johnson, "but it would be vain to seat ourselves in that distant land if the arm of the King is to follow us. It avails us nothing to make this great sacrifice unless we have a charter, guaranteeing freedom from interference in matters both civil and ecclesiastical, and such a charter I fear it will be impossible to secure."

"Aye, but may we not use the charter which the King has recently granted our Massachusetts Bay Company?" asks

Humphrey? "This charter gives the stockholders the right to control the government of the colony, and most of them are pious men, who would gladly aid in this good work. Some, no doubt, will wish themselves to remove to America, others can be persuaded to transfer their shares to such as go. In this way we shall come into possession of the charter and take it with us to Massachusetts as the safeguard of our liberties and our church."

So it happened that four weeks later twelve men at Cambridge, probably within one of the rooms of Emanuel College, made an agreement to this effect: We bind ourselves to embark with our families for New England, there under God's protection to inhabit and continue: Provided that the government, together with the patent, be first, by order of the court, transferred to us.

As a result, in April, 1630, four sturdy vessels—the *Arbella*, the *Ambrose*, the *Jewel*, and the *Talbot*—weighed anchor at Southampton and set sail for Massachusetts. On board were Winthrop, Johnson, Dudley, Saltonstall, Coddington, and several hundred other colonists. They experienced a tempestuous voyage, rainy, cold, stormy, but the time was spent in preaching and catechising, without "fear or dismayedness." On the sixty-ninth day they came in sight of the rocky coast of Maine. Tacking about, they stood for the south. "We had now fair sunshine weather," wrote Winthrop in his *Journal*, "and so pleasant a sweet air as did much refresh us; and there came a smell off the shore like the smell of a garden." A week later the *Arbella* entered Salem harbor and the tide of Puritan migration to New England had set in in earnest.

During the next ten years, with conditions in England unfavorable for the Puritans, thousands turned to the new state in America. There arose in the wilderness one town, then another, with their simple churches and their clusters of cabins— Boston, Charlestown, Roxbury, Watertown, Medford, Lynn, Dorchester. When the outbreak of the English civil war, in 1642, checked the Puritan exodus, Massachusetts had become a prosperous colony of 16,000 people.

The Puritans did not leave their homes in England and

come to this distant land in order to establish either toleration
in religion or democracy in government. Their chief motive
was to found a Bible commonwealth, a City of God on earth.
Since Puritanism was in danger in Europe, they would build
a safe refuge in America; since they could not control the Anglican Church, they would found a church of their own; since
in England the state was out of sympathy with their religious
views, they would build a new state which would support their
efforts and enforce their tenets. To make such a sacrifice in
order to escape what they considered fatal error, and then not
to exclude error from their new homes, would have seemed
folly to the New England leaders. So they made stern laws
against heresy, and persecuted any who broke them. Some
years later, when the Quaker missionaries forced their way
into New England to make converts, they were subjected to
imprisonment, whipping, and hanging.

As for the government, the Puritans, feeling that it should
be the handmaiden of the church, placed it largely under the
control of the clergy. Representative institutions were established, but none save church-members could vote, and the
ministers alone decided who were to be church-members.
They believed that the Bible contained the whole will of God,
and that the ministers, as trained students of the Bible, were
best fitted to declare God's will. In this way Massachusetts
developed into a little theocracy, a state walled about against
heresy from without and guarded against error from within.
Whatever the motives of this great movement, it brought
to New England thousands of industrious, God-fearing people,
and left an enduring imprint upon the civilization of the
United States.

Had the English begun their settlements in America before
the close of the sixteenth century, they would have found none
save the Indian to dispute with them the possession of all the
expanse of territory from Florida to the Arctic. But when
Captain Newport's little flotilla was making its way up the
James, the French had already planted their standards on the
hills of Port Royal; years before Winthrop set foot on Massachusetts soil, the Dutch had made settlements on the Hudson.

Fate willed it from the first that diverse racial elements should enter into the civilization of North America.

September 11, 1609, the little *Half Moon*, with the flag of the Dutch West India Company at her masthead, floated with the tide between the shores of Staten and Long Islands, and cast anchor in New York harbor. Henry Hudson, her commander, was in search of the long-sought passage to Cathay. Borne by favoring winds, the little ship passed under the Palisades, through the calm waters of the Tappan Sea, on beneath the wooded highlands until the fresh water and the swift current warned the captain that once more he was upon the wrong track. But though Hudson failed to find a passage to the South Sea, he pointed the way for Dutch colonization in America.

During the next few years the merchants of Amsterdam and Flushing continued to visit the region, in order to carry on trade with the Indians. On the banks of the great river, seated in amity with the natives, they bartered for the furs of the fox or the beaver, blankets, knives, glass, and beads. In 1614 the States General granted a charter to a company of merchants for exclusive trade in New Netherlands, and soon after their agents were at work felling trees and building houses for a post at the junction of the Mohawk and the Hudson. In this way the Dutch intrenched themselves at the natural gateway of the continent, and served notice that they must have their share of the great American prize.

Other settlements followed. Late in the reign of James I, George Calvert, Lord Baltimore, turned his eyes to America as a possible refuge for the persecuted Roman Catholics of England. In 1628 he visited Virginia and explored the region north of the Potomac. So pleased was he with what he saw that he returned to England determined to plant here his settlement. Baltimore died in 1632, but his son Cecilius Calvert carried his plans to completion. On November 22, 1633, the *Ark*, a vessel of 350 tons burden, accompanied by a little pinnace, the *Dove*, sailed from Cowes. On board were Leonard Calvert and George Calvert, brothers of the second Lord Baltimore, together with twenty other gentlemen and 200 laboring men.

They landed on St. Clement Island, in the Chesapeake Bay, set up a cross, and celebrated mass. Later they entered the mouth of the St. Mary's, a broad stream emptying into the Potomac, and planted their settlement on its banks. Thus persecuted English Catholics followed the examples of persecuted English Puritans and sought a haven in the New World.

The success of these colonial ventures emboldened the English to place their outposts far to the south, in territory almost touching the Spanish colony of Florida. Soon after his restoration to the throne, Charles II, desiring to reward eight loyal gentlemen, gave them a grant of all the land from Virginia to the thirty-first parallel. Settlements had already been made on Albemarle Sound, and some years afterward this region was organized as North Carolina. South Carolina came into being when a group of Englishmen, many of them from Barbadoes, settled at Charleston and began the cultivation of rice and indigo.

In 1664, English power in America was greatly strengthened by the acquisition of New Netherlands. England had never given up her claim to the region and Charles II now granted it to his brother, the Duke of York. The Duke acted vigorously. He appointed Colonel Richard Nicolls his deputy-governor and placed him at the head of an expedition of three war-vessels and an adequate body of soldiers. When Nicolls arrived at New Amsterdam, in August, 1664, the place surrendered without a blow. Shortly afterward the Dutch forts on the Delaware capitulated, and Holland ceased to be an important factor in the settlement of North America.

The English colonies continued to profit by the arrival of persecuted religious sects. In 1680, William Penn, an influential Quaker, secured a patent for a tract of land west of the Delaware and at once began preparations to found a commonwealth on Quaker principles. The enterprise prospered from the first. Settlers poured in, there were no Indian troubles, the people experienced none of the desperate hardships which played so large a part in the story of the earlier colonies. In 1700 Pennsylvania was second only to Massachusetts and Virginia in population and wealth.

The English settlements now stretched along the north Atlantic shore, although with wide intervening gaps, from the Ashley River to the Kennebec. On the coast of Maine, around the half-moon of Massachusetts Bay, in the Connecticut valley, on either side of Long Island Sound, beside every river and inlet of the Chesapeake Bay, the newcomers built their villages and laid out their plantations.

The separate colonies thus founded presented a remarkable mixture of religions, in which the Puritan of New England contrasted strangely with the Roman Catholic of Maryland; the Quaker of Pennsylvania with the Anglican of Virginia. The various denominations which in England dwelt side by side, in the settlement of America grouped themselves in different colonies, and so added to their distinctiveness and aloofness. Each English colony inherited its traits from the common mother country, but in so exaggerated a form as to render it unlike all the rest. And not all of the colonies were English. It required centuries for the Anglo-Saxon settlers to assimilate the Dutch of New York. They have not yet assimilated the Germans of Pennsylvania.

Equally important were the differences of government, for there were royal colonies, charter colonies, proprietary colonies. Massachusetts from the first fell under the control of a theocracy, Rhode Island was a confederation of little republics; the Governor of Virginia was appointed by the Crown, Connecticut chose her own Governor. And so marked were the contrasts of geography, soil, and climate that each section of necessity developed its own peculiar economic system. The allegiance of the colonies to England was almost the only common bond.

Upon this fact in large measure hinges the history of the country for two and a half centuries. Fate was eventually to make out of these diverse elements a great united nation, but the task was difficult, and was accomplished only after countless trials and perils. The issue which was fought out on the battle-fields of the Civil War, the issue of union or disunion, was in a sense created with the planting of the first colonies in the early years of the seventeenth century.

CHAPTER II

THE SCHEME OF EMPIRE

WHEN Captain Newport sailed up the Thames on his return from Virginia in August, 1607, many patriotic Englishmen were stirred to great enthusiasm. "At last the nation has a foothold in America," they said; "at last we have before us the prospect of economic independence. We have fallen upon a land of promise; instead of milk we have iron, potash instead of honey. In this new Virginia has been found all that is needed for producing pitch, tar, masts, cord, iron, copper, glass." And, hard upon the trail of the *Sarah Constant*, the *Goodspeed*, and the *Discovery*, came mechanics to set on foot an infant industrial community—iron-workers with the machinery for building furnaces, Poles and Dutchmen skilled in making potash, Italians for the manufacture of glass.

But the able men of the London Company had failed to realize that the scarcity of laborers in Virginia would make it impossible for the colony to compete with the established industries of the Baltic. "Is not England crowded with poor and idle men?" they had asked. "Will not these people flock across the ocean, relieving the overcrowding here and supplying the colony with workers?" They could not see that cheap labor in England became dear labor in America. The voyage across the Atlantic was costly, and those who came over were in such demand that they could secure wages far above those of Europe.

Captain John Smith seems to have been the first to grasp the truth clearly. He wrote that the workmen had begun to make pitch, tar, glass, and potash, but that little real progress could be hoped for. "If you rightly consider what an infinite toyle it is in Russia and Swetland," he said, "where the woods are proper for naught else, and though there be the helpe both of man and beast . . . yet thousands of those poor people can scarce get necessaries to live . . . you must not expect from us any such matter."

With much bitterness of spirit, after repeated failures, the leaders in the movement for English colonization abandoned their plans for supplying the country with raw materials. England had gained a footing in the New World, but had failed in the chief purpose of the undertaking.

In the years to come the colonies proved for England a source of prosperity and wealth. They purchased her manufactured goods, gave employment to her craftsmen, instilled new life into her shipping centres, supplied her with articles for export, but they never filled the place designed by Hakluyt and the other empire-builders. In the end the mother country was forced to accept from each colony the products for which that colony was fitted by geography, soil, and climate.

The Puritans who followed Bradford and Winthrop to the American promised land were for the most part simple country folk, tillers of the soil, who expected to remain tillers of the soil in their new homes. With them they brought all that was essential to the farm—hoes, spades, scythes, pitchforks, axes, horses, cattle. They went to work, building barns and fences, breaking the ground and planting crops of rye, barley, oats, wheat, and Indian corn. But they found the struggle hard, for the winters were severe and the soil rocky and stubborn. Many began to cast their eyes out over the near-by sea, and to wonder whether a life on the water might not offer a larger return.

Years before, when the Pilgrim band was still at Leyden, Captain John Smith, while cruising off the New England coast, had marvelled at the number of cod and herring. "Let not the meanness of the word fish distaste you," he said, "for it will afford as good gold as the mines of Guiana and Tumbatu." Soon the hardy men of Dorchester and Marblehead and Ipswich were pushing their little craft through the breakers, or struggling with the cold Atlantic winds to make their daily catch. Before the seventeenth century was half completed hundreds of boats were engaged in this industry, while fish by the tens of thousands were going out to the Canaries, the West Indies, Spain, and Portugal.

While some of the early settlers were casting their nets,

others busied themselves building the needed vessels. In every harbor and inlet and river's mouth from the Penobscot to the Connecticut, keels were laid, frameworks fashioned, planking and decks nailed on and the masts set firmly in their sockets. With her forests supplying timber, pitch, and tar in large quantities, New England was destined to become an important shipbuilding centre.

For the ships that were turned off the ways there were always purchasers. The great bays of New England, her fine harbors and her central location marked her for the habitat of a seafaring people. The Yankee clippers found their way to the Chesapeake Bay, New Amsterdam, the West Indies, England. Taking on their consignments of fish, lumber, provisions, and horses at the wharves of Boston or Providence, a few weeks later they would be seen tied up to some private landing on the James or the Rappahannock, or unloading beside the warehouses of Port Royal, or riding at anchor in the Severn or the Thames. They took their profit where they found it. The sugar and molasses of the Indies they exchanged for the tobacco of the Virginia planter; the wines and silks of Spain for the valuable pelts of the Delaware or the Mohawk. They were daring traders, and their ventures brought rich profits to themselves and prosperity to New England.

It was of importance to the Puritan colonies that their basic industries—fishing, ship-building, commerce, intensive agriculture—demanded the work of skilled laborers. The savage Africans, destined so soon to swarm in the tobacco-fields of the South, found no place in the economy of New England; they were unsuited for the arduous work of the Massachusetts farm, they could not supplant the skilled shipwright, the life of the fisherman was too dangerous, even as sailors their lack of training restricted their usefulness. The small farmer and the skilled artisan for 200 years were the backbone of the New England economic structure.

Far otherwise was it in Virginia and Maryland. The richness of the soil and the mild breezes from the Chesapeake Bay made this region especially suited for agriculture. At any time during the summer of 1612 an English gentleman might have been seen with his servants upon his Virginia plantation, busily engaged with a little crop of tobacco. They strewed leaves and boughs over the plants to protect them from the sun, freed them from weeds, broke off superfluous leaves, gathered in the precious harvest, removed it to the barn, and hung each leaf upon a peg to dry. Then, after some weeks, the planter crumbled a leaf in his hand, filled his pipe, and blew forth a cloud of smoke. "Ah!" he cried, "at last I have a product as strong, sweet, and pleasant as any under the sun." Thus did John Rolfe, celebrated as the husband of the Princess Pocahontas, by curing the unpalatable native tobacco, give to Virginia and Maryland a staple whose cultivation was to absorb the energies of the people and mould the structure of their civilization.

Tobacco determined the character of labor, of immigration, of the land system, of social intercourse, even of religious life. To its cultivation the settlers of the James and the Potomac turned with enthusiasm, the merchant deserting his ship, the blacksmith his bellows, the physician his medicine-chest, at times even the minister his Bible. Soon the population had distributed itself upon plantations, not large in extent, but scattered about along the rivers and creeks, wherever the soil was most fertile. Here they raised crops of Orinoco and Sweet-scented, shipped them each year to England, and received in return articles essential to their life.

It was the event of the year on the plantation when the cry went up, "The ship, the ship is coming," and through the trees which lined the river-bank her masts and spars became visible as she slowly approached the wharf. There was a rush to meet her—from the dwelling the planter, his wife, the children, the domestics; from the fields, hoe in hand, the white workers, with perhaps here and there an African slave. The vessel was tied up to the wharf, the captain came ashore to confer with the planter, and then the unloading began. First came six or seven indentured servants, in ragged suits of canvas, their faces pallid from the long voyage; next the crew brought out the merchandise—wooden ploughs, axes, hoes, shovels, knives, hinges, nails; kitchen-utensils—pots, kettles, pans, spits, wooden platters; boxes of clothes—shirts, stockings, shoes, caps, leather doublets; for the mistress silk stockings and a new gown, for the master a brace of pistols, a silver decanter, an hour-glass, and a score of books. When all was off the sailors helped the plantation hands roll the tobacco hogsheads from the warehouse to the wharf. It was a tiresome task under the hot sun, and called forth many an oath. As the last cask was placed on board, the ship was made loose and began the return journey to England.

Many thousands came as indentured servants. By agreeing to work four or five years in the tobacco-fields they had their ocean passage paid for them, and so gained admission to a new country where labor was dear and opportunity for advancement unlimited. Sturdy, hard-working, enterprising folk most of them were, who left England of their own will, with the hope of winning an honorable place in this new land. Many, after their terms of indenture, acquired a little capital, bought fifty or a hundred acres and joined the ranks of the independent planters. Soon Maryland and Virginia were filled with the farms of these freedmen, who tilled the soil unaided by servant or slave. When Sir Francis Nicholson made out his rent-roll, in 1704, he found that the number of plantations in Virginia was about 6,000 and the population about 60,000. Thus the average plantation contained but ten persons.

The eighteenth century brought a startling change. The creation of the Royal African Company had won for England a share in the slave-trade, and the blacks now began to arrive in large numbers. During the years from 1699 to 1708 nearly 7,000 came to Virginia alone. In 1730, of a total population of 114,000, no less than 30,000 were negroes. Slavery, which in the seventeenth century was not an important factor in the life of the tobacco colonies, in the eighteenth became the foundation of the economic system.

An ill tide it was for America, this black tide which broke upon the shores of the Chesapeake. Not only did it presage the day of internal strife and of civil war, but it brought immediate disaster to the small tobacco planters. Placed in competition with slave labor, many a freedman was reduced to poverty, became what the negroes themselves called "poor white trash." Others sold their little holdings to migrate north, where skilled labor received an adequate reward; still others bought negroes and so entered the privileged slave-holding class. The number of wealthy planters, small in the seventeenth century, increased until all tidewater Virginia and Maryland was dotted with their mansions. Tobacco brought upon the region the curse of slavery, and slavery in turn bound the region to tobacco to the exclusion of commerce, manufactures, and intensive farming.

When South Carolina and other Southern communities were founded, they too imported slaves and set them to work in the fields of rice and indigo. In later times, after the invention of the cotton-gin, the Far South found its greatest profit in cotton. This served to swell the number of slaves and to fix the institution more firmly. Like the tobacco colonies, this region developed none of the industries requiring skilled labor, but devoted itself entirely to great staple crops.

In this way the differences between the various sections of British America, differences of religion, race, and institutions, were made more emphatic by the diverging lines of economic development. Between the Anglican slaveholder of Virginia and the Puritan ship-builder or fisherman of New England, between the Dutch fur-trader of New Amsterdam and the rice-planter of South Carolina the contrasts were striking. Could these diverse elements be drawn together under one government, or would they develop into independent nations? Were the English colonies to duplicate the unfortunate conditions existing in Europe, with its network of national boundaries, its conflicting ambitions, its standing armies and frequent wars? Should it prove possible to form a real union, would the divergent interests in the end tear it asunder? Upon the answer to these questions hung the fate of the continent.

The distinctive development of the various colonies and their economic independence of England caused many an earnest debate in the Council for Foreign Plantations, created by Charles II in 1660. A distinguished group it was, among them the Lord Chancellor Clarendon, the Lord Treasurer Southampton, the Lord Chamberlain Manchester, Sir Anthony Ashley Cooper, Lord Willoughby, Lord John Berkeley, Thomas Povey, and Edward Digges.

On all sides complaint arose at the lack of imperial control and the failure of the colonies to fulfil the mission for which they were founded. "Of what service to England are these American plantations?" it was asked. "They do not supply the articles we most need: potashes for our woollen manufactures, masts, tar, and cordage for our ships, iron and copper for our foundries. The West Indies send us only sugar, Virginia the Indian weed, while New England vies with our merchants, ship-builders, and fishermen. Nor do they take from us their share of our fabricated goods, for the Hollanders trade in the Chesapeake, and the New Englanders manufacture for themselves. Is it not time for us to benefit by our colonial ventures? Let us draw to England the exports of the colonies, and preserve for our own manufactures the colonial market to the exclusion of all foreigners, so that British artisans may have employment and British merchant vessels a full loading."

These views took form in the Navigation Acts. There is nothing novel in these laws; they merely crystallize what from the first had been England's imperial policy. Their importance lies in the fact that these policies were now largely enforced, whereas formerly they had often been disregarded. The Acts provided that all tobacco, sugar, indigo, and other colonial products should be exported only to England or to an English colony, that with few exceptions foreign imports to the colonies must first touch at England, and that all colonial commerce must be carried on in English or colonial vessels.

These measures were extremely injurious to the tobacco colonies. Having built up a European market for their staple, they could not restrict themselves to England without disastrous results. The tobacco piled up in the warehouses, the price collapsed, and the planters were reduced to poverty. Virginia sent Governor Berkeley to England to use his influence at court for the repeal of the acts, but in vain. The government would not budge from what had become its fixed policy. The Navigation Laws remained, retarding the growth of the tobacco colonies, driving thousands of poor persons into Pennsylvania, Delaware, and New Jersey, and arousing a spirit of resentment which later flared up in Bacon's Rebellion.

In the meanwhile, England had been striving to make herself the distributing centre of tobacco for the continent. Before the end of the seventeenth century much success had attended her efforts, English tobacco flooded all northern Europe, and prosperity returned to Virginia and Maryland. As the planters of Old Point Comfort paused at their work to look out over the waters of Hampton Roads, it was not unusual for them to see gathering the great tobacco fleet. This group of merchantmen lying at anchor is the contingent from the Rappahannock and the York; to the right, just rounding the point of Newport News, are the James River vessels; the flock of distant sails coming down the bay is the Maryland fleet. And now that all are united, perhaps under the protection of a frigate or two, the signal sounds for the start, sails are hoisted, and the great fleet passes out through the capes and disappears over the horizon. Some weeks later they will arrive in England, to part company again, some unloading at Bristol or Southampton or London, some crossing the Channel to France, others heading for Amsterdam, still others for the distant Baltic ports.

During the eighteenth century the Chesapeake Bay colonies prospered greatly, their populations multiplied, and many of the planters grew rich. They had at that time no serious grievance, and their revolt against the Crown in 1775 was based on political, not on economic reasons.

As for the New Englanders, from the first they found the Navigation Acts more beneficial than harmful. The exclusion of the Dutch from the British colonial trade opened new opportunities to the merchants and brought rush orders to their ship-builders. At the same time their foreign commerce was not greatly injured, for some of their exports and imports were not included in the enumerated lists, while the restrictions on others were frequently evaded.

On the other hand, the interference of the British Government with such New England manufactures as competed with the mother country, proved a severe hardship. In 1700 a partial prohibition was placed on the making of woollen goods in the colonies, while in 1732 Parliament passed an act to put an end to the manufacture of hats. In 1750 the English iron-workers became alarmed at the growing competition of New England, and at their instance Parliament dealt a decisive blow at that industry also.

According to the standards of the day, the British colonial policy was neither narrow nor unenlightened. There is much to be said for the idea of one great empire knit together by bonds of commercial interest, the colonies supplying the mother country with raw materials, the mother country sending them manufactured products. It seemed so reasonable for England and her colonies to supplement each other, not compete, that on some occasions the very men who came to London to plead against the system returned to America as its defenders.

Despite this fact, there were two serious defects in the British policy—its failure to take account of natural conditions of climate and soil in the colonies, and its insistence that colonial interests should be secondary to those of England. The first led to costly attempts to force the colonies into lines of develop-ment for which they were not suited, the second inflicted un-told injury, tended to chill their affection for the mother coun-try, and played an important part in driving them into revolt. The English vision did not embrace the idea of a Britain actu-ally extended across the Atlantic. To Englishmen Virginia and Massachusetts were not parts of a greater England; to their minds the Britisher, the moment he migrated to America, gave up some of the rights and privileges he had enjoyed at home. Eventually the colonists themselves came to accept the view that they were a separate people, recognized that they had interests different from those of the mother country and de-fended them vigorously, first in the legislative hall and then on the field of battle. From the first the system contained the germ of disintegration.

CHAPTER III

THE STRUGGLE FOR SELF-GOVERNMENT

WHEN the Spanish spy Molina was captured in 1611 and brought to Jamestown, he was amazed at the harshness of the English Governors. They treat the people like slaves, he said. At the whipping-post in the fort he saw men shot down by the firing squad, or hanged, or broken upon the wheel. One week a poor wretch, for stealing a few pints of oatmeal, had a hot iron thrust through his tongue, the next a soldier who had fled to the woods was brought back, tied to a tree, and left there to starve. A sad beginning this for the British Empire, a beginning which boded ill for personal liberty and self-government in the New World.

The first charter of the London Company had promised that those who went to the colonies would relinquish none of "the liberties, franchises, and immunities of Englishmen." Yet from the first the King not only denied the settlers representative government, but subjected them to tyranny. James I, who resented bitterly the opposition of the House of Commons, made up his mind that in Virginia the people should be obedient. With his own hands he drew up a framework of government in which all authority was intrusted to rulers appointed by the Crown.

But the immediate future brought better things. In the London Company the pious and able Sir Edwin Sandys, backed by a group of liberals, labored for the cause of American liberty. Many were the secret conferences in his house near Aldersgate, in which the despotism of the King was denounced, and the means of thwarting his designs discussed. "The times are dark indeed," says Sandys. "His Majesty is unceasing in his attacks upon the House of Commons, and the day may be at hand when England will be forced to submit. Is it not necessary, then, that in this new land across the ocean there be established a refuge for the downtrodden? Many worthy patriots, among them lords, knights, gentlemen, and wealthy merchants, are laying hold on Virginia as a providence; they will join us in erecting there the structure of liberty." Sandys had his way. The liberal group secured a majority in the London Company, drew up the Virginia Magna Charta, and assigned to the patriotic Sir George Yeardley the task of putting it into operation.

August 9, 1619, the new Governor, accompanied by the Council of State, entered the church at Jamestown, and took his seat under the rough-hewn beams of the choir. On either hand sat the Councillors, while directly in front was the Speaker. Then the Burgesses filed in and stood respectfully, while Mr. Buck, the minister, implored God's blessing on their deliberations. When the prayer was ended, John Twine, the clerk of the Assembly, called each Burgess by name, and administered the oath of supremacy. Thus was instituted the Virginia Assembly, the first representative body in America.

When James I heard of this bold step he was greatly angered. So, after, when the London Company was in session, a royal messenger appeared. "His Majesty bids me inform you," he said, "that you must choose between your charter and representative government in Virginia. Abolish the Assembly, restore the old régime, and all will be well. Otherwise immediate proceedings will be instituted in the courts against your charter." But the company would not yield. They would show the King that they valued liberty more than money. Let him annul their charter if he would; they refused to destroy the plant of liberty so recently set in the soil of America.

Though James carried out his threat, though the charter was revoked and the Virginia Magna Charta became void, their resistance eventually won the day. James died the next year, and Charles I gave recognition to the Assembly by summoning the Burgesses. In this way became fixed in the colony the principle of limited self-government. The King appointed the Governor and the Council, but the people made their will felt through the Lower House of Assembly. Out of this situation, a situation soon duplicated in most of the royal colonies, grew the struggle between Crown and people, which lasted a century and a half and ended in complete victory for the Americans.

Four hundred years ago, in the days of Henry VIII, the Crown was almost supreme in the English Government. He who offended the King was likely to pay with his head; the nobility feared him, the Commons obeyed him. But time wrought a great change. Year after year, decade after decade, the King's power was whittled away, until to-day little remains. Honored as the legal head of the nation, the occupant of the throne is ignored in all important decisions. England is ruled by the representatives of the people.

The Commons won this victory with one great weapon—the taxing power. To govern, a King must have money, and when money can be had only from Parliament, he finds it difficult to deny whatever Parliament demands. The struggles of the British monarchs to gain financial independence were incessant. Now it was the Ship Money of Charles I, now the cajoling of Charles II, now the corruption of George III. But all to no avail. In the end the victory of the people was complete.

Across the Atlantic this struggle was duplicated in miniature. When Governor Yeardley called to order the first Virginia Assembly, the Burgesses, as a matter of course, assumed the control of taxation. The planters of James City were just as insistent as the London merchants that their money be taken only with the consent of their representatives. The Governors soon found themselves in the same predicament as their royal masters. In Virginia Lord Howard of Effingham might threaten, in Massachusetts William Shirley might plead; they could not govern without funds, and the Assemblies would grant nothing until they had yielded to every demand.

The New Englanders escaped this struggle for half a century. When the ruddy-cheeked John Cotton and the pious John Winthrop first came to Massachusetts Bay, the charter which they had safely stored away protected them from interference. So they erected their government, chose their rulers, and gave to far-off England only a shadowy fealty. As for Rhode Island and Connecticut, they early succeeded in securing liberal charters which gave them also a large degree of freedom.

In the years from 1642 to 1660, when Charles I was contending with Parliament, or Oliver Cromwell with a ring of enemies, all the colonies drifted still farther from the control of the mother country. For several years Sir William Berkeley, in Virginia, and Lord Baltimore, in Maryland, defied Parliament and acquired a temporary independence. Even after a powerful naval and military expedition had appeared in Chesapeake Bay and awed the planters into submission, British control remained lax. The overthrow of the royalist groups in both colonies resulted in the establishment of little republics, in which the people chose their Governors and managed their own affairs. With the restoration of Charles II, British control became more real. The new King had no love for republican institutions, no patience with semi-independent colonies. Once firmly established on the throne, his aggressions were limited only by the grip which the Commons held upon the taxing power. Though Charles felt his position too insecure to inaugurate at once a despotic régime, he tightened the reins of colonial control, both in trade and in government.

Consequently when Sir William Berkeley, upon opening the despatches which came in the tobacco fleet of 1661, found his new commission as Governor of Virginia, he was greatly elated. He would convince these base republicans that their day had passed, he would show them that there was a real King in England, that he as Governor, and not the House of Burgesses, was master in Virginia. So began the Berkelean despotism.

Sir William accomplished his ends, not by openly attacking the representative institutions of the colony, but by undermining them by corruption. When the Burgesses assembled he was all cordiality, all smiles. This prominent planter he appointed as collector on the York River, this rather rustic-looking farmer from one of the back counties he made a sheriff, this large man from Gloucester with the sword at his side he named colonel in the militia, to this wealthy landowner he whispered that a seat in the Council of State was not beyond his grasp. The people began to murmur that the Burgesses were no longer their servants, but Sir William's, that the Governor was defying their laws and doing whatever he pleased. Having corrupted the representatives, Berkeley refused to permit a new election, but kept them on year after year for a decade and a half.

The Virginia planters were already in despair over the fall of the price of tobacco caused by the passage of the Navigation Acts; they were in no humor to submit to the subversion of their liberties. An Indian war proved the tinder which set off the magazine. In the spring of 1676 a crowd of rough frontier planters, their homespun stockings and their ragged suits betraying their poverty, their faces bespeaking anger and determination, stood gazing over the murky waters of the James River. A boat came across from the other side, and out of it stepped a man of twenty-nine, his hair raven black, his eyes deep and masterful, his air pensive and taciturn, his figure slender. As he joined the throng a shout arose: "Bacon! Bacon! Bacon must be our leader." Thus began the movement known as Bacon's Rebellion.

A few weeks later the people of the quaint little village of Jamestown were startled by the cry: "To arms! To arms! Bacon's men are marching on the town." The old Governor rushed about trying to collect a few soldiers, ordering the construction of barricades and directing the mounting of cannon. But it was too late. Bacon was at hand, and Berkeley's men laid down their arms. The motley crew streamed into the little capital: frontiersmen, in buckskin suits; ragged yeomen, deep in debt, denouncing the Government and demanding relief from taxes; freedmen in coarse canvas clothes, whose release from bondage had brought them little save hardship. Sixteen years of oppression were bearing their natural fruit—rebellion.

As the band rested on the green before the new state-house, the Governor rushed out to Bacon, gesticulating wildly, and crying out: "Here, shoot me, 'fore God fair mark." Then drawing his sword, he shouted: "Let us settle this difference singly between ourselves." Bacon tried to calm him. "Sir," he said, "I come not nor intend to hurt a hair of Your Honor's head. And for your sword, Your Honor may please to put it up, it will rust in the scabbard before ever I shall desire you to draw it."

Though he was gentle with Berkeley, he was firm in forcing

through the Assembly a series of acts to redress the people's wrongs and end the period of despotism. When the Burgesses seemed tardy in carrying out his orders, he used force. At a window of the Assembly room a number of faces appeared, looking out upon the exciting scene below. Bacon called up to them: "You Burgesses, I expect your speedy result." His men cocked their fusils and took aim at the crowded window. "For God's sake hold your hands!" cried the Burgesses. "Forbear a little and you shall have what you please." In this way were Bacon's laws placed upon the statute-books. Though with the death of Bacon and the collapse of the rebellion they were declared void, they had served a useful purpose. Their enactment was a warning to despotic Kings and their Governors that Americans would not submit to the overthrow of their liberties.

This warning was repeated in words as blunt as they were bold at the trial of Anthony Arnold, one of Bacon's supporters. We can picture Arnold as he faced the court, calm and unmoved, his head erect. Before him sat Berkeley, his resentment and hatred apparent, on either side the stern, dignified members of the Council of State. "How can you justify your treason before your God?" the Governor asks. "The King rules by Divine right. Do you not resist his authority at the peril of your soul?"

"Sir, you are wrong," replies Arnold. "Kings have no rights but those they got by conquest and the sword. He who can by the sword deprive them thereof, has as good a title to them as the King himself. If the King should deny to do me right, I would make no more of it to sheathe my sword in his heart than in that of any other man." For a moment the court sat horrified. Then Berkeley rose to impose sentence. "For your treasonable words," he said, "which mark you as a horrible and resolved rebel and traitor, you are condemned to be hanged in chains."

Though Arnold and many of his fellow patriots perished on the scaffold, the spirit which animated them lived. In the decades to come the cause of American liberty for which they contended on the field of battle was stanchly upheld and advanced in the legislative halls of every colony. When again the cry to arms sounded, it was to bring victory and independence. The standard which fell from the hands of Bacon and Arnold was raised again in triumph by George Washington.

While Berkeley was pursuing his despotic course in Virginia, Charles II was making futile efforts to establish his authority in Massachusetts. The harsh rule of the theocracy, with its persecution of the Quakers and the narrow limits it set upon the franchise, had created a growing party of opposition. Had the King coupled with his endeavors to bind the province more closely to the mother country a promise to respect the rights of the people, he would have secured a strong following in the colony. At first it seemed that this might be his policy. For two decades Charles felt his position in England too insecure to set up despotism in the colonies. Then suddenly occurred a unique incident, which changed the entire situation.

One day, early in 1681, Charles and the French Ambassador, Paul Barrillon d'Amoucourt, slipped away from the throng of courtiers and retired to the Queen's bedroom. There, in the narrow space between the bed and the wall, safe from spying listeners, they held a whispered conference. "Promise that in your foreign policies you will take no action hostile to France," Barrillon said, "and Louis XIV will grant a pension, sufficient to free you from your Parliament." The shameless bargain was struck. Charles bartered away his nation's foreign interests for a weapon with which to crush the people's liberties.

Louis's gold is the key to the second Stuart despotism, a despotism far more dangerous than that of James I and Charles I. Soon the King had dissolved Parliament, struck at the Whig leaders, limited freedom of speech, and begun to undermine the power of the Commons by tampering with the suffrage. All the gains of a century, won partly in the Commons, partly on the battle-field, hung in the balance.

The assault upon liberty was carried on in the colonies with equal vigor. The King forbade the Virginia Governors to call the Assembly without his permission, and instructed them to deprive the Burgesses of their right of initiating legislation, to challenge their control over taxation and expenditure, to annul their laws by proclamation, to end their long-established judicial powers. Had these commands been carried out in full, the representative institutions of Virginia would have been completely undermined. But the Burgesses resisted so bitterly, were so open in their threats, that Lord Culpeper and Lord Howard of Effingham dared not force matters to the limit. Culpeper, in 1680, put through a bill granting the King a perpetual revenue, but the amount was not large enough to make the Governors independent of the Assembly. Virginia emerged triumphant from this critical period, ready for the great liberal developments of the eighteenth century.

Some years later Philip Ludwell, Senior, came before the Board of Trade to testify concerning the ill government in Virginia of Sir Francis Nicholson. "What bears up the spirit of the people of the colonies despite the discrimination against their trade," he told this dignified body, "is that they have the happiness to enjoy the English laws and constitution, which they reckon the best of governments. But if once their Governors be suffered to break in upon them in this tender point, and to treat them with the arbitrariness of France or the insolence of Morocco . . . it is easy to imagine how ill this will go down with Englishmen who have not forgotten the liberty of their mother country." It would have been well for the English Kings had they reckoned with this spirit in the colonies. But Charles II and James II went blindly ahead with their policy of subversion.

In New England they revoked the Massachusetts charter, did away with representative government, taxed the people without their consent, and took control of the courts. Sir Edmund Andros, who was appointed Governor-General of all the colonies east of the Delaware, disregarded the people's rights, threatened to annul their land deeds, issued laws by proclamation. New England, which from the day when the *Mayflower* cast anchor off the Plymouth shore, had been practically independent, fell under an oppressive yoke.

Early on the morning of April 18, 1689, soon after the arrival of despatches announcing the landing in England of William of Orange, rumors spread through Boston that important events were afoot, and bands of men and boys began to gather under arms. A flag was run up on Beacon Hill, as a signal to the patriots. At nine o'clock drums were heard, and a military company marched up King Street, escorting several members of the former government to the old wooden town house. After a long conference these gentlemen appeared in the east gallery, above the crowd which filled the neighboring streets, and read a "Declaration" condemning the Andros despotism. Thereupon the armed companies shouldered their fusils and marched off to Fort Hill, where Andros had taken refuge.

Near by was a royal frigate—the *Rose*—and as the patriots approached they saw that her pennants had been hoisted, and her ports opened. Undaunted they drew up on either side of the fort, and, dragging cannon into position, summoned the Governor to surrender. Seeing that resistance was useless, Andros came forth, and was led through the streets to the town house. Now the country people swarmed into Boston, muttering threats and demanding that the Governor be put in chains. The fort surrendered, and the next day the castle and the frigate also yielded. Thus the people of Massachusetts threw off the yoke and reasserted their right to "the liberties, franchises, and immunities of Englishmen."

Perhaps the second Stuart despotism would have lasted longer had not James II been less unprincipled than his brother. Charles had sacrificed his religious beliefs for security upon the throne, James not only remained loyal to the Catholic Church, but began active measures to restore it as the established faith of England. He appointed so many Catholics to high positions in the army, in the government, and on the bench, that the Anglicans, who had been passionately loyal to Charles, turned in anger from his successor. England had submitted to the subversion of its liberty; it would not submit to the subversion of its religion. When James's Protestant son-in-law, William of Orange, landed in England, he was welcomed as a deliverer. Deserted by army and people, James sought shelter with Louis XIV, while Parliament declared William and Mary joint monarchs.

This revolution, the "Glorious Revolution," as the English

called it, was of even greater importance to America than to the mother country. Not only was it the signal for the expulsion of Andros, but the overthrow of Nicholson's government in New York, for Corde's rebellion in Maryland, and for revolutionary movements in Virginia. The colonies were as prompt as England itself in resisting encroachments upon their liberties. And now that more liberal monarchs ruled in England, and the supremacy of Parliament had been demonstrated, there followed a long period of liberalism in colonial control. Three-quarters of a century were to pass before again a British King defied the rights of the colonists, and by that time they had grown strong enough to resist even upon the field of battle.

The new Massachusetts charter, issued in 1691, provided for less independence than the people had enjoyed under the old régime. The King was to appoint the Governor, who was to have the power of vetoing bills, appointing judges, and confirming members of the Council upon nomination by the Assembly. But what the people lost in independence they gained in liberty. The enhanced power of the King was compensated for by the weakening of the theocracy. Moreover, since experience soon proved it easy for the Assembly to control the Governor, the royal authority was not greatly strengthened. The Andros régime in Massachusetts had substituted temporarily the despotism of the Crown for the despotism of the clergy, but the Glorious Revolution destroyed the former without fully restoring the latter.

Thus, as the seventeenth century drew to a close all the colonies entered upon a period of advancing liberty. Year after year they were to make gains until at the outbreak of the Revolution Washington could describe the Americans as a free people. The Governors soon found themselves, in their efforts to rule the colonies, in the same predicament as the Kings in their quarrels with Parliament. Nothing could be done without funds, and the Assemblies would grant not one penny if the Governor showed an inclination to uphold the royal prerogative. In some of the colonies the Governor was dependent upon the Assemblies for his own salary, and his salary was held in abeyance until he had signed every bill.

The British Government was aware that this situation was undermining its authority, and made repeated attempts to secure in the colonies grants of permanent revenues, to be at the disposal of the Governors. But the people resisted successfully. The Crown could have thwarted the Assemblies by paying its Governors out of the royal exchequer, but this would have strengthened the King's authority in the colonies by weakening it at home. The unequal contest went on without interruption until the Assemblies had obtained a complete victory, and in internal affairs enjoyed practical independence. In the proprietary colonies a similar development took place, with the authority of the proprietors yielding gradually before the assaults of the Assemblies.

In seeking the causes of every great upheaval it is always necessary to go back into the history of preceding decades or even centuries. Therefore no adequate understanding of the American Revolution can be had without a grasp of the salient facts of the colonial period. We must know that before the middle of the eighteenth century the Americans had become practically a free people, and that freedom had been won by the control of taxation by the colonial Assemblies.

CHAPTER IV

THE BATTLE FOR A CONTINENT

LATE in July, 1535, three small vessels, carrying at their mastheads the white pennants with the fleur-de-lis of France, entered the waters of the Straits of Belle Isle, between the bleak shores of Newfoundland and Labrador. Passing through a great inland sea that promised a short route to the Indian Ocean, they found themselves in the broad mouth of the St. Lawrence River. They sailed on between granite walls to the north and the unbroken forest to the south, under the rocks of the Narrows, through Lake St. Peter with its countless islands, past the mouth of the Richelieu River, until they cast anchor at the present site of Montreal. Thus Jacques Cartier, mariner and explorer, took possession of Canada in the name of King Francis I.

Three-quarters of a century were to pass before French settlers followed. In 1608 Samuel Champlain led an expedition up the St. Lawrence. Stopping before a semicircular rock on the north shore, beneath which the river, narrowed to a mile in width, sweeps on deep and strong, he landed his men, erected a few buildings, enclosed them with a wooden wall and mounted cannon. With the founding of Quebec, French civilization took firm root in the soil of the New World.

Champlain little dreamed, as his vessels floated on the waters of the St. Lawrence, how profoundly this great stream would affect the destiny of Canada. Whereas the British colonies remained for a century pinned to the coast, this wonderful natural waterway lured the French onward into the wilderness of the interior. The iron-willed La Salle, with his crew of Frenchmen and Indians, had paddled down the Mississippi until his canoes floated out on the Gulf of Mexico years before Governor Spotswood, of Virginia, and his Knights of the Golden Horseshoe ascended the Blue Ridge and looked down upon the beautiful valley of Virginia.

In New France the explorer went hand and hand with the

trapper and the trader. The *coureurs de bois* set traps for the
fox and the beaver in the far-off woods of Wisconsin, speared
the salmon in the waters of Nipissing, and hunted the moose
on the shores of Lake Superior. Trading-posts were established
in the wilderness, at Frontenac, at Michillimackinac, at Sault
Sainte Marie, and the Western furs began to pour in a steady
stream into Montreal and Quebec. Many a trader, loading his
canoe with furs in Lake Winnebago, skirted the shores of
northern Lake Michigan, passed into the waters of Huron,
through the Georgian Bay, up the French River, and then,
after a short portage, down the Ottawa River to La Chine and
Montreal. This wilderness trade of the *coureurs de bois* was exceedingly lucrative, and tended to monopolize the energy of
the settlers. The St. Lawrence willed it that New France
should be founded, not on agriculture, foreign commerce, or
manufactures, but on the Indian fur trade.

This traffic brought the French into rivalry with the English of New York and involved them in intrigues with the Indians. Not every canoe-load of furs found its way to Montreal,
for the valley of the Mohawk, cutting through the great Appalachian barrier, also offered an inviting highway from the
Great Lakes. Albany became an important *entrepot*, where
the Iroquois, the Miamis, or the distant Pottawattamies met
the Englishman in amity, and exchanged the beautiful peltries
of the fox or the otter for the guns, powder, knives, kettles,
and blankets so indispensable to their life in the wilderness.
Whether the bulk of the fur trade followed the St. Lawrence
or the Mohawk became a matter of prime importance to both
white man and Indian.

In war and in trade the Indians fought side by side with
their white allies. It was recognized that the great struggle
between Britain and France for the possession of the continent
might be decided by the alignment of the various tribes. In
this matter fortune cast her smiles upon the English, for as
allies they had the Iroquois, the so-called Five Nations, unsurpassed for bravery and cruelty. Throughout northern New
York they built their villages, with long bark houses and palisaded walls: at the foot of Lake Canandaigua the Senecas;

next, to the east, the Cayugas; then, spreading over the gentle
rolling country eastward of Lake Skaneateles, the Onondagas,
or "men of the hills"; beyond them the Oneidas, or "men of
the boulders," and last, in the valley between the Adirondacks
and the Catskills, the "people of the flint," known to their
enemies as Mohawks.

Between this confederation and the Algonquins of the St.
Lawrence valley and the Hurons of the Georgian Bay region,
friends and allies of the French, was a long-standing feud.
When Champlain, in 1609, took part in an attack upon the
Mohawks, he brought upon New France the lasting hostility of the Five Nations. The French found these fierce warriors
not only an almost impassable barrier to aggression upon the
British northern frontier, but a constant menace to Canada
itself. More than once the war-whoop of the Mohawk and the
Oneida sounded beneath the very battlements of Montreal,
and the waters of the St. Lawrence were lit up by the glare of
human torches.

Both French and English considered the Indians indispensable in every campaign. "Here in the forests of America we can
no more do without them than without cavalry on the plain,"
wrote Louis Antoine de Bougainville in his *Journal*. But they
added an element of unspeakable horror to the struggle. When
once the call to the war-path sounded, they smeared their faces
with paint—vermilion, white, green, yellow, black—adorned
their heads with feathers, seized the tomahawk and rifle, sang
war-songs, danced, stamped, yelled, and brandished their
weapons. Then away they went slinking through the forests,
eager for battle. After some days they returned, with their
luckless captives held by cords about the neck. This white
man, with great beads of perspiration starting from his brow,
in his eyes a nameless horror, they stripped to the waist and
bound to a stake. Then, dancing round their victim with unearthly yells, they inflicted upon him all the tortures that
fiendish ingenuity could devise. At last, when death came to
bring relief, after cutting out the heart and drinking deep of
the blood, they consigned the distorted body to the flames.

In June, 1754, Benjamin Franklin went to Albany to the

intercolonial conference which met in the court-house of that little frontier city. As he entered the gate of the palisaded wall, a picturesque scene met his eye. Before him were several hundred dwellings, unmistakably Dutch in architecture, of one story, their wooden shutters neatly painted, their gable ends "notched like steps." Beside each door was a settee, "scoured very neat," while over the roof was an ornamental weathervane—a lion, a goose, a horse, or perhaps a ship. A house more pretentious than the others he recognized as the Governor's residence, a square stone building as the old Dutch church, the frowning structure overlooking the town from the eminence beyond as the fort. He saw groups of Dutch traders puffing at their long pipes, many well-dressed gentlemen just arrived for the congress, and scores of Indians, in nodding plumes and variegated blankets, strolling on the streets or seated under the trees before the city hall.

Some of the ablest men in the colonies came to the congress, for the crisis was real and the need of concerted action against the French urgent. We may imagine Franklin in informal manner conversing with the leading delegates upon the issues of the day—with Thomas Hutchinson, of Massachusetts; William Johnson, famous for his influence with the Iroquois; James Delancy, Lieutenant-Governor of New York; Roger Wolcott; John Penn; Benjamin Tasker.

"We have an advantage over the French," says Hutchinson, "in the preponderance of the English population. I doubt whether all New France can boast of 80,000 people. Massachusetts alone has three times that number, Virginia four times. In all the colonies we have over a million souls. It is partly our fondness for agriculture and commerce which has made us grow so rapidly, partly the liberality of our Kings in admitting dissenting sects. Canada has been held back by the fur trade and the exclusion of the Huguenots. The multitude of industrious families whom Louis XIV drove from France, had they come to the St. Lawrence valley, would have made our rival almost invincible. It is fortunate for us that they went to foreign countries—to Germany, Holland, England, and to us here in the British colonies."

"True," replies Franklin, "it is quite true we have a great advantage in numbers, but is this not offset by our lack of unity? What serves it that we have fourteen to one, if we can never induce our fourteen to act together? Is there an attack on the New York frontier, South Carolina and Maryland are as unconcerned as though the fighting were in Tartary; do the French and Indians raid Virginia, New England can in no way be brought to send aid. The French act as a unit, and can hurl their entire force upon any part of our extended back country. I have brought with me a plan of union which, if adopted by the colonies and approved of by the British Government, will render us supreme on this continent."

"Yes," says Delancy, "but union would be unnecessary were it not for the impatience of control in every colony. Were they to obey the King's commands and to cease their opposition to his Governors, harmony and co-operation would be easy. The Assemblies are utterly unmanageable. Even now the Virginia Burgesses refuse to grant the men and money needed to drive the French out of the Ohio valley, merely because Governor Dinwiddie charges a pistole fee for land patents and the use of the seal. Obedience, not union, is what we need."

"I cannot agree that it is necessary to sacrifice liberty for strength," says Franklin, his kindly face assuming a serious expression, "for you know the Virginians consider the pistole fee as a form of taxation without representation. But that immediate measures should be taken to break the chain which the French are forging to keep us out of the great Western country is obvious. So long as their settlements and forts were confined to the St. Lawrence, the Great Lakes, and the Mississippi, the peril was not imminent. But now that Céleron de Bienville has marched through the Ohio region, claiming it for King Louis, and the French have built Fort Le Bœuf on the headwaters of the Allegheny, we must strike vigorously or remain forever hemmed in east of the mountains. The alarming news has just come that young Washington has been defeated at Fort Necessity and that the enemy are intrenching themselves at the forks of the Ohio."

"One would think from your conversation, gentlemen," breaks in Johnson, "that the fate of America is to be decided by provincials. In the war which now seems inevitable I predict that the regulars from Europe will be the chief factors in victory or defeat. Already it is rumored that the Duke of Newcastle intends to send us two fine regiments, and I wager the French will not be long behind."

Several months before the Albany Congress met, Governor Dinwiddie had sent out George Washington, then a youth of twenty-one, with a letter for the French commander, demanding the immediate evacuation of the Ohio valley. With five backwoodsmen Washington journeyed hundreds of miles to the French outposts, wading through deep snow, crossing ice-choked rivers on rafts or in canoes, making his way through forests and over mountain ridges. The tall, dignified young major delivered his message, but received no assurance from the French that they would relinquish their claim to the region.

Early in 1754 Dinwiddie sent a force of men to construct a fort at the juncture of the Allegheny and the Monongahela, which he rightly considered the gateway to the West. But the French came swarming down the Allegheny in bateaux and canoes, drove off the English before the work was done, and built a fortress of their own which they called Fort Duquesne. In the meanwhile the Governor drew together a regiment of colonials, under Colonel Joshua Fry, and pushed them forward to the critical point. They were brave men, and adept in frontier fighting, but hard to discipline, ill-armed, and ragged. Washington, who was second in command, advanced with half the force, first to Wills Creek and later to Great Meadows. Learning that a small body of French were concealed in a near-by rocky hollow, he attacked them, killed ten and captured twenty-two.

News now arrived that Colonel Fry had died at Wills Creek and that Washington was in supreme command. The rest of the regiment came up, together with a company of South Carolinians, a number of friendly Indians, and a company of regulars. Thus reinforced Washington set out for Fort Duquesne. But he was compelled to fall back on Great Meadows upon learning that a superior body of French and Indians was approaching. Here he took refuge behind hastily constructed works which he called Fort Necessity.

It was a strange scene—the crude square fort with its earthen ramparts and shallow pit, the rough colonials, the painted savages, the British splendid in scarlet coats, the crude camp-sheds and wigwams, the surrounding heights and forests, in the distance the lofty green ridge of Laurel Hill. The enemy appeared and, filling the woods in front of the fort with riflemen, opened fire. All day long the battle continued. A drenching rain began. The English, standing in a foot of water at times, could do little more than gaze helplessly at the enemy's position through a gray veil of mist. By evening their powder was nearly spent, their guns foul, they were exhausted and half-starved. When the French commander proposed favorable terms of surrender, Washington was forced to accept.

Early the next morning the English marched out of the fort with drums beating and colors flying, and began the weary journey fifty-two miles back to Wills Creek. It was the fourth of July. As the men stumbled along over the forest path, bearing the wounded on their backs, Washington was deeply dejected. His first expedition had ended in failure, the French were in complete possession of the disputed country, the Western Indians would now draw the scalping-knife against the English. The youthful commander could not realize that his defeat was not without its bright aspects, that it was training him in adversity, and making him a marvel of fortitude, capable of retrieving every disaster.

Eight months later, when General Edward Braddock arrived in the Potomac with two British regiments, the English colonists were confident that the defeat at Fort Necessity would be avenged. Reinforced by 450 Virginia militia under Washington, Braddock prepared to advance on Fort Duquesne by way of Wills Creek. But he knew nothing of frontier fighting, and turned a deaf ear to the advice of Washington. He moved forward slowly, cutting a road through the forest, and bringing with him his heavy artillery and a long supply train.

On a cloudless July day, the advance division of the army

crossed the Monongahela, eight miles from Fort Duquesne, and entered the woods on the north bank. It was a wonderful spectacle—the long lines of regulars, brilliant in their red uniforms, the blue-coated Virginia militia, the mounted officers, the waving banners, the cavalry, the rough axemen, the sailors and pioneers, the cannon, the train of wagons, the pack-horses, the droves of cattle, all moving on through the shadows of the forest.

The advance column had just passed a wide ravine when the guides and six light horsemen who rode beside them saw through the leaves ahead a man, dressed like an Indian but wearing the gorget of an officer, who turned, waved his hat, and vanished in the woods. Braddock was face to face with a force of French, Provincials, and Indians, whom Captain Beaujeu had led from Fort Duquesne to meet the English. Instantly the war-whoop sounded, and the savages, spreading to right and left, poured in a sharp fire. The British formed in line and fired several volleys into the underbrush. But the enemy were entirely invisible. The Indians, hiding behind trees and bushes, crouching in gullies, crawling forward on their stomachs, raked the helpless red lines.

The British fell back in a huddled mass, and the approach of fresh detachments from the rear only added to the confusion. Facing some this way, some that, they did not know how to reach the hidden enemy. Seeing the Virginians scatter to fight behind trees in true Indian fashion, some of the regulars followed their example, but Braddock beat them back into line with the flat of his sword. Such a thing was unheard of on the battle-fields of Europe; he would not permit it here.

The British continued to fire wildly, many of their bullets striking the Virginians in the back and thus destroying the one chance which remained of saving the army. All was horror and confusion. Amid the unearthly yells of the savages, the groans of the dying men, the roar of cannon and musketry, the mob of soldiers stood irresolute, their foreheads covered with sweat, not knowing what to do or where to turn. The officers fought with great bravery, but all their efforts were in vain. Finally Braddock himself fell from his horse mortally wounded, and the soldiers in panic broke away from the scene.

They fled back over the road which Braddock had cut through the forest, urged on by the war-whoops and shrieks in the rear. Each man thought only of safety, unmindful of the wounded left to be tomahawked, scalped, or perhaps burned at the stake, leaving cannon, horses, wagon, munitions. Braddock was borne away in a litter, incapable of realizing the full extent of the disaster. "Who would have thought it?" he murmured. "We shall better know how to deal with them another time." Another time was never to come for him. He expired soon after, and was buried in the road over which the army passed that the Indians might not mutilate the body.

The first attempts to drive the French out of the Ohio valley had ended in disaster. Braddock's defeat left the enemy in possession of Fort Duquesne, and apparently foreshadowed the triumph of French civilization in the West.

For several years the misfortunes of the English continued. Colonel Dunbar, who succeeded to the command of Braddock's army, led his men to Philadelphia, leaving the frontiers open to Indian attacks. For months the tomahawk was busy in the back countries of Virginia and Pennsylvania. Many humble log cabins went up in flames, many settlers were shot down with the plough-handle in their hands, many women and children were murdered or carried off into captivity.

In 1756 the French Government sent over to command their armies in America the noble Louis Joseph, Marquis de Montcalm. Montcalm led a force from Fort Frontenac across Lake Ontario and captured Oswego, together with 1,400 men and 100 light cannon. This was a crushing blow. It cut off the English from the Great Lakes, blocked their fur trade, impressed the wavering Iroquois, and opened New York to invasion by way of the Mohawk valley. The following year the French secured the Lake Champlain passage by the capture of Fort William Henry at the end of Lake George. Here occurred one of the worst horrors of this war of horrors, when Montcalm's wild allies fell upon the English prisoners, took hundreds from their French guards, and carried them off to the woods to be butchered.

At this moment of discouragement the entire situation was

changed by the appointment of William Pitt as British Secretary of State for politics and war. Pitt had a supreme capacity for administration, coupled with an eye for the proper men to carry out his plans. He replaced the incompetent Earl of Loudoun as commander-in-chief by Sir Jeffrey Amherst, gave him the assistance of a remarkably able group of subordinate generals, and greatly accelerated the sending of troops and stores.

The fruits of this activity were soon evident. In the summer of 1758 a British fleet, accompanied by transports carrying 11,000 troops, laid siege to Louisburg. After the French fleet had been burned, the town bombarded, and the fortifications knocked to pieces, the garrison surrendered. An attack on Ticonderoga proved a failure, but this was amply atoned for by the capture of Fort Frontenac by a force of militia under Colonel John Bradstreet. This cut the long-drawn-out line of communications to the south and west, and made it impossible for the French to hold the Ohio valley. When an expedition under General John Forbes marched against Fort Duquesne, that post was surrendered without a blow. The end was now close at hand.

The Canadian peasants, as they came to the door of their cottages or leaned upon the handles of the plough to gaze out over the broad St. Lawrence in June, 1759, were amazed to see passing up the river a great British fleet. Stretched out as far as the eye could see were ships of the line with their tiers of frowning guns; graceful frigates, the union jack flapping at their mastheads; sloops of war and scores of transports. It was Admiral Saunders's fleet, bearing an army of 9,000 men under General James Wolfe, to lay siege to the fortress town of Quebec.

The commander-in-chief, standing on the deck of the *Neptune*, presented a figure so unusual, so unmartial, as to arouse the question of his fitness for his important task. A scarlet coat hung down from narrow shoulders, partly concealing an extraordinarily long and thin pair of legs, while from beneath a three-cornered hat peered a youthful face with receding forehead and chin, upturned nose, and clear, piercing eyes.

After a dangerous voyage up the river, the fleet arrived off the southern shore of the Island of Orleans, a few miles below Quebec, where the army landed. Wolfe, with his chief engineer, Major Mackellar, advanced to the western end of the island and looked up the river at the distant heights of Quebec. What they saw was far from reassuring. Along the banks of the North Channel, from the cataract of Montmorency to the village of Beauport, stretched one earthern rampart after another; further on, from Beauport to the St. Charles River, was a succession of mud flats covered by batteries; behind, on either side of a long line of whitewashed houses, a veritable city of tents, huts, and wigwams. In the distance, just beyond Point Levy, was the giant rock of Quebec; perched on its summit a jungle of palaces, stone dwellings, churches, convents, with here and there a solitary spire, and on all sides, commanding every avenue of approach, a series of frowning batteries.

Wolfe was nonplussed. He felt that in an open engagement he could defeat Montcalm, but the question was, how to get at the French army. "The Marquis de Montcalm is at the head of a great number of bad soldiers," he wrote Pitt, "and I am at the head of a small number of good ones, that wish for nothing so much as to fight him; but the wary old fellow avoids an action, doubtful of the behavior of his army. People must be of the profession to understand the disadvantages and difficulties we labor under, arising from the uncommon natural strength of the country."

On the 29th of June Wolfe landed troops on the south bank of the river, placed a battery on the heights across the narrows and opened fire on Quebec. Many balls fell in the town, setting fire to the cathedral, destroying the pleasant houses of the Rue du Parloir, and driving many of the inhabitants from the capital. This destruction brought the British no nearer their goal. Wolfe spent weeks in inspecting the eastern bank of the Montmorency, but failed to find a vulnerable spot. On the last day of July he landed a large force just above the river, perhaps with the idea of trying out the enemy's lines. When some of his grenadiers charged without orders in a sudden burst of rain, the French drove them back in disorder. Wolfe was at his wits' end. He became ill and began to talk of giving up the siege.

His officers suggested a new plan of attack at which he grasped, hazardous though it was. Above Quebec the St. Lawrence was walled by a series of heights, covered with trees and underbrush and very difficult to scale. On the summit, extending a mile or more toward the St. Charles was the Plains of Abraham, a grass-covered tract, level in most parts, and studded here and there with clumps of bushes. Wolfe determined to climb the cliffs, occupy this plain, interpose his army between Quebec and its base of supplies, and so force Montcalm to fight.

Already a part of the fleet had run under the batteries of the city and were patrolling the river above; other vessels, conveying several thousand troops, now joined them. On a tranquil summer's night, the men climbed into a flotilla of small boats and bateaux and floated silently down the river with the tide. There was no moon, and the stars shone out brightly through the blackness while the procession glided on beneath the cliffs. Wolfe passed the time repeating Gray's *Elegy in a Country Churchyard.* "Gentlemen," he said: "I would rather have written those lines than take Quebec."

The boats ran ashore on a narrow strand, and a party of volunteers clambered up the slope. At the top they overpowered the guard and signalled to their comrades to follow. The troops leaped from the boats, swarmed up to their aid, and when the first streaks appeared in the eastern sky, the army was drawn up along the crest of the heights. A few hours later, as Montcalm hastened out from the city, he was amazed to see the British extending across the plateau—regiment after regiment of regulars, the brilliant grenadiers, Highlanders, their tartans waving.

This sudden crisis threw Montcalm into a panic. Careful deliberation would have convinced him that the British had placed themselves in a trap. Behind them a few miles away, at Cap-Rouge, was Bougainville with 3,000 men; in front the main French army. A concerted attack upon the "thin red line" on the plains, might have brought victory, and a French victory meant ruin for the enemy. But Montcalm felt it necessary to attack instantly, before Wolfe could bring more men up the declivity. So he went forth to battle with what troops were at hand, less than half his total force.

This charge, upon which hung the destiny of a continent, made a brilliant spectacle—the battalions of Old France, a long line of white uniforms and gleaming bayonets; the rough Canadians; far to the right, advancing behind clumps of bushes, the painted savages. The French came on rapidly, shouting and firing. When they were within forty paces there came a tremendous volley from the British. When the smoke cleared, the white line was seen to waver and crumble, while the ground was covered with dead and dying. As the British charged, the French gave way, streaming back, some to the city, others down the slope past St. Rock and over the St. Charles. Wolfe fell with a ball in the breast and died upon the field. Montcalm too was struck down, but his men carried him within the city where he expired early the next morning.

Despite this disaster, the position of the French was not desperate. Their forces still outnumbered those of Wolfe; they held Quebec, were safe in the fortified camp between the St. Charles and the Montmorency. But all was now panic and confusion. The night after the battle the army fled toward Montreal, deserting their tents, munitions, cannon, and stores. Quebec was left to its fate. A few days later the British took possession, and the union jack waved over the capital of New France.

In the summer of 1760 overwhelming British forces closed in on Montreal, the last stronghold of the French. Amherst descended upon the city from Oswego with 10,000 men; from Lake Champlain and the Richelieu River came an army under Haviland; General Murray led a force up the St. Lawrence from Quebec. September 7 these forces appeared before Montreal and Amherst demanded its surrender. The defenses were weak, the Indians and provincials had deserted, and the garrison was but 2,500. Resistance was useless. On the next day Montreal capitulated.

At the Treaty of Paris, signed in 1763, France renounced

all her possessions on the American continent, resigning Canada to England and Louisiana to Spain. Spain in turn was forced to yield Florida to England. Great Britain was left with but one rival in North America, and that rival so weak that it could offer little effective resistance to her civilization. The struggle for the continent had been decided.

For the British colonies the French and Indian War was of surpassing importance, for it bore directly upon the most vital movements of their history, the movements toward union, free government, and territorial expansion. For the first time the colonies had shown ability to co-operate with England and with each other, for the first time there had been proposed a workable plan of union. The fact that men from Massachusetts had fought side by side with men from New Jersey and Pennsylvania foreshadowed the day when a continental army was to battle for American independence; the Albany Congress was the forerunner of the Philadelphia constitutional convention. Moreover, the overthrow of the French power in America relieved the colonists from the dread of foreign conquest, and so made them bolder in freeing themselves from the control of the British Governors. England could no longer demand obedience as the price of protection. And when, on various battle-fields, the colonial troops showed themselves the equal of the royal veterans, there came over the people a feeling of self-reliance and power. Braddock's defeat cost England more than was suspected at the time.

Hardly less important for the future of the continent was the sweeping aside of the French barrier to expansion. The line of English settlements had already broken away from the Atlantic coast, and had begun the westward march which was to end only with the Pacific. Not only had the French holding-line at the gateway of the Ohio broken down, but that of the Mississippi. La Salle's dream of a wall of French settlements from the Gulf of St. Lawrence to the Gulf of Mexico was destined never to be fulfilled, and the way was cleared for the uniting of all central North America in one great nation.

CHAPTER V

THE ASSAULT ON AMERICAN LIBERTY

WHEN word reached the little town of Danvers in April, 1775, that British troops had left Boston to destroy the military stores at Concord, some of the local minute-men seized their guns and ran sixteen miles to aid in driving them back. Nearly seventy years afterward the historian Mellin Chamberlain asked Levi Preston, one of this band, what it was that fired them with the determination to resist. "Oppressions?" asked the old veteran. "What were they? I didn't feel any." "Stamp Act?" "I never saw one of the stamps." "Tea tax?" "I never drank a drop of the stuff; the boys threw it all overboard." "Well, I suppose you had been reading Sidney or Locke about the eternal principles of liberty." "Never heard of them. We read only the Bible, the catechism, Watts's hymns, and the almanac." "Then what did you mean by going into that fight?" "Young man, what we meant in going for those redcoats was this: We always had governed ourselves, and we always meant to. They didn't mean we should."

It would be difficult to explain the causes of the Revolution more accurately than this. The colonists went to war because the English Government tried to end the condition of semi-independence which it had taken them a century and a half to win. Just why this attempt was made requires especial explanation.

The chief cause of trouble was the imperfect way in which Parliament represented the people of Great Britain. For centuries the larger part of the Commons had been elected by limited groups in certain old boroughs. At the time of Edward II these boroughs had been important centres of trade, but with the shifting of population brought about by time many had fallen into decay. Yet they still sent representatives to Westminster, while more recent towns, although often far more important, had no voice in the government. England had what has been called a monstrous system of represented ruins and unrepresented cities. This increased greatly the power of the landed aristocracy, who often controlled the elections in the "rotten boroughs." The House of Commons was becoming less representative of the people, more an appendage of the House of Lords. It was this development which robbed England of the full benefits of the Glorious Revolution and for the moment threatened liberty at home and in America.

So colonies and mother country went different paths. In America liberalism made great gains in the first half of the eighteenth century; in England there was reaction. The members of the Privy Council began to express surprise at the independent spirit of the Americans. There were many conferences in the famous old Cockpit, on Whitehall, or in St. James' Palace, in which clenched fists hit the table and powdered heads shook ominously. "How can we expect obedience to the King's will in England," they asked, "when the colonies defy his commands? The Governors do what they can to uphold the royal prerogative. But what are they? Why, the slaves of the Assemblies, mere figureheads. If they do not sign every bill which comes before them, they get no salary and are starved into submission."

In 1748 the control of colonial administration was placed in the hands of the Earl of Halifax. Able and energetic, but out of sympathy with liberal principles of government, he set to work to weaken the colonial Assemblies and to strengthen the Governors. Had it not been for the French and Indian War, Halifax might have driven the Americans into rebellion. But the good-will of the colonists was vital to success against New France, and the Revolution was postponed a decade.

The accession of George III in 1760 hastened the crisis. Of simple habits, industrious, chaste, religious, he might have served his kingdom well but for his determination to restore the despotic power of the Crown. "George, be a real King," his mother had told him in his youth, and this one lesson he seems never to have forgotten. The new King was not without abil-

ity. By a lavish use of the patronage he built up a royal group
in the Commons, sufficiently strong to give him a large measure of control over the selection of the Cabinet.

In 1763 he appointed George Grenville Premier. Reactionary, precise, of great industry and little vision, Grenville was
just the man to lash the Americans into obedience. A new colonial programme was announced. In February, 1765, Grenville rose in the historic Westminster Hall and proposed a
Stamp Act for the American colonies. "I am well aware," he
said, "that the colonists maintain that this measure is an in-
fringement upon 'the privilege of all British subjects of being
taxed only with their own consent.' But is it really so? Are
not Americans virtually represented in Parliament, just as
various boroughs of England are virtually represented? Is
not Parliament the common council of the whole Empire?"

"Yes," said Charles Townshend, "and should not these
Americans, planted by our care and nourished by our indulgence, contribute their mite to relieve our heavy burden?" Instantly Colonel Isaac Barré was upon his feet. "They planted
by your care!" he cried. "No, your oppression planted them
in America. They fled from your tyranny to a then uncultivated, unhospitable country! . . . They nourished by your
indulgence! They grew by your neglect of them. As soon as
you began to care about them, that care was exercised in sending persons to . . . spy out their liberties, to misrepresent
their actions, to prey upon them." This fiery answer had little
effect, and after a languid debate the Stamp Act was passed.

America was stunned when the spring packet-boats brought
the news from Westminster. In every gathering-place—in the
great room of the New England tavern, in the New York coffee-
house, in the Philadelphia churchyard before the opening of
services, at the Virginia county court—excited groups of men
discussed the change in England's policy.

"It is well enough for the Ministry to say that we should
bear our part of the burden incurred by England in defending
us against the French," says an indignant merchant, "but has
not England used the colonies for her profit ever since their
first planting? Has she not at times injured their prosperity

in order to build up her own industry and shipping? Has she not gotten great sums from them by indirect taxation?"

"Yes," says a dignified squire, dressed in fine Geneva serge lined with scarlet, "and nothing can be more absurd than this talk about virtual representation. In England, although not one-tenth part of the people can vote, every interest is represented. The colonies have interests distinct from those of the mother country, which will go unheeded if Parliament and not our Assemblies is to legislate for us. British subjects, by removing to America, cultivating a wilderness, extending the domain, and increasing the wealth of England at the hazard of their lives and fortunes, ought not to lose their native rights."

"Quite true," says a Middlesex farmer, who has served his time in the Assembly, "and those rights will be gone if Parliament can take the people's money without their own consent. Has it not been by the control of taxation that we have forced the Governors to consent to measures of vital importance? If this Stamp Act goes down, we shall soon find that a part of the funds will be used to pay the Governors' salaries and defray other expenses of the colonial governments. Then will not the gains of a century be lost and the Americans become a subject people?"

At first there was little thought of resistance. "We might as well have hindered the sun's setting," declared Benjamin Franklin. "Since it is down . . . let us make as good a night of it as we can. We may still light candles." But the astute Franklin misjudged the spirit of his countrymen.

This became evident when in May, 1765, a young man arose in the Assembly Hall of the old Virginia capitol at Williamsburg, and moved seven resolutions denouncing the Stamp Act. As the aristocratic members from the tide-water region viewed the speaker's plain dress, ungainly carriage, and embarrassed manner, they could not conceal their contempt. Who was this country bumpkin, that he should defy the King and Parliament? But their scorn soon turned to amazement when the speaker's manner became confident, his figure straightened, and his voice began to carry conviction. Soon all were listening in breathless interest. "Taxation of the people by themselves is the distinguishing characteristic of British freedom," he said, "without which the ancient constitution cannot exist. The people of Virginia are not bound to obey any law enacted in disregard of this fundamental principle, and any man who maintains the contrary should be stigmatized as a public enemy." Thus did Patrick Henry sound the alarm-bell for the continent.

In a few weeks all America was ablaze. The people began to organize to resist the hated law. In meeting-house and town hall they gathered—the blacksmith with his leather apron, the farmer in his buckskin suit, the shopkeeper, the shoemaker, the weaver, the farm-hand, perhaps even the village parson. Sons of Liberty they called themselves.

In New England this agitation began to assume a violent form. At daybreak on August 14, 1765, the people of Boston found suspended from a great elm-tree the effigy of the local stamp officer. There it hung all day, until at nightfall the Sons of Liberty cut it down, bore it on a bier through the streets, and burned it at Fort Hill. In other colonies the stamp officers were threatened and forced to resign, the stamps were destroyed, journals appeared with death-heads in place of the stamps, while leading citizens boycotted English goods.

The general resentment found expression in a congress, summoned by Massachusetts to concert measures of resistance to the Stamp Act. This body convened in New York, October 7, 1765, with representatives from nine colonies. New Hampshire declined to take part, and in Virginia, Georgia, and North Carolina the Assemblies could not consider the invitation because the Governors would not call them together. This remarkable meeting, held under the guns of the British fleet, marked an epoch in American history. It showed that the colonies, despite their diversity of interests, could act together in the face of a common danger. It was a long cry from the Albany Congress of 1754 to the Stamp Act Congress of 1765.

After eleven days of debate, a declaration of rights and grievances was adopted, echoing in more diplomatic language the spirit of Patrick Henry's resolutions. His Majesty's subjects in the colonies were entitled to all the inherent rights of

natural-born subjects, it declared, among them the vital privilege of "not being taxed without their own consent." Since it
was impracticable for them to be represented in the House of
Commons, they should be taxed only by their own legislatures.

This declaration was seconded by continued resistance to
the stamp-collectors. One day in November, 1765, Governor
Fauquier, of Virginia, sat upon the porch of the coffee-house
in the quaint old town of Williamsburg, conversing with a
group of gentlemen, among them Mr. Mercer, the stamp officer
for Virginia. Suddenly the tramp of feet was heard and an
angry crowd was seen approaching. As Fauquier rose in alarm,
he noted that this was no ordinary mob of ruffians, for among
them were distinguished members of the Assembly, colonels in
the militia, sheriffs, and many influential planters. "Resign,
resign," they shouted to Mercer, "resign your office, or take
the consequences." The Governor and his companions advanced to the edge of the porch, ready to defend the astonished officer, and out of respect for his person the crowd held
back. Then Mercer pleaded for time to consider, and after
some parley the angry Virginians dispersed.

A few days later Mercer arose before an assemblage which
pushed its way into the charming old capitol and overflowed
into the green outside, and pledged himself not to distribute
the stamps without the consent of the Assembly. Instantly a
shout of joy went up from the people. Mercer was hoisted
upon the shoulders of his friends and borne away to the public-
house. Here he was toasted to the accompaniment of drums,
horns, and a continuous round of cheers. That evening the
town was illuminated, and bells rang out as though to announce some signal victory.

When news of this furor reached England, it occasioned
surprise and perplexity. A new government was in power,
and on March 17, 1766, the Stamp Act was repealed. Although
this action was accompanied by a resolution reaffirming the
right of Parliament to make laws for the colonies, the Americans accepted it as a complete victory. Everywhere there were
public rejoicings, everywhere liberty poles were erected, and
the King toasted.

But the people failed to realize that so long as conditions in England were unchanged, the menace to their liberties would continue. The passage and repeal of the Stamp Act was but an incident in the clash between two systems—the despotic system of the English Tories and the liberal system of America. The attack upon the colonies was soon resumed.

In May, 1767, Charles Townshend, one of the reactionary members of the Ministry, secured an act levying duties upon glass, red and white lead, painter's colors, and tea imported into British America. This time it was expressly stated that the revenue should be used to pay the salaries of colonial Governors and judges. An act was also passed for the enforcement of the trade laws, and another suspending the New York Assembly for its refusal to furnish supplies at the demand of the Governor.

The colonists now realized that England was determined to crush their liberties. Some felt that the Stamp Act had been passed without a clear understanding of its consequences, but the Townshend measures came when the issues had been fully defined. Again America seethed; non-importation agreements were signed, customs officials were mobbed, orators denounced the law, pamphleteers pointed out its injustice. To make matters worse, Parliament passed an act making it legal to convey persons accused of treason to England for trial.

Once more Virginia took the lead in opposing the Government. At twelve o'clock on May 17, 1769, Governor Botetot sat in the Council Chamber of the capitol at Williamsburg, around him the Council members, resplendent in powdered wigs, silk stockings, handsome suits, and ruffled fronts. The door opened and the Burgesses, filing in, stood before him. Among them were George Washington, the ruddy-faced Thomas Jefferson, the rustic Patrick Henry, Edmund Pendleton, Peyton Randolph, Richard Henry Lee, Thomas Nelson, and others scarcely less distinguished.

"Gentlemen of the House of Burgesses," said the Governor, "I have heard of your resolutions, and predict that they will have an ill effect. You have made it my duty to dissolve you, and you are dissolved accordingly."

The resolutions to which Botetot objected had protested vigorously against taking Americans to England for trial. And now, when the Burgesses found themselves dissolved, they would not disperse, but met unofficially at the residence of Mr. Anthony Hay. Here they drew up new resolutions, more emphatic than the first. The late unconstitutional act imposing duties on tea, paper, glass, etc., they said, is destructive of liberty. We are deeply affected by the evils which threaten us and our posterity, and fear we are to be reduced from a free people to a wretched state of slavery. To emphasize this protest, they signed an agreement to use no English-made goods until America's grievances had been righted. Then, business being ended, in true Virginia style, they drank a series of toasts: to the King, to British liberty in America, to the Governor, to Colonel Barré, to the Earl of Shelburne, to the Duke of Richmond.

The resentment against the government for taxing the colonies was intensified by the Sugar Act of 1764. For decades New England had enjoyed a lucrative trade with the foreign West Indies. In defiance of the Molasses Act of 1733 the merchantmen of Boston and Providence frequently set sail for Martinique or Guadeloupe, laden down with horses, candles, soap, hay, beef, pork, flour, timber, cod, and mackerel. In return the planters gave sugar and molasses. In 1763, 14,500 hogsheads of molasses were imported into New England from the French and Spanish islands. This commodity the colonists made into rum, which gave them an article of exchange for African slaves. New Englanders considered the commerce with the foreign West Indies vital. They were alarmed, therefore, when the Sugar Act was passed, putting prohibitory duties on this trade and creating machinery to enforce the law. Bonds were exacted from exporters, the admiralty courts were strengthened, and all officers of ships of war in American waters were ordered to act as revenue officials.

This reversion to the imperial policies of the seventeenth century had an important bearing on the Revolution. Since the days when the tobacco colonies were so seriously injured by the restrictions on their foreign commerce, the Board of

Trade had adopted a more liberal policy. Walpole winked at the constant violations of the Navigation Acts, and the New Englanders had been left almost free to seek their best market. Now this was to be changed and they were ordered to fit their commercial interests into the imperial system.

But it is by no means true that this was the chief grievance of the colonists. The New Englanders, by breaking with the mother country, lost far more in an economic way than they gained. They lost the protection of the British navy, they lost their free trade within the empire, their ship-builders lost the benefits of the Navigation Acts. As for Virginia, not only had she no serious economic grievance in 1775, but the Revolution threatened her with ruin by interrupting the tobacco trade with Europe. Yet Virginia went hand in hand with New England as the leader of the revolt. In the words of Professor Charles M. Andrews: "Primarily, the American Revolution was a political and constitutional movement, and only secondarily one that was either financial, commercial, or social."

As time passed many incidents occurred, small in themselves but significant of the growing alienation of colonies from the mother country. On the evening of March 5, 1770, a crowd which had congregated in King Street, Boston, showed their resentment against the British Government for sending troops to their city by pelting a lone British sentinel. Captain Preston and seven privates from the 29th Regiment came to his assistance. The angry crowd threw snow in the faces of the soldiers and dared them to fire. Suddenly, apparently without orders from Preston, they discharged their muskets, killing four persons and wounding seven others. Such was the Boston Massacre. The news of this affair created intense indignation and was influential in arousing the spirit of resistance. It did not matter that the soldiers had been provoked and that the fatalities were few; English troops, sent over to force obedience to oppressive laws, had fired on the people.

In the meanwhile the Townshend Acts had been repealed. This would have caused wide-spread joy, had not the tax on

tea been retained as a mark of parliamentary supremacy.
But the Ministry continued to hector the Assemblies, infringe
their privileges, and in other ways make it clear that the conflict had not been abandoned. "We shall grant nothing to the
Americans," said Lord Hillborough, "except what they may
ask with a halter round their necks." Resistance continued.
The patriots bound themselves together by committees of
correspondence, and Samuel Adams filled all Massachusetts
with these bodies. Virginia carried the system further by
using it for intercolonial union. In March, 1773, the Burgesses
appointed a committee for correspondence with other colonies,
and in a few months machinery for co-operation had been
organized from Maine to Georgia. In the face of the common
danger the colonies, forgetting their local differences, were
making rapid progress toward union.

At this juncture the British Government adopted a measure
which shows that they still misjudged the character of American resistance. We will retain the duty on tea at American
ports, they said, but remove the much heavier tariff that it
now pays as it passes through England. Tea will then sell in
the colonies at a lower rate than ever before. We will see that
these patriots, who talk so loudly about their liberties, are
actually concerned only with their pocketbooks. The Ministers had a rude awakening.

On the afternoon of December 16, 1773, a crowd which
jammed the Old South Meeting-House in Boston, and overflowed into the street, was patiently awaiting the appearance
of a certain Francis Rotch. Rotch was the owner of a cargo
of tea which had arrived on the *Dartmouth*, and the meeting
had sent him to the Governor to ask permission to return with
his vessel to London. As the minutes passed some one lit a
few candles, but their flickering light was not enough to dis-
pel the darkness. Finally Rotch returned. The Governor
had refused to grant clearance papers, he said, and the tea
must be landed. "Who knows how tea will mingle with salt
water?" some one shouted. Then Samuel Adams rose and said
simply: "This meeting can do nothing more to save the country." At this moment from the door of the church came a

war-whoop, and a band of men disguised as Mohawk Indians started off for Griffin's wharf, where the *Dartmouth* was moored. Boarding the vessel, they broke open 342 chests of tea and dumped them into the water.

The British Ministry countered with further repressive measures. "They will be lions while we are lambs," said General Gage, who had just returned from America; "but if we take the resolute part, they will prove very meek, I promise you." Lord North, the new Premier, pushed through four new acts aimed at American freedom. The first punished Boston by closing its harbor. The second practically annulled the Massachusetts charter and swept away town government. The third provided that magistrates, soldiers, and revenue officers accused of murder in Massachusetts should be tried in England. The fourth, known as the Quebec Act, extended the boundaries of Canada southward to the Ohio, thus excluding from the Western country the liberal institutions of the older colonies.

These measures led directly to war. The Virginia Assembly called for a congress to uphold the common cause. The response was general, and in September, 1774, the Continental Congress met in Philadelphia. This body recommended a boycott in the form of an association, and every town and county was advised to choose a committee to enforce it. The old governments ceased to function, while the control of affairs fell to the revolutionary committees. Even before the outbreak of hostilities, British authority in America had almost ceased to exist.

In the ten years of strife which preceded the war England had been constantly the aggressor. The Americans asked for no new privileges and were defending rights which their fathers had enjoyed before them. In 1769 George Washington wrote to George Mason that the people must maintain the liberty which they had inherited from their ancestors, at a time when Great Britain was trying to reduce them to slavery.

In every great movement of history there is a tendency to coin phrases embodying the principles for which men fight. Such a phrase often is influential in arousing public sentiment and in steeling men for war. But as an explanation of what really took place it is inadequate, and becomes an element of confusion rather than of clearness. The Americans did not resist England in order to uphold the principle that "taxation without representation is tyranny." They were far too practical to fight for an abstraction. They fought because they knew that the control of taxation had won liberty, and that to retain liberty they must continue to control taxation. When, therefore, Parliament tried to tax them without their consent, they resisted by every means within their power.

It was understood on both sides of the Atlantic that the colonists were defending liberty in England as well as in America. The English Whigs had long pleaded for the extension of the franchise and a reapportionment of representation. If the Americans should be forced to submit, the Crown would find it easier to resist these demands. On the other hand, if George and his Tory ministers should be defeated in their colonial policy, Manchester and Leeds and Birmingham might insist upon having equal rights with the Americans, the rotten-borough system would be swept away, and the despotic pretensions of the Crown rebuffed.

This explains why the great Whig statesmen not only pleaded against the oppressive acts, but encouraged the colonists to resist. Pitt thought that a victory over the patriots would be a great misfortune for England, and warned the Ministry that America, if she fell, would fall like a strong man; "she would embrace the pillars of the state and pull down the constitution with her." Charles Fox openly rejoiced whenever the Revolutionary armies were successful. In 1782, four months before peace was concluded, the younger Pitt stated in Parliament that had not the House of Commons imperfectly represented the English nation, it would have been impossible to carry on that "most accursed, wicked, barbarous, cruel, unjust, and diabolical war."

But the English liberals argued in vain. George III and his ministers drove through the long series of coercive measures and eventually secured a fairly large public backing by beclouding the issue. Franklin wrote in 1775 that he feared "the lying gazettes" would soon turn the English people against the Americans. Thus the colonists, having for ten years defended by peaceful means the cause of liberty, at last had to continue the struggle on the field of battle.

In a sense the Revolution was but the crowning failure of the British colonial system. Had America been a part of a greater England, had her interests been identical with those of the mother country, there would have been no open break. But the government at London always subordinated colonial interests to those of England. This fostered in the colonials the feeling that they were no longer Englishmen, but Marylanders or Pennsylvanians or Virginians. Perhaps this was inevitable. Perhaps different conditions of climate, soil, and geography would have transformed the colonists into Americans, even had there been no inequality in the colonial system.

The Atlantic Ocean was the great barrier to imperial solidarity. In their national period the Americans themselves were to acquire vast expanses of territory, and send out to them as settlers their sons and daughters. But in most cases the territory was contiguous to the United States, and soon was absorbed into the nation. But the ocean which extended between England and her colonies made a similar development impossible for the British Empire.

This fact did not escape observation at the time of the Revolution. "The last cause of this disobedient spirit in the colonies . . . is deep in the natural constitution of things," said Edmund Burke. "Three thousand miles of ocean lie between you and them. No contrivance can prevent the effect of this distance in weakening government. . . . Nothing more happens to you than does to all nations who have extended empire; and it happens in all the forms in which empire can be thrown."

Gradually, England and her colonies had grown apart. Despite the common heritage of blood, language, institutions, and traditions, despite the binding influence of the imperial system, the cleavage became more and more marked. So when George Washington drew his sword against the Tory government, he acted not only in defense of the rights of Englishmen, but also of the right of America to be free of English control.

CHAPTER VI

THE REVOLUTION

AS the moon rose over Boston harbor on a mild April night, a small group of patriots stood at the water's edge at Charlestown, gazing across the Charles River at the Christ Church spire silhouetted against the sky. Suddenly two lights twinkled forth from the belfry. A few moments later the sound of oars came from the river, and a boat grounded on the shore. From it stepped a young man of thirty-two, who joined them in consultation, and then, mounting a horse, galloped away. Thus began the midnight ride of Paul Revere.

General Gage, upon learning that the patriots had collected military stores at Concord, had sent out 800 men under Lieutenant-Colonel Smith to destroy them. At ten in the evening the troops were rowed across to Lechmere Point and proceeded by an unfrequented route toward Lexington. Their purpose was soon divined, their route signalled from the Christ Church belfry, and Revere sent out to give the alarm. At every farmhouse and village inn the lone rider summoned the minutemen to arms. At Lexington were two leading patriots, Samuel Adams and John Hancock, whom Gage had been ordered to send to England for trial. At the house where they were lodging, Revere was stopped by the guard, who ordered him to make less noise. "Noise!" he cried. "You'll soon have noise enough; the regulars are coming."

When the advance-guard of the British reached Lexington, as the rising sun cast long shadows on the village green, they found a small party of Americans drawn up to meet them. "Don't fire unless you are fired upon!" called out Captain John Parker, leader of the patriots, "but if they want war, it may as well begin here." "Disperse, you villains!" shouted the British commander, and as they stood their ground gave the order to fire. With the crash of the muskets eight fell dead and

63

ten wounded. Not a very murderous volley, none the less a volley which was "heard round the world," and changed the history of two continents.

The minute-men retired, and the British went on to Concord, where after hunting in vain for the arms and ammunition, they set fire to the court-house and started back for Boston. They found the return march difficult. The patriots swarmed up, and soon from every stone fence, every clump of trees, every house along the route, came the crack of muskets. The British fought well, but the fire of the farmers soon threw them into confusion. When at last reinforcements came out from Cambridge and formed a square round the fugitives, they threw themselves upon the ground, "their tongues hanging out of their mouths like those of dogs after a chase." On this, the first day of the Revolutionary War, the British lost 73 killed, 174 wounded, and 26 missing.

The news of Lexington and Concord spread throughout New England. At last blows had been struck; at last America was defending her liberties upon the field of battle. From all parts of Massachusetts, Rhode Island, Connecticut, and New Hampshire the militia marched on Boston, and in a few days Gage was besieged by 20,000 men, many of them veterans of the French and Indian War.

North of Charlestown, on the narrow peninsula between the Mystic and the Charles River, rose the eminence of Breed's Hill, connected by a ridge with Bunker Hill. A battery planted here could rake both the town and the harbor, and make Boston untenable. On the evening of June 16 a party of Americans occupied Breed's Hill and set to work throwing up parapets. From twelve till four the men worked, so that with daylight the British in the fleet saw frowning down upon them a formidable system of earthworks.

Gage immediately determined to drive the Americans from this position. At noon 3,000 veteran troops began crossing the river, and at three all was ready for the assault. As the people of Boston crowded every roof and belfry on that cloudless June day to watch the spectacle, the long lines swept up the hill. Charlestown was burning, but the gentle northeast breeze blew the smoke to one side. The redcoats advanced steadily, their colors flying, drums beating, and bayonets set.

The Americans waited calmly, their rifles loaded, the flints ready. When the line had come within fifty yards they delivered a volley so deadly that the British stopped, wavered, and retreated in disorder. Their commanders reformed the lines, and a second time they advanced to the attack. The patriot fighters, now full of confidence, withheld their fire until the distance was less than thirty yards. Then came a succession of volleys, which tore the British ranks to pieces and forced another retirement.

General Howe hesitated to renew the battle. As he gazed upon the hillside covered with red figures, he wondered whether the prize was worth the cost. But to leave Breed's Hill in the hands of the Americans would necessitate the evacuation of Boston, and this would be a sad blow to British prestige. So a third assault was ordered. Throwing aside their knapsacks, without stopping to fire a volley, the regulars rushed on to come to close quarters with the enemy. The American ammunition was running low. When the line of bayonets was but a few yards away, they fired their two remaining rounds, and slowly retreated past Bunker Hill and over Charlestown Neck. Howe for the time being kept his grip on Boston, but at the cost of 1,054 men, the flower of the British army. "I wish we could sell them another hill at the same price," said General Nathanael Greene.

In the meanwhile New Englanders were wondering whether their fellow patriots of the Middle Colonies and the South would come to their assistance. They were not long in suspense. The Continental Congress assumed the conduct of the war, "adopted" the troops around Boston, and appointed as the commander-in-chief a Virginia planter. This would show the solidarity of the country, they thought, and when George Washington arrived at Cambridge he was acclaimed with enthusiasm by the Yankee soldiers.

The army saw a large, handsome man of forty-three, with blue eyes, square jaws, and splendidly formed head, wearing a blue band of silk upon a plain uniform. He sat his horse like one accustomed to riding from early youth, and his quiet dignity, his high bearing, the strength in every line of his features, bespoke the leader of men. "Dignity, ease, and complacency, the gentleman and the soldier, look agreeably blended in him," wrote Mrs. John Adams. Slaveholder, Anglican, aristocrat though he was, the shout of welcome with which the New England soldiers greeted him showed that he had won instantly their confidence. Nor was this confidence misplaced. Throughout the trying years to come, Washington's soundness of judgment, devotion to duty, integrity, determination in the face of difficulties, and clearness of vision made him the acknowledged leader both in winning independence and in erecting the nation. The title of Father of His Country is his by right.

The siege of Boston continued through the fall and winter. Washington's hardest task was to hold his troops together, organize them into a real army, and equip them with siege-guns. But at last he secured enough cannon, tools, stores, and wagons to begin active siege operations. On the morning of March 5, 1776, the British saw on Dorchester Heights, which commanded the town and harbor from the south, a strong force of provincials standing guard, while workmen made trenches and dragged ordnance into place. All that day a storm made it impossible for troops to cross the bay, and soon the heights had been rendered impregnable. On March 17 the British army, 8,000 strong, went aboard the fleet, taking a thousand loyalists, and sailed away to Halifax.

In her attempt to curtail the liberties of the colonies, Great Britain forced them to unite, and so did them an unintentional service. So deep were the differences between colony and colony that nothing save the common peril could have induced them to co-operate. But all alike had representative government; all loved liberty. What the pleadings of Franklin at the Albany Congress had failed to do, the encroachments of George III accomplished easily.

The second Continental Congress, which met May 10, 1775, had been elected to formulate opinion, make recommendations, and suggest means for united action. The news of Lexington forced the delegates to exceed instructions and take over the conduct of the war. They began with the appointment of Washington as commander-in-chief, and then proceeded to create a navy, open negotiations with foreign nations, issue paper money, assume the management of Indian affairs, and finally to declare independence. Although this was revolutionary, it was so obviously necessary that the States gave tacit approval.

But the colonies, even in this crisis, could not discard entirely the traditions of decades by creating a real federal union. Their makeshift Congress dared not assume certain functions vital to vigorous government. A committee served as the executive, there was no judiciary, while the legislative body, if so we may style Congress, could not levy taxes and had contact with the citizens only through the State authorities. For such a government to make war at all was extremely difficult. It might raise armies, but it could not pay them; it might issue orders, but it could not enforce them; it might negotiate with foreign nations, but it could not command foreign respect.

Had a strong government existed, the Revolution would not have lasted eight years. Such a government would have raised an army of 100,000 men, equipped them thoroughly, converted them into an effective fighting machine, and in eighteen months have driven the British out of the country. As it was, Washington at no time had more than a fraction of this number. And such troops as he could collect were ill paid, poorly fed, and poorly equipped. By unending patience he organized his few Continental troops into a real army, but with the militia, over whom he had but partial control and who served usually for a few months only, he could do little. His appeals to Congress for men and for money with which to equip and pay them were incessant. "My forces are melting away," he would write; "those remaining are destitute of blankets and shoes, food is hard to obtain, many of the men have no bayonets, divisions are reduced to the size of regiments, regiments to a corporal's guard." With such a defective military organization it is miraculous that Washington was able so long to hold his own against the British regulars.

Congress was as powerless to command the financial resources of the country as its manhood. America was prosperous, but the States dared not tax to the bone, while the feeble central government had not the authority. Congress tried to keep the armies in the field by requisitions on the States, and by borrowing both from its own citizens and from foreign countries.

At the outbreak of hostilities it sent Silas Deane to Paris to solicit loans. Louis XVI refused to receive him openly, but advanced money secretly, and used his influence at Madrid to secure aid from Spain. In a short while it became known that 250 cannon, 30,000 stands of arms and large supplies of clothing were on their way from France to America. Later, when France, Spain, and Holland entered the war, loans of considerable size were advanced to the revolutionists. All in all, $7,830,517 was received in this way, $6,352,500 from France, $1,304,000 from Holland and $174,017 from Spain. Although these funds were of great value in supporting the desperate finances of the United States, they were but a fraction of the sum needed to carry on the struggle, and Congress was forced to fall back on the miserable expedient of paper money.

In five years the printing-press turned out $241,000,000 with no tangible value behind it. This sum far exceeded the needs of the country, especially since the States also were issuing paper in large amounts, and depreciation set in. In 1778 the dollar sank to twelve cents, in 1780 to two and a half cents. Before the end of the war it had ceased to circulate.

It has been estimated that Congress got about $50,000,000 worth of service from this mass of paper. But it was at a tremendous cost to the country. Since the States made the Continental money legal tender, prices fluctuated, business was disrupted, speculation became rife, and creditors were cheated. One gentleman paid off debts amounting to £80,000 with paper dollars worth only £1,000.

Hardly less discouraging than the impotence of Congress was the British control of the sea. Since the colonies were stretched out along the coast, the water route was the best means of communication. But this route was now denied the Americans, and their troops and wagon-trains had to move by land, often over the dirt roads of the interior. On the other hand, not only could the enemy use the ocean for concentrating quickly upon any colony, but the great bays and rivers led them on into the heart of the country. When Benedict Arnold invaded Virginia in 1781, he had landed his men at Jamestown before Governor Jefferson could notify the militia of his approach. And the rivers which served as highways for the British, proved serious obstacles to the movements of the Americans.

Nor was this all. America lived largely by the sea. The sea gave employment to her traders, ship-builders, and fishermen; it offered an outlet for her grain and tobacco. With the British frigates lurking off the coast, her industrial life was disrupted and thousands thrown out of employment. A people kept always in economic dependence were suddenly cut off from the rest of the world.

Matters were made worse by the fact that many Americans not only refused to join the revolutionists, but aided the British. The loyalists, as they were called, came chiefly from the official classes, the merchants, pronounced Anglicans, and professional men, but among them were some from the humblest walks of life. When a company of revolutionary militia entered Richmond, a shoemaker ran out and shouted for King George. The troops ignored him and, passing through the town, pitched camp in a near-by wood. Here the shoemaker followed, still shouting for the King. Vexed at his persistence, the soldiers seized him and gave him a severe ducking. As he continued to gasp out his hurrahs, they dipped him head first in a barrel of tar and rolled him in feathers. But to the last, though his wife and children pleaded with him to keep silent, with his mouth full of feathers, he cried out: "Hurrah for King George."

The number of the loyalists has been exaggerated by certain historians. In no State were they strong enough to hold their own unaided against the revolutionists. Yet they proved an unending source of annoyance, flocking to the British, forming companies to rob, plunder, and murder, acting as guides to the enemy, kidnapping revolutionists, inciting the Indians to raid the frontiers. "Who hold a traitorous correspondence with the enemy?" asked a patriot appeal in 1779. "Who daily send them intelligence? Who dissuade men from entering the army? Who harbor those who desert? In short, who wish to see us conquered, to see us slaves, to see us hewers of wood and drawers of water? The Tories." One patriot defined a Tory as "a thing whose head is in England, and its body in America, and its neck ought to be stretched."

The American colonies entered the Revolution, not to secure new rights but to preserve old ones. Even after Lexington they would gladly have accepted any arrangement restoring the relations prior to 1765. So late as June 26, 1775, Washington promised that he would exert himself for peace, while three months later Jefferson was still hoping for reconciliation. The patriots demanded liberty, not independence.

Yet on July 4, 1776, Congress declared the colonies "free and independent States." The reasons for this sudden change are obvious. The Americans sent envoys to Europe to ask assistance from the traditional enemies of England. France was sympathetic, but the ministers of Louis XVI made it clear that if the colonies were fighting only for the rights of subjects against their monarchs, he had nothing in common with them; but if they intended to weaken his great rival by seceding from the British Empire, a military alliance might follow. The delegates in Congress voted for independence with visions of French fleets in American waters and French troops on American soil.

Nor was this all. The colonists were angered when England used against them troops hired from the petty German princes and allied herself with the savage Indians. In Virginia the Governor armed the slaves and burned Norfolk. New England reported the destruction of Portland in the midst of the Maine winter. The British officers could not restrain the troops from plundering, robbing, burning, and murdering. The affection of the colonists for the mother country was soon chilled by the brutality of the soldiers, Hessians and English alike.

In May, 1776, a Virginia convention voted to propose to Congress that it declare the colonies independent. This was received in the Old Dominion with a frenzy of joy; church bells were rung, guns boomed, and the British flag was hauled down from the old State-house at Williamsburg. One after another the other States followed, and on June 8 Richard Henry Lee presented a resolution of independence in Congress. Despite vigorous opposition from conservative members, this resolution passed on July 2, and two days later a formal Declaration of Independence, drawn up by Thomas Jefferson, was made by Congress.

A few weeks prior the Virginia convention had adopted a bill of rights, the work of George Mason, which struck at the foundations of the existing régimes of both Europe and America. It declared that all men were free and independent by nature, that all power was invested in and derived from the people, that government ought to be for the benefit of all. This infused into the struggle a claim to new rights hitherto undreamed of. Mason had enunciated principles which were to become the corner-stone, not only of American democracy but of world democracy.

When Jefferson drew up the Declaration of Independence, the phrases of the Virginia Bill of Rights were still ringing in his ears, and he sought to impress them upon America by incorporating them in that historic document. In this way the Declaration became, not only the birth certificate of a great nation, but a noble assertion of the rights of man. Adopted partly in response to the demand of the King of France, it sounded the doom of that unhappy monarch and all others whose power rested on privilege and despotism. In America itself it challenged some of the fundamentals of society—theocracy, aristocracy, slavery, the restriction of the franchise, unequal representation.

In 1776 the English made a determined effort to reduce the colonies to obedience. The Dutch farmers of New

Utrecht and Gravesend, in August of that year, witnessed a spectacle without parallel in American history. Between Norton Point and Staten Island was one of the greatest war fleets ever brought together by Great Britain. The dark outlines of scores of hulls, the forests of masts entangled in their web of spars and ropes, the hundreds of flapping pennants, gave the appearance of a floating city. Here were great ships of the line, with their frowning sides, their three tiers of guns, their high poops and forecastles; groups of graceful frigates, their slender lines suggestive of alertness and speed; a bevy of tenders, bateaux, and galleys, which served as landing-boats; and hundreds of ponderous transports. This great flotilla of nearly 500 vessels, manned by 10,000 seamen and conveying an army of 32,000 men, was Great Britain's answer to the revolt of her colonies.

The British Ministry, after a study of the geography of the Atlantic seaboard, had concluded that New York was the key to the country. The army and fleet, could they gain the Hudson, would cut the united colonies in two, and prevent the movement of troops, munitions, and supplies from one section to another. The conquest of New England and Virginia, the chief centres of disaffection, would then be easy. So General William Howe, with the defeated Boston army, with the troops of Clinton and Cornwallis, with the newly enlisted Hessians, and the Household troops from London, was sent to secure this gateway of America.

To repel the invasion Washington had practically no fleet, and an army of about 20,000 men, many of them untrained and poorly armed. It would perhaps have been wise to abandon New York. The disparity of troops and the British control of the water made failure almost certain, and disaster quite possible. Washington tried to block the fleet by works on Governor's Island, Paulus Hook, and Red Hook, and by obstructions in the channel, but these measures proved ineffectual. The danger remained that Howe might convey a force up the Hudson, land them in the rear of the Americans, and cut off their retreat. The situation was made worse by the fact that Washington had to detach large bodies of men to garrison the defensive posts around the town, some separated by broad bodies of water.

One of these garrisons, numbering about 7,000 men, under General Nathanael Greene, was stationed on Long Island. This skilful leader had spent the summer fortifying the line from Gowanus Creek to Wallabout Bay, and upon this position Howe determined to launch his attack. On August 22 a bevy of small boats under the protection of great war-vessels moved across the Narrows to Gravesend Bay, and the redcoats swarmed out upon the beach. General Greene was ill at the time, and the defense was assigned to General Putnam, who had not yet studied the ground.

In front of the American works, from the bay northeast toward the Sound, was the thickly wooded ridge of hills known as Brooklyn Heights. Through this barrier, which formed a natural outpost, were four avenues of approach—the Bay road on the left, the Flatbush road, the Bedford road, and on the extreme right the Jamaica road. On the Bay road Putnam placed General Stirling, at the Flatbush pass General Sullivan, and at the Bedford pass Colonel Wyllys with a force of continentals and militia. This revolutionary army posted in the Long Island woods presented a unique appearance: Smallwood's Marylanders in coats of scarlet and buff, Haslet's Delaware regiment in uniforms of blue, Pennsylvanians in black hunting-shirts, a company of Lasher's New Yorkers in gray, regiments of continentals, companies of farmers in homespun. Some were armed with old flintlocks, some with fowling-pieces, some with rifles, a few with good English muskets captured from the enemy.

The British could reach Jamaica pass, far out to their right, only by a circuitous march, and Putnam had left this post unguarded save by a party of five scouts. This oversight cost him the battle of Long Island, and the Americans New York. Displaying excellent qualities of generalship, Howe sent General Grant to engage Stirling, and De Heister's Hessians to hold Sullivan, while he himself with Clinton, Cornwallis and Percy swung far around to the east and came down upon the rear of the Americans.

Between two and three o'clock on the morning of August
27, the five American scouts east of Jamaica pass were captured. When brought before Clinton they refused to divulge
the disposition of Putnam's men, though he threatened to
hang them. But the British soon found that the road ahead
was unguarded. Some hours later when Stirling and Sullivan
were hotly engaged with Grant and De Heister, a scout rushed
in to the American camp to warn Putnam that the enemy
were approaching. As he spoke Putnam could see the long
red line, the dragoons in the lead, then the light infantry, next
a regiment of Highlanders, then a battalion of artillery, and
behind, just emerging from the woods, company after company of Cornwallis's grenadiers.

All was now lost, for this force was in the rear of Sullivan
and Stirling, and only instant retreat could save them. The
forces of De Heister and Grant pressed on as the Americans
gave way. Hundreds of fugitives came streaming out along
the road from Flatbush, or struggling in the Gowanus marshes,
in a desperate effort to reach the Brooklyn works. Had it
not been for the heroic rear-guard fighting of Smallwood's
Marylanders and several other detachments, all would have
been captured. As it was, 400 were killed, while Sullivan and
Stirling, together with 1,100 men were taken.

Washington was deeply moved, and with a heavy heart
took up the task of saving the remnants of Putnam's force.
Had the British made an immediate assault upon the Gowanus
position with the army and fleet, it is probable that they would
have captured them. But they hesitated, while Washington
acted. Collecting every sloop, fishing-smack, yawl, and rowboat
to be found, he kept them busy all through the night of August
29, in ferrying the troops across the East River. It was a moment of the gravest peril, and Washington was greatly relieved
when the last man had set foot on Manhattan.

Now followed a series of hasty retreats, with severe fighting
and heavy losses. Washington retired first to Harlem Heights,
then to White Plains, and finally to New Jersey. Great quantities of stores had to be abandoned, whole companies were
cut off, frequent desertions thinned the ranks. A crowning

disaster came with Howe's capture of Fort Washington in northern Manhattan, with 3,000 continental troops.

When Washington began his retreat across New Jersey late in November, his army had been reduced to 3,000 men, disorganized, disheartened, and ill-equipped, and had Howe pursued relentlessly, he must have dispersed them. But again the British hesitated and Washington, whose abilities always showed most clearly when the difficulties were greatest, placed the Delaware River between his troops and the enemy. He then sent out urgent calls for the Pennsylvania militia, and prepared for a stubborn defense. It was obvious, however, that the American cause was desperate. New York, the lower Hudson, and New Jersey had been lost; the enemy in overwhelming numbers were approaching; Congress, in alarm lest Philadelphia be captured, had fled to Baltimore; everywhere the Tories rejoiced, and the revolutionists despaired.

At this juncture Howe decided to suspend operations until the spring, and distributed his regiments throughout New Jersey in anticipation of a quiet winter. He possessed a mortgage on the American army but fortunately did not foreclose. Washington was quick to improve this opportunity. Realizing that only an unexpected victory would revive the spirits of the Revolution, he sought for a weak spot in the enemy's armor. Across the Delaware at Trenton were stationed three regiments of Hessians under Colonel Rall. This officer had such contempt for the Americans that he felt it unnecessary to prepare against a surprise. It was here that Washington decided to strike.

On Christmas evening he began moving a force of veterans across the Delaware nine miles above Trenton. A fierce northeaster was blowing, sleet and snow beat in the faces of the men, while floating ice impeded the boats. At last men and guns were safely landed on the Jersey side, and at four in the morning the army advanced on Trenton. Throwing Greene's troops around the village, Washington placed his artillery in a position to rake the principal streets.

The enemy were surprised and made but feeble resistance. Rall tried to form them in the streets, but his situation was hopeless. Huddled together, unable to bring their artillery into play, the Hessian regiments were forced to yield to the despised enemy. One hundred were killed, while among the prisoners were 30 regimental officers and 861 men. The effect upon the country was overwhelming. The news spread that the long string of American defeats had come to an end, that Washington had shown himself more than a match for the British generals, that the dreaded Hessians were rather poor stuff.

This heightened morale meant much to Washington, and he decided to strike again while his men had the spirit of victory. By New Year's evening several thousand Pennsylvania militia under General Cadwalader had joined him at Trenton, poorly equipped and almost without training, yet confident of clearing south New Jersey of the enemy. But the British now acted with a promptness which surprised Washington. When the news of the capture of the Hessians reached Howe, he gathered 8,000 veterans and rushed them south under Lord Cornwallis to drive the Americans into the Delaware.

Upon learning that this formidable army was approaching, Washington drew up his men on the east bank of the Assunpinck Creek and prepared for resistance. Late in the afternoon of January 2, Cornwallis entered Trenton, driving ahead of him certain detachments of Americans sent forward to delay his approach. It was still daylight, and had he attacked at once, it is almost certain that he could have broken through the militia in the centre, crumpled up the wings of the American army and destroyed each in detail.

But Cornwallis delayed, while Washington watched anxiously for the coming of darkness which he knew meant for his army the difference between defeat and victory. That night, while the British commander slept, the Americans stole away, moved by back roads around his left flank, and at dawn were approaching Princeton twelve miles away. By this brilliant manœuvre Washington not only eluded Cornwallis, but he got upon his line of communications, threatened his base at New Brunswick, intercepted his reinforcements, and established connection between his own army and the northern forces at Morristown.

That midnight march through the woods and over the waste lands of New Jersey tried the souls of Washington's weary men. In front was a division of tattered continentals, with Moulder's jack-tars, dragging two four-pounders over the frozen roads; next the confused line of the Pennsylvania militia, many without uniforms, all poorly armed; behind them Hitchcock's New Englanders; and, last of all, Hand's riflemen. During the frequent halts, made necessary by the narrowness of the road, many of the soldiers, leaning upon their rifles, fell fast asleep.

Cornwallis had left Colonel Charles Mawhood at Princeton with orders to hasten to his support early on the third. As this officer was leading two regiments south on the post road to Trenton, he saw at a distance, through an opening in the woods, the bayonets of the Americans, glistening in the sunlight. Returning to investigate, he encountered a small detachment commanded by General Mercer, whom Washington had sent to break down a bridge over Stony Brook. There followed an encounter in an orchard. Mercer's troops were veterans who had done heroic work at the battle of Long Island, and for some time they withstood the more numerous enemy. But they were poorly armed, and when the redcoats charged with fixed bayonets their line gave way. The gallant Mercer was fatally wounded.

Washington now came up, leading the main body of the American army. But he had great difficulty in forming a line in the face of Mercer's fleeing men and the advancing British. In the confusion there was danger that Mawhood's two regiments would carry off the victory. But Washington rallied his men, brought up fresh regiments, formed them in a wide semicircle, and moved forward against the foe. An inspiring sight it was: far out to the right Hand's crack riflemen, to their left Hitchcock's ragged continentals; next a motley band of militiamen, flanked by Moulder's battery; and in front, waving his hat and cheering his men on to victory, Washington himself. The British fought stubbornly. Many stood until the Americans broke into their ranks, clubbing and bayoneting. Even then, at intervals, the red line reformed, fired, and retreated again. In the end they broke and fled over the country in confusion. Washington, elated at this success, urged on the pursuit. "What a fine fox-chase it is, my boys!" he cried to his men. The army then pressed on through Princeton, sweeping aside another regiment left to defend the town, and formed a junction with the northern army at Morristown.

When Cornwallis awoke on that cold January morning to find that he had been outwitted, he came back to Princeton, the men "running, puffing, and blowing and swearing." He failed to overtake Washington, but he succeeded in heading him off from New Brunswick and in gathering up the fragments of Mawhood's regiments. The situation was now greatly changed. Washington was on Howe's flank with a strong force, recruits were flocking in, and the heartened revolutionists were making vigorous preparations for resistance. The British were forced to withdraw from south New Jersey behind the Raritan.

The occupation of New York and the lower Hudson by the British was a terrible blow to the American cause, but it did not cut the colonies in two. Above the beautiful Tappan Bay, where the Hudson winds beneath wooded heights, a network of forts made it impossible for hostile vessels to pass, and kept open the communications to New England. But the British, aroused to the difficulty of the situation, now made elaborate plans for conquering New York. They decided to invade the State with three armies, operating upon converging lines. General Burgoyne, with 8,000 men, was to descend from Canada, take Ticonderoga, and proceed to Albany; a smaller force, under Colonel St. Leger, was to land at Oswego, on Lake Ontario, capture Fort Stanwix, and join Burgoyne by way of the Mohawk; Sir William Howe, with an army from New York, was to open the Hudson by capturing the Highland forts.

This plan, which, no doubt, was suggested by the successful triple Canadian campaign of 1760, was unsound. The distances to be covered were great, the country sparsely settled, the roads bad. The Americans, operating upon interior lines, could easily shift their forces to the point of greatest danger, but the British detachments were hopelessly isolated. Without perfect timing they might be overwhelmed in detail. It would have been better to concentrate all the troops at New York and proceed up the Hudson in overwhelming force. But George III rejected this plan. "I greatly dislike that idea," he said; "the force from Canada must join him (Howe) at Albany."

Burgoyne started south in June, 1777, with 4,135 British regulars, 3,116 Hessians, 250 Canadians, and 400 Indians. A month later his army reached Fort Ticonderoga, and forced the Americans to retire. Ticonderoga was considered the key to northern New York, and the news of its capture caused great exultation in England. The King rushed into the Queen's apartment, clapping his hands and shouting: "I have beat them! I have beat all the Americans!"

But Burgoyne's difficulties were just beginning. The country before him was covered with swamps, creeks, and dense woods, and the Americans, as they fell back, broke down bridges and felled trees across the road. Burgoyne could cover no more than a mile a day. The militia of New York and New England, angered at the outrages of the Indians, and eager to defend their country, poured into General Schuyler's camp, while General Lincoln gathered a force on Burgoyne's flank. On August 16, 1,000 Hessians, sent out to capture food and ammunition at Bennington, were practically annihilated by General John Stark. It became difficult for the British army to advance; food was scarce, and the line of communication to Canada was lengthening. Burgoyne looked anxiously for signs of Howe and St. Leger.

But he looked in vain. St. Leger had met stubborn resistance from the Tyrone County militia, and when news arrived that General Benedict Arnold was approaching with a large force, his Indian allies mutinied and, after pillaging his camp, dispersed. St. Leger, with a handful of Tories, was fortunate to escape to Canada. As for Howe, he had disrupted the plans of the Ministry and left Burgoyne in the lurch, by leading his men off for an attack on Philadelphia.

In the meanwhile General Gates took command of the American army and intrenched himself on high ground overlooking the Hudson in the path of the British army. Twice Burgoyne attempted to dislodge him; and twice the Americans,

despite the incompetence of Gates himself, threw him back.
Burgoyne could advance no farther. On the night of October
8, with camp-fires burning to deceive the Americans, he retreated north. It rained hard, the wagons stuck in the mud,
and it was the evening of the 9th when the troops, weary and
cold, pitched camp at Saratoga. Further progress was impossible, for the Americans had posted artillery on the heights on
the east bank of the river and had occupied every available
ford. Gates came up, and, throwing his troops to the west
and south of the British position, opened an artillery fire.
Burgoyne was effectually trapped.

The British army was greatly reduced in numbers. Many
had been killed or captured, hundreds were ill, and the Indian
allies had slunk away in the forest. From the woods and heights
around the camp the American artillery kept up a continuous
fire. There was no safe place for the baggage, the ground was
strewn with dead horses, the wounded sought shelter in the
vaulted cellars of Saratoga or dragged themselves to a quiet
corner of the woods. The Baroness Riedesel, wife of the Hessian commander, passed six nights and days with her three
little children, crouching in a basement corner. The room was
crowded with maimed men, while at intervals cannon-balls
crashed through the rooms above. Burgoyne was forced to
yield, and on October 17 signed articles of surrender. That
afternoon the defeated army marched to a level plain between
the Fishkill and the Hudson, where they grounded arms and
emptied their cartridge-boxes.

The news from Saratoga brought deep discouragement to
England, and the Ministry sued for peace on terms which
would have been joyously accepted had they come two years
sooner. Everything was conceded save independence—freedom from taxation by Parliament, the restoration of the Massachusetts charter, the withdrawal of the military and naval
forces.

But the offer came too late. France too had its eyes on the
northern campaign, and Burgoyne's surrender created enthusiasm in Paris. The Americans had shown themselves formidable opponents, it was said; England's resources would be

strained to subdue them, the British Empire was on the point of disruption. Now was the time, Louis's Ministers told him, to strike a blow at the traditional enemy of his house. So France acknowledged the independence of the United States, signed with them treaties of alliance and commerce, and came to their aid with troops and ships. Feeling that success was assured, Congress rejected the British proposals.

In the meanwhile Lord Howe had won a Pyrrhic victory by capturing Philadelphia. Setting sail from New York with 228 vessels, conveying an army of 18,000 men, he entered Chesapeake Bay and proceeded up to Elkton. Washington learned of his intentions in time to take up a strong position at Chads Ford, on the Brandywine, southwest of Philadelphia. Howe dislodged him by repeating his flanking manœuvre of Brooklyn Heights. While a part of the army engaged Washington at the ford, Cornwallis with 10,000 men crossed higher up the river and came down upon his rear. Only a skilful retreat prevented disaster, and on September 26 the British entered Philadelphia.

A few days later Washington planned an attack upon the British camp at Germantown, comparable to the battle of Trenton in the brilliancy of its conception. Closing in on the enemy from converging roads, for a while the Americans carried all before them. But when a decisive victory seemed assured, a panic seized the army, and despite the heroic efforts of Washington, they retired in disorder. Following this disappointing engagement, the Americans went into winter quarters at Valley Forge.

Here, in striking distance of the enemy, the army passed several months of hardship. The cold was intense, supplies of clothing were not to be had, provisions were scarce, it was impossible to care properly for the sick. Cold, hungry, and half-naked, the men moved about like ragged spectres. So many of the horses died that the soldiers were forced to yoke themselves to the wagons, to haul firewood and food into camp. Washington was deeply moved. "For some days past there has been little less than a famine in camp," he wrote in February. "A part of the army has been a week without any kind of flesh, and the rest three or four days. Naked and starving as they are, we cannot enough admire the incomparable patience and fidelity of the soldiery."

Despite all this suffering the time was spent to good purpose, for Baron von Steuben kept the men busy drilling. When spring came, for the first time during the war Washington took the field with a well-organized fighting-machine. Important work lay before him. The French alliance was already bearing good fruit in that it forced the evacuation of Philadelphia. When the British heard that a fleet under Count d'Estaing was on the way to America, they at once made preparations to retire to New York, for with the Delaware blocked, Philadelphia would be untenable. Washington was watching them closely, ready to move at a moment's notice. When he learned that Sir Henry Clinton, who had succeeded Lord Howe, had crossed the Delaware and was heading for New York, he started in pursuit.

Clinton's men had reached Monmouth Court House and were stretched out on the road to Middletown when Washington's vanguard struck them. An American victory seemed certain until all was spoiled by the treachery of General Charles Lee. Instead of attacking vigorously, as Washington had ordered, this officer gave several confusing commands and then retreated. Washington, galloping ahead of his main body, met Lee several miles west of the Court House, and upbraided him for his cowardice. He then stopped the retreat, formed a new line along a deep ravine, and halted the advancing British. Soon the main body of the American army came up and the day was saved. But the opportunity to destroy a large part of Clinton's force had been lost.

In the meanwhile important events were happening in the West. Even before the outbreak of the Revolution the flood of immigration was ready to pass over the mountains into the Ohio valley. But the Indians guarded the country, and the settler who built his cabin in the Kentucky plains had reason to dread the tomahawk. In the summer of 1774 a series of outrages precipitated Dunmore's War, and the struggle for the Ohio region began in earnest. The initial victory rested with the white men, for Andrew Lewis's Virginians inflicted a terrible defeat upon the famous chieftain Cornstalk, and the way was opened for settlers.

Though defeated, the savages were not crushed, and in many an angry conference the chieftains plotted revenge. "We must strike at once to save our hunting-grounds," they said. "The Great Father in England has promised aid; soon his warriors will be marching south from Canada. To delay is to invite more white men to cross the mountains." When Colonel Henry Hamilton moved from Detroit with a force of British and Tories, the Indians put on their war-paint and hurried to join him. It seemed that the Kentucky settlements would be overwhelmed.

Such was the situation when there appeared before Governor Patrick Henry at Williamsburg the figure of a young backwoodsman. His ruddy cheeks, auburn hair, blue eyes, athletic tread, broad shoulders, confident and open manner, bespoke the frontier leader. He told the Governor of the threatening situation in the West and pleaded for assistance. "Let us carry the war into the enemy's country," he said, "and by conquering the British posts in Illinois, acquire a vast territory and free Kentucky from the savages. Give me permission to collect a few hundred men at Pittsburg, and I will lay Kaskaskia and Vincennes at your feet."

A few months later hunters and Indian runners spread throughout the Northwest the news that 180 riflemen under George Rogers Clark, after journeying 1,000 miles down the Ohio, had captured the Creole village of Kaskaskia. Clark had performed this part of his task in heroic style. But to take Vincennes seemed impossible. Colonel Hamilton held the post with a strong force, winter was at hand, 230 miles of wilderness intervened. Yet the buoyant, confident young leader laughed at every difficulty.

Collecting a force of 170 men, he struck out through the frozen wastes of southern Illinois. For some time all went well. Game was abundant, and when the day's march came to an end the men built fires and feasted on bear, elk, venison, and wild turkey. With dawn, when the march was resumed, the air resounded with the Creole's chant or the Kentuckian's hunting-song. Then, at the moment of greatest enthusiasm, they encountered what seemed an insurmountable obstacle. They had reached the forks of the little Wabash, and there, as far as the eye could see, was an unending series of lakes. The rivers had overflowed and the region was covered with three feet of icy water. How was it possible for human beings to wade through this watery wilderness in the dead of winter! A few spoke of turning back. But Clark plunged in and bade his men follow.

The band presented a strange appearance as they battled through the water—groups of Kentuckians floundering up to their armpits, holding their guns and powder-horns above their heads; canoes full of weak and exhausted men, pushing through trees and bushes; huge frontiersmen aiding benumbed and weary comrades; in front, giving commands or singing a cheery song, the indomitable Clark. When at last the men straggled out on dry land, many fell on their faces, too exhausted to drag themselves to the fires kindled by their comrades. The little band had completed one of the most difficult marches in history.

The amazed British garrison made a stubborn resistance, but the Indians deserted, while the inhabitants of Vincennes refused to take sides. After sustaining the fire of the Virginia riflemen for some hours Hamilton surrendered. Clark had made good his promise to Governor Henry.

These victories were of prime importance. Not only did they relieve Kentucky from the Indian menace and encourage settlement in the "Dark and Bloody Ground," but they gave the United States a claim to the Northwest which proved invaluable in the peace conference. In 1782 Vergennes might plan what he would for the Ohio basin, but the Americans were in actual possession. The youthful Clark and his frontiersmen had conquered for the United States an imperial domain.

Before the end of 1778 the British showed signs of discouragement and perplexity. They had gained many victories, but had made little progress in conquering the country. Boston had been lost, Philadelphia taken and abandoned, the upper

Hudson was still closed, and all four years of war had gained was New York and its immediate vicinity. The British Ministry did not realize that the heart of the Revolution lay, not in cities or States, but in Washington's army. Had they followed the patriot forces relentlessly, their chances of success would have been better. Fortunately they failed to adopt this plan. Instead, they now decided to assume a defensive attitude in the North, and to devote their chief efforts to the conquest of the South.

In December, 1778, a British fleet appeared off the Georgia coast and landed an army which captured Savannah and soon overran the State. They then turned their attention to South Carolina. In this State the large planters of the lowlands, with the small farmers of Scotch-Irish descent, were ardent revolutionists, but the Scotch Highlanders, who were recent arrivals, remained loyal to the Crown.

After months of indecisive fighting, marked by marching and counter-marching, the British under Sir Henry Clinton closed in on Charleston. The city was defended by the able General Lincoln, but after the besieging force, numbering no less than 14,000 men, had captured the defensive works, he was forced to surrender. It was the greatest disaster of the American army during the war. The British took 5,466 prisoners, including seven generals, with 391 guns, 5,316 muskets and 15 regimental colors. No wonder Horace Walpole could say: "We look on America as at our feet."

Though South Carolina was overrun after this disaster, the United States was far from submitting. In South Carolina itself patriotic bands of light troops under the dashing leadership of Thomas Sumter, Andrew Pickens, and Francis Marion made no end of trouble for the enemy. There were midnight marches, surprises, and desperate combats, followed by hasty retirements to the swamps or the mountains.

At last Congress sent aid from Maryland and Virginia, but they rendered it almost useless by appointing the incompetent Gates to the command in the South. Charles Lee, made cynical by his own disgrace, wrote him in a spirit of prophecy: "Take care that your Northern laurels do not change to Southern willows." Gates came into contact with Cornwallis at Camden in August, 1780, and was disastrously defeated. The army was almost entirely destroyed and Gates escaped only by covering 160 miles in three days.

Cornwallis now sent Colonel Patrick Ferguson, with a company of British light infantry and a body of Tories to scour the highlands and secure recruits. Ferguson made the mistake of pushing too far into the wilderness. Suddenly, when it was too late to escape, he learned that several large bands of backwoodsmen were pouring through the defiles of the Alleghanies to cut off his retreat. Retiring to the South Carolina border he took up a position on King's Mountain, a lofty ridge covered with boulders, underbrush, and trees.

The frontiersmen, in fringed hunting-shirts, with sprigs of hemlock in their hats and armed with long knives and rifles, closed in on the enemy from three sides. The British regulars charged down among the encircling Americans, but they were impeded by the roughness of the ground and were cut to pieces. As the survivors fell back up the slope, the backwoodsmen followed, rushing from one bit of underbrush to another, and firing with deliberateness. The Tories fought well, but they too were overwhelmed. At last a rifle-ball struck the brave Ferguson, and his followers laid down their arms. In this engagement the British and Tories lost 1,105 men, the revolutionists 88.

Following the defeat of Gates at Camden, Congress asked Washington to select a new commander for the Southern army, and Washington, with his accustomed wisdom, named General Nathanael Greene. There began now a series of marches, sieges, and battles, which continued for eight months and ended in the reconquest of all South Carolina, save the territory around Charleston, and all Georgia save Savannah. During this time Greene marched nearly a thousand miles, fought three battles, conducted five sieges, and took nearly 3,000 prisoners. This he accomplished in the face of armies outnumbering his own three to one, composed of veterans, thoroughly equipped and supplied.

Greene operated without a base, living off the country, and

frequently was without tents, equipage, or proper clothing and food. His men were undaunted by the snows and cold rains of the winter or the heat of the summer. He was always busy, now forcing a garrison to surrender by erecting a wooden tower, now cutting off small detachments, now hastening across country to gain the protection of some deep river. In all his chief engagements—Guilford Court House, Hobkirk's Hill, Eutaw Springs—he was defeated, but each time he wrested from his enemy the fruits of the victory. "We fight, get beat, rise and fight again," he wrote, and in the end complete success was his. Greene's campaigns in the South are among the most brilliant in American history.

In the autumn of 1780 an incident occurred which filled the country with anger and caused Washington many forebodings. Among the ablest of the American generals was Benedict Arnold. Energetic, impetuous, quick in formulating plans, prompt in putting them into execution, he early won Washington's confidence. But Arnold now considered himself a wronged man. In 1777, when Congress had appointed five new major-generals, he was passed over in favor of Stirling, Mifflin, St. Clair, Stephen, and Lincoln, none of them his equal. Later he was tried by court-martial on a number of charges, found guilty on two minor counts, and sentenced to public censure.

While stationed at Philadelphia, he had married the beautiful Margaret Shippen, the daughter of a gentleman of Tory sympathies. This drew him into the society of loyalists. General Reed wrote that Arnold had given a party to which he invited "not only common Tory ladies, but the wives and daughters of persons proscribed by the State." To make matters worse, Congress disallowed many of his claims for money advanced to the army for supplies, so that he faced financial ruin.

These accumulated misfortunes, with the influence of his wife's friends, easily explain Arnold's treason; they cannot excuse it. Had he retired to private life, trusting that in time justice would be done, he would rank to-day high among the heroes of the Revolution. Instead he tried to right his private injuries by the betrayal of the revolutionary cause.

In July, 1780, when Arnold asked for the command of West Point, Washington complied, glad of an opportunity to show his continued confidence. West Point was the key to the North. Here Washington had built a chain of forts to guard the Hudson and preserve communications between New England and the Middle States. Could this position be delivered up to the British, they would extend their lines to Canada, cut the country in two, and gain all that Burgoyne's army had been sacrificed in the attempt to accomplish.

The traitor arrived at West Point in August, and requested Clinton to send an agent up the river to arrange the surrender. The mission was intrusted to Major André, a young officer of promise and popularity. Ascending the Hudson on the *Vulture*, he came ashore at midnight in a rowboat sent out by Arnold.

There followed a conference in the bushes at the foot of Long Cove Mountain, two miles below Haverstraw. Throughout the autumn night, in the shadow of the heights, with the river at their feet, the plotters continued their whispered conversation. When the gray streaks appearing over the tree-tops of the eastern shore warned them that dawn was breaking, many details still remained to be settled. So they slunk away to a private residence four miles away within the American lines. Here André remained throughout the day, ready to go back at dark.

In the meanwhile, a battery on the east bank opened fire on the *Vulture*, and compelled her to retire down the river. Thereupon Arnold's boatmen refused to row André back, and he had to make the return journey to New York by land. André took with him six papers with descriptions of the fortifications and the disposition of troops, concealing them in his boots. He then exchanged his uniform for civilian's dress, took a pass from Arnold, and set out on horseback.

Upon this lone traveller, in the Westchester woods, depended the course of American history. Had he reached the city, the plot would probably have succeeded, and with the loss of the Hudson the cause of liberty would have been almost hopeless. But fate determined otherwise. André was stopped by three young men, members of one of the free-lance bands which operated in this vicinity, the papers were discovered and he was brought back within the American lines.

On the morning of September 25 Arnold sat down to breakfast in the dining-room of the Beverly Robinson house at the foot of Sugar Loaf Mountain. Despite the merry blaze in the fireplace, which cast shadows over the rough-hewn beams of the low ceiling, the company seemed overcast with gloom. Suddenly a young lieutenant came in and handed Arnold a despatch. No trace of emotion was discernible on the traitor's face as he read the letter. Excusing himself he went up to Mrs. Arnold's chamber, and in hurried tones told her that he must flee for his life. Leaving her in a swooning condition, he mounted his horse and dashed down an unfrequented path to the river. He then entered his barge, and directed the six oarsmen to pull for the *Vulture*. He was proceeding under a flag of truce, he explained, to open negotiations with the enemy. A moment later he was gliding beneath the Highlands in the red, yellow, and brown of autumn, past Fort Clinton, past Anthony's Nose, past Peekskill, past Stony Point, out into the beautiful Tappan Sea. A few minutes later he was on board the *Vulture*.

Arnold received £6,300 from the British Government, he was made a brigadier-general, and escaped his creditors in America. But he gained this at the cost of the detestation of Americans and the scorn even of Englishmen. "What would be my fate," he is said to have asked an American captured during his campaign in Virginia, "if my misguided countrymen were to take me prisoner?" "They would cut off the leg that was wounded at Quebec and Saratoga," was the reply, "and bury it with honors of war. The rest of you they would hang on a gibbet."

As for poor André, he was tried as a spy and hanged. André was young, frank, generous, and brave, and his fate roused the compassion even of his judges. But those English historians who declare his execution unjustified by the laws of war have a very weak case. This is admitted by Lecky, who says that the justice of the sentence "cannot be reasonably

impugned." André came to the American positions to plot
with a traitor, he passed through the lines in civilian dress,
under a false name and with papers conveying military intelligence to the enemy. The fourteen generals who tried his
case, among them Lafayette and Steuben, were right in pro-
nouncing him a spy.

While the country was still wrought up over this affair,
events were rapidly shaping for the culminating campaign of
the war. Difficulties were accumulating for England. In
1779 Spain joined hands with France, and the next year Holland took up the sword against her ancient rival. At the same
time Russia, Denmark, and Sweden united in a league of armed
neutrality to protect their merchant vessels against search or
seizure by belligerent powers. Soon British sailors and British
soldiers were battling against heavy odds in the West Indies,
in the Mediterranean, in India. Many of England's most
valued island possessions fell into the hands of the enemy:
Minorca, St. Christopher, Nevis, Montserrat. This was highly
encouraging to the revolutionists, for it diverted England's
energies from the war on the continent of America and deprived her armies of needed reinforcements. Yet the bright
hopes of French naval co-operation so far had been disappointed. Except for forty-one days in 1779, Great Britain
had continued to control the sea, and the opportunity of those
forty-one days had been thrown away by the incapacity of
the French admiral. But now the French navy was again to
secure supremacy in America, this time for sixty-four days,
and in that interval a blow was struck which ended British
hopes of conquering the country.

In the fall of 1780 Sir Henry Clinton centred his attention
upon Virginia, and sent one detachment after another to conquer that State—Leslie first, then Arnold, and finally Phillips.
Cornwallis marched up from North Carolina, bringing the
total in the Old Dominion to 7,200 men. To oppose them
Washington sent Lafayette, von Steuben, and Wayne. In the
meanwhile, Clinton received word that a French fleet under
Count de Grasse had sailed for America, and that Rochambeau, marching west from Newport with 4,750 men, had united

with Washington at White Plains. He felt that an attack upon New York was imminent, and ordered Cornwallis to take a position on Hampton Roads, ready at a moment's notice to come to his aid. Cornwallis marched down the peninsula to Yorktown, hallowed by the execution of several of Bacon's patriots, and threw up field fortifications.

Washington, on his part, was watching the situation, ready to attack New York if Clinton reinforced Cornwallis, ready to pounce on Cornwallis if he weakened his army in Virginia to aid Clinton. At this juncture De Grasse sent word that he would sail from the West Indies on August 13 for the Chesapeake with 29 vessels of war, an army of 3,200 men, 10 field-pieces, and several large cannons. The supreme moment of the Revolution had come, and it found Washington ready. He decided to transfer his army to Virginia and overwhelm Cornwallis.

Leaving a force to guard the upper Hudson, he marched through New Jersey, crossed the Delaware and headed for the Chesapeake. Clinton was completely mystified, and even after Washington had passed New Brunswick, thought he meditated an attack on New York by way of Staten Island. In the American army itself only Washington and Rochambeau knew where they were going, until at last, as the troops filed through the streets of Philadelphia, the purpose of the expedition became clear. "They are on their way to catch Cornwallis in his mouse-trap," was the exultant cry. It was the first time that the city had seen French and American troops together, and the reception to Rochambeau was hardly less enthusiastic than that which Paris gave Pershing when, with a battalion of the 16th Infantry, he took part in the celebration of July 4, 1917. Windows were thronged with spectators, and the Frenchmen, in their fine white uniforms, were cheered again and again.

Washington did not let this enthusiasm delay his march. Five days after leaving Trenton he had reached Elkton. Embarking on transports provided by the French, the army joined Lafayette at Williamsburg on September 18. It was one of the swiftest marches in history, and can be compared with Napoleon's campaign of 1805, when he marched 400 miles from Boulogne to Ulm in 35 days and overwhelmed the Austrians.

De Grasse played his part perfectly. Entering the Chesapeake, he landed his army and then went out to meet the British fleet. A battle took place off the Virginia capes in which the English suffered so heavily that Admiral Graves was forced to return to New York. The strategy of the British armies was based on the presumption that the communication by sea would not be interrupted, and Cornwallis now was in a desperate position.

The combined American and French armies, amounting to 16,600 men, closed in on Yorktown, while De Grasse kept guard at the mouth of the York River. Parallels were started, siege guns landed from the French vessels, the British outer redoubts stormed, and their lines swept with artillery fire. On October 16 Cornwallis made an attempt to escape across the York River. His plans were frustrated by a storm which scattered his boats. The situation then became hopeless. With 2,000 men sick, with his works crumbling, with the artillery silenced, surrender could no longer be delayed.

At ten o'clock on the morning of October 17 a solitary red figure clambered on a British parapet and began to beat a parley. The noise of the drum was drowned by the cannonade, but the man's purpose was at once divined and firing ceased. Two days of negotiations followed in the old Moore House, on the York, to settle the details of surrender.

On the afternoon of the 19th the French and American armies drew up in two long lines facing each other in a field south of Yorktown. The French troops made a brilliant appearance with their white uniforms, their standards of white silk, embroidered with gilded fleur-de-lis, their plumed and decorated officers. The Americans, while less brilliant, were more picturesque. Regiment after regiment of continentals stretched out along the way, their blue uniforms dingy but showing, by their facings of white, or buff, or red, or scarlet, the services to which they belonged; beside them the light infantry with dark-blue coats and leather helmets decked with a crest of horsehair; in the second line the Virginia militia, some in the variegated uniforms of the independent bands, some in plain homespun.

Then came the British. General O'Hara, who represented Cornwallis, marched up to General Lincoln and presented his sword. Lincoln immediately returned it. Thereupon the British regiments, in new uniforms, their flags cased, the bands playing "The World Turned Upside Down," filed past and grounded arms. It was a great humiliation to these veterans. As the colonels snapped out the orders, "Present arms! Lay down arms! Put off swords and cartridge-boxes!" some were not able to suppress their tears.

When news of Yorktown reached London, Lord North recognized that the blow would be fatal to the hopes of the Tories both in America and England. He walked up and down his office in Downing Street, throwing his arms about and crying: "Oh, God! It's all over! It's all over! It's all over!" The King pleaded for a new campaign, but his henchmen would no longer follow him. In March, 1782, Lord North resigned and a Whig Ministry took office with Lord Rockingham as Premier. In the new government were many friends of America, so that peace became but a matter of arranging terms.

At this moment of triumph the United States found herself involved in new difficulties. As her troops rested on their arms, her diplomats began a contest of wits with the practised statesmen of Europe. The French and Spanish Governments had in common with the American patriots little save hostility to England. The moment independence was assured, they became potential enemies of the United States, and were ready to oppose rather than further her interests. Spain especially was hostile, for she realized that the growth of the young republic was a serious menace to Louisiana and Florida. Count Aranda spoke of the United States as a future colossus, whose growth Spain would watch with grief.

Aranda secured the secret assent of Vergennes to a plan for the region west of the Alleghanies which would cut off the United States entirely from the Mississippi. To England he conceded the country between the Great Lakes and the Ohio, while that south of the river and north of West Florida was to be organized as an Indian Territory. The northern part of this territory he placed under the protection of the United States, the southern part under the protection of Spain. This arrangement, it was felt, would check the Western settlers and give protection to Louisiana and the Floridas.

It was fortunate for the United States that her interests were in able hands. John Jay, John Adams, Benjamin Franklin, and Henry Laurens proved themselves equal to the diplomats of the Old World. Hearing that France and Spain were arranging a peace unfavorable to the United States, Jay and Adams proposed that they open secret negotiations with England. Congress had unwisely instructed the envoys "to undertake nothing in the negotiations" without the concurrence of France, and Franklin was loath to disobey. "What! would you break your instructions?" he is said to have asked Jay. "As I break this pipe," Jay replied, throwing his pipe into the fireplace. He had his way, and when Vergennes awoke to what was going on, all had been settled.

The terms were most favorable to the United States. What her allies refused her, England granted, and the Mississippi became the western boundary from its source to West Florida. The work of George Rogers Clark and his little band had not been in vain. The young republic gained a territory greater than the combined areas of France, Italy, and England. The treaty made it certain that there would be no interruption in the westward advance of the American frontier.

The concessions to the United States did not stop here. England granted the Americans the right to share in the Newfoundland fisheries, while in return she obtained for the loyalists nothing better than the promise that Congress would recommend to the States a programme of compensation. The Americans frankly admitted that such a recommendation would carry no weight, and England was compelled to appropriate large sums for the relief of the exiles. No wonder Vergennes wrote: "The English buy the peace rather than make it. . . . Their concessions regarding boundaries, fisheries, and the loyalists exceed anything I had thought possible."

The changes brought about by the Revolution were many.

The perplexity of Rip van Winkle upon awakening from his long slumber was not overdrawn by Washington Irving, for could one really have slept throughout this period he would have found a strangely altered country. Independence had been won, a federal union formed, expansion had gone on rapidly, democracy had made important gains.

The Revolution fought to preserve old rights, offered an opportunity to gain new rights. It began by resisting the encroachments of the British Government; before it ended it had done much to undermine privilege at home. The Virginia Bill of Rights and the Declaration of Independence committed the republic to the principle that all power is derived from the people. Although democracy was not attained immediately, the pathway of future progress was pointed out. Religious privilege was weakened; slavery was abolished in many parts of the North; primogeniture, entails, and manorial rights were thrown into the discard.

Major Anbury, an officer captured at Saratoga, noted with surprise this trend toward democracy. At Colonel Randolph's, at Tuckahoe, he said: "Three peasants, who came upon business, entered the room where the Colonel and his company were sitting, took themselves chairs, drew near the fire, began spitting, pulling off their country boots all over mud, and then opened their business. . . . When they were gone, some one observed what great liberties they took; he replied it was unavoidable, the spirit of independence was converted into equality, and every one who bore arms esteemed himself upon a footing with his neighbor."

CHAPTER VII

UNDER THE ARTICLES

THE necessity for united action against the British had held the country together prior to Yorktown, and when the armies were withdrawn, many looked for immediate disintegration. Josiah Tucker, Dean of Gloucester, declared that the "antipathies and clashing interests of the Americans, their difference of governments, habitudes, and manners," indicated that they would remain "a disunited people till the end of time. Suspicious and distrustful of each other, they will be divided and subdivided into little commonwealths, according to natural boundaries."

A different vision appeared to Washington and other patriotic Americans. It was a vision of a vast united nation, bound together by the love of its people for liberty, a nation compact enough to defy sectional interests, powerful enough to resist foreign encroachments. Between these two divergent paths, the one leading to discord and weakness, the other to greatness and prosperity, the American people now had to choose.

The powers which Congress at first exercised by common consent later were embodied in Articles of Confederation, and ratified by the States. Unfortunately, the weakness which had hampered the government in war, remained to paralyze its efficiency in times of peace. Each State retained its sovereignty, while the Articles termed the union "a league of friendship for the common defense."

Congress represented not the people but the States; each State had but one vote, while the passage of every bill required nine votes. There was no real executive to put the laws into effect; no judiciary to interpret and enforce them. The President of Congress was merely a presiding officer.

With the Federal Government so inefficient, men began to despise it. Richard Henry Lee, on the floor of the Virginia Assembly, spoke of Congress as "a foreign power." Often men of ability refused to serve as congressmen, and those who accepted were so dilatory that at times months passed without a quorum. When Washington resigned his command but twenty delegates were present, from seven States. To many it seemed that Dean Tucker's prophecy of disunion was to be fulfilled immediately.

But the American people would not have it so. They gave the Articles of Confederation a trial, and after eight years of chaos, discord, and rebellion, threw them aside for a binding federal union. Many useful lessons were learned in those critical days, which hastened the creation of the Constitution and in large measure shaped its character.

Of these none was more important than the insight gained into the relationship between prosperity and a stable, uniform currency. When peace was concluded, and English manufactured goods flowed into the country, all classes rushed to buy. Unfortunately, the effects of the Revolution upon agriculture and trade had left little to give in exchange. In 1784 imports of English commodities amounted to £3,700,000, while exports to England were only £750,000. This unfavorable balance had to be met in part by payments of coin, and so pounds, shillings, pistoles, or whatever else the British merchants would accept, poured out of the country. As gold and silver became scarce, their value rose and the prices of commodities declined. Each coin would now purchase more in wheat or oats or cloth.

But when money becomes dearer, it is the debtor class that suffers, for the dollars they have borrowed at a low level, they have to pay back at a high. This situation has occurred many times in history, and it always brings hardship to multitudes and ruin to some. It was inevitable that a persistent cry for cheaper money should arise. If coin could not be had, it was said, the thing to do was to print paper dollars. This would restore the standard to its former level and answer the need for currency.

Creditors immediately took alarm, for they knew that when once the floodgates had been loosened it would be impossible to check the flow of paper money. In almost every State the opposing factions locked horns and the champions of cheap currency were usually victorious. The case of New Jersey is typical. When in 1785 a bill was introduced in the Legislature calling for £100,000 of paper, letters and articles poured in upon the *New Jersey Gazette*, and the columns of that musty old journal were enlivened with recriminations and charges of disloyalty, of theft, of oppression, of political vice.

"Who is that yonder honest-looking farmer who shakes his head at the name of taxes, and protests that he cannot pay?" asked one scribe. "Why, he is a man whose three daughters are under the discipline of a French dancing-master, when they ought every one of them to be at the spinning-wheel, and who, while they should be dressed in decent homespun, as were their frugal grandmothers, now carry half their father's crop on their backs." Governor Livingston, a bitter opponent of inflation, sent a satirical petition to the Legislature asking that the paper currency be issued "upon such security as you know beforehand that it will infallibly depreciate." Among the signers were Amos Spendthrift, Josiah Workless, Jeremy Grog, Simon Dreadwork, Paul Plowless, Hezekiah Dolittle, Jeronymus Notax, David Neverpay, Jeremiah Put-off, and John Sharper. The Governor's wit was wasted. The bill was passed, the paper issued, depreciation set in, and cheap money became a reality.

The experience of Rhode Island was even worse. Here the bills of credit began to sink almost as soon as issued, creditors were cheated, merchants closed their shops, commerce languished, and the State was thrown into turmoil. With thirteen State currencies in existence, most of them depreciating, some rapidly, others more slowly, with all kinds of foreign coins in circulation—pistoles, guineas, shillings, ninepences, doubloons, pistareens—trade was hopelessly hampered.

This had a telling effect in moulding sentiment for a closer union. In every town the merchants gathered, perhaps in front of their little shops under their swinging signs, perhaps in the nearest tavern, to discuss the remedy for the plague of rag money. And seldom did they disperse without voicing the hope that a real federal government would arise, to sweep away the hodge-podge of currencies and give the country a uniform, stable medium of exchange.

These good men, keenly conscious of their own troubles, could not understand how real were the grievances of the farmers. They were surprised, therefore, to find that they could block inflation only at the imminent risk of rebellion. In Massachusetts especially the evils of the day bore heavily upon the farming classes. At a time when thousands of poor men were struggling to pay off the mortgages on their homesteads, it was unfortunate that taxes should be high and money dear. The fault lay with the wicked traders, thought the country people, for they drained off the specie, made it impossible for the debtor to pay, and then seized upon his property.

Whenever the sheriff came to foreclose a mortgage, to take the farmer's cattle and work-horse, or to lead the farmer himself to the debtor's prison, crowds assembled to denounce and threaten. The delegates from the agricultural districts rode into Boston for the next meeting of the Legislature with stern faces, carrying with them a bill authorizing an issue of paper money. If the merchants expected them to submit to ruin, while sipping foreign wines themselves and dressing their daughters in laces, they would give them a rude awakening.

But the farmers forgot that they were outnumbered by the trading classes. The delegates from the populous Eastern towns listened with impatience to the arguments for cheap money, and rejected the bill by a vote of ninety-nine to nineteen. When word of this reached the farming region, there was an outburst of anger. Seizing the muskets which had done service in the Revolution, the farmers assembled in various places, declaring that they would take the law into their own hands. They would put an end to foreclosures by breaking up the courts and expelling the rascally lawyers. At Concord a certain Job Shattuck addressed the insurgents, demanding the wiping out of debts. "Yes, Job," a voice called out from the crowd; "we know all about them two farms you can't never pay for."

Yet Job was doubtless honest in his outcry against injustice, and his followers were sober, hard-working citizens. Before long, however, every idle fellow who had felt the sting of the lash or the branding-iron began to enroll with the insurgents.

With such followers the leaders could not prevent pillaging, and the rebel bands left a trail of burning barns and ruined homesteads. Although Luke Day was the master spirit of the movement, the most prominent figure was Daniel Shays, a captain of the Revolutionary army.

In January, 1787, Shays led 2,000 men upon Springfield to capture the muskets and cannon stored in the federal arsenal. The Legislature had become aroused by this time, and Shays found 1,200 troops under General Shepard drawn up to defend the town. The jailbirds in the rebel army had little stomach for the fight, and at the first volley beat a retreat, taking with them those of sterner stuff. Shays retired to Amherst then to Pelham, and finally to Petersham. General Lincoln, who now took command of the State troops, marched thirty miles in thirteen hours over ice-covered mountain ridges, and fell upon the insurgents as they were preparing breakfast. Taken by surprise, they fled and the remnants of the army retired through the highlands of Franklin County into Vermont. Shays with 150 men was taken. This broke the rebellion, but another month elapsed before the last embers were stamped out in the Berkshire Hills.

The country stood aghast at Shays' Rebellion. From Maine to Georgia men awaited for the latest tidings from Massachusetts, while many felt that anarchy was at hand. Was it true, as the Tories had said, that liberty in practice meant license, and that the experiment of a federation of republics was doomed to failure? All eyes turned to Congress, but that feeble body gave them reason to despair of the union. The delegates were at a loss what to do. Some argued that they had no authority to send troops into Massachusetts, others that Congress might as well resign if it could not maintain order. In this predicament they decided upon an amazing compromise. The troops were voted, but with the proviso that their destination should be concealed under the cloak of a pretended Indian expedition. In the end but 200 men were enrolled, and these did little in crushing the insurrection. Washington's disgust was unbounded. "Let us have a government by which our lives, liberties, and properties may be secured," he exclaimed; "or let us know the worst." And thoughtful men everywhere echoed his words.

The various Legislatures added to the confusion by erecting tariff barriers against interstate trade. Pennsylvania discriminated against the Delaware farmers, Connecticut placed duties on goods from Massachusetts, while every Yankee sloop which came down the Sound to East River had to pay entrance fees and obtain clearances at the New York custom-house. The case of New Jersey was the worst of all. This State was peopled with hard-working farmers, who made a living by selling eggs and butter or wheat and Indian corn to the people of New York and Philadelphia. When once the Jersey man had turned his produce into shillings and ninepences, he wandered into the shops of Cortlandt or Market Streets to replenish his farm. Seldom indeed did he turn his boat homeward across the Hudson or the Delaware without a supply of muslins, taffetas, pots, and nails, which perhaps had just come in on the latest ship from London.

When the Legislatures of New York and Pennsylvania placed duties on foreign imports, there was much indignation throughout Jersey, for the merchants added the amount of the tariff to the price charged the consumer. The annual amount paid in indirect taxes by New Jersey to her two great neighbors was estimated at £40,000, a fabulous sum to the farmer. The State was likened by Madison to a cask tapped at both ends. At the next session of the Legislature at Trenton there was much heated debate, much denunciation of the greed of the New Yorkers and Pennsylvanians.

At Governor Livingston's suggestion it was decided to encourage foreign merchants to bring their goods directly to New Jersey, by establishing ports at Burlington and Perth Amboy, and making them duty free. But the attempt failed. The Jersey men had to sell their produce in New York and Philadelphia, for there were no other available markets, and where they sold they had to buy. Moreover, New York retaliated by placing a duty on New Jersey farm goods, and by requiring every Jersey shallop of twelve tons or over to enter and clear like any foreign vessel.

As a rejoinder the Legislature at first could think of nothing more effectual than placing a tax of $1,800 a year upon the few acres of Sandy Hook on which New York had built a lighthouse. Later they hit upon a plan, which, although more likely to succeed, was fraught with the gravest peril to the union— they refused to pay New Jersey's quota for the support of the Federal Government. New York and Pennsylvania were taking by their tax laws more than the full quota, they complained, and they intimated that Congress ought to make them disgorge.

This was equivalent to secession, and Congress at once sent a delegation to Trenton to remonstrate. Charles Pinckney pleaded for the withdrawal of the measure. He could sympathize with the wrongs of New Jersey, he said, but other States too were having troubles, and Congress, in its present enfeebled condition, was powerless to see justice done. But the time might not be distant when the country would have a real government, intrusted with the control of commerce, and then all local customs duties would be swept away. New Jersey would do better to hasten this bright future than to ruin all by breaking up the present union. He won his case; the Legislature agreed to pay its quota. From that day the Jersey farmers looked to a stronger constitution as their hope of release from the exactions of their neighbors.

At the same time the ship-builders and ship-owners of New England were also clamoring for united action in commercial matters. It had always been the policy of England to exclude foreigners from the trade of her colonies, and this rule she now applied against the United States. The Yankee merchantmen were cut off from their commerce with the British West Indies, which for a century had been vital to New England. Before long the idle shipyards of the Piscataqua and the slackened activity among the wharves of Boston, Providence, and New London gave evidence of real distress.

The unpleasant task of pleading with the British Government for a more liberal commercial policy fell to John Adams. The first minister to represent the independent American people at the court of St. James's, Adams was not a little embarrassed when, on May 30, 1785, Secretary Carmarthen led him through a gauntlet of ministers, lords, and bishops to the King's closet. George greeted him courteously and put him at ease. He seemed deeply moved when Adams expressed a hope that the "old good-nature between the peoples" would soon be restored, and promised to do his part.

This was a good beginning, but Adams discovered that the British idea of reconciliation did not contemplate the admission of the New England traders to the English colonies. Protracted conferences followed with Carmarthen and later with the younger Pitt, but Adams found both obdurate. England must stimulate ship-building at home, not in America, they said, otherwise the time might come when the Admiralty would have to send to the New Hampshire yards every time a frigate was wanted for the navy.

Adams was keenly disappointed. He pointed out that if England refused to open the old channels of trade, the Americans in turn might make a navigation act, excluding British ships from their ports and placing duties on British imports. "If monopolies and exclusions are the only arms of defense against monopolies and exclusions, I would venture upon them without fear." But Adams knew, and the British Ministry knew, that such a policy could not be carried out, while American commerce was regulated not by one government but by thirteen.

In practice, even the four commercial States of New England could not unite on a common plan of action. In 1785 Massachusetts and New Hampshire agreed to pass navigation acts prohibiting British ships from carrying goods out of their harbors, and imposing heavy duties on such goods as they should bring in. Rhode Island fell into line with alacrity. But Connecticut ruined all by throwing her ports open to the British.

If the commercial States, whose interests were practically identical, worked at cross purposes, it was hopeless to secure the co-operation of the agricultural States of the South. The planters of Virginia or of South Carolina could see no reason why they should exclude the British merchants, who acted as carriers and distributors of their tobacco or indigo, because the Yankee shippers were injured by the British Navigation Acts. Charles Thurston went so far as to declare, in the Virginia Legislature, that it was doubtful "whether it would not be better to encourage the British than the Eastern marine." Though he was hissed down, his words showed the gulf between the different sections.

Thus hardship and misfortune were rapidly winning over to the cause of unity one powerful group after another. To the creditor class a strong central government meant protection against the cancellation of debts; to the Jersey men it meant escape from the exactions of neighboring States; to the New England trader the opening of foreign ports; to the property-holders the ending of the threat of anarchy.

Nor was this all. South Carolina and Georgia began a dispute over the navigation of the Savannah; Virginia and Pennsylvania could not agree upon the possession of the Pittsburg region; Pennsylvania and Connecticut were upon the point of hostilities over the Wyoming Valley; while New Hampshire, New York, and Massachusetts each laid claim to what is now Vermont. At the same time Congress found it impossible to raise funds, Washington's veterans could not be paid, the interest on the debt fell far in arrears, while the national credit sank to the lowest depths.

Yet so strong was the feeling of localism, so great the differences of race, custom, and religion, so divergent the economic interests of the sections, that all these accumulated evils were not enough to make the demand for a strong government unanimous. In New England, Pennyslvania, and Virginia the small-farmer class looked with suspicion upon the federalizing movement, while New York, under the leadership of George Clinton, was chiefly concerned with its own future power.

The gazettes swarmed with letters, articles, and satires, in which "Cato" or "Plain Truth" warned the public of the pitfalls of union. Surely the people had not thrown off the yoke of England, they said, only to place their necks under the yoke of Congress. Congress had been called supine, but was it? Congressmen rolled in their carriages, voted salaries, gave away pensions, and demanded money from the States. No! The need was not for a stronger government, but hard work, economy, and obedience to the laws. If people would be content with homespun and would stop sending pistoles and guineas out of the country in exchange for luxuries, all would soon be well.

But while they were thus arguing, events in a remote part of the country were lending powerful support to their opponents. During the years from 1765 to 1783, when all eyes were fixed upon the struggle with the mother country, an event of surpassing importance had taken place upon the frontier almost unnoticed—the birth of the West. Even before the French and Indian War the hardy Scotch-Irish immigrants had carried their settlements to the foot-hills of the Alleghanies, and the more restless spirits were ready to move out into the valley of the Mississippi. Now and then some Indian trader, in coonskin cap, fringed hunting-jacket, leather trousers, and moccasins, stopped at an outlying farm to tell of the marvellous region beyond the mountains—a region abounding in stately rivers, fertile fields, tall trees, and all kinds of game.

The border settlers had listened eagerly. Already they felt crowded, for the best land had been taken, and they were dissatisfied with the sterile soil of the mountain region. In 1769 a small group of families had pushed out through the narrow valleys of southwest Virginia, to settle upon the headwaters of the Tennessee at Watauga. Others followed, until in 1772 no less than thirteen separate settlements had been made in this region. The opening of the West had begun.

Almost at the same time scattered bands, led by the famous woodsman Daniel Boone, had gone out to make their homes in the beautiful blue-grass district of central Kentucky. Driven out temporarily by the scalping-knife, they had come back in 1774, when Andrew Lewis's Virginia riflemen defeated the savages at the Battle of Point Pleasant. Town after town now arose, until, when the Revolution came to an end, the population of Kentucky exceeded 25,000.

The westward migration profoundly influenced the movement for a closer union. A new section had been added with

interests different from those of the older communities. The
settlers in most cases were not Virginians or Pennsylvanians or
Marylanders, but Scotch-Irish, who now felt themselves to be
Westerners and Americans. They looked to Congress to protect them from unfriendly State legislation.

During the Revolution a number of conflicting claims had
been advanced to the region west of the Alleghanies. North
Carolina had taken possession of what was afterward called
Tennessee, and Virginia had organized Kentucky into one great
county. Upon these points there was no cavil. But a sharp
dispute arose as to the disposal of the territory north of the
Ohio River.

When the charters of Massachusetts and Connecticut had
been framed the English Government had no idea of the vast
extent of the North American continent, and fixed the Pacific
as the western boundary of those colonies. It was now urged
that these ancient charters gave Massachusetts and Connecticut the right to a part of the prize. New York, of course, interposed its bulk between the Yankee States and the western
lands, but they would not admit that this vitiated their claims.
The New Yorkers, on the other hand, scoffed at these pretensions. The region was theirs, they said, because of the Indian
treaties which made them the protectors of the Six Nations.

To Virginia the claims of all three Northern States seemed
unworthy of consideration. Did not her charter of 1609 embrace all the Northwest region, and did not that charter ante-
date those of Massachusetts and Connecticut? Moreover, had
not Andrew Lewis with his Virginia riflemen opened the region
at the battle of Point Pleasant? Had not the Virginian, George
Rogers Clark, wrested the Northwest from the British? Had
not Virginia organized the district from Vincennes to Kaskaskia as the County of Illinois?

While this dispute was in progress, the other States looked
on with growing alarm. Maryland, Delaware, Rhode Island,
New Jersey, and New Hampshire were already overshadowed
by some of their neighbors. If they must sit idly by while these
neighbors doubled their territory, there was no telling what
injustice they might have to submit to. After all, they said,

the trans-Alleghany country would remain in American hands only if England were defeated, and all alike were fighting for this end. Fairness demanded that all should share equally in the rewards of victory.

In 1777 Maryland brought matters to a head by proposing that the western region be organized as a national domain. Receiving only rebuffs, she refused to ratify the Articles of Confederation until her demands were met. This aroused such indignation that there was talk of dividing Maryland between the neighboring States. But the hot-heads finally cooled down, some of them admitting that the Marylanders were right.

In February, 1780, New York set a good example by ceding to Congress her claims to the Western lands. Connecticut followed, while early in 1781 Virginia made a provisional promise to relinquish the region north of the Ohio. Maryland had won. In March, 1781, she ratified the Articles, and the new Confederation went into operation possessed of a great national domain. The union became more than a league of friendship; it became a partnership. Each State now had an interest in the West, and the Federal Government grew in power as settlement developed that region.

Keenly conscious of its new importance, Congress set to work to organize the domain. In 1783 it was still inhabited only by Indians, with here and there a sleepy French village or isolated military post, and Congress could work out a colonial policy in advance of colonization. What this policy was to be had already been outlined by Thomas Paine in his pamphlet *The Public Good*. Congress was to lay out the boundaries for new States, he suggested, which in time should be admitted to the Union on an equal footing with the original members.

This was a path-breaking thought. In previous history colonies had existed in part at least for the benefit of the mother country, and persons migrating to them had to submit to the dictation of those who stayed at home. Here was a plan under which new territories were to be integral parts of the nation. Such a policy, if carried out consistently, not only would eliminate many possibilities of injustice but would give promise of unparalleled growth.

It was no light thing for the East to admit so many States as partners in the Union, and there were numerous predictions of disaster. The West would draw off the population of the older States, it was said, undersell Eastern corn and wheat, control Congress, and impose its will upon the country. But the far-sighted men with whom the decision lay ignored these warnings.

In 1780 Congress promised to divide the domain into territories, to provide republican governments, and eventually to admit them to the Union, with "the same rights of freedom, sovereignty, and independence as the other States." Four years later Thomas Jefferson presented to Congress a plan of organization. The versatile Virginian was fascinated by the possibilities of the great domain, and he pictured the day when prosperous farms and cities would supplant the Indian and the woodsman. Unmindful of the balance of power in Congress, he proposed to divide the domain into no less than twelve or thirteen States. In each the settlers should establish a local government, under the control of Congress, and when the population should have become equal to that of the smallest of the older States, it might be admitted to Statehood.

Strangely enough, Jefferson failed to provide for a bill of rights, but he stipulated that the new States must have manhood suffrage, remain forever a part of the United States, have republican governments, and pay their share of the national debt. He proposed also that slavery be prohibited, not only north of the Ohio, but in the entire trans-Alleghany region. Had Congress passed the measure and had the Southern States acquiesced, slavery would have been cooped up in one corner of the country, and there would have been no contest for new slave territory, no Civil War. Unfortunately it failed, although by the narrowest margin. Virginia and South Carolina voted "No"; North Carolina was divided; New Jersey, Delaware, and Georgia were absent. But for the sickness of a delegate from New Jersey, that State would have cast its voice in the affirmative, and the measure would have passed. Upon such small incidents at times hinge the mightiest movements.

There was dissatisfaction with the ordinance of 1784 because it gave Congress no convenient means of control, and promised to make the future influence of the West too great. Accordingly, in 1787 the Northwest Ordinance was passed, providing that the region north of the Ohio be divided into not more than five Territories, that when any Territory had 60,000 inhabitants it should be admitted to the Union, that education should be encouraged and slavery prohibited. Under this ordinance the new type of American colony was first established.

While Congress was debating this measure, plans for the settlement of the region had begun. In the winter of 1787–1788 a band of forty-five New Englanders, led by General Putnam, made the arduous western journey as far as Fort Pitt. They built a great boat, fitted with bullet-proof bulwarks, named it the *Mayflower*, and when the ice broke up upon the Ohio, floated down to the mouth of the Muskingum. Here, in a great forest, dotted with the terraces of the ancient moundbuilders, they erected a fort which they called the Campus Martius. This band was the vanguard of an army of settlers, and in the next decade so many came to Ohio that in 1802 it was admitted as a State.

In the fall of 1784 a man on horseback, accompanied by one servant, made his way through the wilderness between the Cheat River and the Potomac. The rain-soaked bushes along the buffalo trails tore his clothes and deluged him with water. Once he was without food for a whole day; once he slept on the mountainside with only his cloak to protect him from the rain. It was George Washington.

He was bent not upon personal business, but as usual upon a mission of deep concern to the nation. With the first settlement of the trans-Alleghany region he had grasped the meaning of the lack of communication with the East. Unless the mountain barrier could be pierced by highways and canals, the new country would trade with foreign lands, learn to consider its interests different from those of the rest of the nation, and some day demand separation. Washington was searching out the best route between the Potomac and the Ohio.

Six days after his return to Virginia he sent a report to Governor Harrison, explaining this vital question. The flanks of the United States were touched by formidable powers, he said, which might gain a dangerous influence over the Western people, unless interest was applied to bind them to the Union. "The Western States, I speak now from my own observation, stand as it were upon a pivot; the touch of a feather would turn them any way."

Indeed, the Kentucky settlers were so highly excited that they were threatening secession. The Spaniards, who held the mouth of the Mississippi, had warned them not to bring their barges and rafts south of the Yazoo. Yet it was alone through the Mississippi and the Gulf that trade with the rest of the world was possible. While indignation was still high, Gardoqui, the Spanish Minister, took the matter up with John Jay, then acting as secretary for foreign affairs. He had learned, he said, that the Americans wanted two things: the navigation of the Mississippi and a treaty of commerce. He was ready to grant one, but not the other. The Yankee shippers might trade in the Spanish Indies, but only on condition that the United States relinquish the right of sending boats down to Natchez or New Orleans.

Whether or not Gardoqui tried to set one section of the country against the other, his proposal had that result. To the New England trader whose ship had for months been tied up at the wharf, it seemed foolhardy to hesitate. A treaty with Spain would open new avenues of commerce, relieve unemployment, and lead to a return of good times. As for the Mississippi, of what use was it? The whole Western region was a wilderness, and one might travel through it for days without chancing upon a human habitation.

But the Westerners insisted that this view was short-sighted. True, the region was as yet sparsely settled, they said, but who could view its broad valleys, fertile prairies, mountains, and rivers, without picturing for it a glorious future? To permit the West to be strangled for the sordid gains of trade, would be a sorry bargain. If Congress consented to the policy of exclusion, they might be forced to throw off their allegiance, and seek protection from England or Spain.

While this controversy was in progress, Washington busied

himself with his scheme for creating an avenue of commerce over the mountains. In 1785 he became president of a company for the improvement of the navigation of the Potomac. As nothing could be done until Virginia and Maryland agreed to a uniform policy of tariffs for the Chesapeake, commissioners from the two States met in conference at Mt. Vernon. An agreement was reached, and then, at Washington's suggestion, they requested Pennsylvania to become a party to a compact, consenting to the passage of goods through her territory from the Potomac to the Ohio.

When the Virginia Assembly met that fall, the delegates were asked to consider the question of giving Congress power to regulate commerce. This measure, which seemed the only means of securing unified trade regulations, required the unanimous consent of all the States. Everywhere its fate in the Legislatures was watched with deep interest. If it went through there was still hope in the Confederation; if it failed, continued discord seemed inevitable.

Madison opened the argument for the bill. Pointing out that the measure was needed to revive trade, enforce better treatment abroad, reconcile State duties, and raise a national revenue, he implored the delegates not to strike a death-blow at the union by defeating the bill. Could they sit complacently by while the fruits of the Revolution were lost and America fell asunder? he asked. Did they not dread a future marked by the clash of armies, crushing taxes, and national humiliation? But he pleaded in vain. The State-rights men mutilated the measure until its own advocates turned from it in disgust, and then laid it on the table.

Madison did not despair. In this crisis his mind reverted to the Mt. Vernon conference. If two States could agree on commercial matters, why not all? And if all agreed on this question, why not upon others? Who knew but that great things might come from this modest beginning? So he prepared a resolution, proposing an interstate convention to consider means of regulating commerce. To disarm suspicion he persuaded John Tyler, a strong State-rights man, to make the motion. At first it was brushed aside with contempt.

At this juncture a message came from the Maryland Legislature, announcing their adoption of the Potomac compact and suggesting a national conference to secure uniform custom duties. So others than Madison, it appeared, were in favor of this plan. Madison found support also from the Virginia merchants who were demanding that something be done to aid foreign trade. The Madison-Tyler motion was taken up as a compromise measure on the last day of the session, and rushed through with but two dissenting voices. The State-rights men who voted for this resolution little dreamed that it would lead to the formation of a real federal union.

The convention was to be held at Annapolis, far from the influence of Congress, far from wicked centres of trade, such as Boston or New York. There was to be no buttonholing of the delegates by the merchants, to make them believe that large grants of power to Congress were needed. When the appointed day arrived, commissions appeared from only five States—Virginia, Delaware, Pennsylvania, New Jersey, and New York. Massachusetts, New Hampshire, Rhode Island, and North Carolina had named commissioners, but they were not there, while Georgia, South Carolina, Connecticut, and Maryland had failed to name delegates.

With less than half the States represented the convention could not proceed, but before adjourning it took one step of supreme importance. New Jersey, in her eagerness to rid herself of the oppressions of her neighbors, had instructed her delegates to consider, not only the commercial laws but any other matter conducive to good government and harmony. Taking their cue from this action, the meeting sent out a call for a new convention at Philadelphia on the second Monday in May, to change the Federal Government in such a way as to make it adequate for the country. The delegates then went home.

Had this unauthorized invitation been issued a year earlier, it would probably have met only with rebuffs. But the same post-riders who carried the message to the Legislatures, brought alarming news of confusion in all parts of the country. Rhode Island was rent with the paper-money craze, the West was threatening secession, the dispute over Vermont was waxing hot, while staid old Massachusetts was ablaze with rebellion. The country had before it the alternative of union or anarchy.

Despite the opposition of the anti-Federalists, Madison persuaded the Virginia Assembly not only to name delegates but to include George Washington among them. This aroused great interest in all parts of the country. Might it not be that Washington was destined to lead the nation out of the present wilderness of discord, as he had led it safely through the perils of the war? New Jersey hastened to appoint delegates, and Pennsylvania, North Carolina, and Delaware followed in succession. Massachusetts for a time hesitated. The farming sections of the State were distrustful of the Federal Government, while many had scruples as to the legality of the proceedings. But when Congress, on the motion of Rufus King, itself gave its sanction, the Bay State finally chose delegates. Matters had gone so far now that other States were afraid to be unrepresented, and New York, Georgia, South Carolina, Connecticut, and Maryland fell into line. New Hampshire hesitated until June, while Rhode Island wiped its hands of the whole proceeding.

By an extraordinary chain of events this all-important assemblage was called into being. Washington's solicitude for an avenue of commerce across the Appalachian barrier led to the Mt. Vernon conference; out of the Mt. Vernon conference grew the Annapolis convention; the Annapolis convention sent out the call for the constitutional convention at Philadelphia. But the Constitution of the United States was not the result of accident. The conferences and conventions merely attested the change of sentiment, the loosening of local prejudices before the fear of anarchy. It was the condition of the currency, the interruptions in trade, the boundary disputes, the danger of disunion, the insecurity of property, the fear of internal disorder and foreign intervention which were responsible for the convention. The people had given the Articles of Confederation a fair trial, and now were voicing their desire for an efficient federal government.

CHAPTER VIII

THE CONVENTION

THE constitutional convention held its meetings in the plain but charming brick building in Philadelphia where eleven years previously Congress had passed the Declaration of Independence. On May 25 delegates from nine States having arrived, Robert Morris, on behalf of the Pennsylvania delegation, proposed George Washington for president of the convention. The choice was unanimous, and the General was conducted to the chair by Morris and Rutledge.

As he took his seat he saw before him an assemblage unsurpassed for experience and wisdom in the science of government. Franklin was indisposed that day and had not yet taken his seat; Thomas Jefferson and John Adams were in Europe; Patrick Henry, Samuel Adams, and Richard Henry Lee disapproved of the convention and stayed at home; John Jay had been excluded by the strong anti-Federalist party in New York; Oliver Ellsworth, John Dickinson, Roger Sherman, Luther Martin, and Elbridge Gerry had not arrived. Yet Washington must have felt that these illustrious men could be spared in a gathering which included James Madison, Alexander Hamilton, James Wilson, Robert Morris, Edmund Randolph, George Mason, George Wythe, Rufus King, William Paterson, Charles Cotesworth Pinckney, Charles Pinckney, and John Rutledge.

This wealth of ability was needed, however, for the convention was confronted with a task of great difficulty. Seldom in history has it been possible to form a voluntary union of semi-independent States, and never before with such divergent elements. Could the delegates prove superior to sectional prejudices, religious differences, and State loyalties; could they reconcile the interests of East and West, of mercantile and farming classes, of big and little States, of free labor and slavery? Was it possible to allay all fears, to gather all groups in one household?

The delegates themselves, union men though most of them were, had serious misgivings. Delaware, New Jersey, Connecticut, and other small States feared that in the Union they might be oppressed by their larger neighbors; Virginia and Maryland that their foreign trade might be sacrificed to build up New England shipping; the New Englanders that the West might grow into a dangerous rival. Repeatedly the convention came near shipwreck upon these vital points, and only the dread of anarchy kept the delegates at their task.

On May 29 Edmund Randolph rose and presented, on behalf of the Virginia delegation, the framework of a new federal government. The convention saw a handsome man of thirty-two, whose tall figure and confident, dignified manner commanded instant respect. Speaking in a clear, pleasing voice, he enumerated the misfortunes which had befallen the country under the Articles of Confederation, and dwelt on the need which now existed for a stronger union. He then read the Virginia plan. Under it the national legislature was to consist of two branches, the first to be elected by the people of the country as a whole, the second to be chosen by the first. It was to have jurisdiction in all cases for which the States were incompetent, it could veto State laws inconsistent with the new Federal Constitution, and use the army and navy to compel a State to obey. To carry out the laws there was to be a national executive chosen by the legislature, and to enforce them a national judiciary.

Various emotions passed over the convention as Randolph took his seat. To many the plan seemed far too radical. True, the old Confederation had been incompetent, but was it wise to rush to the other extreme? Could not stable government be secured without setting up a despotic Congress, with the powers to veto State laws and enforce its will at the bayonet's point?

It was not long before David Brearly, of New Jersey, rose to give vent to this dissatisfaction. He objected chiefly, he said, to the proposal to make the national legislature represent the people rather than the States. This had a superficial appearance of fairness, he admitted, but a deeper examination would show it to be unjust. Why should Virginia have six-teen votes in Congress while Georgia had but one? If this provision went through, Massachusetts, Pennsylvania, and Virginia, by uniting their votes, could make all the other States submit to their will.

Brearly was followed by William Paterson. Speaking with great earnestness, he declared that the people of New Jersey would never consent to the Virginia plan. Rather than be swallowed up in one compact nation, they would submit to a monarch. It had been hinted that the large States might con-federate among themselves. Let them. As for him, he would not only oppose the plan here, but he would do everything in his power to defeat it in New Jersey.

The small States had placed their case clearly, and it was now the turn of the large States. They had no reason to com-plain of their first speaker—James Wilson, of Pennsylvania. We have been told that each State is sovereign and equal, he said. But is it not also true that each man is naturally a sover-eign over himself, and therefore equal with every other man? What justice is there in giving 50 citizens of New Jersey the same weight in the government as 150 citizens of Pennsyl-vania? If the small States insist upon so unequal an arrange-ment, there can be no hope of agreement.

June 15, the small-States men took the offensive when Pat-erson submitted a plan for the amendment of the Articles of Confederation. It proposed a legislature of one House, rep-resenting not individuals, but the States. In this respect it left the old government unchanged. But it provided for an executive council and a federal judiciary, and gave Congress the power to regulate foreign and domestic commerce, levy duties on imports, and raise revenues by a stamp act. For a week the convention as a committee of the whole considered this scheme, and then, by a decisive vote, rejected it in favor of the Virginia plan.

The small-States men were not to be so easily downed. For weeks they continued to attack the provision for representa-tion by population, more than once threatening to bring the deliberations to a close. Gunning Bedford, of Delaware, was especially violent. His rotund figure vibrating with nervous energy, his gestures showing the depth of his emotion, he threw down the gauntlet. We have been told with a dictatorial air that this is our last hope of securing a good government, he thundered. It will be the last, indeed, if the propositions reported from the committee go forth to the people. We have no fear of what the large States will do. They dare not dissolve the Confederation. But if they do, the small States will find some foreign ally of more honor who will take them by the hand.

During this heated debate the aged Benjamin Franklin hung on every word, his gentle face alternately lit up with hope and overcast with apprehension. He had long been the champion of union. At a time when few dreamed of a federal government, he had planned it, argued for it, and worked for it. Now, in the evening of his life, when his fondest hopes seemed upon the point of realization, these dissensions were threatening to ruin all.

Rising, he asked why the convention, while groping in the dark, had not thought of applying to the Father of Light to illuminate their understandings? "I have lived, sir," he said, turning to Washington, "a long time, and the longer I live, the more convincing proof I see of this truth—that God governs in the affairs of men. And if a sparrow cannot fall to the ground without His notice, is it probable that an empire can rise without His aid?" He moved that each day's deliberations should be opened with prayers, imploring the assistance of Heaven. But Hamilton and others feared that to begin such a practice might betray to the public their embarrassments, and the motion was lost.

The fears of the delegates from the small States might have been spared had they listened to the prophetic words of James Madison. As this remarkable man rose to address the convention there seemed little in his appearance to mark him as a leader of men. Slight in stature, his manner shy, his voice low, to many it seemed that a diffident boy stood before them to make his first school declamation. But the clearness of the speaker's reasoning, the breadth of his understanding, his wealth of information soon made them aware of their mistake.

Madison showed that there was no reason to fear a clash between the large and the small States. Was it reasonable to suppose, he asked, that the fishermen of Massachusetts would unite with the wheat-growers of Pennsylvania or the tobacco-planters of Virginia, to oppress Connecticut or Rhode Island? No. The real line of cleavage lay between the North and South, with their contrasting climates, industries, and labor systems. It would be wiser for the delegates to begin at once the consideration of this situation, in which lay so real a menace, than to spend time contending over the imaginary differences of big and little States.

A test vote was taken on July 2. The first ten States were tied, five to five. Georgia had still to vote, and as Rhode Island and New Hampshire were unrepresented the decision lay with her two representatives. What were they to do? They both sympathized with the large States group, but if either party won, the other might organize a separate convention. To save the day Houston cast his ballot one way and Baldwin the other, the Georgia vote was nullified, and the result left a tie. This gave time for heated passions to cool. Roger Sherman rose, and in his awkward, uncouth manner suggested that a committee be appointed to devise some compromise. "We are now at a full stop," he said, "and I suppose nobody meant that we should break up without doing something."

After some debate a committee of eleven was chosen, one from each of the States present, consisting of Gerry, Ellsworth, Yates, Paterson, Franklin, Bedford, Martin, Mason, Davy, Rutledge, and Baldwin. It was a victory for the small States. Madison, Randolph, Gouverneur Morris, Wilson, King, and other strong advocates of the Virginia plan were passed over for more moderate men. The convention then adjourned for three days.

There was breathless excitement when, on July 5, Elbridge Gerry arose to report for the committee. With his thin, shrewd face, long nose, big mouth, and heavy white wig, he presented a grotesque figure. But the delegates were interested in his words rather than his appearance. The committee recommended, he said, that the Lower House of the Legislature should represent the people, with one delegate for every 40,000 inhabitants, and the Upper House the States, each State having an equal vote.

The large-States men settled back in their seats with a grunt of dissatisfaction. So this was all the committee had to offer. Several times before the Connecticut delegates had made this proposal, and it had received scant attention. Was it likely that it would succeed now? The irreconcilables were for going home. But an adjournment for a day gave time for blood to cool, and on July 6 a caucus of the large States agreed to abide by the vote. Even then, when the final vote was taken, the compromise was adopted by the narrowest margin. Connecticut, New Jersey, Delaware, Maryland, and North Carolina voted aye; the noes were Pennsylvania, Virginia, South Carolina, and Georgia; Massachusetts was divided; New York and New Hampshire were absent.

At this outcome the small-States leaders rejoiced; Madison and Wilson were dejected. Yet the compromise was a nationalist victory. What mattered it that the States stood upon an equal footing in the Senate, so long as they were indissolubly united in the Lower House? Congress was no longer to be a shadowy affair, touching the individual citizens only through the State governments. Elected in part directly by the people, it was to pass laws for the people, and enforce them through the agency of the federal courts.

The fears of the little States having been relieved, it remained to reconcile the interests of the sections. As the delegates pondered over the new structure of government, they peered anxiously into the future to determine its effect upon this group of States or that. Would the balance of power remain equal between North and South, or would the day come when one or the other of these sections could control the Lower House? Might not the West become the most populous part of the country and dictate to the older States?

July 14, Elbridge Gerry proposed that the number of representatives from new States should never exceed those from the original thirteen. "It is well enough to be just to the West," he said, "but we must not put ourselves at their mercy. If they acquire power, like all others they will abuse it, and we must expect them to tax commerce and drain our wealth into the Western country."

"Yes," said Gouverneur Morris, "we have had experience of this matter in Pennsylvania. Since the settlement of the back counties, the eastern part of the State has had to struggle to keep the upper hand. Moreover, is it to be expected that the uncouth Western country can produce men fit to administer the affairs of the nation? No. The busy haunts of men, not the remote wilderness, constitute the proper school of political talent."

These illiberal views were combated by Sherman, Mason, Madison, and others. "Are not the Western settlers our own sons?" they asked. "Shall we deprive them of an equal voice in the government? We ourselves have just won our independence because Great Britain kept us in a position of subordination. Shall we now adopt for our own colonies the narrow policy which caused us to break the tie with England? If so, it will be impossible long to hold the Western region." These arguments prevailed. The convention voted to treat new States as equals, to place no limitation on the number to be admitted, and to reapportion representation on the basis of population every tenth year.

Even before this decision the battle began between North and South. It was a moment full of evil portent; just how evil even the astute Madison could not foresee. The convention had succeeded in reconciling big and little States, because their differences were largely imaginary. But the conflict between the two great sections was based upon contrasting economic and social systems. No compromise could eradicate these fundamental differences. Compromise might bring North and South under the same roof, might guarantee a temporary balance of power, but it made all the more certain the ultimate fight for supremacy. It was a bitter trick of fate that the train of events which led to Gettysburg should have had its origin in the old State House at Philadelphia, where Northern and Southern delegates shook hands in token of perpetual friendship.

From the first the South felt at a disadvantage in the Union, because her population was less than that of the North. Had it not been that the growth of the Southwest was expected to turn the scale, the Southern leaders would probably have insisted upon guarantees to offset Northern preponderance. As it was, they demanded that in apportioning representatives, slaves be counted equally with freemen.

Against this the North protested. "I can see no just ground for such a provision," said William Paterson. "The slaves are not free agents, have no personal liberty, no property, but, on the contrary, are themselves property. In the South negroes are not counted in fixing representation in the State Legislatures. Why should we adopt such a principle in the Federal Government?" He was followed by Gouverneur Morris. "I can never agree," he said, gesticulating violently, despite his crippled arm and his wooden leg, "to put a premium upon the slave-trade by allowing the Southern States representation for their negroes. Sooner would I submit myself to a tax for a fund to free all slaves, than saddle posterity with such a constitution."

The boyish but polished Charles Pinckney rose to defend the Southern contention. "It must be remembered," he said, "that the negroes are the laborers, the peasants of the South; that the work of a slave in South Carolina is as productive of wealth as that of a freeman in Massachusetts, and is, therefore, as valuable to the nation. In a government such as we are now erecting, designed largely for the protection of property, there is no just reason for not counting the blacks."

Four years earlier, when the Continental Congress had been seeking a new basis for making requisitions on the States, it voted that in determining population five slaves should equal three freemen. Madison now suggested the same plan in this wrangle over representation. Despite bitter opposition, the compromise was adopted, and the three-fifths ratio became the standard in apportioning both direct taxation, and representation in the Lower House.

It was an illogical solution, but it saved the convention from disruption. The Southern delegates were satisfied, for they felt that now they would always be strong enough to block hostile legislation. Had they foreseen the rapid development of the Northwest and the growth of population in the North Atlantic region which was to follow the American industrial revolution, they would have drawn back in alarm. Lulled into security by a false estimate of the possibilities in their own economic system, they consented to a union which was to bring annihilation to that system.

The success of the convention was not yet assured. No sooner had this matter been settled than other conflicting interests were brought to light. When the motion was made to give Congress the authority to prohibit the slave-trade, South Carolina and Georgia protested. It is well enough for others to advocate this step, said Butler and the two Pinckneys, for in the industries of the North slaves cannot be profitably employed, while Maryland and Virginia have all they can use. But the development of the far South will be hopelessly retarded if the source of its labor supply is shut off. The Constitution will be rejected by the rice and cotton planters, if such a provision is inserted.

At the same time the Southern States, especially those of the tobacco belt, were opposed to granting Congress unrestricted power over commerce. The North has a majority in both Houses, George Mason pointed out. Is it not certain that they will pass a navigation act to aid the mercantile interests? A navigation act will hamper the tobacco-trade, increase freight rates, and blight the prosperity of the Chesapeake Bay region. "Is it to be expected that the South will deliver itself bound hand and foot to the Eastern States, so that they may exclaim in the words of Oliver Cromwell: 'The Lord hath delivered them into our hands'?"

The counter-proposal that Congress be empowered to regulate commerce only by a two-thirds vote of both Houses, met little favor from the New England delegates. If you fetter the government in such a way that it will be unable to relieve the Eastern States, what motive can they have in joining, asked Gorham? As for the danger to the South from a navigation act, it is entirely visionary. A strong merchant marine is essential, especially to the South, since it would free that section from dependence upon foreign ships.

Here were the materials at hand for a third compromise. At a conference of New England delegates with C. C. Pinckney and others from the far South, it was agreed that Massachusetts, New Hampshire, and Connecticut should vote to prolong the slave-trade for twenty years, and that South Carolina and Georgia should support the clause empowering Congress to regulate trade by a majority of votes. It was a bargain struck between the two geographic extremes of the country at the expense of the centre. "I will confess that I had prejudices against the Eastern States before I came here," said Cotesworth Pinckney, "but I have found them as liberal and candid as any men whatever."

For Virginia the new compromise was a double defeat. Her delegates were angered, not alone because of the threat to her economic system but because it would give an impetus to the growth of slavery, and make emancipation in the tobacco States doubly difficult. The Virginia leaders regarded this institution as a curse, and hoped for the day when their State would be freed from it. "Slavery discourages arts and manufactures," said Mason, in protest against what seemed to him an unholy bargain. "The poor despise labor when performed by slaves. They prevent the immigration of whites, who really enrich and strengthen a country. They produce the most pernicious effect on manners. Every master of slaves is a petty tyrant. I lament that some of our Eastern States from a lust of gain ever embarked on this nefarious traffic." Mason said little about the provision which gave Congress full power over commerce, but so bitter was his opposition that when the Constitution was completed, not only did he refuse to sign it, but fought it in the Virginia ratifying convention.

The foundations of the Federal Government were laid in compromise. The interests of States and sections had been sufficiently reconciled to permit the ratification of the Constitution, but in no case had the convention dared apply the knife. The various parts of the country came under the new roof unchanged, with their economic, social, racial, religious, and political differences as great as ever. The task of making a compact, harmonious people of these diverse elements was left to time. Yet the most dangerous part of the convention's work had now been completed, and the governmental framework was speedily filled in.

In the masterly hands of the delegates the executive and the judiciary took on their permanent form, while the powers of Congress were defined. As the work progressed it became evident that the government was not to be framed in the interests of democracy. In a sense the convention was a partisan gathering, since most of the anti-Federalist leaders refused to have anything to do with it. Moreover, it was laboring under the reaction from Shays' Rebellion, and so tried to check the power of popular majorities. The delegates did not believe in "government of the people and by the people," but in a government by "the wealth and intelligence of the country."

Before the convention had been in session a week Elbridge Gerry declared that the country was suffering from an "excess of democracy," and George Mason, unmindful of his own words in the Virginia Bill of Rights, admitted the truth of this judgment. Randolph thought that the evils of the time came from the follies of democracy, while Sherman said the people were lacking in correct information, were likely to be misled, and so should have as little to do with the government as possible. As for Alexander Hamilton, he told the convention that he did not believe in the republican form of government and wished it were possible to establish a monarchy modelled upon that of Great Britain.

This distrust of the masses was an important factor in shaping the Constitution. The selection of the chief executive was assigned to an electoral college, which the convention supposed would be a select body of men, who could bring superior judgment to the task. It was expected that the Legislatures would appoint the electors, thus refining the judgments of the populace with "two successive filtrations." The development of democracy and the party system in succeeding decades, which undermined the electoral system and made the electors mere "letter-carriers," was unforeseen by the delegates.

They tried also to erect safeguards against the "tyranny of the multitude" with a system of checks and balances, by assigning to the chief executive the appointment of judges and officials, by having Federal judges serve for life, by safeguarding personal property. They probably would have made the President's term fifteen years and permitted none but property-holders to vote, had they not feared the rejection of the Constitution by the States.

Fortunately little harm was done. The conservative temper of the delegates gave the government strength, while in the end it did not prevent the growth of democracy. The political wisdom of the fathers kept them from trying to make their work proof against change, and the more liberal spirit of later times easily impressed itself on the government.

The task of the convention was now finished. After three months of anxiety and toil, throughout the scorching Philadelphia summer, it had drawn up the greatest of written constitutions. But the delegates had misgivings as to the success of their work. Too close to the great structure to judge correctly of its splendid proportions, it seemed to them a patchwork of conflicting views and half-reconciled interests. They could only hope that it would end chaos and lend strength to the government.

When the work was over Washington sat with head bowed. The members then came forward to sign the document. As the last signatures were being affixed, Benjamin Franklin, his face alight with hope, pointed to the back of the President's black armchair, where was emblazoned a half-sun. "As I have gazed on that figure throughout the sessions," he said, "amid the conflict of my hopes and fears, I have often wondered whether it represented a rising or a setting sun. But now I have the happiness to know that it is a rising sun."

Now that the good ship Constitution had been launched, it remained with the people to decide whether it should sail on, or sink in the waters of disunion. Hardly had the delegates left when the venerable Franklin laid the document before the Pennsylvania Legislature. Here it received a warm welcome, and some of the members were for calling immediately a ratifying convention. But Congress had not submitted the Constitution to the States, and they had to curb their impatience.

Two days later a draft of the Constitution, with a letter from Washington, was placed before Congress, in session at New York. Instantly, several anti-Federalists were on their feet to oppose it. They were amazed at the document, they said. The convention had been called to revise the Articles, not to create a new government. Was it reasonable to expect Congress to end its own existence? When this plea fell on deaf ears, they tried to clog the measure with amendments. But Madison, who arrived from Philadelphia in time to rally the Federalists, soon carried all before him. After eight days of heated debate, Congress voted to place the Constitution before the Legislatures.

In the meanwhile, the Pennsylvania Federalists, weary of waiting for word from New York, decided to go ahead. On the morning of September 28 George Clymer rose, and without previous notice moved to call the State ratifying convention. The anti-Federalists were furious. An election was at hand, and they hoped for a majority in the new Legislature hostile to the Constitution. The motion was out of order, they said. Until Congress had sent them the Constitution, they could not act on it. The Federalists were well aware that it was a rule of the House that every bill should have three readings, yet they were clamoring for the passage of an all-important measure, sprung upon the Assembly without warning. But their voices were drowned by cries of "Question! Question!" The question was carried by forty-three to nineteen. The House then adjourned until four in the afternoon.

But the nineteen dissenters, before going to dinner, held an indignation meeting, and with furious whispers agreed upon a plan to foil the enemy. It took forty-seven to make a quorum. If they stayed away there would be but forty-five, and it would be impossible to name the place and date of the proposed convention. When four o'clock came, every anti-Federalist seat was vacant, and there was nothing left for the Federalists to do but adjourn till morning.

That evening all Philadelphia buzzed with excitement. Angry crowds filled the taverns and coffee-houses until far into the night, while on every street-corner Federalists and anti-Federalists held wordy battles. Soon after breakfast the next morning a group of determined men broke into the lodgings of two of the absentees, dragged them cursing and struggling through the streets to the State-house and held them in their seats. This made a quorum, and the date for the convention was set. With a shout of joy the crowd which filled the lobby and stood about the doors dispersed to their homes, while the church bells pealed out the tidings.

Now began a war of letters, pamphlets, stump speeches, and addresses. The new Constitution was a device to rob the people of their liberty, the anti-Federalists declared. A body of wealthy aristocrats had drawn it up, behind closed doors, so that nobody could know what was going on. And well they might. For they had left out all mention of a bill of rights. What was there to safeguard the liberties of the citizens, to guarantee them jury trial and protect them against the ambition of intriguing men? As for this James Wilson who was trying to pull the wool over the people's eyes, he was a Scotchman, James de Caledonia, a patrician who scorned the common people. Some had said that the character of those who drew up the Constitution was a guarantee that all was well. But was it not true that Hamilton, Madison, and many of the others were mere boys, and that Franklin was in his dotage? As for Washington, of course he was a great soldier, but what did he know about politics? At last one writer, in an article signed "Centinal," so far forgot himself as to declare that Franklin was a fool from age and Washington a fool by nature.

When the Pennsylvania convention met in the old State-house, it was obvious that the anti-Federalists had not succeeded in winning a majority. Yet they made a bitter fight. When the logic of Wilson seemed likely to bear down opposition, they resorted to filibustering. Five days were wasted in trying to settle the meaning of the two words "annihilation" and "consolidation." Several times the overwrought delegates were on the point of resorting to blows. Finally, after three weeks, the vote was taken and the Constitution ratified by forty-six to twenty-three.

Once more Philadelphia celebrated. The Supreme Council, the convention, and the faculty of the University of Pennsylvania formed in procession and proceeded to the court-house, where the ratification was read. That evening some sailors rigged up a boat, and, placing it in a wagon, dragged it through the streets. A man standing in the bow from time to time threw out a sounding line, exclaiming: "Twenty-three fathoms, foul bottom; forty-six fathoms, sound bottom, safe anchorage."

The protracted debates in Pennsylvania deprived that State of the honor of being the first to ratify. In Delaware equal representation in the Senate had silenced opposition, and on December 6 the convention at Dover voted unanimously to accept the new government. Pennsylvania ratified on December 12, New Jersey December 18, Georgia January 2 and Connecticut January 9.

All eyes now turned to Massachusetts. Should this State refuse to ratify, the friends of the Constitution would be in despair. The convention met first in the Brattle Street church in Boston, but soon after, "on account of the difficulty of hearing," moved to the meeting-house in Long Lane. Here assembled 355 delegates, representing every walk of life—learned judges, weather-beaten farmers, a Revolutionary general, blacksmiths, rich Boston merchants, shopkeepers, a noted minister, an old sea-captain, a former Governor, a Berkshire saddlemaker, a Barnstable fisherman. The delegates from Boston and other mercantile towns were strongly Federal, but they had to face the opposition of the small farmers and petty traders.

No sooner had the convention been called to order when the anti-Federalists opened fire on the clause which fixed the term of representatives at two years. Such a thing would be extremely dangerous, they said. Annual elections, which had always been the practice in Massachusetts, were necessary to safeguard liberty. If members were to be elected for two years, how could the people make them obey? "Oh, my country," burst out one delegate, "never give up your annual elections; young men, never give up your jewel."

Then there was the clause giving Congress power to regulate the place and manner of holding elections. If evil men crept into the government, could they not deprive the people of their rights by setting up the polls in remote places? Suppose they ordered the Massachusetts election to be held in the Mohawk valley or in Georgia, what redress would the people have? "Suppose they should say that none should be electors but those worth fifty or a hundred pounds sterling," roared out Abraham White, of Bristol, "can they not do it? Yes, they can, and if any lawyer can beat me out of it, I will give him ten guineas."

"Congress will have power to keep standing armies," said General Thompson. "The great Pitt says standing armies are dangerous. Don't let us go too fast. Let us amend the old Confederation. Why not content ourselves with permitting the present Congress to regulate trade? Other governments have learned how to pick the subjects' pockets without their knowing it, and so will ours. In fact, that is just what Congress is after. To those who deny this I ask, where is the bill of rights? The safety of the people depends on a bill of rights. There are some parts of this constitution which I cannot digest; and, sir, shall we swallow a large bone for the sake of a little meat? I say, let us pick off the meat and throw the bone away."

Such arguments were borne down by the convincing logic of Rufus King, Fisher Ames, Nathaniel Gorham, Judge Dana, and other able Federalists. None struck nearer the heart of the matter, however, than Captain Isaac Snow, of Harpswell, an old sea-dog, the veteran of many a voyage. "Suppose, Mr. President, I have a chance to make a good voyage, but I tie my captain up to such strict orders that he cannot take advantage of the best market in which to sell my cargo or my vessel. If, then, I find on his return that the voyage has been unprofitable, I have only myself to blame. Thus, sir, Congress cannot save us from destruction if we tie their hands and give them no power."

As the debates waxed hot, both parties waited for some

expression of opinion from Samuel Adams. So evenly divided were the factions that his great influence would decide the result. For some weeks Adams refused to commit himself, and sat silently listening to the arguments. At last it became known that his chief objection to the Constitution was the lack of a bill of rights. This made the prospect of ratification extremely dark. Changes in the document could be made only by calling another national convention, and another convention might undo all that the first had accomplished. Washington wrote urging the delegates not to make this fatal mistake. But he reminded them that when the Constitution had been adopted, the people could pass any amendment they desired. Acting upon this suggestion, Governor Hancock, who was presiding, proposed a compromise. Let us ratify, he said, without conditions, but with a resolution urging the passage, at an early date, of an amendment guaranteeing the liberties of the people. Adams gave instant approval, and a few days later the Constitution was accepted by 187 votes to 168.

Six States had now come under the new federal roof, and only three more were needed to put the government into operation. April 28, Maryland ratified sixty-three to eleven, and a month later South Carolina followed. As it was almost certain that New Hampshire would come in, the situation for Virginia, New York, North Carolina, and Rhode Island now took on a new aspect. These States had to choose, not between the old Articles of Confederation and the Constitution, but between accepting the Union or staying out.

The Virginia convention assembled at Richmond, in the New Academy on Shockoe Hill. The delegates presented striking contrasts—wealthy tobacco-planters in fine broadcloth, laced ruffles, silk stockings, and silver buckles; poor farmers clad in homespun; Kentucky pioneers, unabashed in buckskin coat and fringed trousers. Foremost among the Federalists were Madison, Randolph, and John Marshall, while the opposition was led by Patrick Henry and George Mason. Washington was not present, but the fact that he was so heartily in favor of the Constitution exerted a powerful influence upon the delegates. Henry, who had done so much to arouse the country against

Great Britain, now pleaded against ratification. He was the leader of the small-farmer class of the southern and western counties, and the small farmers were anti-Federalist.

Henry declared that the Constitution would create, not a federation, but a "consolidated government." This was obvious, he said, from the wording of the preamble: "We, the people of the United States . . . do ordain and establish this Constitution." "I have the highest veneration for those gentlemen," he declared, "but, sir, give me leave to demand, what right had they to say: 'We, the people'? My political curiosity, exclusive of my anxious solicitude for the public welfare, leads me to ask, who authorized them to speak the language of 'We, the people' instead of 'We, the States'?"

This matter had been debated in the national convention, and all had agreed that ratification should be by States. But the delegates wished the assent of each State to rest upon the final depository of sovereignty in that State, which they considered to be the people. The preamble had at first read: "We, the people of the States of New Hampshire, Massachusetts, Rhode Island," etc. But when it was decided to put the new government into operation when nine States had ratified, it was obviously impossible to mention them in advance, and all names were omitted. No change of meaning was intended.

Madison rose and explained this matter to the Virginia convention. "Who are the parties to the Constitution?" he asked. "The people—but not the people as composing one great body but the people as composing thirteen sovereignties. . . . No State is bound by it, without its own consent. Should all the States adopt it, it will then be a government established by the thirteen States of America, not through the intervention of Legislatures but by the people at large." The anti-Federalists were satisfied, and the discussion turned to other points.

Henry continued to denounce the new Constitution, and to picture the miseries it would bring. The delegates could see the tyrant sitting upon his throne, could hear the tread of mercenary troops, the cries of the oppressed people, the clank of chains, the grating of the prison doors as they opened for their victims. The President would make himself King, he would use the army to oppress the people, he would send his tax-collectors to take their property, he would be a Cæsar, a Cromwell. As for the proposal to adopt the Constitution upon the chance of getting it amended afterward, to mention such a thing was to insult one's understanding. You agree to bind yourself for the sake of what? Of being unbound. You go into a dungeon—for what? To get out.

Henry's pleadings were in vain. Early in the debates Edmund Randolph, in an address unsurpassed for logic and clearness, had explained that Virginia dared not undertake a career as a separate nation. What would be our situation, he asked? On the east the Chesapeake Bay and our many wide rivers afford an enemy access into the heart of Virginia, while the lack of a navy makes it impossible for us to oppose them. It is an ancient maxim that he who commands the sea will command the land. We have no manufactures, we depend upon other nations for our supplies, and our exports are carried entirely by foreigners. To the north and south we should be surrounded by the new Union, while on the west we should have to fight the savages unaided. In our vitals there is a fatal weakness, for an enemy could easily attack us through our slaves. Virginia must either confederate with her sister States, or enter upon an independent career the most perilous ever undertaken. These arguments prevailed. When the question was put, eighty-nine were for ratification, seventy-nine for rejection.

New Hampshire had already ratified, so that ten of the thirteen States were now safely under the new roof. Everywhere the people rejoiced, and the coming Fourth of July was set aside for festivities. Philadelphia celebrated with a monster procession. After the manner of the mediæval parades, every trade was represented—doctors, merchants, brewers, gunsmiths, saddlers, tanners, shipwrights. There were wagons carrying emblematic devices, bands of music, gorgeous banners. The crowds were aroused to enthusiasm when the good ship *Union* came in sight, fitted with masts and sails and manned by four boys. That night the taverns and coffeehouses were filled with revellers, while many a lusty bumper was turned off to Washington and the other builders of the Constitution.

Although the new government was now to be put into operation, without New York, North Carolina, and Rhode Island, the Union would be far from complete. The anti-Federalist sentiment was strong in all three States, but it was hoped that their isolation eventually would force them to ratify. In the New York convention, at Poughkeepsie, the brilliant Hamilton struggled against the anti-Federalist majority. Week after week, he fought the battle for the Union. But the opening address of Chancellor Livingston, explaining how foolish it would be for New York to launch out upon a separate career, was also a powerful factor in deciding the result. How could you defend Long Island? he asked. How keep a hostile army and navy from taking Staten Island, and perhaps Manhattan? How could we expel the British garrisons from the posts in the Northwest, how subdue the hostile Indian tribes? How defend the east bank of the Hudson from an attack from New England? These questions could not be answered. When the final vote was taken, the Constitution was ratified, thirty to twenty-seven.

North Carolina and Rhode Island still held out. The North Carolina convention which met July 21, adjourned August 1 without reaching a decision. As for Rhode Island, she had refused even to summon a convention, contenting herself with a direct popular vote upon the Constitution. Since the Federalists stayed away from the polls in protest against these proceedings, the count stood 2,708 to 232 in favor of rejection. But it was obvious that sooner or later the two States would have to yield. When Congress assembled, a revenue act was passed placing duties on goods from Rhode Island and North Carolina. This was enough for the Carolinians, and on November 21, 1789, they ratified. A threat to cut off Rhode Island from all commerce with the United States finally brought that State to terms. The vote of ratification was taken May 29, 1790, and the Union was complete.

CHAPTER IX

LAUNCHING THE GOVERNMENT

WHEN the sun rose over New York City on March 4, 1789, the guns at the Battery fired a salute. They were celebrating the death of the old Confederation and the birth of the new Union. The members of Congress and the presidential electors had been chosen, and the day had come for putting the government into operation. There was a note of anxiety, for many of the members had not arrived, and without them no business could be transacted. As the day wore on, crowds gathered at the ferries watching for the absentees. When night came, only eight Senators and thirteen Representatives were on hand.

The roads were bad, some members were delayed by personal business, others by contested elections. The next week passed and the next, and still neither House had a quorum. The anti-Federalists began to scoff, the friends of the Constitution to become alarmed. After all, the new government was showing no more life than the old. It was a month after the appointed date before enough members assembled for Congress to organize. On April 6, both Houses repaired to the Senate chamber for the opening of the electoral ballots. There had never been any doubt as to who would be President. When the votes were counted, it was found that George Washington had been chosen without a dissenting voice. Next on the list was John Adams, who became the first Vice-President.

On April 14 messengers arrived at Mt. Vernon to inform Washington of his election, and two days later he set out for New York. He had hoped to pass the remainder of his days on his plantation, but now he was summoned again, this time to take the lead in launching the government. Though his mind was weighed down with this responsibility, his heart was gladdened by the signs of respect which greeted him upon his journey. He was escorted from town to town by troops of horse. At Alexandria, at Georgetown, at Philadelphia, at

Trenton, he was entertained. Everywhere were triumphal arches, flags, fireworks, cheering crowds, and addresses of welcome. Upon his arrival at New York he was greeted by Governor Clinton, Senators, and Representatives, and conducted to his lodgings. On the 30th came the inauguration. At noon Washington repaired to Federal Hall, where he was presented to Congress. As he emerged upon the balcony for the ceremony, a shout arose from the crowd which packed Wall Street and overflowed into Broad Street. Washington wore a suit of dark-brown cloth, white silk stockings, and shoes adorned with silver buckles. As the secretary of the Senate held out the Bible upon a velvet cushion, a hush fell upon the assemblage. Chancellor Livingston administered the oath of office, and then, leaning over the balustrade, shouted: "Long live George Washington, President of the United States."

Now ensued a dispute over matters of ceremonial and style. Washington came before Congress with an "opening" speech, and each House began the preparation of an "address of thanks." How was the President to be styled? After much deliberation the Senate recommended that he be addressed as "His Highness, President of the United States of America and Protector of the Liberties of the Same." This was too much for the more democratic House. They would have nothing to do with what they called an attempt "to ape monarchic practice" and insisted upon addressing Washington as "President of the United States."

Congress then turned to the business of organizing the government. This was second in importance only to the forming of the Constitution itself. The Constitution was a skeleton, an admirable skeleton it is true, but still a skeleton. It remained for the President and Congress to equip it with flesh and blood, and to endow it with vigor. Had this task fallen to weak men, or to men of strong State-rights sympathies, great injury might have been done.

Before Washington reached New York Madison had attacked the problem of raising a revenue. Brushing aside all plans for direct taxation, he proposed to meet the government's needs by a 5 per cent ad valorem duty on imports. The members of Congress readily agreed to this scheme in outline, but when it came to arranging details, sectional differences flared up again.

The suggestion that rum, because injurious to morals, should be subjected to an exceptionally high duty, aroused the Eastern members. Lay such a tax, said John Lawrence, of New York, and in a few months every creek, secluded bay, and swamp along the coast from Maine to Georgia, will be a nest of smugglers. There, in the dark of each moon, hogsheads will be run ashore and hidden. There will spring up on land an army of custom-house officers, on sea a navy of ships, hailing every schooner, giving chase to every shallop that comes in sight.

We are not in church nor at school, added Fisher Ames, to sit listening to harangues of speculative piety. When we take up morality, then let our system look toward morality and not confound itself with revenue and the protection of manufacturers.

But when it came to laying a tax on the importation of slaves, the Northerners not only favored it, but expressed their regret that the Constitution limited the duty to ten dollars. The Southerners, in turn, were opposed to any tax on their imports, especially imports of slaves. As for a tonnage duty to encourage the Eastern ship-builders, they were sure it would increase freight rates and ruin the planters. Pierce Butler, of South Carolina, "flamed away and threatened a dissolution of the Union, with regard to his State, as sure as God was in the firmament."

Nor were the Middle States less sensitive of their interests. When it was proposed to admit steel free of duty, George Clymer protested because in Philadelphia there was a furnace capable of producing two or three hundred tons a year. On another occasion when the demands of Pennsylvania were attacked in the Senate, Robert Morris became so angry that one "could see his nostrils widen and his nose flatten like the head of a viper." Despite this wrangling, the bill was passed, and funds poured in. But the debates had shown that the germ of disunion still existed, and that sectional interests were dangerous even under a vigorous central government.

Congress now took up a series of important measures. Twelve amendments to the Constitution were recommended embodying the principles of a bill of rights; a system of courts was created which in its main features has lasted to the present day; executive departments were established for foreign affairs, finances, and the army and navy. So vital were these matters, that the first Congress, like the French Estates-General which was meeting at the same time, assumed the character of a constituent assembly.

The President's Cabinet was the creation of neither the Constitution nor of Congress. When the heads of departments were appointed, it was taken for granted that the President would consult them singly. Before long, however, Washington began to treat them as an official family, calling them into council as a body. It was his desire that his government should represent no single party, and for the Cabinet he sought the man best suited for each post.

The two most important folios he intrusted to men of the most antagonistic views. To Jefferson the political creed of Hamilton was anathema; Hamilton was sure that Jefferson, if he ever had his way, would bring the country to anarchy and ruin.

It is unfortunate that no word has been left of the early Cabinet meetings, but we may picture the little group, gathered around Washington, gravely discussing the future of the nation. On one side was the tall, loose-jointed Jefferson, his complexion ruddy, like one accustomed to out-of-door life, his hair sandy, his features clean-cut and strong, his expression always pleasant and friendly. He sat in a lounging manner, with one shoulder elevated, from time to time shifting his weight from one hip to the other. Beside him was Hamilton, small in stature, distinguished in bearing, and correctly, if not elegantly, attired. His features, rather severe when in repose, lit up pleasantly when he spoke. With them sat General Henry Knox, Secretary of War, and Edmund Randolph, Attorney-General.

"Mr. President," Hamilton says, "the new government is in every way an improvement upon the old. It is not what I should have wished, for in my opinion the British Constitution is the best in the world, yet if its provisions are carried out with vigor it will go far toward attaining stability. The Constitution permits the widest latitude of interpretation. Should we not avail ourselves of this to tone our government as high as possible, give power to the executive, and cement closely the Union of the States?"

"Most assuredly not," replies Jefferson. "What right have we to distort the Constitution in order to rob the States of the powers reserved to them? The wording is clear; it is our duty to adhere to the obvious intent of those who framed it. As for the strength of the government, it already has every power essential to law and order. If we establish the principle you advocate there will be no end until all things have been drawn into Federal hands. Will not the people then lose the art of self-government? Will they not be oppressed? What the nation needs is not centralization but democracy. Every government degenerates when intrusted to a limited number of rulers. The government of Great Britain has been corrupted because not one man in ten has the right to vote."

"On the contrary," Hamilton replies, "good government depends upon the intelligence of the rulers; if the masses be rulers, there will be bad government, because the intelligence of the masses is low. Your people, sir, are a headless mob, easily led by demagogues, incapable of correct decisions, swayed by passion and prejudice. A beast, sir, a stupid beast."

"Must we, then, purchase efficiency at the cost of liberty?" Jefferson asks. "Must the people be delivered into the power of the few, merely because the few are more adept in the art of government? Better, far better, will it be to instruct the people. Yes, sir, I look to the diffusion of light and education as the one great means of preserving liberty. When every citizen has been rooted in the fruitful soil of knowledge, he cannot be deceived by the designing."

In these debates we may picture Washington listening intently, the gravity of his face reflecting the seriousness of his responsibility. The President felt keenly that the nation needed strength. No doubt Jefferson was right in much that he said, but with the government still untried and disunion possible, he felt it wise not to reject the constructive programme which the Secretary of the Treasury laid before him. Gradually, Hamilton became the active force in the administration, while Jefferson's advice went unheeded. Finally Jefferson withdrew from the Cabinet, feeling that he could not assist in carrying out policies of which he disapproved.

Jefferson's resignation did not mean that he had given up the battle; it meant only that he had shifted the battlefield. He took his case to the people, whom he so greatly trusted, and asked them to decide. There were two points of conflict between Hamilton and Jefferson, the conflict between centralization and localism, and the conflict between aristocracy and democracy. In the first, the victory fell to Hamilton; in the second, Jefferson had his way. These two men, despite the antagonism of their views, succeeded each in his own way in moulding the plastic structure of the young nation. One gave it the strength to withstand the shocks of the future; the other converted it into a democracy. It has been said that if America is right, Thomas Jefferson was right; but had it not been for Hamilton, there might have been no nation for Jefferson to democratize.

Hardly had Hamilton entered upon his duties as Secretary of the Treasury when Congress called upon him for a report on the state of finances. Nothing could have been more to his liking. On January 14, 1790, his plan for restoring the national credit was read before the Houses. This report, which is regarded as the corner-stone of American public credit, recommended that the Federal Government pay at once the national debt, by issuing new bonds and exchanging them at par for the old. In this funding operation he included the debts contracted during the Revolution by the States. In the common war, he said, a defense of any part of the country contributed to the safety of the whole. If local expenses are not met by the central government, the sections which have been most severely ravaged will have to bear the heaviest burden.

The State-rights men listened to the reading with astonishment. Who is this boy, they asked, that he should talk so glibly of shuffling back and forth tens of millions of dollars?

The old bonds were selling for a fraction of their face value; was it just to pay twenty shillings in the pound to one who had given no more than three? As for assuming the State debts, such a plan was a "monument of absurdity." Virginia had already paid off a large part of her debt; why should she have to help her more tardy sisters? Assumption would run the national obligations up to $75,000,000; could the government bear such a burden?

But the mercantile and financial interests rallied to the support of the measure. The national credit must be restored, they insisted, and every creditor paid to the last cent. Soon it became obvious that nothing could block the first part of Hamilton's plan. But the assumption bill hung fire. New England as a whole favored it; the Middle States were divided; Virginia, Maryland, Georgia, and New Hampshire fought it. Madison argued against the bill, and finally it was rejected by the House.

The result was received with exultation by the enemies of the measure, with chagrin by its supporters. "Sedgwick, from Boston, pronounced a funeral oration over it. He was called to order; some confusion ensued; he took his hat and went out. When he returned, his visage bore the visible marks of weeping. Fitzsimmons reddened like scarlet; his eyes were brimful. Clymer's color, always pale, now merged to a deadly white; his lips quivered, and his nether jaw shook with convulsive motions; his head, neck, and breast contracted with gesticulations resembling those of a turkey or goose nearly strangled in the act of deglutition. . . . Wadsworth hid his grief under the rim of a round hat. Boudinot's wrinkles rose in ridges and the angles of his mouth were depressed and assumed a curve resembling a horse's shoe."

But Hamilton was not yet defeated. A controversy was in progress over the selection of a site for the Federal capital. This meant nothing to Hamilton, who was devoted to the task of adding strength to the government, but to Congress and to the public it was a question of intense interest. The Southern members favored a site on the banks of the Potomac; the New Englanders would hear of no place farther south than New

York; Robert Morris suggested Philadelphia, while William Maclay argued for a spot on the Susquehanna, which he knew to be the best because he lived there himself.

One day, as Jefferson was on his way to Washington's residence, he met Hamilton on the street, and a conversation ensued over the matter of assumption. The two men walked back and forth in front of the house for a half-hour, while Hamilton pleaded for his pet measure. Finally, he intimated that if enough Southern votes could be brought over to insure the passage of the bill, he would undertake to have the site of the government in the South. The next day Hamilton and Madison dined with Jefferson, and it was arranged that the capital should remain in Philadelphia for ten years, after which it was to be permanently in a Federal district on the Potomac. Two of the "Potomac members," though "with a revulsion of stomach almost convulsive," were induced to vote for assumption, and this bit of log-rolling went through without a hitch.

"Now," said Jefferson, "couriers and relay horses by land, and swift-sailing pilot-boats by sea, were flying in all directions. Agents were employed in every corner of the land to buy up the State bonds at five shillings in the pound, before the holders knew of the action of Congress. Immense sums were thus filched from the poor and ignorant." Perhaps Jefferson was a prejudiced witness. Evils unquestionably attended the Assumption Act, but the benefits also were great. As Hamilton had foreseen, it strengthened the Federal Government in that it arrayed the propertied interests behind it by forcing thousands of creditors to look to the national Treasury for payment.

Hamilton did not stop here. He secured an excise on the manufacture of spirituous liquors, established a mint, and recommended the founding of a national bank. It was this last measure which most aroused the State-rights men. They were opposed to banks, they said. Banks were aristocratic institutions which robbed the poor, took coin out of circulation, encouraged usury, and set up false credits. The government would do well to destroy the banks already in existence rather than to create one of its own. Moreover, the whole thing was unconstitutional, for the powers of Congress were clearly enumerated, and the establishment of a bank was nowhere to be found among them.

Hamilton argued that such a grant was implied in the "necessary and proper" clause of the Constitution. The Federal Government had the power to borrow money and care for the national finances. The bank was designed to aid in carrying out these functions. True, it was not absolutely necessary, but "necessary" in the sense here used meant only suitable. Jefferson pleaded with the President to veto the bill. Hamilton's argument of loose interpretation would make possible an unlimited increase of Federal authority. If this thing went through, every time Congress wished to pass a law prohibited by the Constitution, it would bring out the "necessary and proper" clause, twist it to suit the occasion, and claim that it gave the desired authority. Washington was long undecided, but at last he signed the bill, and the first Bank of the United States was established.

The government now faced the first real test of its strength. In January, 1791, Congress had placed an excise on whiskey. This angered the Western farmers, and drew vigorous protests from the Legislatures of North Carolina, Virginia, Maryland, and Pennsylvania. Was it right that a staple product of one section, the poorest section of all, should be singled out for this burden? Every one knew that it was impossible for the people of the West to market their grain until it had been turned into whiskey. A pack-horse could carry only four bushels of grain over the mountains, but in the form of whiskey he could carry the product of twenty-four bushels. In western Pennsylvania a Federal collector was waylaid by armed men, stripped, tarred and feathered, his hair cut off, and his horse stolen. A half-witted messenger who began serving writs upon the perpetrators of this outrage was robbed, whipped, tarred and feathered, and left tied to a tree in the woods. For two years this defiance of Federal authority went unrevenged, while bands of disguised persons, known as Whiskey Boys, patrolled western Pennsylvania, beating those who paid the tax and burning their stills. Collectors visited the region at the risk of their lives.

The issuing of fifty writs against the lawbreakers in the summer of 1794 brought matters to a head. A mob gathered at Braddock's Field to attack the garrison at Pittsburg. The next day they crossed the Monongahela, and marched through the streets of the town. But they did not molest the soldiers, and after a few acts of violence dispersed.

The Federal Government now aroused itself. Hamilton advised the President to send a strong force into the disaffected region. "The new government is on trial," he said, "and if it fails in this crisis, the people will despise it. We must show them that it has the power to make its laws respected." The President agreed, and on August 7 issued a call for the militia of Virginia, Pennsylvania, Maryland, and New Jersey. There was a prompt response, and a few weeks later the army, in two long columns, was winding its way over the Alleghany Mountains.

There was no resistance. Awed by this force, the insurgents sent in their submission. A few wretches were dragged out of bed by the soldiers, beaten with scabbards, and hustled off half-naked to prison. Later they were sent to Philadelphia and paraded through the streets with the word "Insurgent" on their hats. Two were condemned to death, but Washington pardoned them. As Shays' Rebellion exposed the helplessness of the old Congress, so the vigor with which the Whiskey Rebellion was put down made it evident that the new government was fully able to preserve order.

In foreign relations the results of the closer union at first seemed disappointing. England showed no inclination to modify her commercial laws; Spain was still determined to stifle the Ohio region by closing the mouth of the Mississippi. Yet in reality the new government added strength to our diplomacy at a time when it was most urgently needed. While Washington was taking the oath of office as President the first rumblings of the French Revolution were heard. A few years later that movement had convulsed Europe, and the republic was confronted with all kinds of dangerous diplomatic questions.

There had been trouble from the outset with Great Britain over the fulfilment of the treaty of 1783. Article IV stated that "creditors on either side shall meet with no lawful impediment to the recovery . . . of debts heretofore contracted." The Revolution had found the balance-sheets greatly in favor of the British, for the Americans habitually bought goods on credit. The ink on the treaty was hardly dry before the agents of the English creditors were swarming in every State, trying to collect these old debts and urging the courts to carry out the treaty in good faith.

They met strenuous resistance. The debtors filled the gazettes with denunciations of this feature of the treaty. Part of the goods for which payment was demanded had been stolen by the British troops, they said. The British in many cases had carried off the very tobacco, or rice, or wheat which the Americans had intended to send in return. Now they demanded payment for goods they themselves had seized, and the American commissioners had been stupid enough to assent. These arguments carried great weight with the judges. Soon the British agents were complaining that some of the States, contrary to the intent of the treaty, were blocking the collection of the debts, while scores of debtors turned their property into cash, and hastened off to Tennessee or Kentucky.

To this controversy was added another over the treatment of the loyalists. The treaty had stipulated that Congress should recommend to the States the granting of amnesty to all Tories and the restoration of their property. Congress promptly complied, but their recommendation was ignored. The evil done by these people was fresh in the memory of all —how they had aided the enemy, had stirred up the savages, had plundered, robbed, and burned. For Great Britain to ask leniency for them seemed a bit of effrontery. They ought to migrate to England, it was said, where they would at last be under the protection of their beloved King. If they remained in America, nothing could save them from their merited punishment.

The British retaliated by refusing to evacuate the posts at Oswego, Erie, Detroit, and other points in the northwest. John Adams protested, but he found Carmarthen and Pitt adamant. The posts would be surrendered, they said, when the agreement relating to the debts and loyalists were carried out. England retained control over the Great Lakes region, and diverted down the St. Lawrence hundreds of thousands of dollars worth of furs which should have gone to Albany. The Canadians began to talk of holding the posts permanently, while irresponsible spirits supplied the Indians with arms and invited them to attack the Americans.

The savages needed little urging, for they were alarmed at the encroachment of the Ohio settlers upon their hunting-grounds, and the war-whoop was soon resounding on the Maumee and the Wabash. The government acted promptly. A force of 2,300 men was gathered at Cincinnati, under General Arthur St. Clair, and pushed forward through the Indiana forests. In comparison with the little band with which George Rogers Clark had worked such wonders, this was a formidable host. But Clark's men had been seasoned frontiersmen, while St. Clair's men were ignorant even of how to oil a rifle or to put in the flint.

When the army reached the Wabash it was attacked by the savages under the chieftain Joseph Brant, and cut to pieces. A bare 600 escaped. The remnant, in their flight, abandoned guns, tents, equipage, wounded comrades. The savages pursued several miles and then returned to enjoy the torments of the prisoners. Some they tore limb from limb, some they put to death by driving stakes through their bodies. This defeat was a severe blow to the new government. Its first military effort had ended in failure, and the old anti-Federalist group was quick to charge incompetence.

Some days later when Washington was entertaining guests at dinner, an officer galloped up to his door, threw his bridle to an orderly, and rushed up the steps. He was told that it was impossible to disturb the President, but he insisted so vehemently that Washington finally came out. The President received the news apparently without emotion and quietly returned to his seat. The dinner and reception over, he dismissed his guests with dignified courtesy, and then broke forth furiously. "It's all over! St. Clair is defeated, routed. Here in this very spot I told him to beware of an ambush.

And yet to suffer that army to be cut to pieces, hacked, tomahawked, by a surprise, the very thing I guarded him against!
O God! he is worse than a murderer! How can he answer
it to his countrymen?" Then he added more calmly: "General St. Clair shall have full justice, he shall have full justice."

But Washington lost little time in vain repinings. A new
army was gathered, placed under the veteran, James Anthony
Wayne, and drilled in the art of Indian-fighting. Moving far
into the hostile region, it encountered, August 18, 1794, 1,300
savages two miles from a British fort on the Maumee. The
Americans charged and the savages fled to the fort, hoping
that the British would take them in. Finding the gates closed,
they disappeared in the woods. Wayne followed, taking occasion to shout his defiance at the British as he passed. "I know
of no war between Great Britain and America," Major Camp-
bell, the commander, called out to him. "How dare you approach so close to my garrison?" "If you are entitled to any
answer," replied Wayne, "you may have it from the muzzles
of my guns." Yet he did not molest the fort, for he had accomplished his purpose in chastising the Indians and did not wish
to add to the tension between the two countries.

In the meanwhile, war had broken out in Europe. England
became a member of the alliance formed to crush the revolution which in France was running to such dangerous extremes.
Using her naval superiority to weaken the enemy, she had
almost driven the tricolor from the seas. Before many months
great quantities of sugar began to pile up at the wharves in
Santo Domingo and Guadeloupe, waiting for neutral carriers
to take them to France. The shippers of New London and
Boston, seeing an opportunity for good profits, sailed for the
French West Indies. But their joy was short-lived. England
refused to sanction a traffic which would weaken her blockade
of France. Before long British frigates were overhauling American vessels, examining their papers, and towing them off to
the prize-court. In the Indies, Yankee seamen were arrested,
stripped of their clothing, insulted, locked up, and browbeaten
by the island officials.

The American press rang with complaints. In certain quarters there was talk of war. But in New England, the section which had suffered most, a rupture with Great Britain was dreaded above all else. A successful voyage from Santo Domingo to France brought such profits that the merchants could afford the occasional loss of a vessel. The Yankee ports were becoming prosperous; why ruin all by bringing a swarm of British men-of-war off Cape Cod or Martha's Vineyard?

Washington, too, was for peace. The United States was still young, still weak. Time was needed for development. War would put to hazard all the gains of the two past wonderful decades—independence, expansion, union. The President felt that an effort should be made to adjust peacefully the differences with Great Britain, and sent John Jay to negotiate a new treaty.

When Jay arrived in England in June, 1794, he was treated with marked cordiality. "Well, sir, I imagine that you begin to see that your mission will probably be successful," the King told him. But when negotiations began he found that the British Government had lost none of its old obstinacy. It agreed to surrender the Northwestern posts in return for the appointment of a joint commission to settle the question of debts. But the treaty of commerce which it granted stipulated that American ships of more than seventy tons could not enter British West Indian ports; that no American trader could carry to Europe the molasses, sugar, coffee, cocoa, or cotton of the islands; but that English ships were to have access to the ports of the United States, navigate her rivers and enjoy trade under the most-favored-nation clause.

A hard bargain this, so hard that Washington hesitated long as to the advisability of accepting it. The Senate struck out the objectionable provisions concerning the West Indian trade before it would ratify. Then, and not until then, was the treaty made known to the public. It was the signal for a burst of indignation. Jay became the most unpopular man in America. He was burned in effigy, while revellers mingled their denunciations with puns upon his name. "A perpetual harvest to America," said one; "but clipped wings, lame legs, the pip, and an empty crop to all Jays."

Despite this condemnation, Jay had served the country well.
Not only did the United States gain possession of the northwest region, but what was needed above all else—time, time
in which to grow, time for the development of her resources,
time for the consolidation of the Federal Union. When, seventeen years later, hostilities broke out with Great Britain, it
brought the United States to the verge of collapse; had war
come in 1795 it would probably have meant ruin. The Jay
treaty permitted an honorable escape from a perilous situation.

Early in April, 1793, a frigate was seen to pass Sullivan's
Island, and drop anchor in Charleston harbor. From her fore-
mast head hung the red liberty cap, while her quarter galleries
were adorned with the letters R. F. She was the *Ambuscade*,
bringing the Minister of the French Republic, Citizen Genêt.

The outbreak of the European war had caused Washington
great perplexity. What should be the attitude of the government to the contending nations? The treaty of 1778 had
accorded France the right to bring prizes to American ports
in time of war, it had prohibited the fitting out of privateers
in America by powers hostile to France, and pledged the United
States to guarantee French territorial possessions. The President felt that to carry out these provisions literally would involve the country in war with England. Yet to repudiate the
treaty would seem not only a breach of faith but the grossest
ingratitude to our old ally.

America was strongly pro-French. The successive acts of the
great drama of the Revolution were hailed with enthusiasm
by the people—the meeting of the Estates-General, the adoption of a liberal constitution, the storming of the Bastille, the
defiance of the league of Kings, the creation of a republic.
When word arrived that Dumouriez had defeated the allies at
Valmy, the people celebrated with banquets, processions, and
speeches. Everywhere Americans sang the Marseillaise, wore
the French cockade, began addressing each other as Citizen
This or Citizen That. In the face of this sentiment, it was hard
for the government to remain passive, while France struggled
with our old enemy.

Yet Hamilton thought that it must. American economic life drew its nourishment chiefly from the sea; we could not afford to break with the mistress of the sea. As for the French treaty of 1778, it contemplated a defensive war, he told Washington, not a war in which hostilities had been started by France. Wisdom demanded a policy of strict neutrality. Jefferson, too, thought it would be folly to provoke England to war, but he pleaded against an open repudiation of the treaty of 1778. In the end Washington issued a proclamation forbidding Americans to take any part in the hostilities and warning them against acts unfriendly to any of the warring powers.

In the meanwhile, Genêt, taking for granted that he could use our territory as a base against Great Britain and Spain, had been sending provisions to the French West Indies, stirring up rebellion in Canada, arming the Kentuckians against New Orleans, and converting American merchantmen into privateers.

The Democratic-Republican party which Jefferson was organizing promised him their hearty co-operation. At Charleston he was fêted; his journey to Philadelphia was a triumphal procession. The farmers gathered along the road to assure him of their friendship for France, and to proffer gifts of corn and wheat to help the cause of liberty. As he approached the capital a great crowd met him at Gray's Ferry, and, with much cheering and singing of liberty songs, conducted him to his lodgings.

Genêt's elation was dampened by the cold civility with which the President greeted him. "Old Washington," he wrote, "cannot pardon my success, and the enthusiasm with which the entire city rushed to meet me. He embarrasses my movements in a thousand ways." Indeed, Washington was determined not to permit this irrepressible Frenchman to embroil the country in war with the coalition. Already he had set George Rogers Clark to work raising volunteers to attack Louisiana, and had sent out fourteen privateers. In June, 1793, the President informed Genêt that though he could not object to the fitting out of French privateers, they must leave as soon as commissioned and not use our ports as a base of operations.

At this Genêt became red with rage. He would appeal to Congress over the President's head, he said, and if Congress proved stubborn he would take his case to the people. This was wild talk, but the conduct of the more ardent Republicans in Philadelphia made him feel that the action of the government was generally disapproved. Angry crowds paraded the streets, threatening to drag Washington out of his house, demanding a new alliance with France and war with England. John Adams was so alarmed that he brought several chests of arms from the war office to his residence to defend it from the expected attack.

Washington regarded these demonstrations with indifference, but he was deeply hurt by the biting personal criticisms of the Republican press. On one occasion he quite lost his temper, defied any man to produce one single act of his which was not done from the purest motives, and declared that he had never repented but once having failed to resign his office, and that was every moment since. He would rather be on his farm than emperor of the world, he said, yet they were charging him with wanting to be King.

Jefferson knew that abuse of Washington could but react on those who indulged in it, and he became alarmed lest the French Minister should do serious harm to the Republican party. Never was so calamitous an appointment made, he complained. Hot-headed, all imagination, without judgment, passionate, disrespectful, and even indecent toward the President, urging the most unreasonable and groundless propositions in the most dictatorial style, his conduct, if ever it becomes known to the public, will excite universal indignation. In fact, Genêt was nearing the end of his rope. In July, 1793, it was whispered about that *The Little Sarah*, a prize sent in by a French man-of-war, was being armed for the sea. Jefferson sought out Genêt and made him promise that she should not sail without notice. Despite this promise, a few days later the vessel slipped out to sea. Washington felt that matters had now gone far enough. "Is the Minister of the French Republic to set the acts of this government at defiance," he asked, "and then threaten the executive with an appeal to the people?" Gouverneur Morris, our Minister to France, was instructed to ask for Genêt's recall.

This action probably kept the nation out of war, but it did not free American politics from foreign interference. The Americans themselves were partly to blame. They had not yet been able to throw off the colonial attitude of mind. To them Europe still seemed the centre of the universe, and the tremendous events which were happening there engaged their thoughts and influenced their actions. All America was divided between the pro-Gallicans and the pro-Anglicans. The Republican leaders regarded the Ministers of France as their natural allies, and went to them for advice and assistance. The Federalists only too often shaped their politics in accordance with the desires of England.

When, in 1796, Thomas Jefferson and John Adams were the rival candidates for the Presidency, the French Minister, Pierre Auguste Adet, took an active part in the campaign. In letters published in the *Aurora* he alternately pleaded and threatened. He told of how Frenchmen had braved the tempests to see the land of freedom, of the tears that dimmed every eye as the Stars and Stripes were unfurled in the French Senate, of the American farmer's turning up with the plough the bones of his countrymen shot down by British mercenaries. But these touching scenes he reinforced with threats of war in case Adams was elected. He succeeded in arousing such resentment that thousands of votes switched from Jefferson to Adams.

The President sent as Minister to France James Monroe, a stanch Republican and friend of the Revolution. He was received with marked honors by the Convention. But when the news leaked out that Jay was at work in London negotiating for an Anglo-American commercial pact, the French Government turned reproachfully to Monroe for the facts. Did the United States propose to ally herself with England, he was asked, and denounce the treaty of 1778 with France? Monroe, who had been left in the dark in regard to Jay's proceedings, assured them that nothing of the kind was contemplated. When, therefore, a copy of Jay's treaty was received in France in 1795, Monroe found himself in a most embarrassing position.

French resentment was apparent. Diplomatic relations were suspended and French officials began seizing American vessels. When C. C. Pinckney arrived in Paris in 1796 as successor to Monroe, he was slighted, threatened with imprisonment, and practically expelled from the country. It looked as though we had avoided war with England at the price of war with France. But President Adams was determined to prevent this catastrophe. He sent a commission to France with instructions to restore, if possible, our friendly relations with that country, without giving Great Britain cause for complaint.

October 8, 1797, three Americans sat impatiently in the Foreign Office at Paris, waiting to see M. Talleyrand. One was a man about forty years of age, whose dark complexion and thick black hair gave a tinge of sombreness to an otherwise pleasant countenance. His plain and untidy clothes hung loosely upon a frame that was as awkward as it was large. Altogether he seemed a rather commonplace American farmer. Of his two companions, one was a thin man whose solemn face was set off by a large nose and a peculiar white wig; the other a well-dressed man of fifty, with pleasant, clear-cut features, clear eyes, and erect, dignified bearing. They were John Marshall, Elbridge Gerry, and Charles Cotesworth Pinckney, on their mission of peace to the French Republic.

After a lapse of ten minutes Talleyrand's door opened and the Foreign Minister stood before the Americans. A pair of cold gray eyes looked out resentfully from beneath bushy brows. As he gazed, the haughty uptilt of his nose showed his contempt for these rustic amateurs in the art of diplomacy. After a stiff salutation he informed them that he would confer with them later, and, with a mocking bow, ushered them out.

Some days afterward a mysterious person accosted Pinckney, and confided to him that the United States was expected to make a liberal loan to France and provide a private "gratification" for the Directory. Pinckney was so amazed at these insolent demands that it was with difficulty that he concealed his resentment. But he desired to place the responsibility upon Talleyrand, and at the slightest sign of truculence he feared that subtle person would deny knowledge of the mysterious interview. So he maintained a calm exterior. But he insisted that the proposals be laid before his fellow commissioners.

This was done at a dinner in Marshall's room by Monsieur Bellamy, a confidential friend of Talleyrand. This gentleman suggested that the United States buy at double their value certain Dutch securities then in the possession of France, thus providing in secret the desired loan, together with the $240,000 *douceur* for the Directory. Feeling that they had now brought the insulting proposals to the door of the French Government itself, the commissioners ended the proceedings with an abrupt refusal. Bellamy retired in confusion, uttering threats against the United States. But even then Talleyrand did not give up, and sent M. Hottinguer back to demand a more explicit answer to the demand for money. "We have already spoken to that point very explicitly," was the response. "No, you have not," said Hottinguer, "what is your answer?" "It is no, no," burst out Pinckney. "Not one sixpence." A few months later all America was echoing his sentiments in the slogan—"Millions for defense, but not one cent for tribute."

Despite this rebuff Talleyrand continued to press his demands through a new agent—a certain M. Hauteval. Finding that Gerry was becoming nervous over his threats of war, he began to confine his attentions to him, and intimated that Pinckney and Marshall would do well to return to America. This they lost no time in doing, warmly advising their colleague to accompany them. But Gerry was now persuaded that the safety of his country depended upon his remaining, and so continued single-handed the duel with the subtle Talleyrand.

Meanwhile, the cipher report of the envoys reached the United States. Adams announced to Congress the failure of the mission, and recommended that steps be taken to defend the country. War measures were accordingly voted. But the Republicans denounced the President's message as hasty and unnecessary and called for the publication of the documents. This Adams was quite ready to do. Concealing the names of Talleyrand's agents under the letters X, Y, Z, he laid bare the story of their insults to the United States. Instantly the country flamed with anger. The friends of France were silent before the storm of indignation, the people rallied to the government and enthusiastically prepared for war.

The army was recruited to its full strength; Washington was called from his retirement at Mt. Vernon to command the troops; the navy was prepared for action and sent to sea; forts and earthworks were erected on the coasts. Subscription lists were started to build new ships for the navy. Boston laid down the hulls of two frigates, New York raised $30,000 in an hour; at Portland, at Salem, at Charleston, at Philadelphia, at Baltimore, the shipyards soon began to hum. The old love for France was forgotten. Everywhere the slogan was repeated: "Millions for defense, but not one cent for tribute." On the ocean hostilities actually began. *The Constellation* captured the French frigate *L'Insurgente*, on February 9, 1799; and later fought a drawn battle with *La Vengeance*. In two years and a half of fighting, our ships took eighty-four French vessels, most of them privateers.

Talleyrand was deeply hurt. He had been bluffing; that he was willing to admit. But was it necessary to draw a pistol in order to call a bluff? Before long negotiations were opened once more, this time through the American Minister at The Hague, and assurances given that if this country would send a new representative to Paris, he would be received in a spirit of conciliation. Despite the opposition of Hamilton and other Federalists, Adams appointed another commission to France, which negotiated an acceptable treaty. Long afterward Adams asked that on his tomb be inscribed this epitaph: "Here lies John Adams, who took upon himself the responsibility for peace with France in the year 1800."

When Thomas Jefferson realized that he could not gain the support of President Washington for his democratic ideas, he decided to appeal to the people. It was for the right of the people to govern themselves that he was contending; when his case had been presented to them, he was sure they would rally around him. He would organize them into a new party, a party free from the taint of anti-Federalism, but demanding a strict adherence to the letter of the Constitution, advocating the extension of the franchise, opposed to the rule of the privileged few, sympathetic with the French Revolution. He was prepared to encounter opposition from the wealthy—merchants, financiers, the large planters of Virginia and South Carolina; but he hoped to win the thousands who earned their livings by manual labor—small farmers of the Piedmont region, Western frontiersmen, skilled mechanics of the North and East.

Jefferson was an adroit politician and organizer. His followers should be called Republicans, he said, to indicate their opposition to the monarchical tendencies of the Federalists. By means of an extensive correspondence he selected able lieutenants in every section, furnished campaign issues, directed their activities, and held out the prospect of distinguished political careers. He founded gazettes, which placed his principles before the people. In imitation of the Jacobites, he covered the country with a network of clubs, which gave unity to the party. Before many years these efforts had proved so successful that Washington exclaimed in despair: "Let that party set up a broomstick, and call it a true son of liberty—a democrat—or give it any other epithet that will suit the purpose; and it will command their votes *in toto*."

In 1796, when Jefferson ran against John Adams for the Presidency, this work of organization was incomplete. Moreover, the Federalist party still enjoyed the prestige lent by Washington, and by its services to the nation—the drawing up and ratification of the Constitution, the organization of a vigorous government. Adams was elected by seventy-one to sixty-eight. Washington, worn out by long public service, had refused a third term. On the day of the inauguration his elation was so evident that Adams could not help remarking on it. "He seemed to me to enjoy a triumph over me. Methought I heard him say: 'Ay! I am fairly out, and you fairly in! See which of us will be the happiest.'"

Adams had frequent occasion to remember this incident. He at once became the butt of an abusive partisan press. He was an egotistical old man, almost in his dotage, it was said, better fitted for the madhouse than the presidential chair. He was avaricious, despotic, and fond of ridiculous pomp. Thomas Callander, William Cobbett, William Duane, Thomas Cooper, Joseph Priestly, Collot, Volney, and other radical editors vied with each other in vilifying the administration.

The Federalists were not only angered but alarmed lest this abuse bring the government into contempt. It was wrong, they felt, that every petty scribbler should be free to drag in the mire the names of the men who represented the majesty of the nation; that a group of aliens, converted in the twinkling of an eye into champions of American liberty, should criticise those who had won the Revolution and established the Constitution.

The Federalists, in dealing with this situation, soon went to unjustifiable lengths. Oliver Ellsworth grouped "the quintumvirate at Paris" with "the Vice-President and minority in Congress, as apostles of atheism and anarchy, bloodshed, and plunder." In June, 1798, an act was hastened through Congress, raising from five to fourteen years the period of residence before an alien could be admitted to American citizenship. Next came a measure empowering the President to send out of the country such aliens as he judged dangerous to the government. Worse was to follow. On July 14, 1798, an act was passed making it a crime to publish malicious statements against the President or Congress, to bring them into contempt, or to "stir up sedition within the United States."

Hamilton saw the folly of these measures. "Let us not establish tyranny," he said. "Energy is a very different thing from violence." But his fellow Federalists, heedless of this warning, made use of the Alien and Sedition Acts as a weapon of persecution. The convictions, although few in number, created serious misgivings. Matthew Lyon, of Vermont, was fined $1,000 and held for three months in a loathsome prison for charging Adams with "unbounded thirst for ridiculous pomp, foolish adulation, and a selfish avarice." A Jerseyman, who had expressed a wish that the wad of a cannon, fired as a salute to Adams, had lodged in the seat of his breeches, was lucky to get off with a fine of one hundred dollars.

Thomas Jefferson looked on with much the same feelings as

a chess-player who sees his opponent make a fatal move. In his letters there was a note of triumph. "Let there be no violence," he wrote to his lieutenants, "no open insurrection, and in the end public opinion will sweep from power the party responsible for these acts." In public he sounded the alarm-bell. "Not only freedom of speech is in danger," he said, "but republican institutions themselves. If this goes down, we shall see attempted another act of Congress, declaring that the President shall continue in office during life, reserving to another occasion the transfer of the succession to the heirs, and the establishment of the Senate for life."

Jefferson's voice was but one of many thousands. The Republicans were furious. "Who is to decide what constitutes a libel against the government?" they asked. "Why, the Federalist government itself—the President, the judge, the grand jury. Does any man hope for an impartial trial before a tribunal made up of the very men who claim to have been libelled? Will it not be a travesty on justice? Will it not put an end to free speech? Soon they will begin arresting people for laughing at the cut of a Congressman's coat."

Jefferson and Madison fanned the flames by forcing through the Legislatures of Kentucky and Virginia resolutions condemning the Alien and Sedition Acts. The Constitution is a compact to which the States are parties, they held, and "each party has an equal right to judge for itself as well of infractions as the mode and measure of redress." The Kentucky Legislature, in supplementary resolutions, proposed steps by which protesting States might concur in declaring the acts void, and preventing their going into effect.

Neither Jefferson nor Madison had ever been in sympathy with the anti-Federalists. Jefferson had approved heartily of the Constitution; Madison, more than any other man, had been responsible for its existence. They had little intention of carrying to their logical conclusion the principles of the Virginia and Kentucky resolutions, for that would have destroyed the Constitution. The resolutions were campaign documents, containing an expression of the State-rights theory as an antidote to Hamiltonian centralization. Madison had explained his position when discussing his estrangement from the Secretary of the Treasury. "I broke with Colonel Hamilton," he said, "or he broke with me; in a word, we parted, when I discovered that he was trying to administration the Constitution into something which he knew and I knew was not intended."

Jefferson was by nature a localist. He hated the paternalism of the old Bourbon France, and lauded the town meetings of New England. But there was nothing in his philosophy fundamentally opposed to vigor in government. At this time he and Madison and the other Republican leaders espoused the State-rights doctrine, because it was the weapon ready at hand with which to combat the party in power. They wished to curb the Federal horse, because Hamilton was in the saddle, riding down the interests they represented. A few years later, when themselves directing the Federal Government, both Jefferson and Madison were responsible for measures justifiable only under the loosest interpretation of the Constitution. In American history the State-rights doctrine has been a weapon of defense with which men have fought rather than a sacred principle which they have fought for.

While the Federalist party was still suffering from the effects of the Alien and Sedition Acts, dissensions broke out within their own ranks. John Adams became President under unfortunate conditions, for Washington remained the nominal head of the Federalist party, Hamilton its actual leader. Adams made matters worse by retaining Washington's Cabinet, all of them devoted to Hamilton. From the first he was not master in his own household.

These men wrote to Washington and Hamilton for advice, and endeavored to manage the President by concerted action. Wolcott or Pickering frequently received instructions from the former Secretary of the Treasury, placed his ideas before the Cabinet, and secured their inclusion in the President's message to Congress.

The rupture came in 1799, over the question of peace or war with France. Hamilton and the Cabinet were opposed to reopening negotiations with Talleyrand after the humiliating X-Y-Z incident. But when information came that France would welcome a new mission, the President, without consulting the Cabinet, nominated William Van Murray as Minister to France. The Federalists were dumfounded. It meant mutiny against Hamilton, a breach of party discipline. "Had the foulest heart and the ablest head in the world," wrote Senator Sedgwick to Hamilton, "been permitted to select the most embarrassing and ruinous measure, perhaps it would have been precisely the one which has been adopted."

A year passed after Adams's declaration of independence before he mustered courage to purge the Cabinet entirely of Hamilton's influence. In May, 1800, James McHenry offered his resignation, after an altercation with the President. To his surprise it was accepted. Adams then turned on Pickering, demanding that he too withdraw. Pickering refused, with an allusion to the expected election of Jefferson; whereupon he was dismissed. Wolcott was not suspected of being a "Hamiltonian spy," and remained till the end of the year.

This split in the Federalist party proved fatal. A caucus of Federalist Congressmen had already promised to support Adams for re-election. "For my individual part, my mind is made up," said Hamilton. "I will never be responsible for him by my direct support, even though the consequences should be the election of Jefferson." Adams retorted by insinuating that Hamilton was subordinating American interests to those of Great Britain. The former Secretary of the Treasury called this a "base, wicked, and cruel calumny; destitute even of a plausible pretext" to excuse its folly, and revenged himself by trying to swing votes from Adams to C. C. Pinckney.

The tide was already turning in favor of the Republicans, and their victory in 1800 would have been overwhelming, had not the Federalists, by various devices, thwarted the public will in several States. In Massachusetts and New Hampshire, the law required electors to be chosen in districts by popular vote. The old Legislatures, both still Federalist in character, were summoned in special sessions and, repealing the law, made the selections themselves. In Pennsylvania the House of Representatives was Republican, the Senate Federalist.

The Federalists refused to permit a popular election, holding out until a compromise gave them seven of the State's fifteen electors. In New York the law required that electors be chosen by the Legislature. When it became known that an election had just given the Republicans a majority, Hamilton urged Governor Jay to call the old Legislature in special session to repeal the law. If the electors were chosen by districts, he pointed out, some would surely go Federalist. Jay refused, declaring that he could not lend himself to so partisan a measure.

For weeks the voting continued, while the nation waited in suspense for the outcome. When it became known that the Republicans had won, Jefferson's followers celebrated with bonfires, bells ringing, speeches, toasts, and songs. The people had triumphed, the Republic was saved, the pro-Anglicans and monarchists thwarted.

The Federalist leaders were in despair. The rule of the enlightened and best was over, they complained, henceforth the rabble would reign. What, then, would the government be? Why, a government by Jacobins, by the ignorant, by blockheads and knaves. As for Jefferson, he was a cowardly wretch, prating about humanity, yet feeling an infernal pleasure in the destruction of his opponents. With such a man as President the country must expect civil war, desolation, and anarchy.

In the midst of these repinings they saw a gleam of hope. Under the Constitution every elector cast two votes; the candidate receiving the largest number becoming President, and the next in order Vice-President. The Republicans had intended Jefferson for the Presidency and Aaron Burr for the second place, but it became known that each had received the same number—seventy-three. Neither had been elected, and the Constitution provided that the old House of Representatives, which was still Federalist, should decide between the two.

Now began a series of conferences among the Federalists to decide what to do. Why not create a deadlock in the House until March 4, some asked, when Congress might declare the government at a standstill, and make some Federalist President? This scheme smacked so of revolution that it was discarded for a solid Federalist vote for Burr. Burr was a demagogue, of course, but if he accepted the Presidency at Federalist hands, he could not be over-harsh in his dealings with them.

On February 11, 1801, Jefferson sat in the presiding officer's chair in the Senate chamber, his gaze wandering from the throng in the galleries to the serious faces of the Senators. Presently the door opened, and the Representatives filed in and took their seats. The electoral ballots were opened and counted. Then Jefferson announced that no election had taken place, and that it remained for the House of Representatives to decide between himself and Aaron Burr. The Representatives retired to their own chamber, and the balloting began at once. On the first vote eight States were for Jefferson, six for Burr, and two divided. Six more ballots were taken with the same result. The eighth ballot was held at the end of an hour, and then eight more without intermission. The sixteenth ballot came at nine in the evening, the seventeenth at ten, the eighteenth at eleven. The members now began to drop off to sleep in their seats, but they were awakened at twelve, one, two, and two-thirty by the tellers, as they went the rounds with their boxes.

In the meanwhile, Hamilton was exerting himself to swing votes to Jefferson. "If there be a man in this world I ought to hate, it is Jefferson," he said. "With Burr I have always been personally well. But the public good must be paramount to every private consideration." Hamilton knew Burr to be a political adventurer whose election would be exceedingly dangerous. For some days he was unable to break the deadlock and the balloting went on. At last, after the thirty-sixth ballot, Maryland, Delaware, and Vermont switched to the Republican column, and Jefferson secured ten States.

The defeated Federalists now hastened to intrench themselves in the judiciary. February 13, 1801, they passed a law creating sixteen new judges and increasing the number of marshals, attorneys, and clerks. To these posts the President appointed trusted Federalists. They were hastily confirmed by the Senate on March 3, and Adams sat up late that night signing the commissions. This done, he began to pack up his belongings, for he could not bear to be present at the installation of his successor. Early the next morning, while the citizens of Washington still slept, he ordered his coach and drove hastily out of the town.

Thus was the Federalist party overthrown. It had done splendid work—it had drawn up the Constitution, secured its adoption, launched the new government, rallied the propertied classes to its support, and endowed it with the strength to withstand the shocks of future sectional clashes. But this accomplished, its usefulness was over. The trend of the day was toward democracy. The X-Y-Z fiasco, the Alien and Sedition Acts, the Virginia and Kentucky resolutions, the reconstruction of the Adams Cabinet were but incidents in the Federalist overthrow; the real cause of defeat was the fact that Federalism was out of step with the age.

CHAPTER X

DEMOCRACY TRIUMPHANT

ON March 4, 1801, at noon, an ill-assorted trio sat on the rostrum of the new Senate chamber at Washington. In the centre was Jefferson, plainly dressed, an expression of mingled triumph and diffidence on his face. To his right sat Vice-President Burr. Small in stature, neatly dressed, courtly, dignified, he presented a contrast to the awkward, ruddy-faced man beside him. On Jefferson's left was Chief Justice Marshall, his bearing erect and steady as ever, his small black eyes twinkling beneath his broad forehead. It was strange that the administration should be ushered in by three men so divergent in their ideals, who in the future were to fight each other so bitterly.

After taking the oath of office, Jefferson began his inaugural address. A hush fell over the audience, and persons in the back seats leaned forward to catch the low-spoken words. As the President proceeded a murmur of surprise passed over the room. Some had expected violent utterances—threats to overthrow the work of his predecessors, threats of vengeance against the Federalists. Instead there was talk of "exact justice to all men," of conciliation and brotherhood. "We have called by different names brethren of the same principle," said Jefferson. "We are all Republicans—we are all Federalists."

Of his own political philosophy there was much. "Sometimes it is said that man cannot be trusted with the government of himself. Can he then be trusted with the government of others? Or have we found angels in the form of kings to govern him? Let history answer this question." He gave, however, some hints of the policies he was to pursue. The government must be frugal, the civil authorities must control the military, debts must be paid, the freedom of the press preserved, there must be peace with all nations, entangling alliances with none.

In letters to his friends Jefferson explained what was meant
by this olive-branch inaugural. The mass of the people were
at heart Republican, he said, and those who had wandered
into the opposing party had been deceived by the artifices
of the Federalists. "You know that the manœuvres of the
X Y Z carried over from us a great body of the people," he
wrote James Monroe, "real Republicans, and honest men
under virtuous motives." These wanderers from the fold he
now sought to win back. The "leaders of the late faction,"
he abandoned as "incurables," declaring that he would never
turn an inch out of his way to reconcile them, but the rank
and file of Federalists belonged under the Republican banner.
The conciliatory sentiments of the inaugural concealed a threat
not suspected by his opponents, a threat to hack away at the
Federalist party, until it had become a mere faction, a head
without a body. Two decades later, when Republicanism had
won New England itself, the Federalist leaders at last realized
what Jefferson meant when he spoke of conciliation on that
momentous March 4.

It was a lasting joy to Jefferson that in his official household there was kinship of thought and personal affection.
The appointment of James Madison as Secretary of State was
inevitable, for the two Virginians had long worked in the closest
harmony. "I do believe," exclaimed a lady, "father never
loved son more than Mr. Jefferson loves Mr. Madison." For
his Secretary of the Treasury the President turned to Albert
Gallatin, second only to Hamilton as a financier. Though a
foreigner, Gallatin knew America well, and his knowledge of
practical affairs was of inestimable value to the administration. Like Jefferson and Madison he was born a gentleman,
and like them he believed ardently in man's ability to rule his
own affairs.

It is easy to imagine this triumvirate, for they were long
the moving spirits in the government, sitting in the newly
finished White House, discussing the issues of the day. Jefferson, lounging in a large chair, attired in a "blue coat, a thick
gray-colored hairy waistcoat, with a red under-waistcoat
lapped over it, green velveteen breeches with pearl buttons,

yarn stockings, and slippers run down at the heels"; Madison in his habitual suit of black, his breeches short, with buckles at the knees, black silk stockings, his hair powdered and brought to a point above the forehead to conceal his baldness, a smile on his wizened features; Gallatin, entering fully into the conversation despite his foreign accent, his prominent nose, his lofty forehead, his expressive hazel eyes, his swarthy face, giving an appearance of ruggedness lacking in his companions.

"The storm through which we have passed was tremendous," says Jefferson. "The tough sides of our argosy have been thoroughly tried. Her strength has withstood the waves into which she was steered with a view to sink her. We shall put her on her Republican tack, and she will now show by the beauty of her motion the skill of her builders."

"Yes," replies Gallatin, "first we must pay off the enormous national debt. The habit of mortgaging the future to support present waste will ruin the Republic. But in reducing the debt, let us not make the mistake of increasing taxes, especially the unjust excise tax. The thing may be accomplished by economy, eliminating useless expenditures, and reducing the army and the navy. Debt, taxes, army, navy—they are all pillars of corruption."

"Quite so," says Madison. "And we must take advantage of our geographical isolation to avoid entanglements in European affairs. This nation is rapidly growing stronger. The census which has just been taken shows that our population is a third larger than it was ten years ago. If we can but have peace, it may be that within our time we can compel justice on the sea. In the meanwhile, let us avoid foreign alliances, trusting to the mutual interest of commerce to secure us fair treatment. But, Mr. Jefferson, what will be your policy concerning the removal of Federalists from office and the appointment of Republicans?"

"Ah!" replies the President, "that is a troublesome question. The Federalists have a monopoly of public offices. That some ought to be removed, all will agree. But it is difficult to draw the line. I shall consider null all appointments made by Mr. Adams after the event of the election was known; I shall remove officers guilty of mal-conduct. No one will be dismissed merely because of a difference of political principle. As offices become vacant through resignation or death, we will appoint Republicans until an equality has been reached between the parties. With what joy will we hail the day, when the only question concerning a candidate shall be: Is he honest? Is he capable? Is he faithful to the Constitution?"

Unfortunately in practice Jefferson found it impossible to follow this programme. From all sides came pressing requests from political lieutenants asking offices for themselves and their friends. Reluctantly he yielded, until at the end of his second term hardly a Federalist remained. Jefferson did not hesitate to use the patronage to further his political views and manage the Republican party. He was angered at Burr when the House was balloting to break the tie in the election of 1800, for not making a statement that he would not accept the Presidency. Burr had equivocated, and Jefferson felt that he had been ready to betray both himself and the Republican voters. Later, when Burr sought favors for his political faction in New York, he met with rebuff. Appointments were handed out to Burr's enemy, DeWitt Clinton, while the powerful Livingston family were adroitly detached from the Burr interests. Before long it dawned on the Vice-President that Jefferson intended to drive him out of the Republican party.

The policy of retrenchment was pursued relentlessly. The Secretary of the Treasury estimated the annual income at $10,600,000. The repeal of the excise law would leave $10,000,000, of which he proposed to use $7,300,000 for the payment of principal and interest on the national debt. For current expenses he put aside $1,100,000, while to the army he doled out $930,000, to the navy $670,000. That this made it necessary to cut both services to the bone, in no wise disturbed the administration. War is a possibility, Jefferson admitted, but we are not justified in taxing our fellow citizens to accumulate treasure for wars to happen we know not when. As for the navy, we will lay up the seven frigates in the Eastern Branch, where they will be under the eye of the department, and require but one set of plunderers to take care of them.

The Federal judiciary presented a difficult problem. The Supreme Court was instituted by the Constitution; its members served for life. John Marshall, the Chief Justice, presumably had before him a long career in which to oppose the Republicans and perpetuate the ideals of Hamilton. He might be impeached, but only for high crimes and misdemeanors. There was no constitutional obstacle to an act to increase the number of justices, thus permitting the President to pack the court with Republicans, but Jefferson would not set so dangerous a precedent, even to unloose from the neck of his party the grip of this "Old Man of the Sea."

But in dealing with the inferior Federal courts which had been established by Congress, he felt no such restraint. "We may well doubt . . . whether offices and officers have not been multiplied unnecessarily," he said, in his first annual message. "The judiciary system of the United States, and especially that portion of it recently erected, will of course present itself to the contemplation of Congress." In accordance with this hint a bill was introduced to repeal the Judiciary Act of 1801. The Federalists declared the bill unconstitutional and a subterfuge to get rid of the Federal judges. "You shall not take the man from the office," said Gouverneur Morris, "but you may take the office from the man; you may not drown him, but you may sink his boat under him. . . . Is this not absurd?" The Republicans retorted that the courts had become a refuge for decayed politicians, and repealed the act by a strictly party vote.

Jefferson now found himself confronted by important questions concerning the West. Despite his desire for peace and his trust in American geographical isolation, he realized keenly that between the United States and the nation which held Louisiana and the Floridas, there was a serious conflict of interest. The treaty of 1783 cut off the Western territory from the outer world. There was no seacoast, for Spanish America still held the Gulf of Mexico; no outlet into the Gulf, for Spanish officials closed the mouth of the Mississippi to Yankee goods. For Spain it was a question of stemming the tide of American migration before it swept over her frontier line; for the settlers in the Ohio region, a question of forcing a passage to the sea or of slow strangulation.

For years the Spaniards were the aggressors in this conflict. They let loose the Indians upon the frontier of Tennessee, they set West and East to quarrelling by the proposed Gardoqui-Jay treaty, they fanned the flames of discontent by holding out the bait of independence under Spanish protection. But with the advent of Genêt in American affairs they found that they were playing a dangerous game. When news reached Madrid that George Rogers Clark had been made an officer in the French army, and that thousands of crack riflemen were awaiting the word to march on New Orleans, they became more conciliatory. If the young American bear meant to take what he wanted, perhaps it would be better to yield. October 27, 1795, a treaty was signed in Madrid, giving the Westerners the use of the Mississippi, and permitting them to deposit their products in New Orleans for transfer from river boats to ocean-going merchantmen.

From the contemplation of this diplomatic victory Jefferson was aroused by the rumor that Spain had ceded Louisiana to France. Could this be true? If so, it opened the liveliest possibilities of trouble. The United States had been content to leave the western part of the Mississippi basin in the nerveless hands of Spain, while her own settlers were filling up the eastern part. But France, under the restless Napoleon Bonaparte —that was another matter. Jefferson and Madison had visions of French immigrants pushing up the Mississippi, of fleets of French merchantmen loading and unloading at New Orleans, of Napoleonic armies holding a series of posts from the Lake of the Woods to the Gulf. French occupation would mean the building up of a powerful rival to the United States, the blocking of Western expansion, the end of freedom from entangling alliances. "The day that France takes possession of New Orleans fixes the sentence which is to restrain her forever within her low-water mark," declared Jefferson. "It seals the union of two nations who in conjugation can maintain exclusive possession of the ocean. From that moment we must marry ourselves to the British fleet and nation."

The subtle Talleyrand had been trying for years to secure Louisiana for France. Frenchmen still lamented the loss of their possessions in America, still dreamed of a colonial empire on the Mississippi. When Talleyrand had visited the United States to escape the Terror, plans for recovering the province took shape in his mind. No sooner had he become Minister of Foreign Affairs under the Directory than he broached the matter to the stupid Spanish monarch, Don Carlos IV. "The cession of Florida and Louisiana to France would be for you a masterly bit of diplomacy," he argued. "The Americans constitute a serious threat to your colonies, and you should hasten to enlist our aid in holding them back. Give us Florida and Louisiana, which are a small part of your American domains, and we will be like a wall of brass, to protect you alike from the United States and England."

Perhaps the brain of Don Carlos was too dull to grasp the force of this subtle reasoning; perhaps his Spanish pride would not permit him to consent to a division of his empire. Talleyrand went away empty-handed. But a new opportunity came with the accession to power of Napoleon Bonaparte. The Corsican was fascinated with the picture Talleyrand drew of a French empire in the New World, and sent a certain Citizen Alquier to Madrid to broach the matter. Napoleon's methods were different from those of Talleyrand. He intimated that he expected immediate compliance with his wishes, at the same time offering in exchange a principality in Italy for the Duke of Parma, the King's son-in-law. Don Carlos not only consented, he was transported with joy. "Congratulate me," he cried to his Prime Minister. "The Prince-presumptive of Parma . . . is invited by France to reign on the delightful banks of the Arno, over a people . . . who once were the controlling power of Italy—a people mild, civilized, full of humanity; the classical land of science and art." The bargain was closed by a treaty signed at San Ildefonso, October 1, 1800. Spain had yielded an imperial domain for the illusory promise of a few small Italian provinces.

A year later Napoleon signed the preliminaries of the Peace of Amiens, which removed the menace of the English navy and made it possible for him to proceed with his colonial project. There stood in his way still one obstacle—the negro chieftain of San Domingo, Toussaint L'Ouverture. In the French empire of Napoleon's plans San Domingo was indispensable. The sugar, coffee, indigo, and cotton of this rich isle were needed for the upbuilding of the merchant marine, its ports were wanted as half-way stations to Louisiana. But San Domingo was no longer under the rule of France. Nine years before, its half-million negro slaves had risen, and in a deluge of blood had made themselves masters of the country. Out of this turmoil had emerged one strong figure, Toussaint, the black Napoleon of the Indies. Seizing the Spanish as well as the French part of the island, he proclaimed a new constitution, and bade defiance to France.

The First Consul prepared to deal with this savage usurper. Gathering a fleet and an army of 10,000 men, he despatched them under General Leclerc, the husband of his beautiful sister Pauline. As Toussaint looked down from his Dominican hills, he is said to have exclaimed: "We must perish. All France is coming to San Domingo." None the less he was resolved upon resistance, and attacked the veterans of France to good purpose. In September, 1802, Leclerc wrote that his situation was critical, that the negroes were fighting fiercely, that disease had thinned his ranks, and that fresh troops must be sent over. Had Toussaint received the loyal support of his lieutenants, it is probable that he would have wrung from France the recognition of Dominican independence. But he was betrayed by his supporters and duped into giving himself up to the French. Napoleon had him imprisoned in a damp fortress in the Jura, where in a few months he perished. None the less he had accomplished what it falls to the lot of few men to do—he had changed the fate of two continents. The negroes rose again under new leaders, disease swept the ranks of the French, Leclerc himself succumbed to the yellow fever. In disgust Napoleon turned from his American enterprise and directed his energies toward the conquest of western Europe.

Perhaps the First Consul was influenced also by the possibility of a war with the United States. To hold Louisiana in the face of an attack by the frontiersmen of Kentucky and Tennessee might prove costly. "The Westerners are undisciplined and lack the proper equipment for an extensive campaign," wrote a Louisiana planter named Pontalba to Napoleon, "but they are skilful in shooting, are masters of woodcraft, and are accustomed to fatigue. Twenty or thirty thousand of these hardy fighters, coming down the river on flatboats, could sweep everything before them."

In truth the Westerners were highly excited over this new peril. When it became known that Napoleon had closed the Mississippi again, they were for striking before the French legions could arrive. But Jefferson, the man of peace, lulled their fears, while he took the matter up with the French Government. Appointing James Monroe Minister Plenipotentiary to France and Spain, he directed him to do what was possible toward protecting American interests in the Mississippi River.

While Monroe's vessel was still on the ocean, Robert Livingston, the American Minister to France, witnessed a memorable scene in Madame Bonaparte's drawing-room. There, in the presence of a brilliant assemblage, Bonaparte came up to Lord Whitworth, the British Ambassador, and said: "I find, my lord, your nation wants war again!" "No, sir," replied Whitworth, "we are very desirous of peace." "I must either have Malta or war!" rejoined Bonaparte and turned away. Within a few days all Europe was talking of the approaching war, and the Louisiana enterprise was forgotten.

Out of this situation came a great surprise for Livingston. For months he had been hanging around Talleyrand, urging him to sell to the United States New Orleans and West Florida. A bit of waste land, he repeated, useless to France but important to my country, because it contains the mouths of some of its rivers. Talleyrand had been more inscrutable than ever, listening attentively, but giving no reply. One day he made a proposal of his own which took Livingston off his feet. "Would you not like to purchase," he asked with his baffling smile, "not only New Orleans, but the whole of Louisiana?" Livingston gasped. "I have been instructed to negotiate only for New Orleans and the Floridas," he replied. "But it is obvious that if we concede New Orleans the rest will be of little value to us," said Talleyrand; "therefore we wish to know what you will give for the whole." "It is a subject I have not thought of," was the reply, "but I suppose we would not object to 20,000,000 francs."

A midnight conference followed between Livingston and Barbé Marbois. "The First Consul says you must pay 100,-000,000 francs," the new agent declared, "together with the claims of Americans against his government." "Such a sum is far beyond our means," replied Livingston, "but we will pay $10,000,000 for New Orleans and the Floridas." Finally Marbois suggested that the United States pay for all Louisiana $11,250,000, together with American claims against France, estimated at $3,750,000. Although this was an amazingly advantageous offer, Livingston would not commit himself, insisting that he must consult Monroe. Prolonged negotiations followed, while the fate of the continent hung in the balance. At last the American commissioners agreed to the terms offered by Marbois, and on May 2, 1803, set their hands to the treaty. For $15,000,000 the United States secured an imperial domain. "We have lived long," Livingston is said to have remarked to his colleague, "but this is the noblest work of our lives. . . . From this day the United States take their place among the powers of the first rank."

Indeed, the cession of Louisiana was an event of the first importance. It made the Mississippi an American river throughout its length, and settled the question of an outlet for the West; it made impossible the building up in America of a rival to the United States; it almost doubled the area of the country; it opened the way to the future acquisition of Texas and the advance to the Pacific. Jefferson had asked Napoleon for a city, and that imperial adventurer had tossed into his lap a province four times the size of France.

Though the Americans had gained so much they were not satisfied. Spain still had the Gulf coast from the Iberville River to the Florida Straits, including the mouths of the Pearl, the Mobile, and the Appalachicola. The wording of the Louisiana Purchase left Livingston and Monroe in doubt as to the extent of the domain they had purchased. The United States was to receive Louisiana "with the same extent that it is now in the hands of Spain, and that it had when France possessed it."

Livingston went to Talleyrand for enlightenment. "What are the eastern bounds of Louisiana?" he asked. "I do not know," replied Talleyrand; "you must take it as we received it." "But what did you mean to take?" "I do not know," was the unsatisfactory answer. "Then you mean that we shall construe it our own way?" "I can give you no direction. You have made a noble bargain for yourselves, and I suppose you will make the most of it."

This advice Livingston followed literally. He wrote Madison that he was persuaded West Florida was included in the purchase. His arguments won over Madison, Madison won over Jefferson, and Jefferson won over a majority in Congress. "We have not only obtained command of the mouth of the Mississippi," John Randolph declared in the House, "but of the Mobile, with its widest extended branches."

One morning, soon after, Don Carlos Martinez Yrujo, the Spanish Minister, rushed into the office of the Secretary of State, waving a copy of a recent act of Congress. So fierce was his expression that the timid little Madison shrank back in alarm. "I had heard that the United States Government would advance a claim to West Florida," cried out Yrujo, "but I regarded it as an atrocious libel. Yet here is an act of Congress which explicitly includes the region in the revenue district of Mississippi. Do you imagine that Spain will submit to this appropriation of her territory?"

Jefferson and Madison soon convinced the irate Minister that they had no intention of seizing West Florida. None the less, they wanted the province very much. They took the matter up with the Spanish Court in a series of exchanges, and relinquished their efforts only when Spain intimated that she would resort to war rather than yield.

In the meanwhile, settlers from Tennessee and Georgia began crossing the border in such large numbers that West Florida soon became more American than Spanish. The newcomers, led by three brothers named Kemper, laid plans to overthrow the local government. When Spain fell into the clutches of Napoleon, and the Spanish colonies began to break away from the mother country, the Kempers gathered a force of fighters, drove out the Spanish Governor, and declared West Florida independent. Hardly had they raised their standard with its seven stripes of white and blue and two stars at the upper end, when they petitioned for annexation to the United States. On October 27, 1810, Madison, then President, ordered the Governor of Louisiana to take possession of the province. The American troops halted before Mobile, however, and that city was occupied only three years later.

At four o'clock on the afternoon of May 14, 1804, in the midst of a pouring rain, a unique little flotilla crossed the Mississippi River a few miles above St. Louis, and entered the mouth of the Missouri. The leading vessel, a keel-boat of fifty-five feet, spread one large square sail, while twenty-two hands pulled away at the oars. There was a ten-foot deck in the bow, another in the stern, and in the middle a series of lockers in the form of a breastwork. Every inch of available space was filled with bundles of clothing, tools, locks, flint, powder and ball, together with all manner of Indian gifts— laced coats, medals, flags, knives, looking-glass, beads, hand-kerchiefs, paints. Behind were two open boats. It was the Lewis and Clark Expedition, starting on its journey from the Mississippi to the Pacific.

Long before Jefferson had thought of purchasing Louisiana he felt an insatiable curiosity about the trans-Mississippi country. In his message of January, 1803, he deplored the ignorance concerning that region, and suggested an exploring expedition to the Pacific. Congress approved, and Jefferson selected as leaders two of his neighbors, Meriwether Lewis and William Clark. These bold adventurers raised a picked force, partly of soldiers, partly of skilled frontiersmen.

Slowly the party made its way up the Missouri, through the dangerous Devil's Race Ground, past the mouth of the Kansas, through the prairies of Iowa and Nebraska; past the mouth of the Platte; under the brown and yellow clay bluffs of Calu-

met, through the country of the Sioux on to the great bend of
the Missouri, where they camped for the winter. With the approach of spring they continued in small boats, until the Rocky
Mountains appeared in the distance with their "several ranges
which rise above each other till the most distant mingles with
the clouds." At the sight of this tremendous obstacle for a
moment even Lewis faltered. But as I have always "held it a
crime to anticipate evils," he wrote in his journals, "I will believe it a good comfortable road until I am compelled to believe differently." Carried on by this spirit, the adventurers
soon crossed the Great Divide, and made their way down one
of the tributaries of the Columbia. On November 7, 1805,
they came "in view of the Pacific, this great Pacific Ocean
which we have been so long anxious to see."

The explorers started on their return in March, 1806. Aided
by their knowledge of the route and by the current of the
Missouri, they accomplished the journey in six months. September 23, 1806, they "descended to the Mississippi, and round
to St. Louis, . . ." and having fired a salute, went on shore,
where they were welcomed by the people of the village. This
expedition opened to American settlers the great Northwest
and foreshadowed the day when the United States was to extend to the Pacific. "Let us do honor to these men," said
President Jefferson, for having made the nation acquainted
with "that vast and fertile country which their sons are destined to fill with arts, with science, with freedom and happiness." Meriwether Lewis and William Clark have taken rank
with De Soto, De Vaca, Coronado, Joliet, Marquette, and
La Salle, as the greatest of American explorers.

While the nation was expanding to the west, events were
happening in the East which threatened the existence of the
Union. The victories of the Republicans were regarded by the
New England Federalists with alarm. It was bad enough that
the hated Jefferson should rule at Washington, but now that
he was winning New England itself, the future seemed dark
indeed. Timothy Pickering, Roger Griswold, and others began
to dream of an independent northern confederacy. But New
England could hardly leave the Union without New York,

and New York was now Republican. In this dilemma the secessionists felt that they could make use of Aaron Burr, who now was ready for anything. Expelled from his own party, he promised to assist in shattering the old Union for a position of prominence in the new. Thus he was put in nomination for the governorship of New York, while his old Federalist enemies worked for his election.

To disunion, especially to disunion under the leadership of Burr, Alexander Hamilton was bitterly opposed. So earnestly did he plead with the New York Federalists not to deliver the State into the hands of this adventurer that Burr was defeated. This not only pricked the bubble of a northern confederacy but ended Burr's last chance to restore his fortunes. Angry, embittered, desperate, he sought revenge by challenging the man who twice had foiled his ambitions.

In the sunlight of a hot July morning two men, one the Vice-President of the United States, the other perhaps its most illustrious statesman, rowed across the Hudson to the duelling ground under the heights of Weehawken. It was one of the most tragic moments in American history, when these old rivals stood facing each other, pistol in hand, in the peaceful setting of the wooded heights, the bright sky, the tranquil river, and the distant city. Hamilton withheld his fire, but Burr took careful aim, and the bullet passed through Hamilton's body. The next day he was dead.

Burr's enemies secured an indictment for murder, and shortly after the duel he left New York, a fugitive from justice. In Washington, while taking leave of political life in a melodramatic address to the Senate, he busied himself with schemes to restore his personal fortunes at the expense of his country. The storm of grief which shook New England and New York at the news of Hamilton's death warned him that he had nothing more to expect in that region. But in the West, where the duel was accepted as an affair of honor, he might yet win distinction.

Burr knew that beyond the mountains there were many elements of discontent. Kentucky and Tennessee were angered because Jefferson would not drive the Spaniards out of Texas;

in Louisiana the planters were protesting against the rule of the American Governor. All this was to Burr's liking. Hamilton had been dead less than a month when Burr surprised Anthony Merry, the British Minister, by offering to sell himself to England, "particularly in endeavoring to effect a separation of the western part of the United States from that which lies between the Atlantic and the mountains." New Orleans was ripe for independence, he explained, and England, by aiding with a squadron of war-ships and a loan of half a million dollars, could strike a heavy blow at the United States.

While Merry was placing this proposal before his government, Burr went to Pittsburg and thence to New Orleans, everywhere perfecting his plans and feeling the public pulse. Finding secession unpopular in Kentucky and Tennessee, he spoke there only of an expedition to conquer Mexico; but to the Creoles of Louisiana he hinted at independence. James Wilkinson, commander of the Western army, a man fully as unscrupulous as Burr himself, he drew into the plot. Then, having put all in readiness, he hastened back to Washington to report to Merry. To his chagrin he found that Great Britain had refused to have anything to do with his schemes.

Burr was now desperate. For the moment he entertained an "insane plan" of seizing President Jefferson, appropriating the public funds, sailing for the Mississippi on the war-vessels at the navy-yard, and proclaiming the secession of Louisiana and the West. In the end he decided to carry out his original plan, even though England had failed him. He drew into his toils Herman Blennerhassett, an eccentric Irishman, who had settled upon an island in the Ohio. Here Burr appeared in the summer of 1806, accompanied by his daughter, the beautiful Theodosia, and her husband Joseph Alston, a wealthy South Carolina planter. Blennerhassett was fascinated by the picture Burr drew of the empire he was to win in Mexico, a picture of marble palaces, of Spanish courtiers, of pomp and power. It was agreed that Theodosia should inherit the throne from her father, but some doubts arose as to whether Alston, as her husband, should also take the crown. "I will win it by a better title," he cried, "by my deeds in council and in field."

Intoxicated by these dreams, Blennerhassett resigned all his property into Burr's hands, and Burr made use of it to launch upon the Ohio an armed expedition, intended either for the alienation of Louisiana or the conquest of Mexico, which one perhaps Burr himself did not know. For either purpose it was ridiculously inadequate, a flotilla of nine bateaux with less than sixty men. Jefferson had had ample notice that Burr was brewing mischief in the West, but his supporters assured him there was no cause for action against him. So for the time he did nothing.

The success of Burr's scheme depended upon the co-operation of Wilkinson, and the general, as the time drew near for action, began to waver. When he learned how small was the force descending upon New Orleans, he decided to save himself by betraying his fellow conspirator. Sending a warning to Jefferson, he threw his forces into the city, arrested Burr's friends, proclaimed martial law, and boasted that he would play the rôle of Leonidas by hurling back Burr's "mighty host!"

January 10, 1807, when the little fleet reached a point thirty miles above Natchez, Burr learned that Wilkinson had betrayed him. For a moment he gave himself up to despair. If he proceeded he would fall into Wilkinson's hands, and perhaps be court-martialed and shot. After some hesitation, he disguised himself in the coarse suit and soiled felt hat of a Mississippi boatman, and, deserting his men, fled into the wilderness. Some weeks later he was arrested in a cabin about fifty miles from Mobile, and conducted to Richmond for trial.

On August 3, 1807, Chief Justice Marshall sat in a room in the old Eagle Tavern at Richmond, to try the former Vice-President on the charge of treason. Around him was an interesting gathering: the prosecuting attorneys, among them the brilliant young William Wirt; Burr himself, urbane as ever; the attorneys for the defense, the witty John Wickham, the eloquent Edmund Randolph, Benjamin Botts, and Luther Martin; the witnesses: Blennerhassett, Andrew Jackson, attired like a frontiersman, and Wilkinson; the grand jury, headed by John Randolph, of Roanoke.

Unfortunately, the trial took on the character of a political contest. Jefferson became the real prosecutor, John Marshall an advocate for the defense rather than the judge. The Republicans clamored for the blood of the accused; the Federalists defended him as a martyr. During the trial Burr had a suite of rooms, where he was allowed to see all comers, and the throngs of visitors at times gave the appearance of a levee. Servants were continually arriving, not only with messages of condolence from the ladies of Richmond but with baskets of oranges, lemons, pineapples, raspberries, apricots, cream, and butter.

In the end Marshall handed down an opinion which made Burr's conviction impossible. The prosecution contended that the assembling of the forces on Blennerhassett's island on December 10, 1806, constituted an overt act against the United States. But on that day Burr had been 200 miles away, and his attorneys pleaded that the act of his associates could not be regarded as his act, even though he had advised it. This argument ran counter to the old common-law doctrine that "in treason all are principals." It ran counter also to common sense, as Wirt pointed out. "This unfortunate man," he said, pointing to Blennerhassett, "thus ruined and undone and made to play a subordinate part in this grand drama of guilt and treason, this man is to be called the principal offender, while he by whom he was thus plunged in misery is comparatively innocent, a mere accessory! Is this reason? Is it law? Is it humanity?" Yet Marshall upheld the contention of the defense, squaring himself with the common-law doctrine by a bit of mental gymnastics. There was nothing left for the jury but to bring in a verdict of not guilty.

CHAPTER XI

WORLD TRADE

HAD President Jefferson visited any one of the shipping centres of New England during the years from 1801 to 1807, he would have found a hive of industry. He would have seen perhaps an incoming merchantman, lowering her mainsail as she glided into the harbor, or a West Indian brig, laden to her gunwales, starting on her journey to Guadeloupe or Martinique; stored on the wharves the products of foreign countries—sugar, coffee, cottons, hides, grain, indigo; in the shipyards the outlines of a dozen vessels, some in skeleton form, others nearing completion. This New England prosperity was the silver lining of the dark clouds of war which hung over Europe.

The British frigates were chasing the merchant vessels of France and her allies from the sea and the demand for neutral shipping had become insistent. A large part of the carrying trade of Europe fell into the hands of Americans. The Yankee ships were everywhere bringing to the embattled nations the products of their colonies, and carrying back the manufactures of the continent. From Cuba, Senegal, Manila, Cartagena, Surinam, St. Christopher, St. Thomas the American merchantmen sailed for the United States, there to take on new clearance papers and then turn eastward to Europe.

Under the stimulus of this trade New England bloomed as never before. The *Neptune*, one of twenty New Haven vessels trading in the South Sea, made a three years' voyage which shows the opportunities of the time. Circling the globe, she brought back a cargo of tea, silk, and chinaware which netted $240,000. With such profits in sight, what mattered it that once in a while the British frigates seized a merchantman! One could afford to run the risk. Money poured into New England, trade boomed, agriculture was encouraged, while every shipyard from the Kennebec to the Hudson hummed with activity.

Shipping advanced by leaps and bounds. In 1789 the tonnage of American-owned vessels engaged in foreign trade was
127,000; in 1796 it had mounted to 675,000; in 1801 to 849,000;
in 1805 to 922,000; in 1807 to 1,089,000. This amazing growth
menaced the commercial supremacy of Great Britain. And
Great Britain was duly alarmed. Her blockades had been designed to weaken Napoleon Bonaparte, not to build up a rival
across the Atlantic. It was axiomatic in England that Britannia must rule the sea or perish, and many felt that the Yankee
skipper was as much to be feared as the Corsican himself.

England was by no means soothed by the discovery that
the American vessels which were elbowing her ships in every
foreign port were in large part manned by Englishmen. The
Americans were not only rivalling her merchant marine, they
were stripping her navy of skilled seamen. Albert Gallatin said
that of the 4,000 seamen required to man the 70,000 tons of
new shipping turned out each year by the American yards,
one-half were British subjects, presumably deserters. Admiral
Nelson had reported that in the war with France which ter-
minated in 1801, 42,000 British seamen had deserted, and
every one knew that if that kind of thing were not stopped
it would undermine British sea power.

The United States needed these foreign sailors because the
training of Americans for the sea lagged behind the building of
ships. The shipwrights of the Kennebec or the Penobscot
could turn out a brig in twelve months; it took years to make
a sailor. You could not ship a lubberly Middlesex farm-hand
or a Boston artisan apprentice and expect him to know the
difference between the jib-boom and the mizzenmast. Unless
the vessels which the shipyards were turning out were to be
woefully undermanned, foreign sailors had to be taken on by
the thousand.

Nor was it difficult to induce the English jack-tar to exchange
his berth in the Royal Navy for one on a Yankee merchantman. Life on board the famous British frigates was hard. The
food was unwholesome, hygiene neglected, the medical service
execrable, wages were low, discipline rigid, punishment brutal.
Had it not been for the press-gangs which swept the wharves

and taverns of every idle sailor, the navy could not have been maintained. Even upon the high seas the British tar was not safe, for many a merchantman was stopped midway on her journey, robbed of her best men, and left to limp into port as best she could.

The deserter found the American masters ready to accord him good wages, comfortable quarters, wholesome food, and decent treatment. Once safe in an American port, he took out naturalization papers, assumed a new name, and felt himself to be as good a Yankee as though he had spent his life within sight of the Cape Cod Highland light. Unfortunately, he could not get the British Government to take the same view of the matter. Once a Britisher always a Britisher, said Pitt. And woe to the deserter who fell into the hands of the royal frigates! Despite his assumed nasal twang, despite his forged papers, he was sure to find himself back in his old job, with his back smarting from the touch of the cat-o'-nine-tails.

Every Yankee skipper, when he saw a British man-of-war looming up, had reason to curse his luck. He knew that he would soon be overhauled, his papers searched, his crew lined up on deck, and every British tar on board carried off, with perhaps an American or two thrown in. Two royal frigates, the *Leander* and the *Cambrian*, cruised for months off Sandy Hook, stopping vessels bound to or from New York. It was a common occurrence for this pair to hold up a dozen or more merchantmen for hours, often causing them to lose their fair wind, their tide, or their market.

Jefferson was deeply concerned at the growing hostility between England and the United States, yet he was sure that all could be amicably arranged. In his philosophy nations could always be brought to do justice to each other, because the path of justice was also the path of self-interest. The United States was growing rapidly; in another thirty years her population would number 25,000,000. What might not such a people be worth to England as customers and friends? What might she not fear from them as enemies? All they asked was justice, and the comity usually observed between nations.

Should England refuse the proffered hand, he felt that he

had the means of bringing her to reason. "Let us not forget," he said to his Cabinet, "that the boycott of 1765 was partly responsible for the repeal of the Stamp Act. Would not an act of Congress for complete non-intercourse be even more effectual in the present crisis? Can England afford to sacrifice a trade of many millions of dollars? Can her colonies exist without access to the American market? No, we will see that she will yield readily enough to our policy of peaceable coercion."

This reasoning had much in its favor. The loss of the American market would have weakened England and brought distress to her manufacturers. But Jefferson failed to see that other factors outweighed this consideration. England was counting on economic strangulation to weaken Napoleon Bonaparte; she considered maritime supremacy the foundation of British power and prosperity. If the American market could be held only by permitting American merchantmen to break the blockade, rob the navy of its ablest seamen, and elbow British traders out of the world's carrying trade, the American market would have to go.

In the quarrel between John Bull and the Yankee merchants, the former relied upon the guns of his powerful frigates. International law was what the British courts made it, and what the British courts decreed the British navy enforced. So the impressments and seizures continued. Yet the profits of the traders and the prosperity of the shipping centres would have taken the emphasis out of the American protests, had it not been for the harshness with which the British proceeded.

On June 22, 1807, at 7.15 A. M., the United States frigate *Chesapeake* left her anchorage outside Hampton Roads, and, spreading sail to catch a fair breeze, moved out to sea. To those who watched from shore as she passed Cape Henry, she seemed in good condition for her voyage to the Mediterranean. But on deck there was much confusion. The gun-deck was littered with odds and ends of rigging; the cables were not stored away; the guns, though loaded, were not all fitted to their carriages; the crew was short-handed and untrained. Commodore James Barron, in command of the vessel, counted upon putting her into trim during the voyage.

As the *Chesapeake* cleared the capes, it was noticed that the *Leopard*, a British frigate of fifty-two guns, also stood out to sea. Commodore Barron supposed she was on the lookout for suspicious merchantmen, and so did not give her a second thought. But at half past three, when both vessels were about ten miles off the cape, the *Leopard* approached to within a cable's length to windward and called out that she had despatches for the Commodore. Barron returned the hail, replying: "We will heave to and you can send your boat on board of us."

A petty officer came on board with a note from Captain Humphrey of the *Leopard*, together with a copy of an order from Vice-Admiral Berkeley, requiring all commanders in the North Atlantic Squadron to search the *Chesapeake* for deserters, if they should encounter her on the high seas. It seems that three deserters from the frigate *Melampus* had enlisted on the *Chesapeake*, but they were native Americans improperly impressed by the English. Therefore Commodore Barron replied that he knew of no such men as were described, and refused to permit the British to muster his crew. Barron did not know that a British tar named Jenkin Ratford had slipped aboard under the name of Wilson.

As the messenger departed, the crew began to clear the deck for action. But it was too late. Humphrey called out: "Commodore Barron, you must be aware of the necessity I am under of complying with the orders of my commander-in-chief." Now thoroughly alarmed, the American replied: "I don't hear what you say." The warning was repeated, but again Barron pretended not to understand. The *Leopard* at once fired a shot across the *Chesapeake's* bow, then another, and finally poured in her whole broadside at 150 or 200 feet.

On board the American frigate all was confusion. The guns were loaded, but could not be fired for want of loggerheads. While the gunners stood bravely at their posts, in the hail of grape-shot, a crowd of men and boys stood about the magazine, clamoring for matches, powder-flasks, and loggerheads. Barron himself, although wounded, stuck to his post, and repeatedly hailed the *Leopard* in the hope of gaining a moment's time. In the midst of the hubbub, Lieutenant Allen picked a live coal out of the galley with his fingers, ran to the deck, and with it fired one of the guns. It was the only shot from the helpless *Chesapeake*.

After fifteen minutes Commodore Barron ordered the flag to be hauled down. The *Chesapeake's* hull had been riddled, her masts injured, her sails cut, three of the crew were dead and eighteen wounded. The boats of the *Leopard* then came alongside, bringing several officers, who climbed on deck and mustered the crew. They picked out the three alleged deserters, and after a search dragged the luckless Jenkin Ratford from the coal-hole. Taking these four men with them, they left the shattered *Chesapeake* to limp back to Hampton Roads.

This unprovoked attack aroused the country to fury. For the first time the people experienced the sensation of national humiliation. Everywhere there were mass meetings, resolutions, preparations for war. Even in New England, where war would have brought great suffering, the people promised to support the President in the strongest measures of revenge. "The affair of the *Chesapeake* put war into my hand," wrote Jefferson some years later. "I had only to open it and let havoc loose." But the President was determined that there should be no war. He would demand disavowal and reparation, he said, and if that failed, he would use his trusted weapon of peaceful coercion.

In the meanwhile England added fuel to the flames by her continued seizures. In 1805 Sir William Scott had rendered a decision which struck directly at the carrying trade of the United States. Hitherto neutral vessels had been permitted to take on goods in the French colonies, bring them to an American port, pay customs duties there, and then transport them to Brest or Bordeaux or Marseilles. The court now decided, in the case of the *Essex*, that the legality or illegality of the voyage must be determined by the intended destination of the cargo. Once more America rang with the indignant protests. "Never will neutrals be perfectly safe till free goods make free ships, or till England loses two or three great naval battles," declared the Salem *Register*.

Jefferson's answer to the *Essex* decision was the Non-Importation Act of April 18, 1806, which forbade the importation of certain specified British goods. John Randolph stigmatized this measure as "a milk-and-water bill, a dose of chicken-broth to be taken nine months hence." In England it was regarded as a threat. The public felt that Congress had left them the alternative of surrendering their commerce and their shipping to America, or of giving up the battle against France. The British Government asked whether the United States would fight, and having satisfied themselves that Jefferson would avoid war at all hazards, treated non-importation with contempt. In December, 1806, the measure was suspended.

Such was the situation when Napoleon issued his famous Berlin decree. Master of western Europe, but checkmated upon the sea, he sought to turn against his foe her own weapon of economic strangulation. The British blockade of the French channel ports he answered with a paper blockade of the British Isles. All British goods were to be lawful prize in any territory held by France or her allies, and all vessels coming from English ports or English colonies were to be confiscated. This was a challenge to a death-struggle, and Britain girded herself to give blow for blow. An order in council of January 7, 1807, declared that England would confiscate any vessel trading between any two ports of France or her allies.

The chief victim was the United States. What the Yankee skipper who crossed the Atlantic had to expect was made clear by the fate of the *Horizon*. Heading for London with South American products, this vessel put in at Lisbon to refit. As she left she was seized by a British frigate. The prize-court condemned the cargo but released the ship. The unlucky master next loaded a new cargo, partly of English make, and set out again for Lisbon. This time the vessel was wrecked off the coast of France, where her cargo was salvaged, and all goods of English origin confiscated. When the American Minister at Paris protested, Napoleon retorted that since America permitted her vessels to be searched, thus recognizing the English blockades, "why should Americans not suffer the blockade laid by France?"

The British press was bitter against the United States. The *Post* declared that "three months' blockade of the Delaware, the Chesapeake, and Boston would make our presumptuous rivals reflect of their puerile conduct." "America is not contented with striking at the very vitals of our commercial existence," it added; "she must also degrade us in the eyes of the world." A new order in council followed, November 11, 1807. Any American vessel would be liable to seizure, it said, if it sailed for a European port from which English vessels were excluded. In addition, all vessels trading with Europe must touch at an English port, where certain designated goods were to pay duty.

While the American press was still protesting angrily, news came that Napoleon had retaliated with a decree even more unjust. "Considering that by these acts the English Government has denationalized the ships of all the nations of Europe," he said, "that it is in the power of no Government to compound its own independence and its rights," it is decreed that every ship searched by an English vessel, or which has paid duty to England, or come from or to any British port, shall be good prize.

In the midst of this fusillade of decrees, counter-decrees, insults, and injuries, Jefferson was calm and confident. Had he not the means of securing justice? Was he not certain of bringing the war-maddened powers of Europe to their senses with his policy of peaceful coercion? Calling his Cabinet around him, he took a loose sheet of paper and drafted a message to Congress, recommending a complete embargo on American trade. Gallatin demurred. "I prefer war to a permanent embargo," he said; "government prohibitions do always more mischief than had been calculated." But Gallatin was overruled. "The whole world is laid under interdict by these two nations," said Jefferson, "and our vessels, their cargoes and crews, are to be taken by the one or the other. . . . If, therefore, on leaving our harbors we are certainly to lose them, is it not better . . . to keep them at home?" Despite these words it was well understood that the intent was to coerce England by the threat to her manufactures. In the Senate a few voices were raised in protest. But the Republican majority forced through the bill almost without debate. "The President has recommended the measure on his high responsibility," said John Quincy Adams. "I would not consider, I would not deliberate, I would act." The bill went through its three readings in the Senate in five hours; the House passed it after two days of debate; and on December 22, 1807, the President affixed his signature.

The embargo, with a few exceptions, forbade the departure of any ships for foreign ports. Coasting ships were required to give heavy bond to put in only at ports of the United States. With a stroke of the pen Jefferson attempted to reverse the economic developments of two decades. American tonnage in foreign traffic was to remain idle, thousands of sailors were to lose their jobs, exports amounting to $108,000,000 and imports totalling $138,000,000 were to be cut off. Many considered this worse than the evil it was intended to correct.

Trouble began at once. Before the law went into effect ships put out to sea, many of them half-manned, badly equipped, without clearance papers. Later, when the Federal officials tried to enforce the embargo, skippers and owners went to extreme lengths to evade their vigilance. Vessels left ostensibly to engage in the coasting-trade, and then turned toward Europe. A brisk trade sprang up across the Canadian border. Great rafts were launched upon Lake Champlain, fitted with little forts, manned by armed companies, loaded with wheat, pork, and potash, and propelled down into the Richelieu for shipment to Montreal. Jefferson was surprised and hurt. "I did not expect a crop of so sudden and rank a growth of fraud and open opposition by force could have grown up in the United States."

Soon every port swarmed with customs officials; gunboats, frigates, and revenue cutters prowled up and down the New England coast; companies of militia guarded the roads to Canada. The President's friends drew back in alarm. Gallatin labored to carry out the law, but with a heavy heart, while Robert Smith, the Secretary of the Navy, was outspoken in his opposition. "Most fervently ought we to pray to be relieved of this said embargo," he lamented.

Indeed, the embargo was bringing the shipping centres to the verge of insurrection. A visitor to New York in 1808 might have imagined himself in a decadent city. In the port scores of ships were lying dismantled, their decks cleared, their hatches fastened down, scarcely a sailor to be found. The wharves were bare of goods, the counting-houses closed, the coffee-houses empty, the streets near the waterside almost deserted. The merchants complained that the act of their own government had done more harm in one year than the seizures of Great Britain in ten.

As a measure of coercion the embargo failed. Although it brought distress to the British West Indies and British manufacturers and workers, it left the English merchant marine without a rival in the carrying trade. The menace to England's commercial supremacy had suddenly been removed by the action of the United States itself; surely it was not the part of England to complain. When William Pinckney, the American Minister at the court of St. James's, asked whether England would revoke her orders in council in return for the repeal of the embargo, Canning replied that to rescind the orders in council would be inconsistent with the interests of the British people, but he would be happy to aid in restoring American commerce and in removing the effects of the embargo as a measure of inconvenient restriction upon the American people.

This was a terrible blow to Jefferson. His pet policy had been a failure. New England was clamoring for its repeal. There were threats of nullification, resistance to the Government, secession. The Republicans in Congress began to waver. Madison and Gallatin tried to hold them in line, but they could not stem the tide. March 1, 1809, three days before his retirement, with much bitterness of spirit, Jefferson signed the bill which ended his great experiment.

March 4 James Madison, pale, nervous, unimposing, arose to deliver his inaugural address before a great crowd in the new Hall of Representatives at the Capitol. He was ill at ease, and his voice was so low that few could hear him. When he was done, and Chief Justice Marshall had administered the oath, he passed the militia in review. That evening he attended an inaugural ball, where "the crowd was excessive, the heat oppressive, and the entertainment bad." "Mr. Madison seemed spiritless and exhausted," wrote one of the ladies present. Jefferson, on the contrary, was in high spirits. His countenance beamed, and every demonstration of respect to Madison seemed to give him more pleasure than if paid to himself.

No wonder Jefferson was happy. At last he was free of the cares of office, free to get away from the turmoil, hatreds, and backbitings of public life. The policies so dear to his heart were still to prevail, the administration would remain in the hands of his closest friends and disciples. So with mingled relief and satisfaction he mounted his horse as the red maple, the weeping willow, and the lilac were announcing the approach of the Virginia spring, and rode off over the muddy roads to his beloved Monticello.

Madison continued the well-nigh hopeless negotiations with Great Britain over seizures and impressment. The task was not new to him, for as Secretary of State he had had the misfortune to deal with George Rose, sent by Great Britain to settle the *Chesapeake* affair. With patronizing courteousness Rose had informed Madison that before reparations could be considered the President must recall the proclamation issued after the attack on the *Chesapeake*, denying our ports to British war-vessels. Although much surprised, Madison agreed, provided the withdrawal and the announcement of British atonement be issued simultaneously. But when Rose demanded various other pledges and disavowals, he broke off negotiations. "The United States cannot be expected to make as it were an expiatory sacrifice to obtain redress, or beg for reparation," he said.

Despite this experience, Madison was able to announce a few weeks after his inauguration what seemed to be a great diplomatic victory. He had signed an agreement with the new British Minister, David Montague Erskine, promising satisfaction for the *Chesapeake* outrage and setting the date for the withdrawal of the orders in council. The Republican press was jubilant. Jefferson had been vindicated, they said, peaceful coercion had won, the embargo had not been in vain. Every American port awoke from its long slumber. Runners set out to summon the idle crews, vessels were reconditioned, laden with goods from the warehouses, and sent out to sea. Then came disappointment. The British Minister had exceeded his instructions, and Canning refused to sanction the agreement.

Madison was thoroughly discouraged. Non-intercourse with Great Britain was revived by proclamation, and when another Minister arrived the President let him wait in Washington while he enjoyed a well-earned rest at Montpelier, his Virginia home. Francis James Jackson was overbearing, supercilious, noted for his bad temper and his bad manners. No one could be less fitted to smooth over the differences of England and the United States. When Madison returned to Washington, Jackson donned his "afternoon frock" and went to the White House to pay his respects. He could hardly conceal his contempt for this "plain and rather mean-looking little man," and smiled condescendingly when "a negro servant brought in some glasses of punch and a seed-cake." What an audience this, he thought, for one who has been received by most of the sovereigns of Europe!

He would have been still more annoyed had he guessed that the "mean-looking little man," feeling that negotiations with him would be hopeless, had decided to bring him to the point and send him home. When Jackson intimated that the American Government in its dealings with Erskine had inveigled him into breaking his instructions, he drew from Madison a sharp rebuke. "Such insinuations are inadmissible in the intercourse of a foreign minister with a government that understands what it owes itself." "You will find that in my correspondence with you," Jackson retorted, "I have carefully avoided . . . uttering an insinuation where I was unable to substantiate a fact." Whereupon the President wrote that no further communications would be received from him, and in due time Canning sent word for him to return to England.

Madison and Jefferson were now to find that the paths of peaceful coercion lead but to war. In 1798, when the United States, smarting under the X-Y-Z insults, let it be known that it was ready to fight, open war was avoided; in the chronic squabble with Great Britain, when the impression was universal that the United States would not fight, war followed. In 1816 Jefferson pointed out to Noah Worcester that the cost of the War of 1812 to Great Britain far outweighed the benefits of her seizures and impressments. It is equally true that had Jefferson, instead of trusting in peaceful coercion, expended on frigates a fraction of what the war cost America, war would probably have been avoided.

In 1807 the government, at Jefferson's earnest desire, built a large number of little gunboats as America's chief line of sea defense. Gallatin protested that this "mosquito fleet" would be useless against frigates, that they would "decay in a given number of years," and that the cost of maintenance would be excessive. He was overruled and the gunboats were built. The few frigates remaining in service were kept afloat only to serve as "receptacles for enlisting seamen to fill the gunboats occasionally" in case of war. Such was Jefferson's idea of preparedness at a time when Europe was convulsed with the Napoleonic wars, when the United States was competing for the world's carrying-trade and when injuries by foreign powers had become almost an every-day occurrence.

Britain was not intimidated by this toy flotilla. Her seizures and impressments continued, and Madison was at his wits' end to know what to do next. Finally, Congress hit upon a new plan of coercion, which it embodied in what is known as Macon Bill No. 2. This measure left commercial relations free with all the world, but authorized the President, in case either Great Britain or France should revoke her edicts against the United States, to prohibit intercourse with the other. This was in fact a surrender to England. Voluntary non-intercourse with France would have completed the blockade of western Europe, and probably have brought the United States into the war as an ally of England.

But England hesitated and Napoleon acted. "The Milan and Berlin decrees are revoked," the Emperor informed the American Minister, "and after November 1 they will cease to have effect, it being understood that . . . the United States, conformably to the Act you have just communicated, cause their rights to be respected by the English." This was fair-sounding language. But Napoleon sought only to hoodwink Madison. He had no intention of permitting freedom to American vessels unless the United States went to war with England. Madison fell into the trap, for it seemed to him the last chance to test the effectiveness of peaceful coercion. November 2, 1810, he issued a proclamation ordering a cessation of commercial intercourse with Great Britain.

It was on Washington's Birthday, 1810, that Henry Clay, hitherto a stranger in the Senate, arose and made his bow to Vice-President Clinton. He was over six feet in height, his figure thin but erect, his nose prominent, his mouth large, his forehead high and sloping backward, his hair light, his eyes blue. In a voice so rich and powerful that it reached every corner of the Senate Chamber, he began by protesting against the surrender of American rights at the dictation of Great Britain. "The conquest of Canada is in your power," he said. "I trust I shall not be deemed presumptuous when I state that I verily believe that the militia of Kentucky are alone competent to place Montreal and upper Canada at your feet. . . . The withered arm and wrinkled brow of the illustrious founders of our freedom are melancholy indications that they will shortly be removed from us. Their deeds of glory and renown will then be felt only through the cold medium of the historic page; we shall want the presence and living example of a new race of heroes to supply their places, and to animate us to preserve inviolate what they achieved. . . . Will you set the base example . . . of an ignominious surrender of our rights?"

These words form a dividing line between the old school of political leadership and the new. Clay represented a group of young statesmen devoted to the Union and sensitive of the national dignity who were to dominate American political life for forty years. It was this group who now forced the sword into the hand of President Madison.

In this they were aided by continued acts of aggression by Great Britain. While the *Chesapeake* outrage was still unredressed, the admiralty sent two frigates, the *Melampus* and the *Guerrière*, to lie off Sandy Hook and search American merchantmen. The Secretary of the Navy warned Commodore Rogers, who was cruising off the coast with an American squadron, to be on his guard. "What has been perpetrated may be attempted again," he was reminded. Every tar'in the service hoped that the time was at hand to avenge the *Chesapeake*.

May 16, 1811, Rogers in his frigate, the *President*, sighted a British war-vessel about fifty miles off Cape Henry, which he believed to be the *Guerrière*. Giving chase to the stranger, the *President* came within range at dusk. When the British fired a shot, Rogers opened his batteries and in fifteen minutes rendered his adversary helpless. Then, to his chagrin, he learned that he had disabled, not the *Guerrière* but the sloop-of-war *Little Belt*, a vessel of but twenty guns. But the American public was jubilant. At last British insolence had been rebuked. When the new British minister, Augustus J. Foster, arrived to settle the *Chesapeake* affair, he found the government singularly apathetic. The shots which had riddled the luckless *Little Belt* did more to remove the sting of Humphrey's attack than all the long-delayed offers of disavowals and reparations.

The final impetus which forced the country into war came not from the maritime East, but from the Ohio valley. To the end New England protested against a war which could but ruin her carrying-trade; but the West expected a great American triumph. They would summon their frontier fighters, press north to the border and down the St. Lawrence to Montreal and Quebec. Every Westerner regarded England as his enemy. "Is it nothing to extinguish the torch that lights up savage warfare?" demanded Clay in the Senate. "Is it nothing to acquire the entire fur trade connected with that country, and to destroy the temptation and opportunity of violating your revenue and other laws?"

With the opening of the year 1811 the war clouds hung heavy over the Northwest. William Henry Harrison, Governor of the Indiana Territory, had secured from several chieftains title to large tracts in the valleys of the Wabash and the White. Two Shawnee chieftains, Tecumseh and "the Prophet," protested against this cession. It would drive the game out for many miles beyond the actual limits, they argued, and bring starvation to their people. The federation of tribes under their leadership would resist in arms the occupation of the Wabash valley. In the fall Harrison led a force of about 1,000 men into the disputed territory. Early in the morning of November 11 the Indians, under "the Prophet," attacked him. At first they were successful; but he rallied his men, and after two hours of fighting drove the savages into a neighboring swamp. The battle of Tippecanoe was the prelude to the conflict with England. "War is not to commence by sea or land," it was declared; "it is already begun, and some of the richest blood of our country has been shed."

In the meanwhile Henry Clay and the other "war hawks" were clamoring for preparedness. "Let us fill the ranks of the army and add ten regiments," they said; "call for 50,000 volunteers, permit merchantmen to arm, and put every available war-vessel into commission." Langdon Cheves, of South Carolina, recommended the construction of twelve seventy-fours and twenty frigates. "I only know of one principle to make a nation great," said John C. Calhoun, "to produce in this country not the form but the real spirit of union, and that is to protect every citizen in the lawful pursuit of his business."

But these enthusiastic nationalists found that the old Republicans would not part with the cherished Jeffersonian traditions, while the Federalists were intent only on overthrowing the administration. All Congress would do was to provide 25,000 additional men for the army, and call into service 50,000 State militia. They refused either to increase the navy or to levy new taxes.

On June 1, 1812, President Madison sent his annual message to Congress. The British cruisers had long been "in the continued practice of violating the American flag on the great highway of nations," he said, "and of seizing and carrying off persons sailing under it." They had hung upon the American coast, harassing entering and departing commerce. American vessels had been plundered under color of "pretended blockades." Congress must decide, he concluded, whether the United

States should oppose force for force. June 4 a bill declaring war on Great Britain passed the House by a vote of 79 to 49; and three days later the Senate concurred by the narrow margin of five votes. June 8 Madison signed the War Act, and the United States had at last been drawn into the Napoleonic wars.

The fundamental cause of the War of 1812 was the expansion of American trade during the period of disturbance in Europe. The demand for neutral shipping made the United States a competitor for the world's carrying-trade, and this brought her into conflict with the British merchant marine and involved her in the net of European blockades. Washington had warned against entangling alliances, but it was the entangling foreign commerce which proved more dangerous to American peace.

Jefferson saw this clearly. It is folly "for us to carry on the business of one-half the world at the expense of eternal war with the other half," he wrote in 1816. "No one can doubt that this alone produced the orders of council, the depredations which preceded, and the war which followed them. Had we carried but our own produce and brought back but our own wants, no nation would have troubled us." To Jefferson's mind the choice lay between "licentious commerce and gambling speculations for a few, with eternal war for the many; and restricted commerce, peace, and steady occupations for all."

To the New England merchants this point of view seemed monstrous. Commerce was the basis of their economic life. If commerce expanded they prospered; if commerce languished they suffered. It was a wholesome, honest occupation, necessary to man's welfare, and it was the duty of the government to encourage it and to protect it from foreign interference. If this involved us in unpleasant complications, we must make the most of it. The war with England might have been averted, they felt, but for the bungling diplomacy of the Republican administration, and the state of unpreparedness in which they kept the country. But if foreign commerce could not be had without war, let there be war. In the end the price would not be too great.

CHAPTER XII

WAR OF 1812

HAVING signed the declaration of war, President Madison put on "his little round hat and huge cockade," and set out to inspect the offices of the War and Navy Departments. These places were almost unknown to him, for in his philosophy administrative preparedness for war had no place, but he now went about "stimulating everything in a manner worthy of a little commander-in-chief." Stimulation was needed.

In the war offices he found William Eustis, of Massachusetts, aided by a few clerks, attempting to discharge the duties of Secretary of War, Commissary-General, Indian Commissioner, Commissioner of Pensions, and Commissioner of Public Lands. Such multiform tasks would have bewildered the greatest administrator, and Eustis was devoid of administrative ability. At a time when he should have been organizing his department, creating armies and planning campaigns, he consumed "his time in reading advertisements of petty retailing merchants to find where to purchase 100 shoes or 200 hats." But the President greeted him with smiles and passed on to the navy offices.

Here he found still greater incompetence. Paul Hamilton, the Secretary of the Navy, was declared by Macon to be "about as fit for his place as the Indian Prophet would be for the Emperor of Europe," while Senator Crawford complained that he was chiefly concerned with making the naval officers supply him with tropical fruits. With two weaklings at the head of military and naval operations, disaster was inevitable. Yet Madison assured them of his favor, and talked about throwing forward the flag of the country, sure that the people would defend it.

If the heads of the departments were bad, the generals were worse. Many were veterans of the Revolution, now old or ruined by drinking. James Wilkinson, notorious for his part in the Burr conspiracy, was as incompetent as he was treacherous; James Winchester, an elderly Tennessee planter, was incapable of leadership; William Hull lacked courage. William H. Winder is described as one who never lost his head because he had none to lose. Nor were the inferior officers better. "Swaggerers, dependents, decayed gentlemen" held most of the appointments and proved unfit for military duty.

Such were the leaders of the army which Clay so confidently expected to march on to Montreal. The army itself consisted of ten old regiments, with half-filled ranks, ill organized and equipped, and thirteen new regiments yet to be recruited. The navy, although led by gallant and able captains, and manned by crews unsurpassed for seamanship and gunnery, was completely dwarfed by the British sea-fighters. The *United States*, the *Constitution*, and the *President* were of 1,576 tons each and carried 44 guns; the *Constellation*, the *Congress*, and the *Chesapeake*, vessels of about 1,250 tons, carried 38 guns; ten smaller vessels varied in size from the *Essex* of 32 guns to the *Viper* of 12. It was a small fleet with which to face Britannia, mistress of the seas.

Even worse was the inability of the government to finance the war. Gallatin still headed the Treasury Department, it is true, but Gallatin could do little in the face of the stupidity of Congress. Despite his pleadings, the Bank of the United States had been allowed to expire in March, 1811, and he was deprived of its services when they were most needed. A bill providing for an increase of duties on imports to meet the deficit was tabled, the suggestion to restore the excise tax was received with sullen disapproval. Congress would authorize a loan of $11,000,000; that was all it would do. The Secretary of the Treasury, to his disgust, found himself a mere "dealer of loans."

The folly of Congress in entering upon a war for which they refused to make any adequate preparation brought upon them the scorn of John Randolph. "Go to war without money, without men, without a navy," he said with a smile of derision, his deep hazel eyes flashing. "Go to war when we have not the courage, while your lips utter war, to lay war taxes! When your whole courage is exhibited in passing resolutions! The people will not believe it."

The young war leaders would not listen to Randolph. "So far from being unprepared, sir," declared Calhoun, "I believe that in four weeks from the time that a declaration of war is heard on our frontiers, the whole of upper, and a part of lower Canada will be in our possession." The country had no idea of what it meant to mobilize the national resources for war. To appropriate the people's wealth, divert capital and labor from the industries of peace into the industries of war, select for the army and navy the ablest and best of the nation's manhood, things to-day considered so indispensable, a century ago were undreamed of. To suggest them upon the floor of Congress would have put one in peril of the madhouse.

Not knowing how to make war, President Madison had to reconcile himself to disaster. Word came that General Hull had been thrown back in his attempt to invade Canada, had retired to Detroit, had been surrounded there by a force of British, Canadians, and Indians, and had surrendered his command without a blow. This was followed by the news that an attack on Montreal had failed because the militia, when they reached the border, refused to leave the country. Next came the announcement that General Van Rensselaer, who was operating on the Niagara, had permitted the enemy to capture 600 of his best men, while he sat still as though in a stupor. Worse was to come. Late in the year the discouraged President heard that the Niagara army had refused to obey their new commander, General Alexander Smyth, and, riddling his tent with bullets in token of their contempt, had returned home.

Madison was crushed. His weak body could not stand the strain of hard work and continued disappointments. In June, 1813, he contracted an intermittent fever. For weeks his friends were in great anxiety, while his faithful wife, the charming Dolly Madison, nursed him back to health. "Even now I watch over him as I would an infant," she wrote to Mrs. Gallatin, after her patient had left his bed, "so precarious is his convalescence."

Perhaps Madison might have stood the shock of disaster in

the field had it not been accompanied by proof that he was no longer presiding over a united people. New England was bitterly opposed to the war. When the news reached Boston that war had been declared, Governor Strong ordered a public fast in Massachusetts. The returning members of Congress who had voted for the measure were insulted, while Charles Turner was seized by a mob at Plymouth and kicked through the streets. Everywhere the people gathered in their town meetings to protest against the war and to devise measures to render it ineffectual. It was uncalled for, they said, the work of an irresponsible minority, and would bring ruin to the country; Madison had sold himself to France; he was destroying the rights of the people and shaking the foundations of the Union.

When the President called for volunteers in New England, enlisting was discouraged; when he asked for a quota of the militia, the Governors of Massachusetts and Connecticut refused. Massachusetts kept 70,000 militia in condition, not to repel the British but to prevent coercion by the government at Washington. There was a general refusal to purchase American bonds, and trade was carried on with the British by way of Halifax. In every New England pulpit the preachers denounced the wicked war, likening Jefferson to Jeroboam, and Madison to Nadab, who made Israel walk in sin.

Madison felt that the conduct of the marine States was indefensible. They had challenged Britain by rivalling her merchant marine and defying her blockades, had brought upon the nation a long series of wrongs, and now, when the nation was aroused to defend its honor, had refused to do their part. The New Englanders, in turn, placed the blame on Madison. Had he built a great fleet of frigates, they said, to dispute the supremacy of the sea, the war might have been worth while. But to declare war without a navy, to leave the Yankee merchantmen to the mercy of the British men-of-war, meant ruin for New England. It was well enough to talk of bringing England to terms by conquering Canada, but the capture of Montreal and Quebec could not restore prosperity to the desolate New England ports. American wrongs could be righted only by a war on the sea, yet for this Madison and Congress had made no preparation. Why? Was it because material was lacking for splendid frigates? Was it because skilled seamen and able commanders could not be found? Certainly not. The truth was that the President, while prating about neutral rights, hated New England and was determined to ruin her.

The war was but a few months old when confirmation came of the contention that with adequate preparation the United States might have made a stand on the ocean. The little American navy accomplished marvels. It could not prevent the British squadrons from blockading the chief ports of the country, but in single actions it demonstrated to the world that ship for ship it was the equal of the enemy, it brought renown to the service, and dealt a blow to the prestige of the English. Had the United States entered the struggle with the twelve seventy-fours and twenty frigates recommended by Cheves in January, 1812, she might have driven every British war-vessel out of American waters.

The war was less than two months old when the *Constitution*, with Captain Isaac Hull in command, sailed out of Boston Harbor. Seventeen days later, while cruising 800 miles off the New England coast, Hull caught sight of a sail upon the horizon. As the stranger drew near all eyes were strained to discover who she was, until at last the cry was raised: "It's the *Guerrière*, it's the *Guerrière*." A thrill ran through the crew of the *Constitution*. At last the opportunity was at hand to avenge the injuries inflicted by this frigate, and to prove that American ships and seamen were inferior to none.

Captain John Dacres, of the *Guerrière*, was not inclined to run from the Yankee. He knew that the *Constitution* was superior in gun-power, but he was confident that British courage and skill would carry the day. He failed to realize that the *Constitution* and her sister ships were the most powerful frigates afloat, their long twenty-four pounders and extremely stout timbers and planking giving them a marked superiority over the usual type of cruiser. As she bore down upon him before the fresh northwest breeze, Dacres backed his maintopsail and waited.

On board the *Constitution* officers and men were keyed to the highest pitch of excitement, but they went about the task of putting everything in readiness for the conflict with coolness and precision. As the fife and drum sounded to quarters, they took their positions beside the wooden gun-carriages, or climbed aloft to furl the sails or to use their muskets. Cutlasses and pikes were neatly piled, ready for use in case the order came to board the enemy, the decks were sanded, while loggerheads were heated in the magazine fire.

For about an hour the two vessels manœuvred for position, while an occasional shot was fired as one or the other took a long chance at hitting a spar or rigging. At last they came together side by side, within pistol-shot. For a moment still Captain Hull withheld his fire, while the gunners of the *Guerrière* were working hard, and his men were beginning to drop. Then, at the distance of a few yards, he poured in his broadside. The British frigate reeled before the terrific blast. Within ten minutes the mizzenmast came down with a crash, the hull was shattered, and the decks swept with ball and grape. "In less than thirty minutes from the time we got alongside the enemy," reported Captain Hull, "she was left without a spar standing, and the hull cut to pieces in such a manner as to make it difficult to keep her above water." When the American sailors set foot on the deck of the frigate, a terrible spectacle met their eyes. The dead lay scattered amid a tangle of spars and rigging, the guns were dismantled, and the carriages surging from side to side, while the groans of the wounded added to the confusion. Two days later as victors and vanquished gazed at the blazing hulk of what had been the *Guerrière*, the *Constitution* set sail for Boston.

August 30, the victorious frigate, with pennants flying, moved into Boston harbor. The entire city celebrated, and Captain Hull with all his crew were paraded up State Street through cheering thousands to a banquet at Faneuil Hall. The navy had been vindicated, the spell of British invincibility had been broken, American seamen had proved their mettle, American ships their power. As the news spread throughout the country, the men of the *Constitution* were everywhere toasted and lauded.

On the evening of December 8 a brilliant ball was held at Washington in honor of Captain Hull and the other officers of the *Constitution*. Upon the wall was hung the flag of the ill-fated *Guerrière*. Hundreds of candles shone down upon beautiful women who chatted and danced with men resplendent in gold lace and epaulets and side-arms. Suddenly the music ceased, the crowd drew back, and a young naval officer entered the room with a British flag over his shoulders. It was Midshipman Hamilton, son of the Secretary of the Navy, sent by Stephen Decatur to announce the capture of the British warship *Macedonian* by the frigate *United States*. A scene of wild enthusiasm ensued. A great shout arose, young Hamilton was lifted by a dozen hands, the *Macedonian's* battle-flag was held over the heads of the officers of the *Constitution*, while the hall reverberated to "Hail, Columbia."

The victories of American frigates in isolated duels, however gratifying to American pride, could have little effect upon the outcome of the war. Soon one squadron after another of great British sea-fighters appeared off the coast, and the Yankee frigates were driven to cover. The *Chesapeake* was captured by the *Shannon*, Decatur with the *United States* and the *Macedonian* was bottled up at New London, the *President* was captured trying to escape from New York, the *Constellation* was held at Norfolk, the *Congress* at Boston. Every port of the United States was guarded; American commerce was swept from the sea. The exploits of Decatur and Hull brought only the bitter reflection of what might have been, had Jefferson and Madison made use of Yankee skill and seamanship to build up a powerful navy.

In the fall of 1813 the people were greatly heartened by several important victories. Kentucky raised 10,000 men, placed them under General William Harrison, and sent them north to Detroit. The Navy Department, at last aroused to the importance of controlling the Great Lakes, launched a small fleet at Presqu'ile, sending to Buffalo and Pittsburg for some of the material and equipment. September 10, the American ships, under the command of Captain Oliver H. Perry, met a British squadron at the western end of Lake Erie. A furious engagement ensued. When Perry's flagship, the *Lawrence*, was reduced to a wreck, he put off in a small boat bearing a blue flag inscribed with the words "Don't give up the ship," and rowed under the British fire to the *Niagara*. With this brig he passed through the enemy, sweeping them with broadsides until all surrendered. "We have met the enemy and they are ours," he wrote Harrison, "two ships, two brigs, one schooner, and one sloop."

This notable victory, which cleared the Lakes of the British, was followed by successes on land. Harrison's army crossed to Canada, inflicted a severe defeat on the British and Indians on the Thames, and forced them to abandon upper Canada north of Lake Erie. United States territory west of the Niagara was not again molested during the war.

Despite these encouraging victories, the crowning humiliation of the war was still in store. In April, 1813, when York, the capital of upper Canada, had fallen into the hands of the Americans, the soldiers set fire to the houses of assembly and other public buildings. General Dearborn reported that this vandalism had been done against his orders. But it served the British as a pretext for a series of raids on the United States coast which spread terror from Maine to Georgia. Rear-Admiral Cockburn landed a force at the mouth of the Susquehanna, laid the country waste, and burned the villages of Havre de Grace and Fredericktown; Admiral Warren pillaged the defenseless town of Hampton; another expedition wrought havoc on Cape Cod, levying contributions on Wellfleet, Brewster, and Eastham, and destroying other towns; Stonington, Connecticut, was laid in ruins.

In August, 1814, a large British fleet, under the command of Vice-Admiral Cochrane and General Robert Ross, sailed up Chesapeake Bay and entered Patuxent River. Their immediate aim was to capture a flotilla of Jefferson's gunboats, commanded by Commodore Joshua Barney. This officer had no idea of sacrificing precious guns and still more precious sailors in defending these useless vessels, so he promptly dismantled and blew them up. Thereupon the British commanders landed an army of 4,500 men, veterans of Wellington's peninsular campaign, and marched on Washington.

The defense of the city had been left to the incompetent Winder. Although he had had six weeks to make preparations, when the British began their leisurely march through eastern Maryland not a ditch had been dug, not a rampart constructed, not a cannon planted. At the last moment a force was brought together, consisting of a few regulars, Barney's jacktars, 120 light dragoons, and several thousand volunteers and militia. This motley force might have saved Washington had Winder concentrated them at Bladensburg, through which the British had to pass. But Winder thought the enemy would attempt to cross the Eastern Branch, and so held his men on its western bank at the navy-yard.

When news came at ten o'clock on August 24 that Ross was well advanced on the road to Bladensburg, there was a wild scramble to head him off. Away went the President, the Cabinet, the corps commanders, with the long line of troops streaming out behind. As the men came up, an effort was made to form them in line, but nothing could be done with such amateurs in the face of the British regulars. "A few companies only," says an eye-witness, ". . . presented some appearance of regular troops. The rest seemed country people who would have been much more appropriately employed in attending to their agricultural occupations than in standing with muskets in their hands on the brow of a bare, green hill."

When the British charged, the few regulars acted well, and greeted them with a heavy discharge of artillery and musketry. But the militia gave way, and, running westward toward Georgetown, carried the reluctant veterans with them. Meanwhile Barney's sailors, who had refused to remain behind, came up on the run and took a position on a hillside a mile from Bladensburg. They sent a few contemptuous oaths after the fleeing militia and limbered up their guns. Four hundred against four thousand were terrible odds, but, though they could not save Washington, they could prove that Americans, when properly drilled and commanded, were inferior to none. Three times the British charged Barney's battery and were thrown back. There was deadly work with cutlasses and handspikes, and the men stood their ground until some were bayoneted with fuses in their hands. Not until Barney had been wounded, until they had been deserted and were in danger of being surrounded, did they quit the field.

As evening came on, the British advanced to the outskirts of Washington. Here the main body pitched camp, while a detachment, led by Cochrane and Ross, marched through the deserted streets to the Capitol. This building, which all Americans regarded as symbolic of their growing greatness, they immediately set on fire. As the flames crept up over the Senate Chamber and the newly completed Hall of Representatives, the troops proceeded to the White House. After ransacking the mansion, they piled the furniture in the drawing-room, and applied the torch. The Americans fired the navy-yard and the vessels in the Eastern Branch to prevent their falling into the hands of the enemy. On the hills of Virginia the disheartened President paused in his flight to watch the three great conflagrations, as they shone out in the night and glistened in the waters of the Potomac. His was a humiliation such as no other President of the United States has ever been called upon to bear, the humiliation of a great national disaster brought on by incompetence and lack of preparation.

Yet the capture of Washington had little influence upon the outcome of the war. The British troops soon evacuated the city, Madison returned, and things went on much as before. The danger which oppressed the mind of the President was the threat of New England secession. In October William Wirt came to Washington, and after viewing the blackened walls of the White House, which he regarded as a "mournful monument to American imbecility," called on Madison. "He looks miserably shattered and woebegone," he said. "In short, he looks heart-broken. His mind is full of the New England sedition. He introduced the subject and continued to press it, painful as it obviously was to him."

Indeed, the discontent in the maritime States was nearing the breaking-point. From the day Jefferson took his seat as President, the northern Federalists had rgearded the future with despair. What hope was there for a nation presided over by men so far sunk in democratic heresies, so destitute of ad-

ministrative ability, so deaf to the people's real interests, so
blinded by sectional prejudice? Both Jefferson and Madison
were Southerners, with Southern interests and points of view.
For the New England industries—the carrying-trade, ship-
building, and fishing—they cared nothing.

"The people of the East cannot reconcile their habits, views,
and interests with those of the South and West," said Timothy
Pickering. "The latter are beginning to rule with a rod of
iron." All the important measures of the Republican administration they opposed as injurious to the interests of their
section—the annexation of Louisiana, the occupation of West
Florida, non-importation, the embargo, the refusal to rechar-
ter the bank, Macon Bill No. 2, the War of 1812. Many were
the meetings in which the Federalist leaders gave free rein to
their hatred of Jefferson and talked of the day when New
England would secede from the Union. Is our status not that
of a conquered people, they said? Does not the Virginia dynasty rule us as the master rules his slaves? Are not our oppressions worse than those we suffered from George III and
his Tory Ministers? There is no hope, save in the formation
of an independent confederation, composed of the mercantile
States.

Nor did they hesitate to take the position of Jefferson and
Madison in the Kentucky and Virginia resolutions. "I believe
the assent of each individual State to be necessary for the admission of a foreign country as an associate in the Union,"
declared Pickering, at the time of the Louisiana purchase, "in
like manner as in a commercial house the consent of each
member would be necessary to admit a new partner into the
company." In the days when Hamilton was leading them on
to one victory after another, they had been committed to the
doctrine of loose construction; but now they demanded adherence to the letter of the Constitution. "Whenever the national
Legislature is led to overleap the prescribed bounds of their
constitutional powers," declared Governor Turnbull, of Connecticut, "on the State Legislatures in great emergencies
devolves the arduous task—it is their right, it becomes their
duty—to interpose their protecting shield between the rights

and liberties of the people and the assumed power of the general government."

It was a singular trick of fate which made it possible for Madison's enemies to use his own words against him, and force him to defend the position which formerly he had assailed. In American history the State-rights doctrine has seldom been a sacred principle which men defend because they believe it legally correct, or best for the interests of the nation. It has been a utilitarian doctrine, accepted or rejected by the various sections as it served the purpose of the day. Virginia and Kentucky turned to it in 1798 to protect themselves against the acts of the Federalist majority in Congress; New England seized upon it in 1808 and 1812 as a weapon with which to oppose the Virginia dynasty; and later, when the South's interests were threatened by the increasing Northern population, her statesmen once more became ardent State-rights men.

On December 15, 1814, a small group of men met in the Council Chamber of the dignified old State-house, at Hartford. Their serious faces and the secrecy of their deliberations showed the momentous character of their business. In the president's chair sat George Cabot, his large figure, white locks, and calm, dignified features giving him a striking resemblance to George Washington; before him were Harrison Gray Otis, easy, polished, courtly, handsome; James Hillhouse, his large, bony frame and aquiline features not unlike an Indian; the short, bulbous John Treadwell; Benjamin Hazard, easily singled out by his swarthy complexion and long frizzled hair, and others equally distinguished. In all there were twenty-three men. It was the Hartford convention, called by Massachusetts, Connecticut, and Rhode Island to press the grievances of the East.

After three weeks of deliberation, the delegates drew up and published their report. "A sentiment prevails," they said, ". . . that the time for a change is at hand . . . events may prove that the causes of our calamities are deep and permanent . . . they may be traced to implacable combinations of individuals, or of States, to monopolize power and office, and to trample without remorse upon the rights and interests of commercial sections of the Union. Whenever it shall appear that these causes are radical and permanent, a separation, by equitable arrangement, will be preferable to an alliance by constraint, among nominal friends but real enemies, inflamed by mutual hatred and jealousy."

A list of proposed amendments to the Constitution followed, all tending to weaken the Federal Government and strengthen the States. Embargoes must be limited to sixty days; the concurrence of two-thirds of both Houses of Congress should be necessary for a declaration of war, for the passage of non-intercourse acts and the admission of new States; the President should be ineligible for a second term. If the demands of New England were ignored and the war persisted in, another convention was recommended "with such powers and instructions as the exigency of a crisis so momentous may require."

The extreme Federalists were disappointed. They had expected the convention to recommend the secession of New England and the formation of a northern confederation. All it had done was to use secession as a threat to enforce the demands of the East. But that threat was serious. The Massachusetts Legislature appointed a commission, consisting of Otis and two others, and early in February they set out to place their ultimatum before Madison.

A few days before their departure Pickering wrote to Lowell: "If the British succeed in their expedition against New Orleans—and if they have tolerable leaders I see no reason to doubt of their success—I consider the Union as severed. This consequence I deem inevitable." But Pickering did not reckon with the leadership of Andrew Jackson. When it became known that a British fleet of 50 sail, carrying perhaps 1,000 guns and 8,000 troops, was descending upon the city, this veteran of the Indian wars was called upon to take charge of the defense. The task seemed almost hopeless. To oppose an army of selected British troops, led by the brilliant Pakenham, Old Hickory at first had only 800 regulars and 1,000 volunteers. True, the Tennessee frontiersmen were approaching, men who had done service against the Cherokees and Creeks, and now rejoiced at the prospect of coming to close quarters with the redcoats. They came marching through the quaint old

streets of New Orleans, dressed in buckskin shirts, fringed leggings, and coonskin caps, and armed with hunting-knives and
long rifles.

Jackson rushed them down the river to the Villeré plantation, to attack a force of 1,600 British. Pakenham had brought
his army across Lake Bargue, and was advancing up a bayou
and across a swamp to the Mississippi. Jackson proposed to
destroy the advance-guard before the main body could arrive.
Old Hickory himself attacked in front, while General Coffee
with his Tennesseeans fell on the enemy's flank. It was a weird
fight, that foggy December night beside the quiet river, when
the bayonet of Britisher and Highlander clashed with the
backwoodsman's hunting-knife or the Creole's musket-butt.
Reinforcements came to Pakenham at the critical moment, and
the Americans fell back.

The next day Jackson selected a line of defense along a dry
canal connecting the swamp and the river, and put his troops
to work fortifying it. Pakenham waited for reinforcements
before advancing. When, at last, he reached Jackson's line,
he found it too strong to be carried without artillery. So he
ordered another halt, while the sailors, with great toil, brought
heavy guns from the fleet. As the mists cleared away on New
Year's morning, the British batteries opened fire, while the
infantry stood under arms, ready to advance. Every man in
the army was sure that the American guns would be silenced
and the wall of earth and cypress battered to pieces. To their
surprise they received an answering fire, which surpassed their
own in rapidity and precision and increased in intensity as the
moments passed. By noon all of the British batteries had been
put out of action, and most of the men killed or driven away.
"Never was any failure more remarkable or unlooked for,"
said one of the British officers.

Pakenham now decided to send a force across the river to
storm the poorly manned works on the right bank, in the hope
of flanking Jackson's main line and forcing him to retire. Several days were spent in extending the Villeré canal through
the levee, so that the boats could be brought into the Mississippi. By the evening of January 7 all was in readiness, and

Colonel Thornton with 1,200 men crossed over. Had Paken-ham made this his main attack, leaving only a holding force on the left bank, he might have swept on into New Orleans. But he subordinated it to a frontal assault on Jackson's posi-tion. At six on the morning of the 8th two long lines of red-coats, one along the levee and the other stretching out from the swamp, advanced in solid formation, with flags flying and bayonets glistening in the early sun.

Behind Jackson's rude intrenchments a weird array awaited them—Tennessee riflemen, in buckskin suits; a battalion of Creoles in brilliant uniforms; grouped around one gun a few grizzled old French soldiers, around another a squad of dra-goons; the Kentucky frontiersmen, the freebooters of Pierre Lafitte, a group of bluejackets, and a company of San Domingo negroes. Every man in this little army was confident of vic-tory.

As the British threw aside their knapsacks and came on cheering, a deadly fire greeted them, and the red lines staggered and fell back. This was to be no repetition of the Bladensburg affair. Pakenham himself reformed his men and led them on to a fresh attack. Again the riflemen took careful aim, again the British regiments wilted. The gallant Pakenham was killed and the trumpeters sounded the retreat. Stretched out on the sugar-fields before the American line lay 2,000 men, among them 3 generals, 7 colonels, and 75 other officers. The Amer-ican loss was 71.

Jackson's elation was turned to anxiety when the sound of firing warned him that the enemy were attacking the small American force on the right bank. Hastening to the levee he peered through the river fog to watch the struggle. He could see nothing of the combatants, but the flashes from the guns were easily discernible, and their continued progress up the river made it clear that the Americans were retreating. For a while he was sure that Thornton would press on to New Orleans, and force him to abandon the lines which Pakenham had tried to storm. But the British felt that their terrible losses rendered their position critical. General Lambert, who succeeded Pak-enham, relinquished the idea of capturing the city, at once recalled Thornton, and a few days later took his troops to the mouth of the bayou, where they re-embarked.

In the meanwhile, the three New England commissioners were proceeding to Washington with their ultimatum to the Federal Government. They momentarily expected to receive word that New Orleans had been captured and that England had refused to consent to peace save on humiliating terms. Staggering under two such blows, the Administration would be powerless to refuse their demands. They were greatly surprised, upon reaching Baltimore, to learn that the British had been defeated and that Louisiana was safe. "The miraculous success of our armies at New Orleans . . . will probably put the Administration on stilts," said Otis, "and augur no favorable issue to our mission." On the night of February 14, two days later, the commissioners, from their lodgings in Georgetown, noted that Madison's residence was illuminated as though in celebration. Going out to inquire the reason, they found that peace had been concluded, and that the United States had emerged from the war on honorable terms, with "not one inch ceded or lost." Their mission was now hopeless, and after venting themselves by referring to Madison as a "pigmy" and "a mean and contemptible little blackguard," they began their return journey to Massachusetts amid the jeers of the Republican press.

Along the route they found the people celebrating the return of peace. Amid the ringing of bells and the parading of military bands, patriotic speakers dwelt upon the deeds of the young nation. They had punished the insults of the British Empire, they had fought for two and a half years upon equal terms, they had forced their adversaries to an honorable peace. As for New England, Otis discovered that it had forgotten the Hartford convention amid preparations for sending out the idle merchantmen over the deserted trade-routes.

In August, 1814, American and British envoys met at Ghent to negotiate peace. The British began by making harsh demands. The United States must cede territory in Maine and New York, abandon the Great Lakes, form the Northwest into an Indian state, and give up the right to fish off Newfoundland. The American delegates—Clay, Gallatin, John Quincy Adams, Thomas Bayard, and Jonathan Russell—received these proposals with astonishment and began preparations to return home. Fortunately, the news of important American victories and the possibility that a new European war might grow out of the Congress of Vienna induced the English to become reasonable. Point by point they receded from their demands until they consented to a return to the status before the war. Impressments and seizures were passed over, and the questions of boundaries, fisheries, and the navigation of the Mississippi were left open for future adjustment. On December 24, 1814, fifteen days before the battle of New Orleans, the envoys signed the treaty.

England and the United States made peace because there was no longer any serious matter over which to fight. The American war was an outgrowth of the great European conflict. That conflict was now over; commerce was seeking its old channels; blockades, decrees, embargoes, and impressments were matters of the past. England was burdened with too great a debt to think of wasting men and money to secure an empty revenge; for the United States peace was necessary to prevent bankruptcy and disunion.

CHAPTER XIII

THE NEW ENGLAND REVOLUTION

IT was in 1789 that a handsome young Englishman stole out of his home at Derby disguised as a farm laborer, and set out for London. Here he secured passage to New York, and, on September 13, sailed down the Thames. He was not a culprit fleeing from justice, but a specialist in the intricate machinery used in the manufacture of cotton cloth. England guarded jealously the inventions of Arkwright and Hargreave, which were responsible for her supremacy in weaving and spinning, and had any one suspected that this youth had served for four years as superintendent of the great Milford factory his detention would have been certain. For this reason he took neither patterns nor drawings. It was Samuel Slater, forerunner of the American industrial revolution.

Slater was invited to Providence by the wealthy merchant Moses Brown, who promised him adequate backing and prophesied that by perfecting the first water-mill in America he would win lasting fame. The difficulties were many. Not only had Slater to rely upon his memory in making the delicate machinery but he had to fashion some of the tools with which he worked. At last all was in readiness, and the machines were set up in an old fulling-mill. The first yarn was produced late in 1790. A new era had begun in American industry.

Yet several decades were to pass before New England could turn with a whole heart to manufacturing. Labor was too dear, the competition of Great Britain too keen, the profits from commerce too great, for the factory system to attain immediate success. Although here and there mills were started not only for cotton and woollens but for paper, tinware, iron, flaxseed-oil, glass, rope, shoes, and guns, hand-manufacture in private homes still accounted for most of the industrial output.

The long winter evenings in the New England farmhouse

were not wasted. Around a small furnace set in the chimney-corner, which glowed with every puff of the bellows, were grouped the men and boys hammering out nails and tacks; the housewife made the spinning-wheel hum as she fed out the wool, cotton, or flax; the daughter worked at the old-fashioned loom. The skilled New England artisans—blacksmiths, carpenters, coopers, millers, tanners, wheelwrights, shoemakers—still went about their work, undisturbed at the impending competition of labor-saving machinery.

Yet the time was near when this competition was to become so keen that many were driven out of business. Skill and industry could no more save the New England workers in the face of the industrial revolution than they had saved the craftsmen of Britain.

The change came with the long interruption of foreign trade brought about by non-intercourse, the embargo, and the War of 1812. For nearly two centuries England had supplied the American market with manufactured articles—farm-implements, cloth, clothing, tableware, household utensils, paper, glass, pottery, tinware, powder, firearms, buttons, hats, wagons, carriages. This stream of goods was now largely cut off and the people had to supply their own needs or do without. Home production received a tremendous impetus. Even Jefferson, who looked upon agriculture as the only entirely wholesome occupation, became an advocate of domestic manufacture. He who now opposes it, he said, must be either in favor of reducing us to dependence on foreign nations or to clothing ourselves in skins.

The passage of the Non-Intercourse Act was the signal for a burst of enthusiasm for American industries. The United States would retaliate against England for her seizures and impressments, it was said, by depriving her permanently of the American market. In the cities people formed associations called Societies for the Encouragement of Domestic Manufactures, and pledged themselves to wear only American-made garments. At Baltimore there was a great industrial parade on the Fourth of July. Everywhere the press urged the people to discard imported finery and dress in domestic raiment. Tradesmen filled their shops with American wares. The State Legislatures declared it the duty of every citizen to give preference to American goods, while the politician who did not clothe himself from head to foot in domestic articles was courting defeat. Even Madison, at his inauguration as President, thought it wise to wear a suit made of American cloth.

The results were startling. Factories multiplied. The swift streams of New England were well suited to supply power. At the end of the first decade Connecticut alone could boast of 67 cotton-mills, 66 woollen-mills, 225 fulling-mills, 15 powder-mills, 24 paper-mills, 17 oil-mills, 5 glass-works, besides several factories for guns, buttons, spoons, combs, ploughs, tinware, hats, leather goods, iron, silk, and anchors. "The traveller's eye is charmed with the view of delightful villages," wrote one observer, "suddenly rising as it were by magic along the banks of some meandering rivulet; flourishing by the influence and fostered by the protecting arm of manufactures." In parts of Massachusetts and Rhode Island, all over New York and Pennsylvania factories were established for cotton and woollen cloth, knives and axes, carpets, glass, paper, type, shot, ironware, salt, thread, and a hundred other articles. The American industrial revolution, which was to effect so many changes in the life of the people, had begun.

Not the least of these changes was the breaking of the old commercial ties with England and the acquisition of a degree of economic independence. "The longer peace is delayed," wrote Jefferson in November, 1813, "the more firm will become the establishment of our manufactures. The growth and extent of these can be conceived by none who does not see them. Of coarse and middling fabrics we never again shall import. . . . This single advancement in economy, begun by our embargo law, continued by that for non-importation, and confirmed by the present total cessation of commercial intercourse, was worth alone all the war will cost us." As the Revolution brought political independence, so the trade restrictions of 1807–1815 brought partial economic independence.

Important also was the shifting of population from the country districts to the manufacturing towns. Many farmers, unable to withstand the competition of the West in agricultural products, and of the new factory itself in their household manufactures, abandoned their farms and began life anew as mill-hands. In like manner the skilled jack-tar, who had commanded high wages during the days of New England's commercial supremacy, now turned his back on the deserted wharves of Boston or Providence, to seek employment in the cotton or woollen factories. The North, especially New England, was diverting its labor and capital from trading and agriculture into manufacturing.

With commerce dead it was necessary to invest funds in manufactures, or permit them to lie idle. "The banks are at their wits' end to lend their capital," said John Lowell, "and money is a drug." So new factories continued to rise. "Wheels roll, spindles whirl, shuttles fly,". reported *The Connecticut Herald*. In the year 1814 alone Massachusetts chartered thirty companies for the manufacture of cottons, woollens, glass, files, wire, and other articles. The industries of America were now turning out goods to the value of fifteen or twenty million dollars.

But this rapid growth of manufactures was dependent upon the trade restrictions of the war period; when these restrictions were removed by the Treaty of Ghent, American industry received a temporary setback. In May and June, 1815, English merchantmen began to arrive. They came laden with manufactured goods—earthenware, muslins, taffetas, silks, linen, kerseys, soap, nails, watches, farm implements, stoves, grindstones. For years the British factories had been piling up a surplus of fabricated articles, and this they now dumped upon the American market. Single vessels were followed by great fleets. November 14 twenty square-rigged ships sailed up New York Bay together, while another flotilla of fifteen ships and eight brigs arrived five days later.

It was a new invasion of the United States, a conscious attempt to conquer the lost American market. "What matters it should we have to sell below cost," said Lord Brougham, in Parliament? "It will be worth it to stifle in the cradle the manufactures of the United States created by the war." So England sought not only to get rid of her surplus of goods, but to use that surplus as a weapon to prevent the Americans from freeing themselves from dependence upon British manufactures.

At first success seemed to attend these efforts. The American cotton and woollen industries tottered before the storm. Mills were forced to suspend operations, many companies went into bankruptcy, thousands were thrown out of employment. The new factory towns, so recently humming with activity and radiant with hope, now seemed lifeless. Unless something were done at once, the new industry would be ruined.

Petitions began to pour in on Congress begging for a protective tariff. They had entered upon the manufacture of cloth and other goods in response to a national appeal, the mill-owners said. They had laid out time and money that the people might have clothes in the time of hardship. Now that the emergency had passed, was it just that they should be left to face the competition of the long-established English industries? Moreover, was it wise to relinquish the hope of economic independence just as it was within the nation's grasp? Was it right to force into idleness the thousands employed in the mills?

But now serious opposition developed to a policy of protection. The commercial interests felt that it would interfere with trade, the farmers that it would increase the cost of living. When the matter came before Congress, Daniel Webster, then just rising to fame, spoke against it. "I feel no desire to push capital into extensive manufactures faster than the general progress of our wealth and population propels it," he said. "I am not in haste to see Sheffields and Birminghams in America. . . . I am not anxious to accelerate the approach of the period when the great mass of American labor shall not find its employment in the field; when the young men of the country shall be obliged to shut their eyes upon external nature, upon the heavens and the earth, and immerse themselves in close and unwholesome workshops; when they shall be obliged to shut their ears to the bleating of their own flocks upon their own hills, and to the voice of the lark that cheers them at the plough, that they may open them in dust and smoke and steam to the perpetual whirl of spools and spindles and the grating of rasps and saws."

Despite this appeal, so remarkable for its insight into the evils of the factory system, a protective tariff was passed. The tariff of 1816 marks the end of the old economic era, the beginning of a new. It proved inadequate to end the influx of cheap British goods, it is true; it did not set whirling instantly the spindles of New England. But it established the principle of protection for our industries in the face of destructive competition.

It must not be supposed that New England at once turned its back upon the old pursuits. For some years after the War of 1812 commerce continued to absorb the attention of a large part of the people. With the news of the conclusion of peace and the lifting of the blockade, every port from Maine to the Sound burst into activity. Ships were put into commission, sails mended, sides caulked, crews employed, and cargoes taken on. Soon they were starting out over the long-deserted ocean routes to England, France, the Baltic, and the West Indies.

Yet disappointment was in store. New England's commercial ascendancy was born of the urgent demand for neutral shipping during the Napoleonic wars, and the Napoleonic wars were now over. Everywhere the Yankee skippers were elbowed by the merchants of England and France, while many a port, where formerly they had been welcomed, now excluded them by the renewal of the old navigation laws. The American vessels began to come back almost empty. The seaboard took on once more an air of depression, ships were laid up, and shipbuilding languished. Many decades were to pass before American tonnage in foreign commerce was to approach the figures of 1806 and 1807.

This development definitely turned the tide in favor of manufactures. The change which had taken place is illustrated by the attitude of Daniel Webster toward the tariff bills. When in 1828, for the first time, he gave his support to protection, his opponents in the Senate taunted him with his change of front. How is it, they asked, that you now favor the tariff which so recently you denounced? Webster's answer was frank. Hitherto New England has held back from protection, he said, because she considered it wise for manufactures to make haste slowly. But now that so much capital has shifted into this growing industry, popular sentiment has shifted with it from free trade to protection. New England for two centuries has centred her activities upon commerce, but to-day she is primarily a manufacturing community.

No one at the time, not even the far-seeing Webster, grasped the full meaning of this change. Not only did the industrial revolution transform the economic life of New England, but it altered her relations with the rest of the country. Hitherto her interests had been so distinct as to make her in a sense an isolated community. At any moment the Southern and Middle States might force through legislation hostile to her commerce, fishing, or ship-building. It is this which made her so dissatisfied under the unsympathetic rule of the Virginia dynasty. But when she began to place her faith in manufactures, her isolation vanished. The Middle States, too, had been touched by the magic wand of the industrial revolution, and henceforth were at one with her in protecting industrial interests. The developments of this period tended to destroy the East as a distinct factor in American history and create the North. The Pennsylvania coal-miners and iron-founders reached over the Hudson to extend the hand of fellowship to the cotton and wool spinners of Hartford and Providence. When the Southern States, with their peculiar agricultural interests founded on slave labor, began to protest against fostering legislation for the industrial system, they found themselves confronted by a united North.

The industrial revolution, with its attendant change of occupation for thousands and the shifting of capital and population, was influential in precipitating a no less profound social and political revolution. The people were no longer content to submit to the theocratic and aristocratic groups who had so long ruled in Massachusetts and Connecticut. The champions of the old order were fully conscious of the impending change. There were many conferences upon the evils of the time, many denunciations of Jefferson and his new democracy, many lamentations for the good old days when New England never questioned the moral and political leadership of the "best and most enlightened."

We may imagine them assembled around one of the great New England fireplaces, their faces betraying their gloomy thoughts. The huge man in the plain black suit, with the thin, silvery hair, aquiline nose, fierce eyes, firm mouth, and prominent chin is Timothy Pickering. Beside him sits Fisher Ames, his figure erect, his hair long and curly, his features pleasing and regular, his manner cordial and easy. Here is George Cabot, dressed in black, with knee-breeches and silk stockings, his hair drawn back and tied in a queue, his large frame and firm mouth indicating force and power. With them might be seen Theodore Dwight, George Griswold, and Oliver Wolcott.

"The nation has fallen upon evil days," says Ames. "The Jacobite principles of Jefferson are sweeping the country, and New England, the last stronghold of good government, is now threatened. Here we have a happy combination of the most enlightened—the clergy, propertied men, and men of education, which hitherto has saved us from the excesses of democracy. Constitutions are but paper; the state of society is the real factor in preserving liberty, and society in New England is superior to that of other parts of the country."

"Yes," says George Cabot, "but if the old order in New England is destroyed by demagogues and knaves, if power is intrusted to the mob, there will be bad government here also. While among the body of our people there is more wisdom than elsewhere, we too are full of errors which no reasoning could eradicate, even though there were a Lycurgus in every village. We are democratic altogether."

"Which but emphasizes the necessity for the formation of a northern confederacy," chimes in Pickering. "The democratic contagion which has swept over the rest of the country cannot be repelled from New England so long as the Union continues. We differ from the States to the South, not only in pursuits and interests but in morals, manners, and government. A separation would unite congenial characters, promote public happiness, and make it possible for us to preserve the state of society handed down by our ancestors."

"I fear separation will not effect a remedy," replies Cabot, "for the evil exists within ourselves. Even now the rabble in Connecticut, led by the base Abraham Bishop, are seeking to overthrow the unwritten constitution, under which the State has so long prospered, to make way for a pure democracy. They wish to destroy the influence of the clergy, give every base fellow the right to vote, sever the tie between church and state, do away with the religious test for office-holders, and abolish church tithes. It will come, of that I am sure. We are destined in this country, as in all free states, to sacrifice the essence of liberty to the spirit of democracy, and democracy places power in the hands of evil and designing men."

The old structure of society which these men defended so vigorously was extremely illiberal. A survival of the colonial period, changed somewhat to meet the needs of independence, it was still theocratic and aristocratic. The Revolution, although it brought separation from England, had failed to bring real liberty. None could vote save those who owned land, rented a house, or paid taxes, while the restrictions upon the holding of public offices were even more narrow. No atheist, Jew, freethinker, nor man of meagre income could be Governor of Massachusetts; no Roman Catholic could be Governor of Connecticut. In Massachusetts one must have a freehold of £300 or personal property valued at £600, to be eligible for election to the Upper House of the Legislature, while New Hampshire required a freehold of £200. And everywhere the force of tradition, the reverence for the clergy, the fear of the rich, tended to uphold the old order. The voter who turned from the Federalist leaders to hearken to the seductive voice of Jefferson was likely to incur the denunciations of the ministers and the enmity of his rich neighbors. "We have lived in a State which exhibits to the world a democratic exterior," said the reformers, "but which actually practises all the arts of an organized aristocracy, under the management of the old firm of Moses and Aaron."

The storm centre of the struggle was Connecticut. In other States the frontier, with its democratizing tendencies, had already done much to break the power of the aristocracy. But Connecticut had no frontier. There the ruling classes were intrenched behind a barrier of statutes, patronage, election devices and customs. The Republicans, led by Abraham Bishop, attacked this antiquated structure. Before a great gathering at Hartford, May 11, 1804, Bishop startled the Federalists by declaring the old charter of Charles II, from which the government still derived its authority, null and void. "When independence was declared," he said, "the people should have been permitted to draw up a new constitution. But the General Assembly usurped their rights, retained the charter as the fundamental law, and perpetuated the old restrictions and inequalities." "Twelve men make the Council," he pointed out, "seven make a majority. These seven have a veto on legislation and control the Lower House by corrupting the members. Is this an instrument of government fit for freemen? Let us sweep it away for a constitution based on the will of the people, in which every honest man has the franchise."

Everywhere the Republicans denounced the influence of the clergy in politics. What are they but a pack of privileged reactionaries, they asked, strutting around in queues, shoe-buckles, and cocked hats? We are tired of these aristocratic ministers with their long faces, prating about government by the wisest and best. By the wisest and best they mean themselves and those who aid in upholding their privileges.

The conservatives resisted bitterly. Would you carry desolation through the fabric erected by our fathers? they asked. Would you place the government in the hands of fanatical atheists, bent on ruining the church? The issue lies between religion and infidelity, morality and debauchery, legal government and disorganization. This man Bishop is a fool and a Jacobin, a disciple of Jefferson—Jefferson, the "man of sin," the enemy of the church, the "infidel and liar."

Despite the desperate resistance of the Federalists, the reformers carried the day. In the election of 1817 the Republicans placed Oliver Wolcott, Jr., in the Governor's seat, and secured a majority in the Lower House. The next year a new constitution was adopted, guaranteeing religious freedom, shearing the Council of much of its power, extending the suffrage, separating church and state, making all Christians equal before the law, abolishing tithes and the religious test for office. The last remnant of the old Bible commonwealth, the structure erected by the Puritan fathers, had crumbled before the new democracy. The day after the ratification of the constitution, Lyman Beecher found his father sitting on a rush-bottomed kitchen chair, his head drooping on his breast, his arms hanging limply down. "Father, what are you thinking of?" he asked. "I am thinking of the Church of God," was the solemn answer.

The New England revolution was attended by far-reaching changes in the character of the population, as well as in government and industry. During the first decades of the century thousands of emigrants left the East to seek homes in the Ohio region, while in ensuing years their places were filled by newcomers from Ireland, Canada, and other foreign countries. Thus, soon after the franchise was extended to the lower classes, their ranks were filled up with foreigners, in large part Irish and Roman Catholic. It was the last development in the New England revolution.

Had one stationed himself at any point along the highways leading out of New England in the years immediately following the War of 1812, he would have witnessed a ceaseless movement toward the West.

If we stop this Connecticut farmer who, with his wife and children, is heading for the Western reserve, to ask him why he has deserted the old homestead, we receive a simple reply: "For years I toiled upon my worn-out land. With what result? We lived in dire poverty, and my farm was eaten up in mortgages. In the West land is cheap, it requires little care, it gives a rich return. So when the agent offered to trade a large tract in Ohio for our thirty acres in Litchfield, we did not think it wise to refuse."

Next we turn to a young man on horseback, whom we judge to be a lawyer. "What is your reason for seeking a home in the West?" we ask. "I go because the West is the land of opportunity," he answers. "I am a Republican and a Methodist; at Hartford, whence I came, none gain advancement save Federalists and Congregationalists. I go where there are no Tories, no tithe-gatherers, where ministers preach but do not govern, where no honest man is excluded from voting or holding office."

So the exodus continued. New England was flooded with guides, gazetteers, and books of travel, painting the attractions of the new Eden. Why toil in poverty on the rocky hills of New England, why accept small wages in the cotton-mills, why submit to political and religious discrimination, why pay heavy taxes, when the West beckons on? "Come to us," said the Cincinnati *Liberty Bell*, "come, you poor job-hunting, street-walking Yankee mechanics, and you will find a land of plenty."

The prosperity of New England was threatened. Parts of Massachusetts and Connecticut began to show signs of decay —deserted farmhouses, the shutters off the hinges, the roofs beaten in, the yards overgrown with bushes; tumble-down schoolhouses; ruined churches. In the town of Winchester alone sixty bare chimneys could be counted along one lonely bit of road. In 1820 East Haddam, Stonington, Cornwall, Sharon, Derby, and other towns were no more populous than in 1810; Ellington, Somers, Franklin, Lyme, Norfolk, Roxbury had fewer people than in 1800; Wallingford, Waterbury, Woodbridge, Windham, New Fairfield, and Bolton had made little progress since 1790.

At first this emigration was looked upon as a wholesome movement. President Dwight, of Yale, rejoiced that New England was getting rid of thousands of shiftless families. But sentiment soon underwent a change. Reflection led all to realize that the old States could ill afford to lose so many workers, and press and pulpit began to vie in condemning the "Western madness." Men were advised not to give up the civil, literary, and social influences of New England for a log cabin in the wilderness. Better "tarry at Jericho," they said, than go off after the pot of gold at the end of the rainbow. You will soon be sighing for the old homestead and for old friends in the East.

The feeling of alarm became more intense a few years later when foreigners began to come in to take the places of those who went West. New Englanders prided themselves on the purity of their stock, and were inclined to turn the cold shoulder to newcomers from Europe. The great German migration of the eighteenth century had avoided this section, while the Scotch-Irish Calvinists, who imagined that they would be welcome in Massachusetts and Connecticut, usually found it best to move on to other colonies. "Foreigners rarely reside with us long enough to become inhabitants," wrote David Field.

But New England now had to give up its racial homogeneity in order to preserve its industrial life. As thousands of poor farmers left for the West, as the population dwindled and labor became scarce, a jealous eye was cast upon those States to which the foreign workers were coming. If Connecticut and Massachusetts continued to repel European settlers, it was pointed out, they would be outdistanced in population, wealth, and political influence.

So early as 1815 the foreigners began to straggle in—British mechanics, seeking higher wages; Canadians, tempted by the cheap land of Maine and New Hampshire; industrious Irish, fleeing from high rents and excessive taxes in the old country. For some years, however, the numbers were small. The census of 1830 showed 9,620 foreign-born in all Massachusetts. At that date New England was still essentially Anglo-Saxon in blood. Then the tide set in in earnest. In 1840 the foreign-born of Massachusetts had increased to 34,818, in 1850 to 164,448, in 1860 to 260,114, in 1870 to 357,319. In 1880 the whole number of foreign born in all New England was 793,122, with some 400,000 more born of foreign parentage.

At any time during the fourth or fifth decade one might have seen these foreigners arriving at the Boston piers. Their condition was often pathetic—whole families penniless, ragged, shivering in the cold; lone children, bewildered and frightened; poor sufferers, dying with malignant typhus; ragged mechanics, clutching with one hand a box of tools, with the other a bundle of clothing. They had endured many hardships on board ship, from foul air, crowding, unwholesome food, and sickness. The newcomers, despite their condition, were hardy, patient, hard-working folk, who needed only an opportunity to rise. Victims of poverty and oppression in the Old World, they soon proved their worth.

Some went to work upon canals, roads, and railways; some secured employment as bricklayers and carpenters; some became farm laborers, some domestic servants; some secured jobs in the shops and mills. In a few years many had purchased old run-down farms, which they made bloom. One Irish machine-worker, after three weeks on a small tract, purchased and paid for a cow. "How long would you have had to labor in Ireland to spare enough for a cow?" his employer asked him. "My wife and I have just been calculating that," he replied, "and find that it would have taken exactly one year and ten weeks." Before long foreigners were doing most of the physical work in southern and eastern New England, whether in mill, shop, or farm, and had become the "bone and sinew" of the land.

Thus was the political, religious, and industrial transformation of New England followed by a change no less profound in the character of the people. The strangers who poured into every city and town had no tie with the New England of former days. They knew nothing of the ideals of John Cotton and John Winthrop, abhorred the old theocracy, and cared little for the traditions of Anglo-Saxon constitutional government. Yet, enjoying the extended franchise, and voting at the command of skilful organizers, they became a power in political matters.

To-day one who travels along a typical New England highway will find evidences of two distinct civilizations. Here he enters a charming village, its quaint houses, its rock fences, the church with its white spire, the distinctive accent of the people, all suggestive of the conservative, theocratic, Anglo-Saxon New England, the New England of Cotton Mather, Fisher Ames, and Timothy Pickering. Two miles down the road he finds a factory town on the banks of some rapid stream, the houses small, the people chiefly foreigners. It is the modern New England, the product of the great revolution which a century ago transformed the region.

Often the most profound revolutions are bloodless. The New England revolution was unaccompanied by the stupendous shock of the French Revolution, with its political overturns, excesses, suffering, and great wars. Yet it is doubtful whether the changes wrought in France from 1789 to 1815 were more far-reaching than those in New England in the early decades of the nineteenth century.

Some have said that Thomas Jefferson destroyed the old New England, and it is true that Jefferson led the attack upon the theocracy and the aristocracy. But the real causes of the movement must be sought in the fundamental developments of the time—in the opening of the West, the necessity for economic independence, the termination of the European wars, the spread of liberal ideas, the growth of nationalism. The old New England fell into the crucible of revolutionary times and came out transformed in industry, government, religion, and blood.

CHAPTER XIV

RISE OF THE NEW WEST

LESS than half a century after James Robertson's frontiersmen had settled in the valley of the Watauga, the new West had risen to a position of importance. Kentucky, the dark and bloody ground, where formerly even the Indian dared not cast his wigwam, now boasted half a million people; in the hills and plains of Tennessee were 350,000 settlers; Ohio, so recently a wilderness, had a population of 400,000; Indiana had been admitted as a State, while thousands of home-seekers were pushing on to the regions beyond, up the Wabash, the Kaskaskia, the Mississippi, the Missouri, and the Arkansas. The West—the West which Jefferson dreamed of and Elbridge Gerry dreaded—had suddenly sprung into being, vigorous, democratic, vibrating with life.

Migration had come, not in a steady stream, but in successive waves. In the years from 1783 to 1789, when unemployment was wide-spread, thousands had turned toward the fertile West. But during the Napoleonic wars, when the demand for American shipping and American products was insistent, when profits were large and wages high, migration slackened. It swelled again with the embargo, the War of 1812, and the economic distress following the Treaty of Ghent. In the decade from 1807 to 1817 multitudes sold their homes in the East or South, bundled up their effects, and made their way over the mountains to the Ohio valley.

One would often see a sturdy New England farmer, his boots worn, his clothes covered with dust, trudging wearily along the execrable roads, beside the covered wagon which carried his wife and child and their meagre belongings—hoes, spades, clothes, a gun, a mattress, pots, skillets, pans, blankets, perhaps a bed and a chair or two. Next would come a mechanic on his way to Indiana, dragging his children and goods in a hand-cart; then a Rhode Island blacksmith, pushing a wheelbarrow, the mother with an infant in her arms walking behind. So the endless procession passed on.

The South furnished its full share of emigrants. The tobacco-fields of the Rappahannock and the James, worn out by centuries of wasteful cultivation, no longer yielded a good return, and many young planters, descended perhaps from the proudest Virginia families, left to seek their fortunes in the West. "How many sad spectacles do our lowlands present of wasted and deserted fields, of dwellings abandoned by their proprietors, of churches in ruins!" complained the Virginia Legislature. "The fathers of the land are gone where another outlet to the ocean turns their thoughts from the place of their nativity, and their affections from the haunts of their youth."

The Far South, too, felt the lure of the West, and thousands from South Carolina and Georgia set out for the basins of the Tombigbee and the Alabama. The well-to-do settlers took their slaves and travelled in bands, with pack-horses and cattle and wagons. At night their camp-fires lit up the forests of Tallapoosa or glistened in the Chattahoochee.

Not all the settlers came from the older States. Europe, too, sent her thousands to mingle with the stream which was pouring over the mountains. The Napoleonic wars had left Great Britain exhausted and burdened with debt. New machinery was crowding many out of employment, wages were low, the price of bread high, discontent rife. Many, both in England and Ireland, sought relief by crossing the Atlantic and settling in the West. Industrious and sober, they were well qualified for the task of transforming the wilderness into thriving cities and farms.

If we join the main stream of migration, through Pennsylvania to Pittsburg and down the Ohio, there opens before us a panorama of wild beauty. Packing our belongings in a one-horse wagon, we pass up the streets of Philadelphia, between rows of neat houses with broad porches and projecting roofs, out upon the Lancaster Pike. We find ourselves now in a beautiful country dotted with the neat farms and villages of the German settlers. Our road goes over gentle hills, past woodland and pasture, and fields of red clover and Indian corn;

through forests, with here and there a stone inn; over the Susquehanna; up mountain slopes; through wooded valleys; past crude wooden taverns, where the hosts are rude and the food bad. Then the road emerges from the wood and we look down upon Pittsburg, with its cluster of solidly built brick houses, its mills, its warehouses, the shipping moving up and down the two rivers. We raise a shout of joy, for Pittsburg is the gateway to the West, and the first part of our journey is over.

Entering the town, we take lodgings at the City Hotel at the corner of Liberty and Market Streets, and prepare for our voyage down the Ohio. We engage passage upon a flatboat, and bring our baggage on board. Our vessel is a crude affair, with square hulk, the bottom tightly caulked, the top covered with thin boards, on each side a long oar moving on pivots, at the stern another for steering. Flatboats, we are informed, carry most of the traffic down the Ohio and the Mississippi, but they never attempt the return journey, and are broken up at their place of destination.

The next day we begin our voyage down the river. As we float out upon the Ohio we pass between wooded heights on the left, and gentle, rolling hills on the right. Soon we pass the mouth of the Beaver, where the river twists between precipitous cliffs, or eddies around projecting rocks, until we reach the clustered houses of Wheeling. On we go, past Marietta, past Blennerhassett's Island, past Maysville, standing out boldly in a framework of green hills, on between woods of sycamore, ash, locust, poplar, walnut, and beech, with here and there a log cabin, until at last we reach Cincinnati.

Here we tie up and bring our belongings ashore. Cincinnati we find a town of 10,000 people, with 6 churches, court-house, jail, school, theatre, steam-mill, foundry, four banks, and many brick stores and residences. On the streets we meet tall Virginians, with wide hats and long, loose-fitting coats, New Englanders from Vermont or Nantucket, ragged negroes, barefooted women, Englishmen, Irish, Germans, Canadians. At the wharves steamers, barges, flatboats, and keel-boats are taking on or discharging their cargoes, amid the shouting and yo-hoing of the river-men.

Illinois is our final destination; so we secure horses, blankets, guns, and hatchets for our journey through Indiana. We feel self-conscious in our new clothes—broad-brimmed hat, long trousers, moccasins, shot-pouch, and powder-horn slung from belt, rifle at back, tomahawk in the holster, saddle-bag stuffed with food and an extra shirt or two. Waving good-by to Cincinnati, we start off through southern Ohio.

Indiana we find one vast forest, intersected by two or three open roads and a few trails. There are no towns, and the loneliness of our journey is broken only by an occasional farmhouse or log tavern. Often we spend the night in the open. Then, rolled in our blankets, feet to the fire, hugging our rifles, listening to the wind in the leaves, or starting at the howling of wolves and panthers, we experience a strange dread of the solitary wilderness.

At last we reach our destination, mark out a claim on the Little Wabash, cast our tent and begin our cabin. We bring down oaks, poplars, and sycamores. The straightest trunks we cut into lengths of fifteen and eighteen feet, hew smooth on two sides, notch at the ends, and fit together for walls. Next we affix rafters, raise the frame of the roof, lay down crude board shingles, and fasten them in place with horizontal beams. Our floor we make of boards slit from logs, pinned to round logs with wooden pegs. The door, for there is but one, we construct in an upper and a lower section. Our chimney is of thick timbers covered with clay, while a flat piece of sandstone serves for a hearth. It is a crude structure, but it gives shelter and protection until we can erect a better one.

The furnishings also are primitive. Upon a shelf, made by laying clapboards on wooden pins, we store cooking-utensils, pewter dishes, plates, spoons, water-bucket, powder and ball, food-supplies, seeds, medicines. For a chair we have a three-legged stool. A pair of blankets stretched on the floor serves as the bed, two blocks of wood with a board laid between as the table.

We find that we are not without neighbors, though distances are great and the roads bad. On one side is a veteran hunter, who is as much at home in the forests as the Indians. In dressed buckskin, with homespun hunting-shirt outside, long knife and tomahawk in his belt, moccasins on his feet, a blanket on his saddle, he hunts deer, bear, and elk. Although his life is full of hardship and his home consists of a one-room log hut, he considers himself the happiest of beings. On the other side is a farmer, who came to Illinois three years ago and is now well established, his home built and his fields cleared. He plants crops of tobacco and corn, shears his sheep, tans his hides, all with no help save that of his sons. His lot is not bad. He owns his farm, his table is profusely furnished, and in a few years he will be well-to-do.

But the backwoodsman earns prosperity only by unceasing toil. Labor cannot be had, and he must grapple alone with the difficulties of wilderness life. He must clear the forests, plant crops, care for his stock, build barns and fences, carry his goods to market on pack-horses over forest trails or on crude rafts down creeks and rivers. At times he rests to wipe his brow and sigh for the old life, for relatives and friends, for church, schools, and libraries. And none can depict his agony as he urges his horse through the woods in search of the doctor, while wife or son, struck down by the fever or wounded by wild beast, hovers between life and death.

After all, the brunt of this wild life rests not on the men, but on their wives. We find many a gentle woman working like a beast of burden in her wilderness home. She cares for the children, prepares the food, does the washing, churns the butter, tends the garden plot, dips candles, sews, spins, and perhaps works in the fields. When this home-building is accomplished, we say to ourselves, many women will be prematurely broken or laid in their graves.

Democracy, we soon learn, is the most striking characteristic of this Western country. The judge leaves the court-room, shakes hands with the backwoodsmen gathered in front of the court-house, and retires to his log home. The next day we find him at the plough, or harvesting his crop. The colonel of the militia is a tavern-keeper, the magistrate a small trader. The boatman, the hunter, the storekeeper, the farmer, all stand upon an equal footing, and the newcomer who treats even the roughest individual as an inferior is apt to provoke a volley of oaths. But in the West one looks in vain for the effeminate or feeble man; all alike are manly, vigorous, brave.

We observe that the only note of pessimism touches the matter of transportation. Here we have every natural resource for the building of a prosperous country, the settlers say—timber, coal and iron, fertile lands. But the great Appalachian barrier cuts between us and the East, making communication difficult and diverting traffic down the Mississippi. The cost of shipping the grain and hides of Ohio or the tobacco and hemp of Kentucky by wagon through woods and over mountains is prohibitory. So our faces are turned, not toward the East, but toward the Gulf of Mexico, and this can but lead to disunion.

While the settlers were shaking their heads over this problem, thoughtful men everywhere were turning to the solution suggested by Washington. Let us forestall disunion, they said, by constructing a great artificial waterway between East and West. As for the route, there was divergence of opinion. The Marylanders and Virginians still hoped for a canal to unite the Potomac and the Monongahela, but New Yorkers insisted that the Mohawk valley was a more feasible route.

Nature has here made a pathway through the ranges which elsewhere extend unbroken for hundreds of miles, they said; we need only extend her handiwork to link the waters of the Hudson and the Great Lakes. The only high ground can easily be cut through, intervening rivers can be crossed on aqueducts, there is water in abundance. When all is completed we shall have access, not only to the Great Lakes region, but to the Ohio basin as well.

In 1810 the New York Legislature appointed a commission to explore the route, but no immediate results followed. Then came the war of 1812, and plans for internal improvement for the time were dropped. With the return of peace DeWitt Clinton drew up a memorial on the canal, so brilliant and convincing that it carried conviction to the people and fired them with a determination to push through the great project.

On April 15, 1817, the Legislature passed an act authorizing the construction of the canal. In the Council of Revision,

Acting-Governor Taylor and Chief Justice Thompson were opposed to the scheme, Judges Yates and Platt favored it, while Chancellor Kent was undecided. In the midst of one of the debates Vice-President Tompkins entered the room, and began arguing for a rejection of the bill. "The late peace with Great Britain was a mere truce," he said, "and we shall undoubtedly soon have a renewed war with that country; and, instead of wasting the credit and resources of the State in this chimerical project, we ought to employ all our revenue and credit in preparing for war."

"Do you think so, sir?" asked Kent.

"Yes, sir, England will never forgive us for our victories, and, my word for it, we shall have another war with her within two years."

"If we must have war," replied the Chancellor, rising from his seat, "I am in favor of the canal, and I vote for the bill."

Now began the digging. Thousands of men were put to work with plough and scraper, and the great ditch began its slow progress westward. It went past the Little Falls of the Cohoes, up the Mohawk, through Oneida, past the ancient haunts of the Onondagas, through the quicksands of Cayuga, over the Genesee River, through the rocks of Lockport, on to the Tonawanda, to Buffalo and to Lake Erie. For miles it went through forests so dense that the surveyors could hardly distinguish their stakes in the gloom. But the giant oaks and sycamores soon came down, the stumps were hauled away, and the canal moved steadily on.

At last, in 1825, eight years after Judge Richardson had lifted the first spadeful of dirt at Rome, the great work was completed and all New York celebrated. On the morning of October 26 four boats entered the canal at the village of Buffalo, amid the booming of cannon, the waving of flags, the cheering of the crowds. In the lead was the *Seneca Chief*, drawn by four gray horses, carrying Governor Clinton, the Lieutenant-Governor, distinguished guests, delegations from New York City, and commissions from towns along the route. One boat carried a cask of water from Lake Erie, another, dubbed *Noah's Ark*, was filled with wild animals of the West. The procession was greeted everywhere by salutes of artillery, fireworks, triumphal arches, bands, processions, banquets, and toasts.

At the aqueduct over the Genesee a boat called the *Young Lion of the West* was stationed to protect the entrance. As the flotilla approached some one on board called out: "Who comes there?" "Your brothers from the West, on the waters of the Great Lakes," replied the *Seneca Chief*. "By what means have they been diverted so far from their natural course?" "By the channel of the grand Erie Canal." "By whose authority, and by whom, was a work of such magnitude accomplished?" "By the authority and by the enterprise of the patriotic people of the State of New York."

At New York City a fleet met the barges and escorted them out past Sandy Hook. Here, amid the cheers of the onlookers, Governor Clinton emptied the keg of water from Erie into the ocean, as a symbol of the union of the Great Lakes and the Atlantic. That afternoon the city celebrated. A long procession moved up Broadway and Broome Street to the Bowery, thence down Pearl Street to the Battery. In the lead were trumpeters on horseback, a band, and the grand marshal with his aids; then came foresters with axes, followed by representatives of all the various trades—tailors, butchers, weavers, hatters, tanners, potters, shipwrights, carpenters. Next came the fire department, with its hand-engines, then the lawyers and doctors, and, behind all, the State officials and members of the Legislature. That night the City Hotel, the Coffee House, Pearl's Museum, the Park Theatre, and other buildings were illuminated, while the City Hall was ablaze with fireworks.

Well might they rejoice. The canal was a brilliant success. The products of the West began to pour through, every town along the route bloomed, the water-power was utilized for manufactures, land values in the western part of the State tripled, New York City became the metropolis of the continent. DeWitt Clinton's prophecy had come true. "That city will, in the course of time, become the granary of the world," he had said, "the emporium of commerce, the seat of manufactures, the focus of great moneyed operations . . . and before the revolution of a century the whole island of Manhattan, covered with habitations and replenished with a dense population, will constitute one vast city."

Three years after the opening of the Erie Canal an event occurred at Baltimore which may be regarded as the beginning of a new system of transportation—the laying of the cornerstone of the Baltimore and Ohio Railroad. Early in the morning of July 4, 1828, crowds assembled in Baltimore Street, thronging the pavements and grand stands and peeping down from every window. At eight o'clock a procession started from Bond Street and moved westward to a field near Gwynn's Falls. In the lead were the first Baltimore Hussars, next the pioneers, with implements of labor, then the Masonic fraternity, next several carriages with persons of distinction, then the order of the Cincinnati, a few gray-haired veterans of the Revolution, a band of music, followed by the various trades— farmers on floats, sowing wheat or harvesting; bakers in white; victuallers in white roundabouts, vest, and pantaloons, with a blue ribbon across the breast; tailors in dark coats, white pantaloons, and white gloves; blacksmiths with white aprons, ornamented with the anvil; carpenters, preceded by a car carrying a miniature temple; after them masons, bricklayers, painters, farmers, curriers, cordwainers, hatters, coopers, saddlers, printers, watchmakers, glass-cutters, rope-makers, seamen. At ten o'clock the procession reached Gwynn's Falls and lined up before a pavilion upon a small elevation. Here Charles Carroll, of Carrollton, sole surviving signer of the Declaration of Independence, erect and alert despite his ninety-one years, stepped forth and aided in the laying of the foundation-stone.

The people of Baltimore expected much from this enterprise. New York was securing the lion's share of the Western trade, and their city was being overshadowed. They grasped at the hope held out by this highway of iron, over which some day puffing engines might draw trainloads of wheat, corn, iron, and lumber. "We are commencing a new era in our history," said John B. Morris, one of the directors, "for there are none present who even doubt the great and beneficial influence which the intended road will have in promoting the agriculture, manufactures, and inland commerce of our country. It is but a few years since the introduction of steamboats effected powerful changes, and made neighbors of those who before were far distant from each other. Of a similar and equally important effect will be the Baltimore and Ohio Railroad. While the one will have stemmed the torrent of the Mississippi, the other will have surmounted and reduced the heights of the Alleghany."

Yet many years were to pass before the railroad crossed the mountains. The first section extended from Baltimore to Ellicott's Mills, a distance of only thirteen miles. The roadbed was crude, the rails primitive. Upon cedar ties were laid pieces of yellow pine, six inches square and from twelve to twenty-four feet long. These beams, their outer edges bevelled and covered with strips of flat iron, served as rails. At first it was a matter of doubt whether steam-engines or horses should be used. A year elapsed after the laying of the first rail before Peter Cooper brought from New York a little boiler, and set it up, with a steam-engine, on a four-wheeled car. This contrivance, not much larger than the ordinary hand-car, after repeated alterations, succeeded in covering the distance to Ellicott's Mills in sixty-one minutes. But the *Tom Thumb*, as Cooper's locomotive was called, fell into ridicule when it was defeated in a race with a horse. Engine and horse on parallel tracks, each drew a single coach, one filled with persons hostile to steam locomotion, the other with its ardent advocates. The latter were thrown into gloom at the start as the big gray horse sprang away to a good lead, but they cheered loudly when the clattering mechanism got up steam and overhauled the wagon. Victory seemed sure. But a belt slipped, the locomotive lost its momentum, and the horse came in far ahead.

Though it was soon recognized that steam could be utilized on railroads, and many lines were put into operation, the hopes of Carroll and Morris were slow of fulfilment. Before the lines could reach out over great distances it was necessary for them to pass through a period of experimentation. Proper roadbeds, tracks, motive power, financial organization came only with experience. At first the grades were so heavy, the curves so sharp, the locomotives so lacking in power that it was difficult to make headway when the rails were wet.

The early railways radiated from the cities back into the country and were designed to supply local needs. Trunk lines evolved later by the linking up of many little independent companies. In 1842 one could go from Albany to Buffalo by rail, but only by making use of seven different roads—the Mohawk and Hudson, Utica and Schenectady, Syracuse and Utica, Auburn and Syracuse, Auburn and Rochester, Tonawanda, and Attica and Buffalo. At every terminal-point passengers changed cars and usually had to spend the night. Gradually these little roads consolidated, and the era of trunk lines began.

In 1853 the Baltimore and Ohio was carried to Wheeling, and the first train passed through the gorges of the upper Potomac and the Cheat, where seventy years before Washington had searched for a route for his projected canal. Three years later the B. & O. constructed a line to Parkersburg, where it connected with the Marietta and Cincinnati, which in turn linked up with the Cincinnati and St. Louis. Thus was established an all-rail route from the Chesapeake to the Mississippi. This new union of East and West was celebrated by running a through train from Baltimore to St. Louis, bearing a notable group of officials, editors, Governors, Cabinet members, Congressmen, and other distinguished guests. Along the route the train was greeted with fireworks, banquets, speeches, and processions.

In this way the Appalachian barrier was finally overcome. A few years later a half-dozen lines were bringing to the East the agricultural products of the Mississippi basin, and carrying back the manufactures of New England, New York, and Pennsylvania. When finally disunion came, the line of cleavage was not, as so many had feared, between East and West, but between the slaveholding South and the free North.

The rise of the new West was a movement of surpassing importance. In 1770 the region was inhabited only by Indians and wild beasts; three-quarters of a century later it boasted of a population of over 7,000,000. A vigorous, buoyant, self-assured society it was, still crude, but full of confidence in the future. Men who had seen the wilderness transformed into smiling farms, villages of log huts into cities, streams which formerly knew only the Indian's canoe into important highways of commerce—all within one generation—could set no limit to the ultimate accomplishment of the new West.

The democratic Westerner had little sympathy with the social and political structure of the older States. Thousands of poor men, men of the type of Thomas Lincoln, the father of Abraham Lincoln, had migrated north of the Ohio to escape the competition of slave labor; they brought with them an abiding hostility to the society founded on slavery. The settlers who fled from the reactionary New England governments, hated the waning theocracies of Massachusetts and Connecticut. The people of Ohio and Michigan revered the name of Winthrop, but in practice repudiated his ideals; they regarded Hamilton as a hero and a martyr, but abhorred his principles of government by the "wisest and best."

At first the West felt itself to be a unit in contrast to the East, there being no distinct line of demarcation between the southern and northern region. Although slavery was prohibited north of the Ohio River, thousands of Southerners who settled in Indiana, Illinois, and Ohio brought slaves with them. But with the new tide of settlement from New York and New England by way of the Mohawk and the Great Lakes, which occupied the prairie lands of the Northwest, sectionalism began to take more definite form. The development was accentuated by the contrasting economic systems on either side of the Ohio, and as the struggle over slavery began to wax warm, Western solidarity gave way. The Northwest eventually linked itself in sympathy with the Northeast against the South. In 1850 there were but two sections of the Union—North and South.

CHAPTER XV

THE DIVIDING LINE

THE close of the second decade of the century found Thomas Jefferson at peace with the world. With the principles of democracy to which he had devoted the best efforts of his life sweeping over the country, with his henchmen in control of the government, with the remnants of the Federalist party discredited and ignored, he was content to pass his remaining days at his beloved Monticello. His time was spent in poring over the pages of Cicero, or answering his voluminous correspondence, or receiving his guests with kindly hospitality. Seldom did he read the newspapers.

From these dreams of peace he was aroused by the news that the country had divided itself into two hostile camps over the question of admitting Missouri as a free or slave State. When the bill for statehood had come before the House of Representatives, James Tallmadge, Jr., of New York, offered an amendment prohibiting the further introduction of slaves to Missouri, and providing for gradual emancipation. This had brought on a stormy debate, in which there had been much bitterness, recrimination, and predictions of disunion.

"The banks, bankrupt law, manufactures, Spanish treaty are nothing," wrote Jefferson. "These are occurrences which, like waves in a storm, will pass under the ship. But the Missouri question is a breaker on which we lose God only knows what. I had for a long time ceased to pay attention to public affairs, content to be a passenger in our bark to the shore from which I am not far distant. But this momentous issue, like a fire-bell in the night, awakened and filled me with terror. I considered it at once as the knell of the Union. It is hushed, indeed, for the moment, but this is a reprieve only, not a final sentence. A geographical line, coinciding with diverging political and moral principles, once held up to the angry passions of men will never be obliterated. No man can condemn slavery more fervently than I, but I see no practical means of emancipation. We have the wolf by the ears, and we can neither hold him nor safely let him go. It is my only consolation that I will not live to see the country rent asunder, and this glorious experiment in self-government made futile."

Missouri had been settled chiefly by Southerners who brought slaves, so that the institution was now firmly intrenched in the Territory. Unless Congress made emancipation a condition precedent for admission, Missouri would come in as a slave State. This would push slave territory into the Northwest, add to the political power of the slaveholding section, and threaten Northern preponderance. The people of the North were determined that this should not happen. "I feel much concern for the issue," wrote Rufus King, "which, if decided against us, settles forever the dominion of the Union. Not only the Presidency, but the Supreme Judiciary, at least a majority of its members, will forever hereafter come from the slave region. . . . The slave legion will parcel out the great offices, will determine all questions respecting the general and common welfare, and, in a word, will rule us as they have done in contempt of our rights."

In opening the attack, the Northern Congressmen based their case almost entirely upon the well-known evils of slavery. February 16, 1819, Tallmadge rose in the Hall of Representatives in the temporary brick Capitol, at the corner of First and A Streets, to defend his amendment. "Look down the long vista of futurity," he said. "See your empire, in extent unequalled, in advantageous situation without a parallel, and occupying all the valuable part of our continent. Behold this extended empire, inhabited by the hardy sons of American freemen, knowing their rights, and inheriting the will to protect them—owners of the soil on which they live, and interested in the institutions which they labor to defend. . . . But, sir, reverse this scene; people this fair domain with the slaves of your planters; extend slavery—this bane of man, this abomination of heaven—over your extended empire, and you prepare its dissolution; you turn its accumulated wealth into positive weakness. . . . If the western country cannot be settled without slaves, gladly would I prevent its settlement till time shall be no more."

"Yes," said John W. Taylor, of New York, "history will record the decision of this day as exerting its influence for centuries to come over the population of half our continent. If we reject the amendment and suffer this evil, now easily eradicated, to strike its roots so deep in the soil that it can never be removed, shall we not furnish some apology for doubting our sincerity, when we deplore its existence? . . . Those whom we shall authorize to set in motion the machine of free government beyond the Mississippi, will, in many respects, decide the destiny of millions. . . . Contemplate the States hereafter to unfurl their banners over this fair portion of America, the successive generations of freemen who there shall adorn the arts, enlarge the circle of science, and improve the condition of our species. Our votes this day will determine whether the high destinies of this region, and of these generations, shall be fulfilled, or whether we shall defeat them by permitting slavery, with all its baleful consequences, to inherit the land."

The Southern members were angered at the attacks upon slavery as an institution, and intensely alarmed at the attempt to prevent its expansion into the Far West. The industrial revolution, which was transforming and unifying the North, together with the enormous development of cotton-planting attendant upon the invention of the cotton-gin, had conspired to divide the country into two great sections with contrasting economic systems. Since both were under the authority of one government, which section should control that government became a question of surpassing interest. The Southern States had entered the Union with the expectation that westward migration, then directing itself south of the Ohio, would give them the preponderance, but the recent growth of Ohio, Indiana, and Illinois disappointed these hopes. Rufus King had failed to grasp the meaning of this change, but it dawned upon the South when the Missouri question placed them in the position which New England had occupied during the administrations of Jefferson and Madison, the position of a section with peculiar economic interests which it had not the political power to defend. So when the North tried to weaken the South still further, by blocking its expansion into new territory, the Southern representatives resisted violently.

"On our side of the House, we are contending not for victory, but for our political existence," declared Benjamin Hardin, of Kentucky. "We have already surrendered to the non-slaveholding States all that region of the American empire between the great rivers Ohio and Mississippi; and if you tear from us that immense country west of the Mississippi, we may as well surrender at discretion, crouch at the feet of our adversaries, and beg mercy of our proud and haughty victors. . . . I fear, I greatly fear, Mr. Chairman, that gentlemen are fighting under false colors—that they have not yet hoisted their true flag. As the contest is upon the great theatre of the world, in the presence of all the civilized nations of the earth, and as it is to be viewed by an impartial posterity, would it not be more magnanimous to haul down the colors on which are engraved humanity, morality, and religion, and in lieu thereof unfurl the genuine banner, on which is written a contest for political consequence and mastery? . . . The calculation is this, that the North, having a majority of non-slaveholding States, will give law to this nation.

"I beg the gentlemen who are in favor of this restriction not to push matters to extremities; for although they may have a majority on this floor, we will never submit at discretion. I call upon them to recollect the old proverb, 'Beware of the desperation of a peaceable man.' No, Mr. Chairman, sooner than be delivered over, not to our brethren, either in politics or affection, but a Federal party in the North, bound hand and foot, and to have no voice, no lot, no part in this Union, we will burst all ties and bonds that unite us together and stand erect in our own majesty."

In the main, however, the Southerners defended themselves with the State-rights doctrine, taking once more the ground of the Virginia and Kentucky resolutions. It did not matter that for the past two decades they had played truant to their former theories, that in practice even Jefferson and Madison had proved themselves to be centralists; they pleaded now that

Congress could not force the people of Missouri to free their slaves because Congress had not the constitutional authority. From the moment Tallmadge introduced his amendment until the State conventions of 1860 and 1861 took the South out of the Union, State rights was the shield which the Southerners interposed to the assaults of the Northern majority.

"The question is not whether slavery is, in itself, an evil," said Philip P. Barbour, of Virginia, "but whether, supposing it to be such, we have the power to correct it, in relation to Missouri. . . . If we impose this condition, we should commit a palpable violation of that provision of the Constitution which makes it our duty to guarantee to every State in the Union a republican form of government. . . . We, whose sworn duty it is to guarantee to the people of Missouri a government formed by themselves, are now about to declare that in one important particular their constitution shall not be such as they desire. . . . If we are at liberty to impose what conditions we please upon the new States, our government would present this monstrous anomaly, that the original States had provided a permanent Constitution, as it respected themselves, but as it respects new States had in effect given to Congress the power of making a constitution for them."

"Yes," added James Pindall, of Virginia, "and the treaty of April 30, 1803, by which France ceded Louisiana to the United States, imposes an express obligation on this government to admit the inhabitants of the ceded country as soon as possible to the enjoyment of all the rights, advantages, and immunities of citizens of this country. Our government knew when this treaty was made that the people of the territory held slaves; how is it, sir, that it now attempts to deprive them of that kind of property? How can they deny them the right to create for themselves their own State constitution?"

"And is it just to the States of the Union where slavery is tolerated to prohibit them from a settlement in Missouri, purchased by the common funds of the nation," asked Christopher Rankin, of Mississippi? "If I cannot enter there with my property, which habit, or something else, has rendered necessary to me, I am excluded."

"But let us listen a moment to the other side," replied Timothy Fuller, of Massachusetts. "If slaveholders cannot remove with their slaves, in case the restriction is adopted, so also, if it is not adopted, the industrious citizens of the non-slaveholding States are proscribed, in a great degree, from the benefits of emigration. Where a system of slavery throws all the wealth and all the political influence into the hands of a few, and where labor is disgraceful, as the proper occupation of slaves alone, the independent spirit which is found among citizens in moderate circumstances in the non-slaveholding States will never brook the inevitable consequences of emigration. Freemen, proud of their rights, proud even of their industry, as the basis of their independent condition, will never consent to be ranked by the opulent slaveholder, living by their side, on a level with slaves."

"What is it which excites such fervent sympathy for Missouri?" asked William Darlington, of Pennsylvania. "What is the mighty bugbear which so alarms gentlemen? Is it proposed to bind her hand and foot and deliver her over to the dominion of despotism? Sir, a man of plain comprehension might well be astonished if he were to learn, for the first time, that the simple proposition before you is to enable Missouri to become an independent republican State and to rescue her from the dreadful curse of slavery! We propose to do that for her which we have already done for the States northwest of the Ohio, and for which the citizens of these States will be forever grateful. . . . When we know that the welfare of our descendants in Missouri, as well as the United States generally, requires the restriction of slavery, how can we reconcile it to our sense of duty to permit the unnecessary introduction and diffusion of an evil which we are sure will be the scourge of countless generations."

In the meanwhile the country seethed with excitement. At Boston a great mass-meeting in the State-house affirmed the power of Congress to make abolition a condition precedent to the admission of new States, and urged the Northern delegates to hold firm. Gatherings in New York, Philadelphia, Trenton, Baltimore, and other Eastern cities took similar action. Soon the Speaker's desk in the House of Representatives was piled high with petitions from all parts of the North praying that Missouri be freed of slavery, while each day the crowds which thronged the brick Capitol followed the debates with breathless interest.

On February 17, 1819, came the first test of strength. When the vote was taken in the House of Representatives, it was found that the bill, together with the abolition clause, had passed 87 to 76. An ominous moment it was, for only one Southerner voted for exclusion and only ten Northerners against it. The great struggle between North and South had begun, a struggle which was to continue for forty years in the nation's legislative halls, create unspeakable bitterness, and end in civil war. March 2, the Senate returned the bill to the House with the Tallmadge amendment struck out. The House refused to concur and the session ended in deadlock.

When Congress reassembled in December, 1819, Maine was applying for admission to Statehood, and the Southerners made their consent contingent upon the defeat of the Tallmadge amendment. The Northern delegates were angered at this move, but it was defended by Henry Clay. "A State in the quarter of the country from which I come asks to be admitted to the Union," he said, stepping down from the Speaker's stand. "What say the gentlemen who ask the admission of Maine? Why, they will not admit Missouri without a condition which strips her of an essential attribute of sovereignty. What, then, do I say to them? That justice is due all parts of the Union; your State shall be admitted free of condition, but if you refuse to admit Missouri also free of condition we see no reason why you should take to yourselves privileges which you deny her, and until you grant them also to her we will not admit you."

On January 21, 1820, William Pinkney, of Maryland, rose in the Senate Hall of the restored Capitol, to present the Southern side of the Missouri question. In the balcony men leaned over the balustrade or stood on tiptoe to see the speaker, while the floor was filled with foreign guests or handsomely attired women. Pinkney was considered the ablest speaker in Congress, and his address had been widely heralded. It has been said that Congress "is not bound to admit a new State into this Union," he said. "Be it so for argument's sake. Does it follow that when you consent to admit into this Union a new State you can make it less in sovereign power than the original parties to that Union; . . . does it follow that you can force upon it an additional compact not found in the compact of the Union; that you can make it come into the Union less as a State, in regard to sovereign power, than its fellows in that Union; that you can cripple its legislative competency by what you choose to call a condition?"

Pinkney continued to speak with great effectiveness for hours, much to the delight of the Southerners. "Of the immense power of the orator and his finished delivery no listener could entertain a doubt," wrote John A. Dix. Even John Quincy Adams, who heard the conclusion of the address, thought "the language good, his fluency without interruption or hesitation, his manner impressive." But, he added, his argument was weak, "from the inherent weakness of his cause." Adams was deeply concerned that there were no free-State men able to cope with Pinkney, Barbour, Clay, and Randolph, save perhaps the veteran debater Rufus King. "Oh, if but one man could arise," he wrote in his *Memoirs*, "with a genius capable of comprehending, a heart capable of supporting, and an utterance capable of communicating those eternal truths that belong to that question, to lay bare in all its nakedness that outrage upon the goodness of God, human slavery, now is the time, and this is the occasion, upon which such a man would perform the duties of an angel upon earth."

Some weeks later King rose in the Senate and threw consternation into the Southern ranks by basing the cause of the free States, not on the Constitution but on the laws of nature. "And now, Mr. President, I approach a very delicate subject," he said, in his calm, dignified, but fervid manner. "I have yet to learn that one man can make a slave of another; if one man cannot do so, no number of individuals can have any right to do it, and I hold that all laws and compacts imposing any such condition upon any human being are absolutely void, because contrary to the law of nature, which is the law of God."

The deadlock continued until Jesse B. Thomas, of Illinois, offered an amendment, providing for the admission of Missouri without restrictions, but forever excluding slavery from the Louisiana territory north and west of that State. This compromise had been suggested in substance by Hardin. "It strikes me, Mr. Chairman," he had said, "that this matter can be settled with great facility, if each party be so disposed. . . . Cannot it be done by permitting Missouri to go into the Union without the restriction, and then draw a line from the western boundary of the proposed State of Missouri, due west to the Pacific? North of the line prohibit slavery, and south admit it. . . . Can either party be so vain as to expect a victory? Behold! and see how this nation is divided: eleven States against eleven; a small majority in this House in favor of the amendment, a small one in the Senate against it, and the Cabinet, perhaps, not unanimous."

The dread of disunion and the obvious advantages of excluding slavery from the vast territory north and west of the Missouri now won over a small group of Northern Representatives. "On this question, which for six weeks has agitated and convulsed the House, I have voted with the majority," said Charles Kinsey, of New Jersey. "But I am convinced should we persist to reject the olive branch now offered, the most disastrous consequences will follow. These convictions are confirmed by that acerbity of expression arising from the most irritated feelings, wrought upon by what our Southern brethren conceive the unkind, unjust, determined perseverance of the majority, and to those I now beg leave to address myself. Do our Southern brethren demand an equal division of this wide-spread fertile region, this common property purchased with the common funds of the nation? No! They have agreed to fix an irrevocable boundary beyond which slavery shall never pass; thereby surrendering to the claims of humanity and the non-slaveholding States, to the enterprising capitalists of the North, the Middle, and the Eastern States, nine-tenths of the country in question."

John Randolph so fully agreed with this statement of the case, that he derided the folly of his fellow Southerners in supporting the compromise. Against Henry Clay he was especially bitter, and in an address on Washington's Birthday attacked the Speaker with the biting invective of which he was master. Clay could but writhe. He changed color, pretended to read the newspapers, fumbled with the papers on the desk, took a pinch of snuff, beckoned the attendants, looked down at his shoe-buckles, glanced up in the gallery, called Thomas W. Cobb to take his place in the Speaker's chair, and paced back and forth in the lobby.

But Randolph's pleadings were in vain. The House gave up restriction by a vote of 90 to 87, Missouri came in as a slave State, and slavery was forbidden in all the rest of the Louisiana territory north of 36° 30′. The first great clash between North and South had ended in compromise.

But the aged Jefferson was quite right in saying that this settlement was no more than a truce. The excitement subsided, the voice of recrimination was stilled, there were frequent references in Congress to the days when North and South fought side by side in the cause of liberty, men turned with relief to the affairs of daily life and tried to forget the bitterness of the recent clash; yet the disease which was eating at the heart of the nation, the disease of which the Missouri trouble was but a symptom, since it had not been cured, was destined to break out again more violent than ever. "I take it for granted," said John Quincy Adams, "that the present question is a mere preamble—a title-page to a great, tragic volume."

CHAPTER XVI

PASSING OF THE VIRGINIA DYNASTY

WASHINGTON was astir early on the morning of March 4, 1817, to see the inauguration of James Monroe as President of the United States. At eleven o'clock a troop of mounted citizens formed in front of Mr. Monroe's residence on Pennsylvania Avenue, and escorted him to the temporary brick Capitol at the corner of First and A Streets. He took the oath of office in the Senate Chamber and then stepped out on an elevated portico. There, in the sunshine of the Southern spring, surrounded by Cabinet officers, judges, Senators, foreign diplomats, and handsomely gowned women, he delivered his inaugural address. The people saw a tall, well-formed man, his manner engaging but awkward, with serious face, frank blue eyes, large mouth, well-shaped nose, and broad forehead. He dressed always like the older generation, and we may imagine him in black broadcloth, knickerbockers, silk stockings, and shoes with silver buckles.

He spoke of harmony, prosperity, good-will, and peace. "Discord does not belong to our system," he said. "Union is recommended, as well by the free and benign principles of our government, extending its blessings to every individual, as by the other eminent advantages attending it. The American people have encountered together great dangers and sustained severe trials with success. They constitute one great family, with a common interest. . . . To promote this harmony . . . will be the object of my constant and zealous exertions." Little did he realize that even as he spoke forces were at work to divide the country into two hostile camps, arouse bitterness, and end in civil war. To him the future seemed as serene as the blue sky above.

The address concluded, the booming of cannon at the navy-yard and at Fort Warburton announced that the nation had a new President. Mr. Monroe then made his way through the throng while a body of marines, the Georgetown riflemen, two companies of infantry from Alexandria, and a company of artillery stood at attention. That afternoon he held a reception, while in the evening a throng of ladies, officers, foreign diplomats, strangers, and citizens danced and chatted beneath the flickering lights of the ballroom in the Davis Hotel.

One of the first concerns of the administration was the acquisition of Florida. This peninsula, the fabled land of the fountain of youth, where Spaniards and French had fought before Captain Newport landed at Jamestown, was almost indispensable to the United States. It commanded the entrance to the Gulf of Mexico, was a source of irritation in the hands of Spain, and constituted a threat in time of war.

John Quincy Adams, Secretary of State, so early as 1817 opened negotiations for the cession of the province. He had every hope of success until news reached Washington that Andrew Jackson had invaded Florida, in pursuit of marauding bands of Seminoles, had seized St. Marks and Pensacola and hanged two British subjects, Arbuthnot and Ambrister, who had been active in aiding the Indians. The Spanish Minister, Don Luis de Onis, was highly incensed and came to Adams's office to protest. A strange contrast they presented, these two men who had opened a new chapter in the long diplomatic struggle between the ancient monarchy of Spain and the young republic of the West. One the stern, cold, rugged, honest Puritan; the other proud, cunning, calculating, able, courteous, but cold and overbearing. "Surely this unprovoked attack upon Spain has not been authorized by your government," said de Onis; "surely you will disavow the action of your general. I have just received instructions authorizing me to cede Florida to the United States, but I fear this incident will force me to take a different course."

"You must remember that we have been acting only in self-defense," Adams replied. "Spain has permitted Florida to be used as a refuge for our runaway slaves, and a base of operations both for the Seminoles and the pirates of the Amelia Island. If you cannot protect us, we must protect ourselves. General Jackson's actions, even the taking of Pensacola, have been defensive, and do not constitute an aggression against Spain."

Months of discouraging negotiations followed. Adams sturdily upheld the rights of the United States; de Onis countered with the arts of the veteran diplomat. Adams was embarrassed by a group in Congress who talked of seizing Florida by force, de Onis by the stupidity and pride of the Spanish Government. "You can have no conception of the obstinacy and imbecility of the King's Council," he confided to Adams. "The Ministers themselves are sure of nothing. One day the Council will agree on a certain policy, and the next, by the manœuvres of some grandee, it will be reversed. These men, who know nothing of the matter, are always harping upon the honor, dignity, and glory of Spain, and think they are still in the time of Charles V."

More important than Florida itself was the fixing of the boundary line between the United States and Mexico. Many Americans believed that the Louisiana purchase gave us the great territory between the Sabine and Rio Grande Rivers, but this the Spaniards denied. "If you insist upon having Texas," de Onis told Adams, "the Spanish Court will never consent to the treaty." Monroe proposed that the boundary should follow the Trinity from its mouth to its source, then run north to the Red, which it should follow to its source, thence due west to the Rio Grande. Even this compromise was rejected, and in the end Adams agreed to the Sabine as the dividing line, and the United States renounced its claim to territory as large as England and France combined.

Henry Clay, who had his eye upon the Presidency and saw in Adams a dangerous rival, sought to discredit the Secretary of State by attacking the Florida treaty. "A miserably poor exchange this," he said, in the House of Representatives. "The climate of Texas is delicious; its soil is fertile; it is watered with stately rivers; it has one of the finest harbors on the Gulf of Mexico. Other countries are separated from their colonies by vast seas. Our colonies form a part of our continent. Shall we surrender such a province in exchange for the Florida peninsula? Texas is four times as large as Florida. It is true that we need Florida, but in the course of time it must certainly come to us. The ripened fruit will not more surely fall. As for the vast reaches of Texas, it is a matter of surpassing importance to determine what race shall people them. In our hands they will become the habitat of freemen, with our language, laws, and liberties; in the hands of others, they may become the land of despotism and slaves."

But Clay pleaded in vain. To many our claim to Texas seemed shadowy, while the advantages obtained by the treaty were many and real. The Senate ratified unanimously; the King of Spain, after many delays, signed; Florida became part of the United States, and our claims to Texas were renounced. John Quincy Adams complacently congratulated himself upon the completion of his work. "The change in the relations with Spain, from the highest mutual exasperation and imminent war to a fair prospect of tranquillity and of secure peace," he jotted down in his *Memoirs*, "completed the auspicious character of this transaction, which fills my heart with gratitude. . . . The acquisition of the Floridas has long been an object of earnest desire to this country. The acknowledgment of a definite line of boundary to the South Sea forms a great epoch in our history." But years afterward, when the United States annexed Texas at the cost of a war with Mexico, there were many who thought that in this matter Henry Clay had been more far-seeing than Adams and Monroe.

On November 7, 1823, four men met in one of the stately rooms of the restored White House. At the head of the table, a number of manuscripts before him, sat President Monroe, the seriousness of his face betraying the importance of the matter to be discussed. Beside him was John Quincy Adams, attired as usual in full dress—short small-clothes, silk stockings, and shoes fastened with buckles. His face, round and full, seemed cold, even crabbed, and his small black eyes wandered from one face to another as though divining the thoughts of his colleagues. Frequently he wiped away a tear, for his incessant reading had brought on an affection of the eye. In strong contrast to the stern Puritan was the buoyant Secretary of War, John C. Calhoun. Tall, well-proportioned, handsome, frank, courteous, his complexion dark, his eyes black, he was typical of the South.

Samuel L. Southard, Secretary of the Navy, was the only other Cabinet officer at this historic meeting, for William H. Crawford was ill and William Wirt in Baltimore.

"Gentlemen," Monroe began, "you are aware of the proposals of Mr. Canning, the British Secretary of State, to our Minister in England, Mr. Richard Rush. The people of the United States have from the first shown deep sympathy with the Latin-American states in their efforts to throw off the yoke of Spain and establish the principles of freedom for which we contended in our own Revolution. This sympathy has led us to recognize the independence of Buenos Ayres, Colombia, Chile, Brazil, Mexico, and Guatemala. We learn now with great concern that the Holy Alliance is planning to send armies to America to aid Spain and Portugal. This reactionary body, formed to restore the despotic system which existed in Europe prior to the French Revolution, has undertaken to stamp out liberty in Europe. The troops of Louis XVIII have recently crushed the liberal government of Spain, while Austrian bayonets have restored to his throne in Naples the tyrant Ferdinand. The Holy Alliance denies the sovereignty of the people, abhors representative government, and has declared war on the freedom of the press. In short, gentlemen, it is the enemy of all that we hold sacred. We cannot, without grave danger to our institutions, sit idly by, while it extends its system to the American continent."

"Quite true," said Adams, "and so it is important that we consider carefully our answer to Mr. Canning's proposal. In several notes and conversations he has informed Mr. Rush that Great Britain believes that without aid Spain cannot recover her colonies, that she would consider objectionable any interference with the Latin-American states by foreign powers, and herself disclaims any intention of molesting them. Mr. Canning is anxious for the United States to unite with England in this policy, believing us deeply concerned in the matter. 'If these opinions and feelings are, as I firmly believe them to be, common to your government with ours,' he writes, 'why should we hesitate mutually to confide them to each other, and declare them in the face of the world?' I would have you note, gentlemen, that this joint statement would pledge the United States not to acquire any part of the Spanish-American possessions."

"I should favor giving Mr. Rush a discretionary power to join in a declaration against interference by the Holy Alliance, even though it should pledge us not to take Cuba or Texas," said Calhoun, "because the power of Great Britain to seize them being greater than ours, we should get the advantage in obtaining the same guarantee that we give."

"The cases are not parallel," rejoined Adams. "We have no intention of seizing either Cuba or Texas, but it is possible that those provinces may some day solicit a union with us. They will certainly do no such thing with Great Britain. By joining with England, therefore, we give an inconvenient pledge and obtain nothing in return."

"You are right," said Monroe. "It would be undignified for us to take a position subordinate to that of Great Britain. It would be better to send a special envoy to Europe to protest directly to the Holy Alliance against interference in America."

"I have recently received from the Russian Minister, Baron Tuyl," said Adams, "a communication which affords a very convenient opportunity to take our stand without accepting the British offer. It will be more candid and dignified to avow our principles to Russia and France than to come in as a cockboat in the wake of the British man-of-war."

This met with general approval and Monroe at once authorized Adams to make his answer to the Tzar a vehicle for announcing American principles of government and America's attitude toward foreign intervention in the New World. Thus did this Cabinet meeting of four men reach the decision that the United States must reject the British offer and stand on its own feet in dealing with the reactionary powers of Europe. It was the birth of the Monroe Doctrine.

Several days later the President received a letter on this subject from the venerable Jefferson. "America, North and South, has a set of interests distinct from those of Europe, and peculiarly her own," he wrote. "She should therefore have a system of her own, separate and apart from that of

Europe. While the last is laboring to become the domicile of despotism, our endeavor should surely be to make our hemisphere that of freedom. One nation, most of all, could disturb us in this pursuit; she now offers to lead, aid, and accompany us in it. By acceding to her proposition, . . . we bring her mighty weight into the scale of free government, and emancipate a continent at one stroke."

President Monroe was deeply impressed and began to waver in his decision to reject Canning's offer. He was further influenced by Calhoun, who was now convinced that, if we failed to join hands with Great Britain, the Holy Alliance would restore Mexico to Spain. But Adams was steadfast for an independent declaration. "I no more believe that the Holy Allies will restore the Spanish dominion upon the American continent than that Chimborazo will sink beneath the ocean," he said rather testily.

In the meanwhile, the Secretary of State had completed his note in answer to Tzar Alexander. This visionary monarch had written the United States Government, exulting in the suppression of republican revolutions in Europe, extolling the Holy Alliance, and preaching to us concerning the superiority of the monarchical system. Adams felt that he had bearded us to our faces, and was determined to repay him in his own coin. He read his answer at a Cabinet meeting on November 25. "From all the combinations of European politics," it said, "the United States have studiously kept themselves aloof. They have not sought, by the propagation of their principles, to disturb the peace, or to intermeddle with the policy of any part of Europe. They believe, however, that for government to be lawful it must be founded upon the consent of those who are governed, and that each nation should be the sole judge of the government best suited to itself. The first of these principles is the principle of liberty, the second the principle of national independence. They are both principles of peace and goodwill to men."

"Why, that is a hornet of a note," said William Wirt. "It will surely offend the Emperor."

"He cannot object to it," replied Adams. "Since the Holy

Alliance have thought proper to edify and insult us with their principles, it is due in candor to them and in justice to ourselves to return them the compliment."

"You remind me of a man I know in Virginia," said Wirt, "who declared it his principle that if a man gave him a fillip on the nose, he would knock him down with a brick-bat."

There was more debating over the wording of the note, but in the end President Monroe decided to omit the strongest sentences. Adams was deeply disappointed. Yet the reply which he finally delivered to Baron Tuyl was far from spineless, for it contained, in addition to a declaration of American principles, an intimation that the American continents were henceforth not to be subject to colonization by European powers.

It had now been definitely determined both that the United States should act independently of Great Britain, and that the President, in his annual message to Congress, should announce that we should not tolerate interference in South America by the Holy Alliance. Wirt asked if we were prepared to sustain this declaration by force. "To menace without intending to strike is consistent neither with honor nor with the dignity of the country," he said. "It is possible that Mr. Canning's proposals are a trap to lead us into public declarations against the Holy Alliance, after which Great Britain will leave us to breast the storm alone."

"It is probable that by taking our stand now we will deter the Holy Alliance from forcible interposition in America," said Calhoun, "but if not, we must sustain the ground we now take, even to the extent of war."

To this there was general assent. The President now read to the Cabinet his message to Congress, and, after some discussion, modified parts to meet objections by Adams. All agreed that it should state the position of the United States upon three great issues: that there should be no further appropriation of American soil by European powers; that this country had no intention of interfering in European affairs; that it would regard with displeasure efforts by the Holy Alliance to interfere with independent American nations.

There was intense interest in the House of Representatives

when the clerk rose to read President Monroe's message of December 2, 1823. After touching on minor affairs, it announced in the most emphatic manner the Government's disapproval of foreign interference in American affairs. "The American continents," it said, "by the free and independent condition which they have assumed and maintain, are henceforth not to be considered subjects for future colonization by any European powers. . . . In the wars of the European powers in matters relating to themselves we have never taken any part, nor does it comport with our policy so to do. It is only when our rights are invaded or seriously menaced that we resent injuries or make preparations for our defense. With the movements of this hemisphere we are of necessity more immediately concerned. . . . We owe it to candor and to the amicable relations between the United States and those [the allied] powers to declare that we should consider any attempt on their part to extend their system to any portion of this hemisphere as dangerous to our peace and safety. With the existing colonies or dependencies of any European power we have not interfered and shall not interfere. But with the governments who have declared their independence and maintained it, and whose independence we have, on great consideration and on just principles, acknowledged, we could not view any interposition for the purpose of oppressing them, or controlling in any other manner their destiny, by any European power in any other light than as the manifestation of an unfriendly disposition toward the United States."

This message was received with enthusiasm throughout the United States. Some felt that Monroe was rash in bearding the Holy Alliance, but they were silenced in the chorus of approval. England too was extravagant in praise of Monroe's firm stand. "It is worthy of the occasion and of the people destined to occupy so large a space in the future history of the world," said the London *Morning Chronicle*. "What a contrast between the manly plainness of this state paper and the Machiavellism and hypocrisy of the declaration of the manifestos of the governments of this part of the world." "By one short passage in it is set to rest, we dare presume, whatever may have been in agitation by the Continental allies in reference to the late Spanish possessions in America," said the Liverpool *Advertiser*. "There will be no attempt made, it may be confidently affirmed, to interfere with the present condition of those countries when it is known that such interference would be viewed by the United States as a just cause for war."

As for the Holy Alliance, Von Gentz, the Austrian statesman, fairly expressed their general dismay. "The separation of America from Europe has been completed irrevocably," he exclaimed. As for Prince Metternich, the arch reactionary of Europe, he declared in disgust that the message only confirmed his opinion that great calamities would be brought upon Europe by the establishment of those vast republics in the New World. Canning, though annoyed that the United States had acted independently of England, felt his position strengthened. "I have called a new world into existence," he boasted, "to redress the balance of the old."

The Monroe Doctrine has proved a tremendous factor in the life and development of America. In its main objects it was entirely successful. Russian encroachments upon the northwestern coast of North America came to an end, and eventually Russia withdrew from the continent. The other European powers were forced to abandon hope of building up colonial empires on this side of the Atlantic, for the United States stood always as an insuperable barrier. What might have happened had there been no Monroe Doctrine is shown by the French conquest of Mexico in 1861 when our country was rendered helpless by the Civil War. Monroe and Adams and those who collaborated with them in setting forth the doctrine of the two hemispheres, unquestionably changed the history of the New World and saved America for the Americans.

From the pleasant contemplation of their diplomatic victories in the Florida Treaty and the Monroe Doctrine, which seemed to give them so just a claim to the continued support of the people, the Democratic-Republicans were aroused to the fact that their party was upon the point of disintegration. They had been lulled into a sense of security by the rapid de-

cay of the Federalist party. The principles of Jefferson were everywhere triumphant. In sections of New England groups of irreconcilables still put up candidates and pleaded for government by the "wisest and best," but the mass of the people had become democratic. In 1820 Monroe would have received every electoral vote, had not one member from New Hampshire cast his ballot for John Quincy Adams merely to save for Washington the sole honor of a unanimous election.

But the very completeness of the triumph of the Republicans proved their undoing. Just as ceaseless contact with wood is essential to the proper development of the woodpecker's bill, so is opposition the life of a political party. Although Monroe's administrations have been called the era of good feeling, it was obvious that under the outward calm a fierce political storm was brewing. The conflicting sectional and economic interests, gathered under the wings of the Democratic-Republican party, so soon as they realized that protection from their old Federalist enemies was no longer needed, began to fight among themselves. Jefferson's organization had completed its work; it was time for it to make way for new parties and fresh issues. When the public cast about for a successor to Monroe, five or six leaders came forward, all Democratic-Republicans, all having large followings.

The old party machine, which for decades had named the party candidates, early settled upon William H. Crawford as the only legitimate candidate, but the people refused to submit to its dictation. At seven o'clock on the evening of February 14, 1824, the hall of the House of Representatives was illuminated, while a crowd of over a thousand persons thronged the galleries. There was a buzz of expectation and every now and then a loud thumping upon the floor, as though the spectators were anxious for the show to begin. It was the caucus of Senators and Representatives, called to name the Democratic-Republican candidate. In this way Jefferson had been nominated in 1804, in this way both Madison and Monroe had twice been voted the choice of the party. But now there were present but sixty-six members—ten Senators and fifty-six Representatives. They were henchmen of William H. Crawford, almost all of them, and it was obvious that the others had stayed away because they had no intention of abiding by the result.

From the galleries there now came loud cries of "Adjourn, adjourn." Then a lone voice called out: "Let them go on and commit political suicide." But the members ignored these demonstrations and proceeded to take the ballot. There were sixty-eight votes in all, two by proxy, of which Crawford received sixty-four, Adams two, Andrew Jackson one, and Nathaniel Macon one. When the result was announced, there was some clapping in the galleries, which, however, was drowned out in a chorus of hisses. At this one member rose to remonstrate, but others whispered that it was best to ignore the rabble, for Calhoun had obviously packed the house with clerks of the War Department.

When all was over, many of the spectators repaired to Brown's Hotel to discuss the effect of the nomination. "What was King Caucus like?" asked an old gentleman, raising his spectacles. "Like!" was the reply. "Why, like a cat in a strange garret, frightened at every step it took and alarmed at everything it saw." "I thought they would get into a quandary," returned the old man, replacing his spectacles and walking away.

The mass of the Democratic-Republican party had no intention of permitting this little group of Congressmen to force a candidate upon them. Already the Legislature of Tennessee, in a series of eulogistic resolutions, had placed General Andrew Jackson in nomination. "In him they behold the soldier, the statesman, and the honest man," they said. "He deliberates, he decides, and he acts; he is calm in deliberation, cautious in decision, efficient in action. Such a man we are willing to aid in electing to the highest office in the gift of a free people."

Their action was greeted with enthusiasm in the West. This section, whose growth had been so rapid, felt that the time had come to demand a more important part in the nation's councils. "We are tired of seeing these aristocratic Easterners in the President's chair," they said, "with their stiff, dignified manners and their formal clothes. Jackson is not only a West-

erner but a man of the people. He knows what it means to
win his fortune in a new country; he can wield the woodman's
axe as well as the hunter's rifle, he is not afraid of the frontier
garb, he is not too proud to receive at his table the humblest
citizen. Give us Andrew Jackson, Old Hickory, the hero of
New Orleans."

The Jackson men, organizing themselves into clubs, began a
campaign of stump speeches, editorials, and pamphlets. "The
Hickory Club" of Philadelphia required each member to wear
a black silk vest, stamped with portraits of Jackson. In Sevier
County, Tennessee, a mass-meeting was held to test opinion
concerning the Presidency. Five banners were set up, bearing
the names of Adams, Jackson, Clay, Crawford, and Calhoun.
The people were asked to express their preference by gathering
under the banner of their favorite. When the signal sounded
almost the entire assemblage moved over to the Jackson
flag, and it was found that 616 had voted for the general,
7 for Adams, 3 for Clay, 1 for Crawford, and not one for
Calhoun.

These proceedings alarmed the supporters of Clay. This
noted statesman still wielded great influence, and Kentuckians
felt that his claim was superior to that of Jackson. What did
Jackson know about the complicated duties of the Presidency?
Surely the killing of 2,000 Englishmen at New Orleans did not
fit him to become the head of a great nation. Yet what other
preparation had he had? He was known to be prejudiced, ob-
stinate, headstrong. Why experiment with such a man when a
statesman of Clay's type was available?

The West was torn with the contentions of the partisans of
the two great leaders. Around the tavern fire, on board the
river-boats, at the court-day gatherings, men argued and
quarrelled. And it was impossible to hold a public meeting
without political speeches and the taking of straw votes.

As Jackson and Clay were the favorites of the West, so
Adams was the choice of New England. He was nominated by
a great meeting in Faneuil Hall, February 14, 1824, and New
Hampshire, Connecticut, Maine, and Vermont rallied round
his standard. His services as diplomat and statesman, it was

declared, his integrity, stanch loyalty to the Democratic-Republican party, and splendid ability rendered him the ideal candidate.

In Pennsylvania a party convention at Harrisburg gave hearty indorsement to Jackson. "An able advocate and judge," they called him, "a distinguished legislator and Governor, an incorruptible patriot, a skilful, brave, and successful general, and an enlightened statesman." The convention stigmatized the Crawford caucus as a departure from the usage of the Republican party, since it was held by a minority, contrary to the wishes of the party and the people.

As the election approached the people became more and more excited. It was the custom to choose electors, not all on the same day, but at different dates in different States. This fact, together with the slowness with which news travelled, left the nation in doubt for weeks. By November 13, however, it was known that Adams had carried all New England, that Virginia had gone for Crawford and Pennsylvania for Jackson. Then the Southern and Western returns began to come in, and on November 27 *Niles Gazette* gave the standing as Adams 80, Jackson 69, Crawford 40, and Clay 37, with several States to be heard from.

It was evident that there would be no majority in the electoral college, so that the election would be thrown into the House of Representatives. The Constitution provided that the House must make its selection from the three highest candidates, and all eyes now turned to the race between Crawford and Clay. The influence of the great Kentucky leader was so strong among the Representatives that it was probable that they would declare him President, if his name came before them. As December drew to a close, the returns showed that Crawford had 41 votes and Clay 37, with Louisiana still to be heard from. Finally came the news that this State had split its vote, giving 3 to Jackson and 2 to Adams. Clay was excluded, and the House was forced to decide whether Jackson, Adams, or Crawford should be President.

Jackson had carried the solid vote of New Jersey, Pennsylvania, South Carolina, Alabama, Mississippi, Tennessee, and

Indiana, with a few votes from New York, Louisiana, and Illinois, amounting to 99 in all. Adams, who swept New England, won 26 votes in New York and a few from Delaware, Maryland, Louisiana, and Illinois. His total was 89. Crawford carried Virginia and Georgia, while Clay won Kentucky and Ohio.

"If no person have a majority, then from the persons having the highest numbers, not exceeding three, on the list of those voted for as President, the House of Representatives shall choose immediately the President," says the Constitution. "But in choosing the President the vote shall be taken by States, the representatives from each State having one vote."

Clay now found himself in a position of great power but of no little embarrassment. His following in the House, which he could throw to any one of his rivals, was certain to determine the final decision. Himself deprived of the Presidency, he had become President-maker. It was a dangerous eminence, for, whatever his decision, he was sure to incur the hostility of the defeated parties. But for the time being the factions vied with each other in flattering and cajoling him.

"I am sometimes touched gently on the shoulder by a friend, for example, of General Jackson," he wrote, "who will thus address me: 'My dear Sir, all my dependence is upon you; don't disappoint us. You know our partiality for you next to the hero, and how much we want a Western President.' Immediately after a friend of Mr. Crawford will accost me: 'The hopes of the Republican party are concentrated on you; for God's sake, preserve it. If you had been returned instead of Mr. Crawford, every man of us would have supported you to the last hour. We consider him and you as the only genuinely Republican candidates.' Next a friend of Mr. Adams comes with tears in his eyes: 'Sir, Mr. Adams has always had the greatest respect for you, and admiration for your talents. There is no station to which you are not equal. Most undoubtedly you are the second choice of New England, and I pray you to consider seriously whether the public good and your future interests do not point most distinctly to the choice which ought to be made?' How can one withstand all this disinterested homage and kindness?"

During Monroe's first administration Clay had made an address in the House of Representatives denouncing Jackson for his conduct in the Florida campaign, which the "old hero" had resented bitterly. But now his friends went buzzing about to effect a reconciliation. The Tennessee delegation gave a dinner which both Clay and Jackson attended. When Clay retired from the table, Jackson and his friend Eaton followed him to the door and insisted that he ride home in their carriage. Jackson then invited Clay to dinner, and it seemed that the old feud had been laid to rest.

None the less, Clay had made up his mind to throw his influence to Adams. In temperament Clay had nothing in common with the austere Puritan, while in public matters he had frequently clashed with him. But for Adams's ability, experience, and integrity, he entertained a profound respect. Jackson he distrusted and feared. It would be a dangerous precedent, he thought, to elevate a military chieftain to the Presidency, merely because he had won a great victory. In 1818 Monroe had entertained some idea of making Jackson Minister to Russia, and asked Jefferson what he thought of it. "Why, good God!" exclaimed the old statesman, "he would breed you a quarrel before he had been there a month."

Clay understood that not only the Presidency but the alignment of new parties hinged upon his decision. He was selecting his political associates for the remainder of his career. Now, in an Adams-Clay alliance, Adams might be President, but Clay would certainly be the party-leader. Adams was uninspiring, Clay had the art of winning and holding friends; Adams had little strength beyond New England, Clay was distinctly a national figure. But in any partnership with Jackson, the general would demand complete control, and Clay did not fancy playing second fiddle. Moreover, in the inevitable readjustment Clay felt that the interests which he represented would receive greater support in the East, where Adams was popular, than in the Southwest, where Jackson was popular. Clay had become the champion of the tariff. He must look for support from New England, where manufactures were rapidly increasing.

Hardly had Clay announced his decision when he was subjected to a venomous attack from the Jackson forces. January 28, 1825, the following appeared in the *Columbian Observer*, of Philadelphia: "For some time past the friends of Clay have hinted that they, like the Swiss, would fight for those who pay best. Overtures were said to have been made by the friends of Adams to the friends of Clay, offering him the appointment of Secretary of State, for his aid to elect Adams. . . . I was of opinion, when I first heard of this transaction, that men professing any honorable principles, could not, or would not, be transferred, like the planter does his negroes or the farmer does his team of horses. Contrary to this expectation, it is now ascertained to a certainty that Henry Clay has transferred his interest to John Quincy Adams."

"I believe this letter to be a forgery," wrote Clay to the *Columbian Observer*, "but if it be genuine I pronounce the writer, whoever he be, a base, an infamous calumniator, a dastard, and a liar." Whereupon George Kremer, an eccentric Congressman from Pennsylvania, noted chiefly for wearing a leopard-skin overcoat, admitted the authorship. This made the affair ridiculous, and the whole country laughed at the idea of Clay's hurrying off to Bladensburg to take aim at one of the spots on Kremer's coat. So Clay contented himself with demanding an investigation by the House of Representatives.

Jackson at first refused to credit this charge of bargain and corruption. On February 9 he met Adams at a crowded reception in the White House. The general had a lady on his arm. The two men stood for a moment looking at each other, and then Jackson moved forward and extended his hand. "How do you do, Mr. Adams? I give you my left hand, for the right, as you see, is devoted to the fair. I hope you are well, sir." Mr. Adams took the hand and said, with icy coldness: "Very well, sir; I hope General Jackson is well." But when Jackson learned that Adams had actually appointed Clay Secretary of State, and that Clay had accepted, he became convinced that the charges of corruption were true. "You see," he wrote to a friend, "the Judas of the West has closed the contract and will receive the thirty pieces of silver. His end will be the same. Was there ever witnessed a more barefaced corruption in any country before?"

When the House of Representatives assembled on the morning of February 9, 1825, the galleries were filled with spectators. Of the 216 Congressmen, all were in their accustomed seats save Mr. Garnett, of Virginia, who was ill. At twelve o'clock the members of the Senate filed in and sat down, their presiding officer, Mr. Gaillard, taking his place at the Speaker's desk. The sealed returns were opened by the tellers, who counted them and made their report. Whereupon Mr. Gaillard rose, and announced that no person had received a majority. Since Andrew Jackson, John Q. Adams, and William H. Crawford are the three persons who have received the highest number, he added, the House of Representatives must decide which shall be President. The Senators then withdrew and Henry Clay resumed his seat at the Speaker's desk.

Gathering in various parts of the House in little groups, the members began to ballot among themselves to determine how the vote of each State should be cast. Through the crowded galleries there was a rustle of excitement, for the result, despite Clay's decision, was still in doubt. Some of the delegates on the morning of the election had not made up their minds. It is related that Stephen Van Rensselaer, a pious Congressman from New York, as he sat at his desk, prayed for guidance in casting his ballot. While his eyes were still closed, some one placed on his desk a piece of paper on which was written Adams's name. When he opened his eyes, he felt that he had received his answer, and voted accordingly.

The ballots were now counted by the tellers—Daniel Webster and John Randolph. Amid silence Webster arose, and in his deep voice, which carried to the farthest corners of the room, announced that thirteen States had voted for Adams, seven for Jackson, and four for Crawford. The throng in the galleries could contain itself no longer, and a few persons began to applaud, others to hiss. "Clear the galleries," ordered the Speaker. Thereupon a deputy sergeant-at-arms walked along the broad stone cornice which ran outside the balustrade, shouting: "The Speaker orders the galleries to be cleared; all must retire. Clear the galleries." When the crowd was gone, Clay arose and announced that: "John Quincy Adams, having received a majority of the votes cast, is duly elected President of the United States."

Though Adams took his seat as President, though Clay became Secretary of State, they soon found that they would have to face bitter opposition in Congress. The Calhoun interests immediately joined with the Jackson and the Crawford men, to oppose and thwart the Administration. At first they had no definite programme; they did not profess to constitute a separate party; their only rallying cry was "Revenge for bargain and corruption." They simply waited until Adams made some suggestion or committed himself to some policy, and then fought it. On one important issue, after the Administration had won a victory, Martin Van Buren, the opposition leader in the Senate, remarked: "Yes, they have beaten us by a few votes, after a hard battle, but if only they had taken the other side . . . we should have had them."

Though the schism in the Democratic-Republican party at first seemed personal in its character, soon the two opposing factions began to crystallize into new parties. An important Southern group, with distinct interests, gradually evolved a fixed programme. Since the struggle over the admission of Missouri they had come to understand that State rights was the great bulwark of their safety, and they now consistently demanded the strictest construction of the Constitution. With them developed the Western group, impatient of the old school of statesmanship, demanding social democracy, eager for a Western President. Combining with certain elements in the North, these factions became united under the leadership of Jackson and his advisers. Effective electioneering machinery was built up, and all that was lacking for the new party was a name. For some years they continued to style themselves Democratic-Republicans, but eventually they became known merely as Democrats.

The friends of Clay and Adams replied by organizing on their side. They drew their greatest strength from the North, especially the great industrial centres, but they had also many followers south of Mason and Dixon's line. They dreaded democracy, favored a vigorous administration, and sought legislation favorable to industrial development. At first they took the name of National Republicans, but in later years they became known as Whigs.

Thus, as the aged Jefferson sank into the last sleep, the party which he had created fell asunder. Of the two new parties which took its place, both had for their leaders followers of the democratic faith, both claimed succession from the Democratic-Republican party. Clay and Adams on the one hand, and Jackson, Crawford, and Calhoun on the other, no matter how fierce their contests with each other, alike had learned their political precepts at the feet of the sage of Monticello, alike disclaimed any kinship with the Hamiltonian Federalists.

It was fortunate that in the new political alignment sectional lines were largely ignored. With the embers of the Missouri quarrel still glowing, with slavery more firmly fixed on the South than ever, with Northern industries still expanding, the development of two new parties, one above and the other below Mason and Dixon's line, would have been fatal to the Union. As it was, though the Democrats felt the South to be their stronghold, they counted followers also in every part of the North; though the Whigs were strongest in New England, their presidential candidates often carried Southern States. Since both parties were national in character, both dreaded the sectional issue, and so far as possible both avoided it.

Thus they served as cementing forces to hold the country together. Their efforts to hush the sectional quarrel, their insistence upon less dangerous issues, their willingness to compromise, did much to postpone the threatening conflict. The Whig leaders refused to commit their party to an antislavery platform for fear of losing their Southern followers; the Democratic leaders knew that an uncompromising demand for the extension of slave territory would alienate the Northern vote, without which they could do nothing in Congress. In the end the sectional differences proved too strong for the parties and shattered them both, first the Whigs and then the Democrats. But the parties unquestionably postponed the crash for years, until, when finally the South seceded, the North had become strong enough to force it back into the Union.

CHAPTER XVII

THE REIGN OF ANDREW JACKSON

IN 1829 Jackson got revenge. Soon after the election of 1825 he was nominated by the Legislature of Tennessee. The old Crawford group and the friends of Calhoun rallied around him, and he was recognized as the regular Democratic candidate. The Whigs turned on him a bombardment of ridicule. This man Jackson is not only illiterate, they said, but a firebrand who in the President's chair would involve the country in all kinds of difficulties. They issued a pamphlet entitled *Reminiscences: or an Extract from the Catalogue of General Jackson's Youthful Indiscretions between the Age of Twenty-three and Sixty*, which was filled with accounts of Jackson's fights, brawls, and duels. Their attacks availed nothing. Old Hickory grew in popularity, while Adams, whom the Whigs nominated, aroused no popular enthusiasm. When the election was held, Jackson received 178 electoral votes, to 83 for Adams.

March 4, 1829, broke mild and serene over the city of Washington. Soon after sunrise vehicles of every sort, from the elegant coach to carts filled with women and children, were moving through the mud of Pennsylvania Avenue, while thousands of pedestrians thronged the sidewalks or peeped down from open windows. Here and there in the crowd would be seen a Tennessee hunter in buckskin shirt and coon cap, who had come 500 miles to see the "old hero" inaugurated. When Jackson appeared in an open carriage, escorted only by a band of Revolutionary officers, he received an ovation.

At twelve o'clock the tall figure of the President-elect emerged from the Capitol upon the east portico and ascended a platform. The spectators who covered the portico, the steps, the terraces, and the open space beyond, saw a man, bony and thin, who carried himself with erect military bearing. His face was covered with strong, deep-set lines, his forehead was seamed, his white hair, stiff and wiry, was brushed straight back, his mouth set like steel, while fierce eyes glared from beneath bushy, gray brows. He bowed gravely, took a manuscript from his pocket, and, in a low voice, read his address. When he had finished, the aged Chief Justice Marshall administered the oath, and as the new President bent over to kiss the Bible, a shout arose, followed by the booming of cannon.

Jackson elbowed his way through the throng, mounted his horse, and set out for the White House, followed by a stream of people in carriages, in carts, on horseback, and on foot. At the mansion no police arrangements had been made to preserve order, and the rabble rushed in to help themselves to the refreshments. Laborers, boys, negroes, and dirty children stood with their muddy feet on the damask satin chairs to get a peep at the President, or fought and jostled to reach the punchbowls, breaking the china and glassware and soiling the carpets. Jackson stood with his back to the wall, friends forming a barrier around him, until at last he escaped by a side entrance. A fitting beginning, said the Whigs in disgust, to the era of Jacksonian democracy.

The Cabinet had already been announced. Martin Van Buren, the intriguing political leader from New York, was made Secretary of State. The others were lesser men—John H. Eaton, S. D. Ingham, John Branch, John M. Berrien, and William T. Barry. Van Buren, who was Governor of New York, could not enter at once upon his duties, so Jackson appointed Colonel James H. Hamilton to fill the interim. On the morning of March 4, when Hamilton appeared, Jackson said to him: "Colonel, you don't care to see me inaugurated?" "Yes, General, I do; I came here for that purpose." "No, go to the State House, and as soon as you hear the gun fired, I am President and you are Secretary. Go and take charge of the department." Hamilton complied at once and later, when the cannon at the arsenal and the navy-yard sounded, the danger that Henry Clay might control the affairs of the State Department one minute beyond the appointed time was averted.

Four years before the election of Jackson an event had occurred which created much contention and before long was to convulse the country and endanger the Union. This was the passage of the protective tariff of 1824. The duty of 1816, designed to keep out the cheap goods which poured in after the War of 1812, had proved inadequate. An economic crisis had followed which culminated in 1819. Prices went down, business houses failed, unemployment was wide-spread and discontent rife. The cry for further protection arose more insistent than ever. In 1820 Clay championed a bill to increase tariff rates, but it failed in the Senate. Now, in 1824, he took up the cudgels again for what he termed the "American system," as opposed to a policy of low custom duties which he denounced as "the foreign policy."

On March 31 the eloquent Kentuckian spoke in the House for this bill. "In casting our eyes around us," he said, "the most prominent circumstance which fixes our attention and challenges our deepest regret, is the general distress which pervades the whole country. . . . It is indicated by the diminished exports of native produce, by the depressed and reduced state of our foreign navigation, by our diminished commerce, by successive unthreshed crops of grain, perishing in our barns and barnyards for the want of a market, by the alarming diminution of the circulating medium, by the numerous bankruptcies, . . . by the universal complaint of the want of employment, and a consequent reduction of wages.

"The explanation is found in the fact that we have long shaped our industry and commerce to a foreign market which no longer exists; in the fact that we have depended upon foreign supplies, and have neglected our own resources. Mr. Chairman, our confederacy embraces a great diversity of interests—agricultural, commercial, fishing, manufacturing. If we are to prosper, protection must be extended to all. What a spectacle of jealous rivals do our people now present, all rushing off to the glutted foreign markets the perishable produce of their labor! This bill is intended to transform these competitors into friends and mutual customers, and to place the Union upon a foundation of a common interest.

"All parts of the country will participate in these benefits, although it is probable that the North and East will enjoy the largest share. But I appeal to the South—to the high-minded, generous, and patriotic South—to vindicate the rights of our country. Should it not offer, upon the altar of the public good, some sacrifice of its peculiar opinions? Of what does it complain? A possible temporary enhancement in the objects of consumption. Of what do we complain? A total incapacity produced by ruinous foreign competition. This bill may be defeated, but the cause is the cause of the country and in the end it must prevail."

But the South was not inclined to make any such sacrifice. The East and the North alone benefit from a protective tariff, said the Southern Congressmen. Those regions have capital, they have dense populations and abundant skilled labor. The South has little capital, its population is sparse, its slave labor is unsuited for manufactures. The tariff will add to the cost of necessary goods and will hamper our exports of cotton and tobacco. It will be a tribute laid by one section of the country upon the industry of the other.

Yet in this struggle the dividing line at first did not run between free and slave States. Several of the commercial States of New England, led by the eloquent Webster, were opposed to a measure so injurious to their carrying trade; Kentucky, Missouri, and western Tennessee voted for it because it raised the duties on hemp. "A fine mixture this," sneered John Randolph; "the merchants and manufacturers of Massachusetts repel this bill, whilst men in hunting-shirts, with deerskin leggings and moccasins, want protection for manufactures." None the less the combination was effective, and the bill became law.

But when, four years later, a new tariff bill raised the average duties to the unprecedented height of 49 per cent, the sectional division between North and South became more distinct. Every free State save Maine and parts of Massachusetts and New York voted for the measure; the entire South, save Kentucky and Delaware and the non-slaveholding parts of Virginia and Maryland, opposed it.

The fact that the bill resulted from a bit of political juggling by the Jacksonian leaders did not soothe the ruffled feelings of the Southerners. Pennsylvania, a Jackson State, wanted protection for iron; New England, where Adams was strongly intrenched, demanded a tariff on textiles. The bill was heralded as the work of New Englanders, and later so amended as to remove the protection from textile manufactures. It was expected that the Eastern States would then bring about its defeat, thus making the Pennsylvanians hostile to Adams, and relieving the South of all responsibility. Their plans failed because the New Englanders in the end voted for the bill, believing that before long they could secure changes favorable to their interests.

The South was greatly alarmed. They felt that the Northern majority was using its growing power to build up its own prosperity at the expense of the slaveholder. There was talk of open resistance. "If we are to be reduced again to a condition of colonial vassalage," thundered James Hamilton, of South Carolina, in the House of Representatives; "if we have to purchase in one quarter of the Union all that we consume and sell all that we produce to the same favored portion, we will revert to the principles of the Revolution, repel tyranny by force, and maintain our position as a sovereign people."

In this situation certain prominent South Carolinians became open advocates of nullification. In 1828 John C. Calhoun prepared a paper for the committee of the State Legislature on relations with the Federal Government, which came to be known as "The South Carolina Exposition." If in this compact of States the Federal Government exceeds its powers to the detriment of certain sections, it said, it is the duty of the States to protect their citizens against the operation of its laws. If Congress persists in taxing South Carolina for the benefit of the Northern manufacturers, South Carolina will be forced to prevent the collection of the custom duties in her ports. This doctrine found expression in a debate which took place in the Senate in the early weeks of 1830.

The champion of South Carolina and nullification was Colonel Robert Y. Hayne. His slender figure, graceful carriage, piercing eyes, and musical voice were all typical of the South. It was known that he would speak on January 25, and that day the gallery and lobbies were filled, while many seats on the floor were occupied by ladies and distinguished guests. "The South Carolina doctrine," he said, "is only the Republican doctrine of 1798. It is the doctrine of the Virginia and Kentucky resolutions, the principle which saved the Constitution at the time of the Alien and Sedition Acts; the principle which New England statesmen adopted when they believed themselves the victims of unconstitutional legislation. Sir, as to the doctrine that the Federal Government is the exclusive judge of the extent of its own powers, it is utterly subversive of the sovereignty of the States. It makes little difference whether Congress or the Supreme Court is invested with this power. If the Federal Government is to prescribe the limits of its own authority, and the States must submit, this is practically a government without limitation of powers.

"South Carolina has kept steadily in view the preservation of the Union by the only means by which she believes it can be preserved—a firm resistance to usurpation. The measures of the Government have prostrated her interests and will soon involve the whole South in ruin; but even this evil, great as it is, is not the chief ground of our complaints. It is the principle involved—a principle which substitutes the discretion of Congress for the limitations of the Constitution and brings the States and the people to the feet of the Federal Government."

This able address was answered by Daniel Webster. The Northern champion was a man of commanding presence, sturdy frame, dark complexion, broad forehead, square jaw, firm mouth, and courageous eyes. He wore the conventional Whig uniform—a blue dress-coat with bright buttons, buff waistcoat, and white cravat. A murmur of expectancy swept over the assemblage, followed by silence. "Mr. President," he said, "I understand the honorable gentleman from South Carolina to maintain that it is a right of the State Legislature to interfere whenever, in its judgment, this government transcends its Constitutional limits, and to arrest the operation of its laws.

"May I ask, is this government the creature of the State Legislatures or the creature of the people? If the agent of the State governments, then they might control it, provided they could agree on the manner. If the United States Government were the agent of the people, then the people, and the people alone, could control, restrain, modify, reform it. According to the gentleman from South Carolina, it is the creature not only of the States, but of each State separately, so that each might assert for itself the power to settle whether it acts within the limits of its authority. It is the servant of four-and-twenty masters, of as many different wills and purposes, yet bound to obey all. This absurdity arises from a misunderstanding of the source of the government. It is, sir, the people's government, made for the people, made by the people, and is answerable to the people.

"Who, then, shall construe this grant of the people? Who interpret their will when it may be supposed to be left in doubt? For this the people have wisely provided in the Constitution itself, when they declared that the judicial power should extend to all cases arising under the Constitution and laws of the United States. The very end, the chief design for which the Constitution was formed and adopted was to set up a government that should not be forced to act through State agency or depend on State discretion. The people had enough of that kind of government under the Articles of Confederation.

"As for the doctrine of nullification, talk about it as you will, it goes the length of revolution. It leads directly to disunion and civil commotion. When my eyes shall be turned to behold for the last time the sun in heaven, may I not see him shining on the broken and dishonored fragments of a once glorious Union; on States dissevered, discordant, belligerent; on a land rent with civil feuds or drenched, it may be, in fraternal blood. Let their last feeble and lingering glance rather behold the glorious ensign of the republic, now known and honored throughout the earth, still full high advanced, its arms and trophies streaming in their original lustre, not a stripe erased or polluted, nor a single star obscured, bearing for its motto that sentiment dear to every true American heart—Liberty and Union, now and forever, one and inseparable."

While the echoes of the Hayne-Webster debate were still

reverberating, the State-rights men began laying plans to commit President Jackson to their principles. In case the Southerners actually nullified the tariff, it would be impossible to use force against them without the approbation of the President. And they felt that the President, as a Southern man, elected largely by Southern votes, ought to assist rather than oppose them. It was decided to hold a Democratic love-feast on Jefferson's birthday, with Jackson as the guest of honor, in which the toasts should glorify the doctrine of nullification.

It was a distinguished assemblage which gathered at Brown's Hotel on April 13 for the banquet. Around the tables were President Jackson, Vice-President Calhoun, the Secretary of War, the Secretary of the Navy, General Hayne, P. P. Barbour, and many others hardly less well known. When the regular toasts were completed Jackson rose to give the first volunteer toast. A hush fell over the room, as he drew himself up to his full height, raised his cup, and, looking at Calhoun, said in a crisp, harsh tone: "Our Union! It must and shall be preserved!"

The explosion of a bomb could not have produced a deeper sensation. It was Jackson's way of serving notice that he would have nothing to do with nullification. The toast was drunk standing, and when all had resumed their seats Calhoun offered the second volunteer toast: "The Union! Next to our liberty the most dear." Then after a moment's hesitation he added: "May we all remember that it can only be preserved by respecting the right of the States and by distributing equally the benefits and burdens of the Union."

The incident was quickly over. Other toasts followed, but all zest had gone from the company, and many left the room soon after Calhoun resumed his seat. In its main object of committing the President and the Democratic party to the doctrine of nullification, the banquet had proved a dismal failure. Jackson, soon after, let it be known that he was prepared to use the military forces to compel obedience to the Tariff Law.

None the less, the South still hoped for relief. A new tariff bill was introduced in 1831, and Henry Clay, conciliatory now as always, himself advocated a reasonable reduction of rates. The Southern leaders drew a vivid picture of the distress which the tariff had caused among the planters. It blights our harvests, they said, ruins our fields, impoverishes our people, causes grass to grow on the wharves of our ports; it enhances the price of all we buy and depresses the price of all we sell. But the Northerners replied that any injury to the South from the tariff was immeasurably outweighed by the ruin which its repeal would bring to the manufacturing sections. So strenuously did they resist all attempts at revision that when the bill passed in July, 1832, the protective principle was strengthened rather than weakened.

South Carolina felt that the crisis had arrived. In the election of 1832 they showed their resentment against Jackson by giving the eleven votes of the State to John Floyd, of Virginia. When the general was re-elected, they proceeded to put nullification to the test. "If you will not withdraw your exactions, if you will not live with us upon the terms of equal rights," Thomas Clayton had warned the country, "I will tell you in language of plain truth . . . we shall certainly part from you, and part, I hope, in peace." Now the South Carolina Congressmen called upon the people of the State to decide "whether the rights and liberties which you received as a precious inheritance from an illustrious ancestry shall be surrendered tamely . . . or transmitted undiminished to your posterity."

In a strenuous election the nullifiers carried the State, and the Legislature, which met in extra session in October, 1832, authorized the calling of a convention for the purpose of considering the national tariff laws. The convention met November 19 in the hall of the House of Representatives at Columbia. After five days of deliberation the Ordinance of Nullification was passed by a vote of 136 to 26. It stigmatized the Tariff Law as unauthorized by the Constitution of the United States, declared it "null, void, and no law" in so far as South Carolina was concerned, called upon the Legislature to carry out the Ordinance, and threatened secession in case the Federal Government should interfere.

A few weeks later President Jackson issued a proclamation announcing his determination to enforce the law in South Carolina, and appealing to the State not to plunge the country into fratricidal strife. He had already recommended a downward revision of the tariff, and the Legislature of Virginia, at the suggestion of Jackson's friends, had appealed to both sides to compromise their differences. Leading citizens of South Carolina now arranged to postpone nullification in order to await the action of Congress.

Henry Clay, "the great Pacificator," took charge of the situation in Congress to save his American System and prevent disunion. On February 12, 1833, he offered in the Senate a compromise tariff bill, providing for a horizontal reduction, to be made gradually, until in 1842 the highest rates should not exceed 20 per cent. It was, in effect, a return to the standards of 1816. At the same time Congress took up the so-called force bill, authorizing the President to use force in overcoming resistance to the collection of the duties. Calhoun agreed, in return for the compromise tariff, not to oppose this bill, and the two measures passed together. Thus did the government offer the olive branch with one hand, while it kept a tight grip upon the sword with the other. This proved effective. On March 11 the South Carolina convention reassembled and rescinded the Nullification Ordinance.

Both sides claimed the victory. Calhoun pointed to the fact that one State, unaided by its neighbors, by challenging the constitutionality of a Federal law, had forced Congress to offer a compromise. This seemed a remarkable feat, but it benefited South Carolina only temporarily, while in its far-reaching effects the nullification incident proved a stunning defeat. Calhoun had put to the test the State-rights doctrine as a weapon of defense against unwelcome Federal legislation, and the test had proved it to be inadequate. Concessions had been granted, not because Calhoun had convinced the nation of the correctness of his doctrines, but because of South Carolina's threat to disrupt the Union. The next time North and South were thrown into conflict the same weapon would be less effective, while eventually it would lose its force entirely. Nullification, by proving that the government was ready to coerce a State in order to enforce the laws, showed that where radical differences of interest exist in various sections of a country, no constitutional check can protect adequately the weaker section from the stronger. So the South turned once more to the well-nigh hopeless task of obtaining enough new slave territory to counterbalance the growing preponderance of the North. Upon this attempt hinge the most important chapters of the next twenty-five years.

The deeper significance of the nullification question could not escape Calhoun, and in his heart he knew that he had been defeated. But Jackson, who regarded the affair as a conflict between South Carolina and his administration, never forgave himself for consenting to the compromise. It is related that in his last days, when slowly sinking, he asked his physician what, in his opinion, posterity would most condemn about his career. After the doctor had made a futile effort to guess, the old man rose in bed, his eyes flashing, and said: "I can tell you: posterity will condemn me more because I was persuaded not to hang John C. Calhoun as a traitor than for any other act in my life."

Even before the conclusion of this affair, Jackson entered into a new conflict, which was to shake the country to its foundations. The charter of the second United States bank was to expire in 1836. The institution had proved invaluable in aiding government financing, stimulating business and stabilizing the currency, but it wielded a great power over industry, and had early excited Jackson's suspicion. Old Hickory looked upon it as a monopoly unsuited for a democratic country, which benefited the rich and injured the poor. This opinion became fixed when some of his closest supporters intimated that the directors were using their power to further the ends of the Whigs.

Jackson made his first assault upon the bank in his message of December, 1829. "The charter expires in 1836," he said, "and its stockholders will most probably apply for a renewal of their privileges. Both the constitutionality and the expediency of the law creating this bank are well questioned by a large portion of our fellow citizens, and we submit to the Legislature whether a national bank, founded upon the credit of the government and its revenues might not be adequate." This message was read with surprise. Every one knew that the bank had done good service, many felt that it was essential to the nation's prosperity. Congress affirmed its confidence in the institution, and the Committee on Ways and Means made a report hostile to the President's substitute scheme.

Jackson renewed the attack in December, 1830, and again in his message of 1831, but he did not press the matter. Apparently he had no idea of making it an issue in the approaching presidential campaign. Nicholas Biddle, president of the bank, felt that the institution ought not to become identified with any party, and the question of renewing the charter would probably have hung fire until after the election had it not been for Henry Clay.

The brilliant Kentuckian, whose nomination by the Whigs was now assured, believed that Jackson had presented him with a winning issue. The President's own party would not follow him in an effort to kill the bank, he was sure, for the Cabinet was divided, and many Democratic Congressmen were known to be friends of the institution. Was it likely that Pennsylvania, Jackson's faithful Pennsylvania, which prided itself on being the seat of the bank, would submit to its destruction? Clay determined to press the fight to the limit. He would save the bank, and in so doing win the coveted Presidency.

Biddle, too, tired of trying to disarm Jackson's hostility, decided to stake all upon the election. Joining hands with Clay, Webster, and other Whig leaders, he pressed for a bill to renew the charter. The measure passed triumphantly in the Senate 28 to 20, and in the House 109 to 76. Such a challenge could not be evaded by Jackson. If he had suspected the bank before, from the moment Clay became its champion it assumed in his mind the character of a monster, which he, the people's champion, must beard and kill. The bill was presented to him July 4, 1832, and on July 10 came his veto.

"It is to be regretted that the rich and powerful too often bend the acts of government to their selfish purposes," he said.

"In the full enjoyment of the gifts of heaven and the fruits of superior industry, economy, and virtue, every man is equally entitled to protection by law. But when the laws undertake to add to these natural and just advantages, artificial distinctions, to grant titles, gratuities, and exclusive privileges, to make the rich richer and the potent more powerful, the humble members of society, the farmers, mechanics, and laborers, who have neither the time nor the means of securing like favors to themselves, have a right to complain of the injustice of their government. . . . If we cannot at once, in justice to interests vested under improvident legislation, make our government what it ought to be, we can at least take a stand against all new grants of monopolies and exclusive privileges, against any prostitution of our government to the advancement of the few at the expense of the many."

When Clay heard the reading of this message, a smile of triumph passed over his face. Such irrevelant nonsense would surely react upon Jackson and cost him the election. "It has all the fury of a chained panther, biting the bars of his cage," thought Biddle. "It is really a manifesto of anarchy." The friends of the bank were so confident that it would win converts to their side that they ordered 30,000 copies to be printed for distribution. On the floor of the Senate Clay and Webster thundered against it, picked flaws in its logic, questioned the accuracy of its statements, and derided it as an undignified bit of demagogism.

There was an unpleasant surprise in store for them. The veto message was read by tens of thousands of honest men to whom it seemed neither illogical nor ridiculous. They looked upon Old Hickory as the champion of the oppressed against the forces of monopoly. They were not certain how the bank operated, but they were convinced, none the less, that it was a machine for transferring money from the poor to the rich.

So far from breaking the ranks of the Democratic party, the message knit them more solidly than ever. The bank Democrats discovered that they must either turn face about, or incur Jackson's animosity. "General, I want you to understand that I am your friend," a leading Virginia politician said to

Jackson. "I voted for you in 1829, and I intend to vote for you again this year. In only one point do I differ from you, and that is this matter of the bank." "Hell!" yelled the President, banging his fist down on the table, "you don't call that being a friend, do you?" No wonder certain members of Congress who had voted for the renewal of the charter now assured Jackson they had seen the error of their way, and joined in the battle against "intrenched privilege and corruption."

Clay missed the significance of all this, and on the eve of the election was sanguine. Bitter was his disappointment when the returns showed that his arch-enemy had won a sweeping victory. Of the 288 electoral votes Jackson received 219, Clay 49, John Floyd 11, and William Wirt 7. The people had shown that they wanted Old Hickory back in the White House, and that they did not want the bank.

Biddle still had hopes. To close the bank in 1836 would necessitate the sudden calling in of a great mass of loans, and the consequent derangement of business. Would the country permit this calamity? Biddle thought that, when the time came, he might be able to carry a charter over Jackson's veto. Jackson thought so, too. So he proceeded to meet the emergency by breaking the power of the bank in 1833. Two of his henchmen suggested that he might cripple the institution by withdrawing the public funds. The law required that this should be done only upon order of the Secretary of the Treasury, who must report his reasons to Congress. Jackson shifted Louis McLane, who was unwilling to attack the bank, to the Department of State, and appointed William J. Duane Secretary of the Treasury in his place. Duane was known to be an opponent of the bank, and Jackson took for granted that he would not object to removing the deposits. Yet he did object. He told the President frankly that he thought the measure injurious to the business of the country, and when Jackson insisted refused to comply.

The general was not the man to tolerate insubordination in his official family, so Duane was removed and Roger B. Taney made Secretary of the Treasury. Taney began drawing out the public funds and making all new deposits in selected State banks, which became known as "pet banks." In all $9,891,000 were drawn out, and the bank promptly curtailed loans to the extent of $7,000,000. The effect was instantaneous. The money market became stringent, many banks failed, business languished, and the country seemed to be on the verge of panic.

When Congress assembled in December, Clay, Webster, and Calhoun opened their heaviest artillery on the President. The removal of the deposits was illegal, they said, it was high-handed, it was inexpedient, it was ruinous to business. In the midst of one of his most eloquent addresses, Clay stepped close to Van Buren's desk, and appealed to him to use his influence with Jackson to reconsider his action. "Go to him and tell him, without exaggeration, but in the language of truth and sincerity, the actual condition of his bleeding country," he said. "Tell him that in a single city more than sixty bankruptcies, involving a loss of upward of $15,000,000, have occurred. Tell him of the alarming decline of all property, of the depreciation of all the products of industry, of the stagnation in every branch of business, and of the close of numerous manufacturing establishments which, a few short months ago, were in active and flourishing operation. Depict to him, if you can find language to portray, the heartrending wretchedness of thousands of the working class cast out of employment. Tell him of the tears of helpless widows, no longer able to earn their bread, and of unclad and unfed orphans who have been driven by his policy out of an honest livelihood."

During the delivery of this appeal, Van Buren looked respectfully and innocently at the speaker, as if treasuring up every word to be faithfully repeated to the President. After it was over he went up to Clay, asked him for a pinch of snuff, and, having helped himself, walked nonchalantly away. Though the Vice-President refused to take Clay's appeal seriously, a majority in the Senate supported him in his condemnation of Jackson's conduct. On March 28, 1834, a resolution of censure was passed, declaring "that the President, in the late executive proceeding in relation to the public revenue, has assumed upon himself authority and power not conferred by the Constitution and laws, but in derogation of both."

Jackson was furious. In a special message he defied the Senate. "Your action is nothing less than an impeachment trial," he said, "without the observance of the prescribed constitutional forms. The President is the representative of the American people; he is in no way responsible to the Senate, and for that body to censure his acts is an attack upon the foundations of the government." While the excitement was at fever heat, Thomas Benton, leader of the Jackson forces in the Senate, gave notice of his intention to move that the resolutions of censure be expunged from the journal.

In the meanwhile, the thoughts of the country turned to the approaching presidential election. Many imagined that Jackson would demand a third term. But Jackson was now an old man, his health was failing, and he thought only of ending his days in peace at the Hermitage, his beloved home in Tennessee. Yet so complete was his ascendancy in the Democratic party, that when it became known that he favored Martin Van Buren as his successor, the nominating convention lost no time in carrying out his command.

As for the Whigs, they went into the campaign with shattered ranks, with divided leadership, without holding a national convention, and without uniting upon a ticket. In certain States Whig meetings indorsed General William H. Harrison, the victor of Tippecanoe, while the Legislature of Massachusetts put Webster in nomination. From the first the Whig cause was hopeless. Van Buren received 170 electoral votes to 124 for all other candidates. Thus was Jackson's choice ratified by the people.

The evening of January 16, 1837, found the Senate Hall jammed to suffocation. Many members of the House of Representatives were seated on the main floor, while the galleries and lobbies were so filled that it was difficult to get in and out. As darkness came on, the great chandelier was lit up, casting a brilliant glow over the scene. The last battle was being fought between Andrew Jackson and his enemies. The order had gone forth from the White House that the resolutions of

March 28, 1834, censuring the President, must be expunged from the records.

The night was far spent when Calhoun rose to protest against the violation of the journals. "No one not blinded by party zeal can possibly be insensible that the measure proposed is a violation of the Constitution," he said. "The Constitution requires the Senate to keep a journal; this resolution goes to expunge the journal. If you may expunge a part, you may expunge the whole; and if it is expunged, how is it kept? The Constitution says the journal shall be kept; the resolution says it shall be destroyed."

Clay followed with an impassioned burst of oratory. "Why detain the Senate or waste breath in fruitless exertions?" he said. "The decree has gone forth. The deed is to be done. Proceed, then, with the work which lies before you, and, like other skilful executioners, do it quickly. And when you have perpetrated it, go home to the people, and tell them what glorious honors you have achieved for our common country. Tell them that you have extinguished one of the brightest and purest lights that ever burnt at the altar of civil liberty. Tell them that henceforward no matter what daring or outrageous act any President may perform, you have forever hermetically sealed the mouth of the Senate. Tell them that he may fearlessly assume what powers he pleases, snatch from its lawful custody the public purse, command a military detachment to enter the halls of the Capitol, overawe Congress, trample down the Constitution, and raze every bulwark of freedom."

The final address was delivered by Webster. "This resolution will pass," he said. "We expect it. We collect ourselves to look in silence while a scene is exhibited which, if we did not regard it as a violation of a sacred instrument, would appear to us to be little elevated above the character of a contemptible farce. This scene we shall behold; and hundreds of American citizens, as many as may crowd into these lobbies and galleries, will behold it, also, with what feelings I do not undertake to say."

As Webster resumed his seat, silence fell over the room. For some moments the acting President of the Senate waited, but no one arose to continue the debate. Then came the one word, "Question." The secretary of the Senate called the roll and one by one the Senators arose in their seats and gave their votes. There were 24 yeas and 19 nays, and the motion was carried.

The secretary produced the journal of the Senate, and, opening at the page which contained the censure, drew a square of broad black lines around it, and wrote across the face these words: "Expunged by order of the Senate, this 16th day of January, 1837." As he began this task, hisses and groans arose from the crowd in the gallery over the head of Senator Benton. The President promptly ordered the gallery to be cleared, while Benton, in a rage, demanded the arrest of the "bank ruffians." "Here is one just above me who may easily be identified!" he shouted. The man was brought before the bar by the sergeant-at-arms, but was soon released, after which the Senate adjourned.

The gratification of Jackson was extreme. It was the crowning triumph of his career—this humiliation of the three greatest American statesmen of the period, his arch-enemies all of them. A few days later the White House resounded to the click of glasses, to the laughter of women, to witty speeches and patriotic toasts. It was Jackson's dinner to the "expungers" and their wives. Although the general himself appeared, he was too ill to remain, and after placing Benton in his chair, retired to his chamber.

Even as Jackson and his friends rejoiced, a storm was brewing which was destined to sweep the Democratic party out of power. Clay's predictions of financial ruin were now to find fulfilment. For some years there had been an appearance of prosperity. Immigrants had poured in, railroads had extended their mileage, business had boomed, prices had risen, new enterprises had sprung up. But much of this activity was unsound, the result of inflation rather than of actual economic progress, and a crash was imminent.

The removal of the deposits played its part in creating inflation. Many of the "pet banks" could not resist the temptation to earn high interest rates, and so used the government money to back enterprises of questionable soundness. New banks were created; bank-notes in circulation increased from $103,000,000 in 1835 to $149,000,000 in 1837, while the specie behind the paper shrank from $44,000,000 to $38,000,000. This dangerous situation was aggravated by wild speculation in government lands. Dealers would pay for the land in bank-notes, which then went to the "pet banks" for deposit, and were once more lent out to the dealers to buy more acres. It was a vicious wheel, which added to the inflation and increased the danger with each revolution. In 1832 the receipts from the sale of public lands had been $2,623,000; in 1836 they rose to $24,877,000.

The inevitable collapse was hastened when Jackson issued his famous "specie circular," instructing the land officers to accept only gold and silver in payment for public lands. This would have been a wise measure had it come sooner, but now it served only to shake the tottering structure of credit. The country accepted it as an expression of distrust by the government in the bank-notes which constituted the bulk of the currency. To add to the tension, Congress passed an act lending to the State governments millions of dollars from the surplus which had accumulated in the "pet banks." This made necessary the transfer of large sums with a sudden contraction of loans by certain banks and expansion of loans by others.

Hardly had Jackson alighted from his carriage at the Hermitage amid a throng of welcoming friends and neighbors, when news came of the final explosion. Banks all over the country began to suspend specie payment or to close their doors; gold and silver disappeared; bank-notes sank in value; factories closed down; merchants failed and thousands of workmen were thrown out of employment. Years were to pass before business resumed its normal volume.

The panic of 1837 marked the end of the reign of Andrew Jackson. His trusted lieutenant remained for four more years in the White House, it is true, but the spell had been broken. Clay and Webster were quick to place the blame upon Jackson's shoulders, while many of his former henchmen felt that his actions had been ill-advised. The imperious old general to his dying day continued to send forth his orders from the Hermitage, but they often went unheeded.

The secret of Jackson's astonishing political career is to be found in his ability to win the confidence of the masses of the people—the farmers, the mechanics, the small shopkeepers. They loved him as a man of their own stamp, and looked upon him as their champion against intrenched privilege and greed. They cared not that he was unpractised in statesmanship, that he was prejudiced, egoistic, and pugnacious; they delighted to see him wield the "big stick," were glad to obey his commands. "When I view the arduous administration through which I have passed," said Jackson, in his farewell address, "the formidable opposition, to its very close, of the combined talents, wealth, and power of the whole country, with their corrupting influence, with which we had to contend, I am truly thankful to God for this happy result." Such was Jackson's estimate of his career as President, and such was the estimate of millions of his fellow citizens.

CHAPTER XVIII

MANIFEST DESTINY

THE ink was hardly dry on the treaty with Spain renouncing the claims of the United States to Texas, when Americans began to cross the Sabine to settle in the rich cotton lands of the Trinidad and the Brazos. They were typical frontiersmen, afraid neither of the arduous task of conquering the wilderness nor of facing the scalping-knife. They found a country occupied only by Indians and a few Spanish posts, ready for the axe and the plough—prairies, full of buffaloes and deer; forests of pine, ash, oak, and cedar; great rivers flowing into the Gulf of Mexico; a mild climate and a fertile soil.

In 1820 Moses Austin, pioneer and promoter, obtained a grant of land in Texas, and prepared to plant a colony of Americans. He died on the eve of this undertaking, and to his son, Stephen F. Austin, fell the honor of founding modern Texas. As the younger Austin was on his way to San Antonio in August, 1821, with a company of Americans and Spaniards, he saw several men coming to meet him. "Viva independencia!" they shouted, "viva independencia!" The Spaniards embraced each other, gave cheer after cheer, and celebrated with a breakfast feast. In this way the news that Mexico had declared its independence came to the Father of Texas.

Austin now had to secure confirmation of his grant from the Mexican Congress, and after planting a little group on the Brazos, at San Felipe, set out for Mexico City. He found the country in turmoil. With the collapse of Spanish authority a republic had been founded. This was overthrown by General Iturbide, who in turn gave way in 1824 to a second republic. In the end, however, Austin and other American proprietors received large concessions and hastened north to gather settlers. Thus Mexico gave approval to a policy which could but lead to the loss of her northeastern province. At the moment when the Mexican people were renouncing their alle-

giance to Spain, it is strange that they could have supposed
that Texas, once peopled with Anglo-Americans, would remain
loyal to Mexico. Differences of blood, language, institutions,
religion, and temperament would make it impossible for Mexico to assimilate this new community, and without assimilation,
independence and perhaps annexation to the United States were
inevitable.

A few years later a learned Mexican, Don Manuel de Mier
y Teran, journeyed through Texas and reported his observa-
tions. "As one crosses this province from San Antonio to the
Sabine," he wrote, "he will find Mexican influence less and
less, until at Nacogdoches it is almost nothing. The Anglo-
Americans maintain English schools, and send their children
north for further education. I warn you to take timely measure, for this is a smouldering fire which can throw the nation
into revolution. Our law prohibiting slavery they avoid by
making sham contracts with their slaves before crossing the
border. Yet the mere existence of the law deters many, and
were it repealed wealthy Louisianians would move over in
such numbers as to make Texas a powerful state."

In the summer of 1830 Teran entered Texas once more, this
time at the head of an army to enforce obedience to the laws
of Mexico. Along the one highway which crossed the province
from the Rio Grande northwest to Nacogdoches tramped the
soldiers of the republic—dusky men, most of them, but presenting an imposing appearance in their gaudy uniforms.
From the main road detachments were sent off across the
prairies or through the woods to garrison the villages. As they
passed, the fair-haired, blue-eyed newcomers looked on with
resentment, or gathered before the village store to discuss the
invasion and the possibility of securing aid from Louisiana.

During the eighteen months that the soldiers remained, there
were several clashes, but the people as yet were too weak to
expel them. In the end they were rescued by one of the peri-
odic upturns in Mexico itself. News came that Antonio Lopez
de Santa Anna, a shifty, calculating politician, posing as a
friend of the common people, had started a fresh revolution.
Instantly the soldiers were fired with a longing for glory and

loot. Garrison after garrison threw their hats in the air, vowed loyalty to Santa Anna, and hastened away for the Rio Grande. Unwilling to be laggards in so good a cause, the Texans also declared for the new government, and when Colonel Piedras, commander of Nacogdoches, refused to join in the movement, they attacked his garrison, forced them to surrender, enlisted them in the revolutionary cause, and sent them on rejoicing.

Following this turn of events, Austin set out for Mexico City to demand a State constitution and the setting up of the English common law. To gain time the subtle Santa Anna promised all. But his liberalism was a sham, and he soon threw himself into the arms of the reactionary party, suppressed Congress, and set himself up as a military despot. Austin was thrown into the old dungeon of the Inquisition, while an army under General Cos moved north, to overawe the Anglo-Americans.

Instantly all Texas was ablaze. "Are we going to submit to this tyrant?" the people asked. "Shall we permit our liberties to be overthrown and our homes invaded by Mexican troops?" Throughout the valleys of the Colorado and the Brazos, angry men seized their rifles and made ready to repel the invaders. In September, 1835, a Committee of Safety was organized, while a call was sent out for a great "consultation."

At this juncture Colonel Ugartechea, commander of the Mexican forces at San Antonio, sent a corporal and four men to seize a brass six-pounder at Gonzales. The people of the town sent the soldiers back empty-handed, removed the gun, took their families to a place of safety and issued a call for help. Soon 160 Texans were assembled at Gonzales, and a few days later they crossed the Colorado River, and dispersed a detachment of 80 Mexicans. Thus were Lexington and Concord re-enacted on the plains of Texas.

In February, 1836, a picturesque army made its way across the plains of southern Texas. In the lead was President Santa Anna, his gorgeous uniform, glittering epaulets, wide-brimmed hat, and richly decorated saddle bespeaking the grandiose chieftain. Behind him stretched out long lines of infantry in the showy uniforms of the Revolutionary period; dragoons, their lances swung behind the shoulders, their plumes nodding; cannon, lumbering over the sandy roads; hundreds of wagons, laden, not only with stores and munitions, but with dusky women and children. Mexico was sending the flower of her army to punish the daring Texans.

Texas was ill prepared to meet this force. They had elected as their commander the soldier and frontiersman Sam Houston, but he wielded a shadowy authority over some of the independent bands. The troops, instead of being concentrated, were scattered, with no co-ordination and no plan of campaign. One of these companies, led by the brave W. B. Travis, was stationed at the quaint Spanish village of San Antonio. When the Mexicans closed in on the town, instead of falling back, Travis led his men into an old mission called the Alamo, and awaited the assault.

On March 3 he sent off a message to the people of Texas. "With 145 men I have held the place against a force variously estimated from between 1,500 to 6,000 men, and I shall continue to hold it until I get relief from my countrymen, or I will perish in its defense. We have had a shower of bombs and cannonballs continuously falling among us the whole time; yet none of us has fallen. . . . A blood-red flag waves from the church of Bexar and in the camp above us, in token that the war is one of vengeance against rebels. . . . These threats have had no influence upon my men but to make all fight with desperation, and with that high-souled courage which characterizes the patriot who is willing to die in defense of his country, liberty, and his own honor. God and Texas; victory or death!"

At dawn on March 6 Travis heard a bugle and, looking out, saw the Mexicans approaching. The bands struck up the Spanish air of "Deguelo," and the troops rushed forward, the front ranks carrying scaling ladders, crowbars, and axes. The defenders were ready. Crouching on the thick stone walls, they poured in a deadly rifle and artillery fire and the enemy fell back. But the officers urged the men on, they were pushed forward by those behind, and at last, after repeated failures, weight of numbers swept them up to and over the wall. In the yard there was hand-to-hand fighting, as the clubbed rifles and bowie-knives of men in hunting-shirts and moccasins clashed with the bayonets of the Mexicans. Before the last little group of defenders were cut down in the mission church, fighting desperately, hundreds of Mexicans had fallen. Not one of the Texans was spared. "Thermopylæ had its messenger of fate," was the proud Texan boast; "the Alamo had none."

After this disaster Houston retreated eastward, attempting to unite his scattered bands as he went. One company, flung far out to the south at Goliad, was surrounded by the Mexicans, and surrendered with the condition that they should be "treated as prisoners of war." The treatment they actually received, however, is vividly told by a Mexican officer. "This day, Palm Sunday, March 27, has been to me a day of heartfelt sorrow. At six in the morning the execution of 412 American prisoners was commenced and continued until eight, when the last of the number was shot. At eleven commenced the operation of burning their bodies. But what an awful scene did the field present, when the prisoners were executed, and fell dead in heaps—and what spectator could view it without horror!" No wonder the frontiersmen as they fell back, first to the Colorado, then to the Brazos, and finally to the San Jacinto, swore revenge for the Alamo and for Goliad.

Some weeks later James Buchanan, while calling at the White House, found President Jackson seated in his office before a map of Texas. He had just finished tracing out the course of the opposing armies. "Here is the place," he said to Buchanan, putting his finger upon San Jacinto. "If Sam Houston is worth one baubee, he will make a stand here, and give them fight."

April 20, 1836, found both Houston and Santa Anna marching for the same point—the ferry over the San Jacinto River. If the Mexicans reached it first, not only would they cut off Houston's retreat, but could carry the war unopposed to the Sabine. Fortunately, the hard-marching Texans won the race, and when Santa Anna arrived, he found them blocking his way. He pitched camp on a hill, with a morass and San Jacinto Bay at his back, fortified his position by piling up a barricade of boxes, baggage, and pack-saddles, erected a slight abatis of boughs, and waited for his opponent to make the first move.

The morning sun of April 21 looked down from a cloudless sky upon the two armies—the Texans in frontier garb, armed with shotguns, rifles, muskets, carbines, some with bayonets, some without, straining their eyes in the glare of the prairie to catch sight of the enemy; the Mexicans in gaudy uniforms, confident that they had trapped the rebels and could end the war. The morning wore slowly away, and neither side showed an inclination to attack. Then, late in the afternoon, the Mexican sentinels observed a line of Texans emerging from a grove of oaks a thousand yards away. Simultaneously came the sound of a solitary fife, and Houston's men swept forward on the run. "Remember the Alamo!" they shouted. "Remember the Alamo!"

The Mexicans were taken by surprise. Santa Anna was resting in his tent, many officers were stretched out for a doze, some of the men were cutting wood, others were cooking, the cavalry were riding bareback to and from water. When the alarm was sounded all was confusion. The Mexicans had barely time to seize their muskets and fire one volley before the Texans burst over the feeble barricade. Now bowie-knife and musket-butt did their work. After resisting for a few minutes, the Mexicans fled. Santa Anna ran around, wringing his hands, and then sprang upon a black stallion and galloped from the field. Some of his men ran toward the morass, where they were shot in the mire, others fell on the bank of the bayou, still others, who fled to the prairie, were cut down by the cavalry. "Me no Alamo! Me no Alamo!" cried the terror-stricken fugitives, but the Texans showed them little mercy. Santa Anna's army was annihilated; 630 were killed, 208 wounded, and 730 captured.

Shortly after the battle Houston was lying in his tent nursing his ankle, shattered in the battle. He was a large, powerful man, with broad, high forehead, gray hair, commanding features, dressed like an Indian. He looked up as the guard entered, bringing a prisoner dressed in citizen's clothing—blue cottonade, coat, and pantaloons. It was Santa Anna. The

fallen ruler was profuse in apologies for his butcheries. He had
been acting under orders from the government, he said; he was
unaware that the forces at Goliad had surrendered under promise of good treatment, and when he was free would execute
Urrea for deceiving him.

Houston felt that he had a valuable asset in Santa Anna.
He restrained his men, who wanted to shoot the prisoner, and
placed a guard around his tent. Eventually Texas entered into
an agreement with the President whereby he promised to suspend hostilities, surrender his prisoners, indemnify the public,
and acknowledge the independence of the State. Although
Mexico repudiated his action, the agreement hastened the retirement of the remaining Mexican troops, and so perhaps
compensated the Texans for not placing Santa Anna before the
firing squad.

The heroic struggle of Texas was watched with interest in
the United States, and hundreds of youths, especially from the
Southern States, seized their rifles and set off for the Sabine.
There had been great enthusiasm at the news from San Jacinto, and when in August, 1837, Texas filed a formal request
to enter the Union, many supposed that she would be welcomed. We must not miss this opportunity of recovering our
lost province, they urged, and of carrying our frontiers to the
Rio Grande! We must not turn our backs upon our brethren
of the Southwest, leaving them the alternative of submitting
to Mexico or forming an entente with Great Britain!

But there stood in the way of annexation one great barrier
—slavery. It was easy for the North to envisage the day when
the basins of the Colorado and the Brazos would be covered
with cotton-fields, when Texas would be divided into several
States, each sending two representatives to the Senate. The
fruits of the Missouri Compromise will be thrown away, it was
said, if, after forbidding slavery in the northern part of the
Louisiana territory, we annex the limitless areas of the Southwest, where slavery is already established.

Sentiment in the North against slavery had become more
pronounced since 1820. Benjamin Lundy, a New Jersey
Quaker, took the lead in a crusade against the institution,

organizing emancipation societies and publishing an anti-slavery paper. He was powerfully seconded by William Lloyd Garrison, whose journal, the *Liberator*, made its first appearance in 1831. Garrison was impatient of compromise or delay. "I shall contend for the immediate enfranchisement of our slave population," he said. Soon he had drawn around him the more earnest opponents of slavery in New England, and had become a power in moulding public sentiment. In 1832 was formed the New England Antislavery Society and the next year the American Antislavery Society.

The abolitionists were bitter in their denunciation of the attempt to annex Texas. I look upon the Texas war as an "invasion of brigands from the United States," said Lundy, with the "avowed purpose of adding five or six more slave-holding States to this Union." His words were echoed in Congress. "In my opinion the people of the United States will not consent to bring into the Union a new, vastly extensive, and slaveholding country," said Daniel Webster, "large enough for half a dozen or a dozen States." James Russell Lowell could see in the matter only a purpose to grasp new pens to cram with slaves. So bitter was the opposition that the Democratic leaders feared it might injure their party in the North, and so were willing to let the matter slumber. Throughout Van Buren's administration the friends of Texas continued to clamor for annexation, but the President turned a deaf ear.

The prospect of success during the succeeding four years seemed equally slight. Van Buren was sure to be nominated again, and the Whig candidate, whoever he might be, would hardly dare offend the antislavery group in that party by coming out for annexation. At first it was supposed that the Whig convention would once more choose Henry Clay. Clay was the undisputed leader of the party, he had been one of its founders, had shaped its policies, had battled for it during its days of adversity. Now that the panic of 1837 had produced a revulsion against the Democrats, and a Whig victory was assured, he could claim the nomination as a right.

But there were strong influences at work to bring about Clay's defeat. Thurlow Weed, the Whig leader of New York, who favored the nomination of General William H. Harrison, played a shrewd trick upon the Kentuckian. He got the politicians in various parts of the State to write a series of letters creating the impression that it would be impossible for Clay to carry New York. "Do what you can for Clay in your district," wrote these pretended friends, "for I am sorry to say he has no strength at all in this." This manœuvre greatly weakened his chances of gaining the nomination. The convention itself was marked by intrigue, and in the end Harrison gained a clear majority. Again Clay had been thrust aside for a military hero, a hero who had accomplished nothing more than a victory over the savages at Tippecanoe.

Clay was bitterly disappointed. When the news reached him he rose from his chair, and walked backward and forward, lifting his feet like a horse string-halted in both legs, and stamping upon the floor. "My friends are not worth the powder and shot it would take to kill them!" he cried. "If there were two Henry Clays, one of them would make the other President of the United States. . . . I am the most unfortunate man in the history of parties; always run by my friends when sure to be defeated, and now betrayed for a nomination when I, or any one, would be sure of an election."

In order to appease Clay, the convention named as Vice-President several of his friends, but one after the other they declined. Then, almost in desperation, they nominated John Tyler, of Virginia. Tyler was a Democrat who had been expelled from the party for resigning his seat in the Senate rather than obey the instructions of the Virginia Legislature to vote for the expunging resolutions. For this, and apparently for this alone, the Whigs honored him with the second place on their ticket. It was a bit of folly which they later deeply repented.

The campaign was a farce. The Whig convention had adopted no platform, and based its claims solely upon the blunders of the Democrats. Yet there was no end of enthusiasm, of stump speeches, monster meetings, and torchlight processions. "Harrison is the typical man of the people," the Whigs declared; "he knows what it means to live in a log cabin and wear the humble garb of the frontier." Everywhere they unfurled their banners, decorated with log cabins and coonskin caps; built log cabin headquarters, drank hard cider, and shouted for "Tippecanoe and Tyler too." When the vote was taken Harrison received 234 electoral votes, Van Buren only 60.

On March 4, 1841, General Harrison rode to the Capitol on a white horse, hat in hand, bowing to the cheers of the multitudes who lined the streets. After the oath of office he stood for an hour and a half without hat or overcoat in a cold wind to deliver his inaugural address. Several weeks later he was caught in a shower and contracted pneumonia. On April 4 he died. Thus one month after the inauguration the crowds again assembled, this time in sorrow, to attend the funeral of their leader. Minute-guns were fired throughout the day, flags floated at half-mast, Pennsylvania Avenue was hung with streamers of black, shops were closed, and the nation mourned for the first President to die in office.

This sad event dumfounded the Whigs. Their victory, won after so many years of waiting, served only to put a Democrat in the White House. Tyler at once assumed the title of President and let it be known that he would not submit to the dictation of Clay, Webster, and the other Whig leaders. After he had vetoed a bill to charter a new national bank, the Cabinet which he had inherited from Harrison deserted him, and a party caucus declared that "all political connection between them and John Tyler was at an end."

These unexpected events inspired Texas with new hope. Tyler was an avowed annexationist. "I give you a hint as to the probability of acquiring Texas by treaty," he wrote Webster, in October, 1841. "Could the North be reconciled to it, could anything throw so bright a lustre around us?" When Webster resigned as Secretary of State, he appointed Abel P. Upshur, of Virginia, who took up the Texas business in earnest.

His task was rendered less difficult by British intermeddling. England used her good offices to induce the Texans to free their slaves and come to an understanding with Mexico. This aroused American suspicions. The growth of an independent

Texas, supplying half the world's cotton, protected by the
British navy and threatening the supremacy of the United
States, seemed an alarming possibility. In vain John Quincy
Adams declared that the rumors concerning Great Britain were
spread about solely to neutralize Northern repugnance to annexation. The British ogre seemed too real, and when Upshur
opened negotiations with Houston for a treaty of annexation,
the current of public opinion was setting his way.

The country was now preparing for another presidential
election. It had long been obvious that Clay would be the
Whig candidate. The misfortunes brought on the party by
Weed's intrigues in 1840 gave him a prestige too strong for the
most wily of politicians. As for the Democrats, it was thought
that they would once more name Van Buren. All this boded
ill for Texas. In May, 1842, Van Buren visited Clay at his
charming home in Lexington, where these old foes indulged in
"a great deal of agreeable conversation, but not much of politics." But it is probable that this "agreeable conversation"
turned on Texas, and that the two leaders reached an understanding to eliminate that question from the campaign. Both
feared it, Clay as a Southern man with a strong Northern following; Van Buren as a Northern man seeking to carry Southern States.

But the question of annexation could not be downed. It
was the most important issue facing the country, and in the
end it obtruded itself to the undoing of both Clay and Van
Buren, causing the latter to lose the Democratic nomination,
and the former to lose the election. The Democratic politicians felt that Texas had become a winning issue, and so, passing over Van Buren, they cast about for a strong pro-Texan.
Their choice fell on James K. Polk, former Speaker of the
House of Representatives and Governor of Tennessee, who
had pronounced "in favor of immediate reannexation of
Texas."

The Whigs nominated Clay, but he killed his own chances
by straddling the issue. Clay had declared that it was "perfectly idle and ridiculous, if not dishonorable, to talk of re-
suming our title to Texas," and had pointed out that annexa-

tion would bring on a war with Mexico. But now he began to have misgivings as to the wisdom of this position. Letters poured in from Southern Whigs, urging him to reverse his stand. Clay hesitated. He wanted the Presidency very much. Could he win the election without Southern votes? In the end he weakened, and on July 27, 1844, wrote a letter in which he stated that he would approve of annexation, could it be done "without dishonor, without war, with the common consent of the Union, and upon just and fair terms." The result was unexpected. Thousands of antislavery men deserted Clay to vote for James G. Birney, candidate of the Liberty party, and the Democrats carried New York State and the country. Polk received 170 electoral votes to 105 for Clay.

A month after the election President Tyler, in his annual message, asserted that "a controlling majority of the people and a large majority of the States" had declared in favor of the annexation of Texas and recommended steps to carry out the mandate. The opposition in the Senate was still too strong to admit of annexation by treaty, but the desired end might be obtained by a joint resolution of both Houses inviting Texas to join the Union. After a bitter fight this was done. On March 1, 1845, President Tyler signed the resolution, and two days later the official messenger set out for Texas with the invitation. Thereupon Almonte, the Mexican Minister at Washington, served notice that his country would maintain its claim to the province "at all times, and by every means in her power," and demanded his passports.

At Mexico the news was received with a tremendous burst of anger. "We must wage war at once to recover our province!" cried the press in unison. "August Houses! President of the Republic!" said *El Amigo del Pueblo*, "the hour of danger for the country has sounded, and she has a right to look to you for salvation. Union and war!" Hasty preparations were made for the struggle. The archives at Vera Cruz were carried into the interior, new guns were mounted on the forts, munitions were hurried to the Rio Grande, and steps taken to float a loan.

Sentiment in Mexico against abandoning Texas was strengthened by the possibility that the United States would become involved in war over Oregon. For years this territory had been occupied jointly by England and the United States, but in 1846 Polk refused to continue the arrangement, and a crisis impended. The people of the Northwest wished to carry the boundary line to the Southern extremity of the Russian possessions, at 54° 40'. They took as their slogan "Fifty-four forty or fight." In the end a compromise was effected by which the dividing line was the forty-ninth parallel from the Rocky Mountains to the middle of the channel between the continent and Vancouver's Island, and through that channel to the Pacific. Thereupon Lord Aberdeen, British Foreign Secretary, declined to interfere with the Texas affair and warned the Mexican Government not to plunge into a war with the United States.

The danger of a clash was increased by the fact that President Polk at heart was not entirely averse to war. The United States had suffered many injuries from Mexico: our citizens had been imprisoned and robbed, our flag insulted, our ministers threatened, agreements had been broken, treaties violated, our claims ignored. "The United States have borne more insult, abuse, insolence, and injury from Mexico than one nation ever before endured from another," declared the New Orleans *Commercial Bulletin*. The administration was determined to end these unending affronts.

Moreover, Polk ardently desired the great provinces of California and New Mexico. Amid the forests and valleys of the far Southwest here and there was a Spanish mission or a dwindling Mexican settlement; save for these the region was as much a wilderness as in the days of Cabrillo and Ferrelo. But now adventurers from the United States were arriving in defiance of Mexican law, and its seemed that the valley of the Sacramento might become another Texas. Could Mexico be induced to part with these provinces, Polk was ready to pay a sum fabulous in the eyes of that impecunious government. Texas he considered a closed incident.

To the Mexicans Texas was still a burning issue. When Polk sent John Slidell to negotiate a treaty, fixing the boundary at the Rio Grande, settling American claims, and, if possible, arranging for the purchase of California and New Mexico, there was a fresh burst of rage. President Herrera had intimated that Slidell would be welcomed, and when the public learned this they turned on him furiously. He is the betrayer of the nation's honor, it was declared, the genius of disgrace; he is seeking to "avoid a necessary and glorious war." Herrera tried to save himself at the last moment by refusing to receive Slidell, but it was too late. His government was overthrown by the war party, and Mariano Paredes, who opposed any agreement relinquishing Texas, was made President.

War was now inevitable. Polk hastened forces to the Rio Grande under General Zachary Taylor, while a Mexican army commanded by Mariano Arista marched north with orders to begin the attack. On April 24, 1846, some Mexican cavalry, under General Torrejón, crossed the river above Matamoras. Hearing of this, Taylor sent Captain Thornton with sixty-four men to reconnoitre. The company fell into an ambush, and after several men had fallen, surrendered to the Mexicans.

This was Polk's opportunity. "The government has made every effort to avoid hostilities," he said, in a special message. "After the annexation of Texas, we sent an envoy to that country to adjust all differences in a friendly spirit. The Mexican Government not only refused to receive him, but after continued menaces have invaded our territory and shed the blood of our citizens. As war exists, and exists by the act of Mexico, we must vindicate the honor of our country." The message was received with enthusiasm. Congress authorized the President to raise 50,000 men and placed $10,000,000 at his disposal.

On May 8, 1846, the American army was moving over the burning plains of southern Texas. At their head was General Taylor, "Old Rough and Ready" his men called him, a middle-aged man with broad forehead and courageous mouth, riding a beautiful white horse and wearing a blue uniform and felt top cap. His army, numbering 2,228 well-drilled men, stretched out behind—dragoons in blue uniforms, guns drawn by lumbering oxen, three regiments of infantry and long lines of supply wagons. Suddenly the men in front saw a dark line across the plain some three miles in front, and the cry arose: "The Mexicans! The Mexicans!"

Arista had taken up a strong position, flanked on either side by dense thickets of thorny shrubs, and in front by boggy pools and wide fields of high, stiff grass. They made a brilliant appearance—long lines of gaudy infantry, Torrejón's red lancers, the horse under Canales, a number of four-pounders, and in front, riding up and down the lines, Arista himself, a tall man with red hair and sandy whiskers, a blaze of gold lace. He harangued the army, and the men answered with loud vivas, while silken banners fluttered and bands played.

The American artillery opened with a roar, and the Mexican four-pounders replied. Arista's pieces were too light, the shot fell short, and as they ricocheted, our men easily dodged them. But the American guns were very effective, opening gaps in the infantry, and leaving the ground strewn with dead and wounded. Arista was greatly surprised. He had expected Taylor to charge, but instead he was decimating his ranks with this long-distance artillery fire. So he sent his red lancers, a thousand strong, streaming off to the left, with trumpets sounding and lance-points glittering, to flank the Americans and crumple up their line. Taylor, sitting with one leg over the pommel of his saddle, ordered his men to "keep a bright outlook for them." The Fifth Infantry marched out to the right and against these the red lancers charged twice and then retired.

The grass now took fire, and a roaring flame swept across the plain between the two armies. The battle ceased for nearly an hour. While the smoke was still rising from the charred grass, Arista sent forward his right flank. But they recoiled from a hot fire, and, when Duncan's battery opened, wavered and finally hastened from the field with the shrapnel bursting among them. Darkness was at hand, and fighting was suspended. Early the next day, as the morning mists slowly dissolved, Taylor was surprised to see the Mexican line move off into the chaparral toward the Rio Grande. Palo Alto, the first real battle of the Mexican War, had ended in victory for the Americans.

Taylor followed slowly, and in the afternoon found the

enemy in camp five miles from the river. Here he struck them again. This time the victory was decisive. Captain May's dragoons swept over the Mexican guns, the infantry charged, and Arista's men, after a stubborn fight, fled to the Rio Grande. There was a wild panic at the ferry, as men fought for places on the boats. Many were drowned. Had Taylor pressed his victory he might have destroyed Arista's army, for the enemy were thoroughly disorganized. May 18 the Americans crossed the river and entered the town of Matamoras.

Taylor now made ready to invade northern Mexico. But reinforcements came in slowly, he was delayed by sickness, lack of guns, and inadequate transport, and it was September before he set out for Monterey. His men were charmed with the country. On all sides were groves of oak, walnut, ebony, and cypress; pastures with herds of sheep, cattle, and goats; villages with flat-roofed houses of rubble; and in the distance the pale-blue summits of the Sierra Madre. On September 19 Taylor and his staff entered the San Juan valley. Before them lay Monterey, beneath towering lilac mountains, its white houses peeping from green groves, the cathedral towers above, on one side the citadel over which floated the green, white, and red flag of Mexico, and beyond, the bishop's palace with its black cross and narrow turrets.

Though all seemed so serene, the town had been converted into a labyrinth of fortresses. The streets were barricaded, the houses loopholed and garrisoned, the cathedral fortified, the foot-hills to the south and west covered with redoubts. Taylor did not hesitate. The next morning a long column left the American camp—Texans in coarse red or blue shirts and buck-skin caps, company after company of infantry in sky-blue uniforms, an artillery battalion in dark blue with red stripes down the legs, a band of Louisiana volunteers, many in citizens' clothes. It was General Worth's command, sent out to cut off retreat and to attack the city from the west.

Several days of fighting followed. Worth's men defeated a detachment of Mexican cavalry who came at them, their lance-points glittering, their green and red pennons fluttering. Then, turning upon the strong defenses on the right, they stormed through chaparral up the precipitous sides of Federation Ridge, swept over the crest of Independence Hill, captured the bishop's palace, and drove its defenders into the city.

But Monterey was not yet helpless. When the two divisions of the American army assaulted the town, Taylor on one side and Worth on the other, they encountered desperate resistance. The Mexicans, behind barricades and on housetops, fired upon the invaders in the streets, and more than one charge was thrown back. Gradually the men in blue worked through the maze of buildings toward the cathedral. The Texans broke into the houses, battered openings through the partitions, drove the enemy from room to room, swept them from the roof-tops, and by night on the 23d were within one square of the plaza. The next morning General Ampudia asked for terms. Taylor permitted the enemy to evacuate the town with their arms, accoutrements, and six field-pieces, and Monterey was ours.

In the meanwhile, the wily Santa Anna had returned to Mexico, and, taking advantage of Taylor's victories to discredit Paredes, once again made himself master of the country. He immediately began massing his forces to drive the invaders over the Rio Grande, and early in 1847 moved north with an army of 20,000 men, by way of San Luis Potosi. Taylor, who occupied an exposed position west of the southern ranges of the Sierra Madre, fell back to a pass between the lofty mountains near Buena Vista. Here he posted his army of 4,750 men, and awaited the Mexican onslaught.

On February 22 Santa Anna arrived. At dawn on the 23d the reveille sounded in the Mexican camp, and infantry and cavalry drew up in line. They made a brilliant spectacle in their bright uniforms, some in red, some in green, some in yellow, some in sky-blue, their silken banners and bright plumes fluttering. Priests now passed along the line, bestowing benedictions, while the bands rendered sacred music. The troops then moved into position, while tremendous vivas rolled up the valley and echoed from the mountains.

Taylor had formed his troops across the valley. His right wing guarded the road to Buena Vista, his left was posted on a stony plain between two deep ravines, at the foot of the tow-

ering Sierra. Santa Anna sent General Blanco down the road
as a feint, and then hastened his heaviest columns up the
southern ravine to crush the American left, swing past their
line, and cut off retreat. As regiment after regiment emerged
upon the plain, it seemed that they must carry all before them.
But suddenly came the crash of the American fire, and the
front columns melted away. The Second Indiana, O'Brien's
battery, and Colonel Marshall's dismounted cavalry, fought
fiercely to hold the line. Fresh bodies of Mexicans now pushed
forward, brushed aside the troops before them, and headed for
Buena Vista far in the rear. All seemed lost. Happily Jefferson
Davis's Mississippi Riflemen, in duck trousers and red shirts,
came hurrying up from Saltillo in time to check the movement.
In the meanwhile, Taylor, stationed conspicuously on the plateau on "Old Whitey," ordered every available man to concentrate on the left, and a storm of shot and shell opened upon
the Mexican column. Isolated from the rest of Santa Anna's
army, they took refuge in the recesses at the foot of the
mountain. Eventually most of them made their way around
the base of the sierra and rejoined their comrades in the broad
ravine.

Thereupon Santa Anna launched another fierce assault upon
the plateau, and once more the American line faltered. But
the Indiana and Mississippi regiments came up, Bragg and
Sherman wheeled their guns into position, and volley after volley was poured into the ranks of the enemy. The Mexicans
could not withstand that fire. With thinned ranks they fell
back down the broad ravine, and the battle of Buena Vista was
won. That night, while the pale moon lit up the jagged mountain peaks and shone down upon the dead, Santa Anna stole
off on a forced march back to San Luis Potosi.

Exactly two weeks after the battle of Buena Vista, an American army of 10,000 men, under General Winfield Scott, landed
on the Mexican coast just southeast of Vera Cruz. It was an
imposing spectacle—the frigates, with long rows of heavy guns
and their network of spars and ropes; the gunboats in close to
the shore; surf-boats loaded down with soldiers; the inky waters of the Gulf; the long yellow line of the beach; to the north

the walls and spires of Vera Cruz; the cloudless sky above; and in the west the sun, just sinking behind the peak of Orizaba. At a signal shot from the *Massachusetts* the bands struck up our national airs, and the surf-boats made for the shore. There was no resistance. The boats grounded, hundreds of men in blue uniforms leaped out on the sand, the cannons were landed, and the Stars and Stripes planted.

The Americans drew their lines around Vera Cruz, and brought up heavy guns. For four days they bombarded the city. With each flash of the mortars, the light would glare for an instant upon the pall of smoke which hung over the American army. There could be heard the crash of a roof, an explosion, screams and wailing. Garrison and citizens became cowed. With shells bursting, many houses burning, steeples and domes tottering, the streets filled with terror-stricken women, surrender was unavoidable. Scott granted easy terms, for he was impatient to reach the mountains before the arrival of the yellow fever. A few days later the defenders marched out in uniforms of blue, white, and red, and after stacking arms, they dispersed under parole.

Now followed days of climbing up the rugged mountain roads, bitter fighting in the ravines of Cerro Gordo, marches over highways lined with hedges and alive with song-birds, through charming villages, with snow-clad volcanoes always in view. After a long delay at the ancient city of Puebla, famed for its cathedral with its two dark towers, the march was resumed through a charming country full of grazing herds, stately country houses, and white churches. The way led past the peaks of Popocatepetl and Iztaccihuatl, through Rio Frio, until the Americans passed over the crest of a mountain range and looked out upon the beautiful valley of Mexico.

To the war-stained soldiers it seemed a bit of Paradise— fields of grain, green orchards and groves, villages, haciendas and churches, roads and canals, glittering lakes, in the middle distance the capital of Mexico, with its stately palace, its cathedral, its park, around all a ring of volcanoes, and in the distance a line of mountains. More than three centuries earlier Hernando Cortez, looking down upon the same valley, then the land of the Aztecs, had vowed to conquer it for Spain. Now the dingy warriors from the North, which in the days of Cortez had been a wilderness, said to each other: "That splendid city shall soon be ours."

General Scott decided to approach Mexico from the south, and so led his men along the southern shores of Lake Chalco and Lake Xochimilco. Santa Anna hurried up to block his passage. The Mexicans took position at Contreras and Churubusco, on either side of a wide lava bed full of fissures, caves, jagged points, and pitfalls. It seemed impossible for the Americans to dislodge them. But Scott struck at Contreras, flanked the enemy, and drove them toward Mexico with a loss of 700 killed and 800 captured. Santa Anna was so enraged that he stood with a whip, slashing at the fugitives as they came rushing in. Soon he regained composure enough to draw in his forces for the defense of Churubusco.

Here the Americans delivered a series of slashing assaults. The Mexicans, now desperate, occupied strong positions, and at first Scott's men were unable to make any impression upon them. At length sheer bravery carried the day. Swarming forward with fixed bayonets, the men took one post after another, until the enemy gave way and fled toward the city. Santa Anna's total loss for the day was probably not less than 10,000, nearly half his available army.

The Americans could now have entered Mexico City almost unopposed, but Scott permitted Santa Anna to trick him by a request for an armistice, pending peace negotiations. While two weeks were wasted in parley, the Mexican reorganized his army and reconstructed his defenses. When hostilities were resumed, the army found its way blocked by a group of massive stone buildings known as Molino del Rey. They carried the place, but at heavy cost in killed and wounded.

Scott next turned his eyes to the heights of Chapultepec. Here a rock rose from the plain like a lone signal-tower, crowned by an old palace of the Mexican viceroys converted into a fortress. Could this be taken, it was thought that Santa Anna would consent to terms of peace. At daybreak on September 13 the American batteries, in a furious cannonade, poured grape, canister, and shells upon the buildings and the approaches at the foot of the hill. At eight o'clock the infantry swarmed forward. There was hand-to-hand fighting in an ancient cypress grove, which dated back to the days of Montezuma, and the approaches to the hill were carried. With a shout the men clambered up the steep slopes, placed ladders against the walls, and came tumbling over into the palace.

Without delay the Americans turned their attention to Mexico. Soon soldiers and guns were clanking over the famous causeways and battering at the inner defenses of the city. Throughout the afternoon Santa Anna's men resisted, but during the night they retired to Guadalupe Hidalgo, and at daybreak the conquerors marched in. The crowds who thronged the streets and looked down from windows, balconies, and house-tops saw a band of grim fighters, devoid of pomp and show. In front were Quitman and Smith, the former with only one shoe, behind them the men, their blue uniforms stained with mud, carrying their guns at various angles. Filing into the plaza, they formed before the cathedral, while the American flag rose over the National Palace. Suddenly a clatter of hoofs was heard, and General Scott, imposing in gold epaulets and white plumes, rode into the plaza with his staff. As he moved along the line of troops, the men presented arms and the bands played the national airs. The Americans had duplicated the feat of Cortez.

On February 2, 1848, Nicholas P. Trist, Luis G. Cuevas, Bernardo Conto, and Miguel Atristain, meeting in secret at Guadalupe Hidalgo, seat of a venerated shrine, signed a treaty of peace. Mexico renounced her claims to Texas, ceded to the United States territory embracing the present States of California, Nevada, and Utah, with parts of Colorado, Arizona, and New Mexico, and in return the United States assumed all obligations due by Mexico to American citizens, renounced her right to indemnity, and paid the Mexican Government $15,000,000. The treaty was submitted to the Senate by President Polk on February 22, where, after a bitter struggle, it was ratified thirty-eight to fourteen.

The three years from 1845 to 1848 are momentous. In this

short period the United States annexed territory equalling the entire area of the original thirteen States. Before we could realize the consequences, we had acquired hundreds of miles of western coast and had become a Pacific power. Unfortunately, the question of whether slavery should be admitted to the new territories caused the smouldering sectional fires to burst once more into flame. It required the strenuous efforts of Clay, Calhoun, Webster, and other unionists to compromise the differences growing out of the Mexican War. And, despite them, the acquisitions of 1848 played an important part in bringing on the War of 1861. The heroes of Buena Vista and Chapultepec—Grant, Lee, "Stonewall" Jackson, Meade, Huger, Jefferson Davis, Bragg, Joseph E. Johnston, Porter, Sherman, Magruder—little realized that the Mexican victories were hastening the day when their guns would be turned against each other.

CHAPTER XIX

CONFLICT IRREPRESSIBLE

JANUARY 28, 1848, a certain James W. Marshall burst into the office of his employer, John A. Sutter, at New Helvetia, California, and requested a private interview. Sutter wondered what could have happened, for Marshall was dripping wet and much excited. "Are you alone?" demanded the visitor. "Yes," was the reply. "Did you lock the door?" "No, but I will if you wish it." "I want two bowls of water," said Marshall. "Now I want a stick of redwood, and some twine, and some sheet copper." "What do you want of all these things, Marshall?" "To make scales." "But I have scales enough in the apothecary's shop," said Sutter. When the scales arrived Marshall drew forth a pouch and poured from it some glittering articles. "I believe this is gold," he said. With trembling hands the two men applied aqua fortis to the metal, and it stood the test. Next three dollars in silver coin were put in one of the scales, and enough gold-dust to balance it in the other. When both were immersed in water, down went the dust and up the silver coin.

A few days before Marshall, while building a sawmill upon one of the tributaries of the Sacramento, had noticed a yellow deposit in the mill stream. He paid little attention at first, but, seeing more, it occurred to him that it might be gold. He sent for a tin plate, and washed out the dirt. "Boys, I believe I have found a gold-mine," he told the workmen. "I reckon not," was the gruff response; "no such luck."

None the less, gold it was, as all America soon knew. Within four months thousands of newcomers had entered the region. Rough men in high boots, flannel shirts, and slouch hats swarmed along every little stream. Some washed the ore in wicker baskets, some used wooden rockers, some the sluice, others picked out gold from the rocks with knives. While Governor Mason was inspecting the gold-fields, a teamster called out to him: "Come here, captain, and look at this man picking out the gold." "He was picking out of the crevice in the slate, across which the water had pitched in winter to a bed some feet below, the gold and earth in lumps, and had his left hand full when I saw him," says the Governor. "I mean, he was picking it out of an open hole in the rock, as fast as you can pick the kernels out of a lot of well-cracked shell-barks. . . . In less than half an hour the man got between five and six ounces of pure gold."

As the tales of rich finds spread, a rush began for the gold-fields. The farmer left his plough, the mechanic his tools, the sailor his vessel, the doctor his drugs, even the preacher his Bible. Some crossed the continent, their covered wagons lumbering over prairies and through defiles, fording rivers, glistening in the desert sun; some chartered vessels for the journey around Cape Horn; others sailed to Panama, and after crossing the isthmus with mules and canoes, waited on the Pacific coast for a chance vessel.

The population of California quadrupled within a few months. San Francisco is "a mass of wooden hovels and cloth tents," wrote a Forty-niner, "pitched without order on sand-banks and what few rocks were not sand-covered, on its northern and middle slopes. People from all parts of the world are here, and every language seems to be spoken, but the babel resolves itself into one great motive, 'Gold! Gold!' and still 'Gold!'" Fifteen months later he found all changed, the streets following a definite plan, the shacks and tents largely replaced by solid buildings. "Still, it was yet a very primitive place, with a population composed mainly of men, bearded and clothed in the roughest attire." In 1848 California had been a wilderness; in 1850 its population was 92,574.

Few of the Forty-niners brought slaves. In the scramble to reach the gold-fields no one wished to make the arduous journey "carrying slave property on his back." The negro might prove useless, not only in the extraction of gold, but in cultivating the soil. "A plough, a yoke of oxen, and a ready will, with a reasonable knowledge of modern discoveries in agricultural chemistry are sufficient to insure any young or middle-aged man who goes to California a golden and peaceful competency for his old age and a handsome legacy for his children," wrote one of the settlers. So the black workers were left behind, and so, in the twinkling of an eye, California had become "free soil," linked in interests with the Northern States.

The settlers proceeded to organize a government excluding slavery. They elected delegates to a convention, which met at Monterey September 1, 1849, and drafted a constitution upon the familiar American lines. The people ratified at once, 12,066 to 811. The first Legislature, which met at San Jose in December, drew up a memorial asking that California be admitted as a free State.

The South was bitterly disappointed. They had hoped that the territory secured from Mexico, much of it south of 36° 30', would be divided into slaveholding States and help redress the balance of power in the Union. When David Wilmot, of Pennsylvania, in 1846 had added to a bill in the House, appropriating money to enable the President to make peace, the proviso that none of the territory acquired in the Mexican War should be open to slavery, their desperate resistance caused its defeat. Already the North had undisputed control in the House of Representatives; the admission of California as a free State would break the tie in the Senate and sweep away the South's last veto on hostile legislation. To make matters worse, the Northwest, from the upper Mississippi to the Pacific, which stood waiting to be moulded into free States, would in time double the population of the North.

It dawned upon the Southerners that they were losing because of the superiority of the Northern economic system. Northern industry could take root in any region suited for human habitation. It could convert the prairies of Nebraska into fields of corn and wheat, line the rivers of Minnesota with factories, reach into the earth for the gold of California or the copper and silver of Montana. But slavery was suitable only for staple crops in fertile soil under sunny skies. Even in the old South slavery did not flourish in the mountain regions. The Appalachian ranges were an island of free labor in a slavery sea. If, then, slavery could not exist in the Blue Ridge or the Alleghanies, what hope was there of planting it on the barren slopes of the Rockies or in the sterile plateaus of New Mexico? As for the great plains of Iowa, Minnesota, and the Dakotas, had slavery found its way there, it is probable that it would have languished or died. The Northwest was little more suited for the institution than the Northeast, and in the Northeast, even in colonial days when New England participated in the slave-trade, it attained but a precarious footing. The Southerners, struggling against the forces which were hemming them in, felt that, if slavery were excluded from the most fertile parts of the Mexican cession, the South would soon become a minor section, ringed about by hostile States, and helpless in the face of unfriendly legislation.

Thus, when General Zachary Taylor took up the duties of the Presidency in 1849, he found the country facing the most serious crisis since the nullification ordinance. Taylor, who was a soldier, not a statesman, was unsuited to grapple with the situation. In his annual message he merely announced that California would soon apply for admission, and recommended her petition for favorable action. An attempt to deny the Californians the right to decide for themselves the question of slavery, he thought a violation of the principles of self-government.

The Southern leaders assailed the President, and precipitated in Congress a bitter debate which took up once more every phase of the slavery controversy. The Northerners demanded not only the admission of California, but reverted to the principle of the Wilmot Proviso in attempting to exclude slavery from all other portions of the Mexican cession. They asked, also, for the settlement of the western boundary of Texas along a line east of the Rio Grande, and the abolition of the slave-trade in the District of Columbia. The South resisted bitterly, and in turn asked for an effectual law for the return of the slaves who had fled to the North. The battle soon was raging with such intensity that disunion seemed imminent.

Henry Clay came to the Senate in 1849 with the determination to remain "a calm and quiet looker-on." But he loved the Union ardently. He could not be the idle witness to its destruction. So he aroused himself for one more parliamentary campaign, the most arduous of his career, to defeat the extremists and effect a compromise acceptable to both North and South.

The great "Pacificator" proposed that California be admitted "without the imposition by Congress of any restriction in respect to the exclusion or introduction of slavery"; that Congress take no action either to introduce or exclude slavery from other parts of the Mexican cession; that Texas relinquish her claim to eastern New Mexico in return for the assumption by the United States of her State debt; that "it is inexpedient to abolish slavery in the District of Columbia" at present; that "the trade in slaves brought into the District of Columbia from places beyond its borders should be prohibited"; that "more effectual provision ought to be made for the restriction" of fugitive slaves; that "Congress has no power to prohibit or obstruct the trade in slaves between the slaveholding States."

On February 5, 1850, Clay, now an old man, tottered up the steps of the Capitol and made his way to the Senate Hall. His head, bald on the top, was fringed with long gray hair, his cheeks were sunken, his shoulders bent. He was dressed in black, and from a high black-satin stock emerged a white collar, which reached to his ears. A few minutes later, as he rose to speak, there came thunders of applause from the throngs in the gallery, on the floor of the Senate, and in the halls and lobbies. Despite his weakness, he was still eloquent, still powerful in his appeal for peace.

"Mr. President," he began, "never on any former occasion have I risen under feelings of such painful solicitude. I have seen many periods of great anxiety, of peril, and of danger in this country, and I have never before risen to address any assemblage so oppressed, so appalled, and so anxious, and, sir, I hope it will not be out of place to do here what again and again I have done in my private chamber, to implore of Him who holds the destinies of nations and individuals in his hands, to bestow upon our country His blessing, to calm the violence and rage of party, to still passion, and to allow reason to resume its empire.

"I am aware of the difference of opinion prevailing between the free States and the slaveholding States. I am aware that while one portion of the Union is pushing matters to the greatest extremity, the other portion is pushing them to an opposite, perhaps not less dangerous extremity. It appears to me that if an adjustment is to be made, it must extract from both parties some concessions—not of principle, but of feeling, of opinion. In regard to California, I propose that it be admitted without restriction in regard to slavery. Well, now, is there any concession in this resolution by either party? No, sir, there is not. If in the struggle for power between the two classes of States a decision adverse to the Southern States has been made, it is a decision not by the general government, but by California itself.

"But, sir, if California has declared against slavery, is it likely that slavery can ever secure a foothold in New Mexico? No, sir, the mountainous character of those regions, the nature of the soil, its barrenness, all lead to the conclusion that slavery cannot be introduced there. I say to you who reside in the free States, what do you want? You want the territories acquired from Mexico to be free of slavery. Well, you already have it in California, and in all human probability in New Mexico also.

"If this confederacy should be involved in civil war, in which one side would try to restrain the introduction of slavery into new territories, and the other to force its introduction there, what a spectacle would we present to the contemplation of mankind! An effort not to propagate right, but I must say an effort to propagate wrong. It would be a war in which all mankind would be against us.

"And, sir, I must say that, in my opinion, there is no right on the part of any State to secede from the Union. War and dissolution of the Union are identical and inevitable. Even if consent were given, in less than sixty days after, war would break out between the slaveholding and non-slaveholding portions of the Union. Ah, sir, the veil which covers those sad events is too thick to be penetrated by any mortal eye.

"Sir, can you lightly contemplate these consequences? Can

you yield yourself to the tyranny of passion amid these dangers? I implore gentlemen, whether from the South or the North, by all that they hold dear—by all their love of liberty, their veneration of their ancestors, their regard for posterity, their gratitude to Him who has bestowed on them such unnumbered blessings, the duties which they owe to mankind and themselves—to pause at the edge of the precipice, before the fearful leap into the abyss below."

As Clay began this address his old vigor returned, his eyes flashed, and his voice filled the Senate Chamber. But on the second day, after he had been on his feet for hours, he showed signs of weakness. Several times his colleagues urged him to consent to an adjournment, but he insisted upon going on to the end. "My strength is greater now than it will be later," he said with unintentional pathos. "If I do not weary the patience of the Senate, I prefer to continue."

A month after this address, John C. Calhoun, now on the threshold of death, made a last appeal for the slaveholding South. His tall, emaciated figure, wrapped in a long black cloak, entered the Senate Chamber, with slow and feeble steps. A thick mass of snow-white hair, brushed back from his brow, fell to the shoulders, while deep, cavernous black eyes looked out from a face seamed with lines. Too weak to stand, he requested his friend, James M. Mason, of Virginia, to read for him his carefully prepared paper. Mason's delivery was excellent, and as his voice rang through the Senate Chamber, Calhoun sat motionless, his eyes at times wandering anxiously from one face to another as though to divine the effect of his appeal.

"Senators, it can no longer be disguised that the Union is in danger. You have thus forced upon you the gravest question that can come under your consideration: How can the Union be preserved? The danger arises from the discontent of the Southern States, and the belief that they cannot remain, as things now are, consistently with honor and safety, in the Union. One cause for this feeling is the long-continued agitation of the slave question in the North. There is another, lying back of it, which is the primary cause—the fact that the equilibrium between the two sections as it stood when the Constitution was ratified, which afforded ample means to each to protect itself against the aggression of the other, has now been destroyed.

"In 1790 the population of the United States was 3,929,971, of which number the Northern States had 1,977,899 and the Southern 1,952,072, making a difference of only 25,827. The number of States, including Vermont, Kentucky, and Tennessee, was 16, of which 8 belonged to the Northern section and 8 to the Southern. There was a small preponderance in the House of Representatives and in the electoral college in favor of the North, owing to the fact that in estimating Federal numbers, five slaves counted but three, but it was too small to affect sensibly the perfect equilibrium. But since that time there has been a startling change.

"According to the census of 1840, the population then amounted to 17,063,357, of which the North had 9,728,920 and the South 7,334,437, making a difference in round numbers of 2,400,000. If we consider Delaware a doubtful State, the Northern section then had 13 States and the Southern section 12, making a difference in the Senate of 2 votes in favor of the former. According to the apportionment of 1840, the North had 135 members of the House of Representatives, and the South but 87. Since the census of 1840, 4 States have been added to the Union—Iowa, Wisconsin, Florida, and Texas. They leave the difference in the Senate as it stood before, but they increase the Northern majority in the House.

"The census is to be taken this year, and will add greatly to the strength of the North. Moreover, two Territories, Oregon and Minnesota, will soon demand admission as free States, and efforts are being made to bring in three more from the territory conquered from Mexico. On the contrary, there is not a single Territory in progress in the Southern section. The prospect, then, is that the two sections in the Senate will soon stand, 20 Northern States to 14 Southern. These great changes, which must take place in the next decade, will effectually destroy the equilibrium which once existed, and give to the North control of all branches of the government.

"Had these changes been the result of time alone, the South

would not complain, but they were caused by the legislation of the common government—first, the series of acts by which the South has been excluded from the territory belonging to all the States; second, the laying of an undue proportion of the burden of taxation upon the South, and, lastly, the measures by which the government has been changed from a Federal republic to a consolidated democracy. As the North has absolute control over this government, it is manifest that on all questions between it and the South, the interests of the latter will be sacrificed to the former. No matter how oppressive the results, the South has no means of resisting through the government.

"But can the Union be saved? Yes, easily; not by the weaker party, for it can of itself do nothing—not even protect itself—but by the stronger. The North has only to will it to accomplish it—to do justice by conceding to the South an equal right to the acquired territory, to carry out the stipulations relative to fugitive slaves, to cease the agitation of the slave question, and consent to an amendment restoring to the South the power she once possessed of protecting herself.

"It is time, Senators, that there should be an open avowal as to what is intended to be done. If you, who represent the stronger portion, are not willing to settle on these principles, say so, and let the States separate in peace. If you are unwilling we should part in peace, tell us so, and we shall know what to do, when you reduce the question to submission or resistance."

The Senators and onlookers listened in profound silence to the reading of this remarkable paper, and at its conclusion Webster arose to say a word of personal kindness to the dying Southern leader. Then gentle hands supported him as he tottered from the Capitol and drove back to his lodgings at Hill's boarding-house. As his last moments approached, his mind dwelt constantly upon the problems which confronted the country. "The South! The poor South!" he murmured. "God knows what will become of her!" On March 31, four weeks after the address in the Senate, a message flashed over the country: "John C. Calhoun is dead!"

The tragic feature of the great Southern leader's career lay in his inability to see that the failure of the South was caused not primarily by hostile legislation, but by the weakness of her industrial and social system. "The equilibrium plan, by which slavery is to repress and keep back the institutions of freedom, is a confession of the weakness of slavery," wrote one free-soil advocate. "It shows what must be its own destiny in case of disunion and if left to itself. Why is it that the slave States need new guards? Simply because free institutions are outstripping them. In this age, can it be dreamed of that freedom shall be kept back because slavery cannot go forward?"

On March 7 Webster spoke. Webster was looked upon as the antislavery champion. It was hoped that he would repudiate Clay's compromise measures, and throw the weight of his influence against opening New Mexico to slavery, and against enacting a stringent fugitive-slave law. He did nothing of the sort. Pointing out that the nature of the soil would make it impossible for slavery to secure a foothold in the territory ceded from Mexico, he held that legal exclusion would be a needless humiliation for the South. The North had been unmindful of their duty in aiding slaves to escape, he said, and offered to support an effective fugitive-slave law.

Secession he denounced as illegal, unpracticable, unthinkable. "I hear with distress the word secession," he said. "Secession! Peaceable secession! Sir, your eyes and mine are never destined to see that miracle. The dismemberment of this country without convulsion! Why, sir, our ancestors—our fathers and grandfathers would reproach us, and our children and grandchildren would cry out 'Shame!' To break up this government, to dismember this great country, to astonish Europe with an act of folly! No, sir! No, sir! There will be no secession. Gentlemen are not serious when they talk of secession."

Despite the unexpected support of Webster, despite Clay's able leadership, the compromise measures at first were defeated. Among them were so many provisions to which certain groups were irrevocably opposed, that there was no hope that all could be passed when linked together. Some were willing to vote for the admission of California, but not for territorial governments in New Mexico without the exclusion of slavery; some would vote for the territorial governments, but not for the Texas boundary. The extreme antislavery men insisted upon reviving the principle of the Wilmot Proviso, the extreme proslavery men would not accept the admission of California. Moreover, President Taylor was opposed to the compromise bill and did his best to defeat it. Broken in health, exhausted, despairing, Clay gave up the battle and went to Newport to recuperate. Then happened the unexpected. On July 9 President Taylor died suddenly from an acute attack of cholera morbus, and was succeeded by Millard Fillmore, of New York, who favored the compromise. At the same time the Southern radicals were weakened by the refusal of the people of the South to follow their leadership. A canvass of the Southern press showed only 50 out of 300 newspapers in favor of extreme measures, while a convention which met at Nashville opposed secession and showed a willingness to compromise. The measures were taken up separately and passed one after the other—the fixing of the Texas boundary line, the admission of California as a free State, the organization of New Mexico without excluding slavery, the fugitive-slave law, the prohibition of the slave-trade in the District of Columbia.

The Compromise of 1850 was a makeshift at best, a settlement of the points of immediate contention. The mortal disease which afflicted the country, the disease which had appeared in the Missouri Compromise, in nullification, and again with the annexation of Texas, this disease the compromise did not touch. It left the nation still divided into two sections, with contrasting economic systems and conflicting interests, sections already fired with hostility, the weaker conscious of its helplessness and apprehensive of the future.

Clay and Webster and other ardent unionists pleaded with the people to give finality to their compromise. Everywhere, North and South, the extremists were denounced as the enemies of the country, and the compromise was extolled as the sole hope of the nation. Webster rebuked the fanaticism of the Northern Abolitionists; Clay thundered against the Southern secessionists as traitors. Under the lulling influence of the old-school statesmen, the people turned to their daily tasks, glad to forget the bitter sectional strife.

The fears of the South were partly allayed by the return to power of the Democratic party. Fillmore executed the compromise measures faithfully. But when the Whig convention met in 1852, the faction in the party opposed to "finality" gained the ascendancy, and, repudiating the President, nominated General Scott. On the other hand, the Democrats named Franklin Pierce, of New Hampshire, who promised to abide by the compromise measures—"the act for reclaiming fugitives from service and labor included." When the election was held, and it was found that Pierce had received 254 electoral votes to 42 for Scott, the country settled back in the expectation of a long period of repose. Bitter disappointment was in store. On January 4, 1854, Stephen A. Douglas, of Illinois, leader of the Northern Democracy, and the keenest parliamentarian of his party, reported to the Senate a bill for organizing the Territory of Nebraska "with or without slavery." Instantly the antislavery men took alarm. Since Nebraska was to be carved out of that part of the Louisiana purchase territory north of 36° 30', the bill was a repudiation of the Missouri Compromise. Salmon P. Chase, Charles Sumner, Benjamin F. Wade, and other antislavery leaders issued an address to the people of the United States denouncing the bill as a violation of a solemn pledge, as a "criminal betrayal of precious rights, as part and parcel of an atrocious plot to exclude from a vast unoccupied region immigrants from the Old World and free laborers from our own States, and convert it into a dreary region of despotism, inhabited by masters and slaves."

It would have been wise for the Southerners to refuse this bait, by reaffirming their allegiance to the Missouri Compromise and voting down the slavery clause in the Nebraska bill. Even should it prove possible to use slave labor in the new Territory, even should the slaveholders gain control of the State, it would not redress the lost sectional balance of power. On the other hand, to repudiate "finality," and begin again the struggle for more slave territory, would unite Northern sentiment and provoke the evil it was designed to prevent.

But the South would not accept the position of a minority section. The Southern leaders rallied around Douglas, induced President Pierce to give his sanction to the new doctrine of "squatter sovereignty," made the Nebraska bill a party measure, and whipped into line the wavering Northern Democrats.

On January 30 Douglas rose in the Senate to defend his bill. A short, thick-set, burly man, with large, round head, heavy hair, and dark complexion, he seemed the personification of belligerency. At present his face was flushed with anger, and his eyes wandered menacingly. "Mr. President," he said, "it is true that the express enactment of the Missouri Compromise Act covered only the territory acquired from France, but the principle of the act required that it should be extended indefinitely westward whenever new purchases should be made. When Texas was annexed, the compromise line was extended through that territory by a clause in the treaty prohibiting slavery in any States formed from it north of 36° 30′. This was done for the purpose of preserving the principle, in order that it might be extended to the Pacific, whenever we should acquire the country that far.

"Then, sir, in 1848, when we acquired California and New Mexico, I proposed a bill to extend the Missouri Compromise line through those Territories. This bill was defeated, and for the first time the principles of the Compromise of 1820 were abandoned. By whom was the bill defeated? By Northerners, with Free-soil proclivities. Who, then, was faithless? The very men who now insist that the Missouri Compromise was a solemn compact were the first to violate it and cause it to be superseded by the Compromise of 1850. Sir, the Compromise of 1850 abandoned the idea of a geographical boundary between free and slave States, and substituted a principle of self-government which allowed the people of any Territory to do as they thought proper in regard to the admission of slavery. Thus was the Missouri Compromise superseded by a principle which was equally applicable to the country north as well as south of 36° 30′."

This reasoning was savagely attacked by Chase. "The truth is," he said, "the compromise acts of 1850 were not intended to introduce any principle of territorial organization to any other territory than that covered by them. Senators, will you unite in a statement which you know to be contradicted by the history of the country? If you wish to break up the time-honored compact of the Missouri Compromise, do it openly. Do not declare it inoperative because superseded by the principles of 1850. You may pass it here, but the effect will be to satisfy all thinking men that no compromises with slavery will endure, except so long as they serve the interests of slavery. This discussion will light up a fire which may consume those who kindle it."

After a bitter struggle, in which sectional animosity was aroused to the highest pitch, the bill was passed; in the Senate 37 to 14, and in the House of Representatives 113 to 100. On May 30, 1854, President Pierce affixed his signature. This rash measure tended to unite the formerly discordant antislavery elements of the North. "The Fugitive Law did much to unglue the eyes," said Emerson, "and now the Nebraska bill leaves us staring." Thousands of earnest men, convinced that there was no hope of blocking the extension of slavery through the medium of the old parties, drew together to organize a party of their own. Republicans, they called themselves. They asserted that neither Congress nor a Territorial Legislature had authority, under the Constitution, to establish slavery in a Territory. So rapidly did they expand that, two years later, in their first presidential contest, they polled 1,300,000 votes.

Douglas's bill divided Nebraska into two Territories, one to retain the name Nebraska and the other to be called Kansas. The Southern leaders had little hope of establishing slavery in the former, but they felt sure that a rush of Missourians into Kansas would win that fertile region for the South. They were doomed to disappointment.

Now that the principle of "squatter sovereignty" had been accepted, the Northerners turned it to their own advantage by pouring free-soil settlers into the new territory. Eli Thayer, of Massachusetts, organized the Emigrant Aid Society, and sent out hundreds of families to take up claims along the Kansas River. This aroused the South, and an agitation was started, marked by public meetings, fiery speeches, and subscriptions, to aid slaveholders to emigrate and so "save Kansas." Two groups of settlements were established in the Territory, the one composed chiefly of pronounced antislavery men, the other of slaveholders.

This development had not been contemplated by Douglas. Trouble could not be avoided. When the first election was held, hundreds of Missourians came across the border, took possession of the polls, and elected a proslavery Legislature. Thereupon the free-soil men refused to recognize the government. They called a convention at Topeka, and drew up a constitution of their own in which slavery was prohibited. Bloodshed followed. The proslavery party attacked the town of Lawrence, looted newspaper offices, sacked stores, and destroyed a large stone hotel. In retaliation John Brown, a fanatical abolitionist, entered the settlements of the slavery party on the Pottawattamie Creek, and summoning a number of men from their houses, one by one, split their heads open with a broadsword. This was the signal for the outbreak of a fierce guerilla war. Bands of men from each side wandered over the Territory, plundering, shooting, burning. Two hundred lives were sacrificed, and two million dollars' worth of property destroyed. This ominous event made many thoughtful men despair of the future, for in the struggle upon the plains of Kansas they saw the prelude to the war between the sections.

The North was highly excited. Newspapers filled their columns with inflammatory articles, public speakers denounced the South violently, preachers in the pulpit made appeals for money and arms with which to fight slavery in Kansas. The effect upon the two old parties in the North promised to be disastrous. Every day voters were deserting both the Democrats and the Whigs, because neither would take a determined stand against slavery. The Republican party, which had denounced slavery as a "moral, social and political evil," grew rapidly. The Democratic leaders, seeing that the Kansas affair was likely to be their undoing, now made strenuous efforts to settle the matter before the election of 1856. Senator Toombs introduced a bill abolishing both governments in Kansas, calling for a new constitutional convention, and guaranteeing a fair election.

This bill was practically a surrender by the Democrats, for the antislavery group in Kansas was now in the majority, but the Republican leaders would not accept it. "So far as the subject of slavery is concerned," said Seward, "the most that can be claimed for the bill is that it gives an equal chance to the people of Kansas to choose between freedom and slavery. . . . The standard of political justice which commends itself to me is a more rigid one. I recognize no equality in moral right or political expediency between slavery and freedom." In this spirit the Republican party nominated John C. Frémont for the Presidency, and entered the campaign, pledged to the abolition in the Territories of slavery and polygamy, "those twin relics of barbarism."

The South answered with an open threat of secession. "If Frémont is elected," wrote Governor Wise, of Virginia, "there will be a revolution. . . . We will not remain in confederacy with enemies." And though the Republican newspapers ridiculed "the stale disunion threat," it had a sobering effect upon the North. The Democratic convention, passing by Douglas, nominated James Buchanan, of Pennsylvania. Buchanan had been in England when the Kansas-Nebraska bill was passed, and so had had no part in reopening the slavery question. He now favored the Toombs bill, with its "recognition of the rights of the people of Kansas to decide upon their own affairs." To many the choice seemed to lie between union and disunion, and when the vote was counted, it was found that Buchanan had received 174 electoral votes to 114 for Frémont. Once more the conservative character of the American people had postponed the crisis, and the country, exhausted by the protracted excitement, relapsed into quiet. Hardly four months had passed, however, when a most unexpected incident once more aroused sectional animosities to the highest pitch.

Two days after the inauguration of Buchanan, an old man in judicial robes, seated in the secluded semicircular room in the basement of the Capitol where for decades the Supreme

Court had held its sessions, began the reading of an opinion. Beside him, seated in stately high-backed chairs, were his fellow justices, while behind, just discernible in the gloom of the ill-lighted apartment, was the portrait of Chief Justice Marshall. The speaker was a tall, square-shouldered man, with large mouth, wrinkled face, and slender hands—a gaunt, ungainly, but none the less impressive man. As he read, his hollow voice, which resounded from the arches of the low ceiling, was audible to all. It was Chief Justice Taney, delivering the opinion on the Dred Scott case, which declared the Missouri Compromise unconstitutional.

Years before, in 1834, Doctor Emerson, an army surgeon, had taken the slave Dred Scott to a post in the Illinois Territory, on soil made free by the Missouri Compromise. Encouraged by some citizens of Missouri, Scott sued for his freedom, basing his claim upon his residence on free soil. The case finally came before the Supreme Court. The majority of the justices were of opinion that Scott had no right to plead, and so the Court could easily have avoided passing upon the dangerous question of the right of Congress to exclude slavery from the Territories. But they persuaded themselves that it was their duty to make a decision which would strip Congress of the power of meddling with slavery, and thus bring peace to the distracted nation. So the fatal opinion was read.

William Pinkney had once said of Taney: "I can answer his arguments, I am not afraid of his logic, but that infernal apostolic manner of his there is no replying to." Certainly the listeners, on this important occasion, were impressed with the sincerity as well as the ability of the aged jurist. "Can a negro whose ancestors were imported into this country and sold as slaves become a member of the political community formed and brought into existence by the Constitution of the United States," he asked, "and as such become entitled to all the rights and immunities guaranteed by that instrument to the citizen?" He cannot. "In the opinion of the Court, the legislation and histories of the times, and the language used in the Declaration of Independence, show that neither the class of persons who had been imported as slaves, nor their descen-

dants, whether they had become free or not, were then acknowledged as a part of the people." "It is difficult, at this day, to
realize the state of public opinion in relation to that unfortunate race which prevailed in the civilized and enlightened portions of the world at the time . . . but the public history of
every European nation displays it in a manner too plain to be
mistaken. They had for more than a century been regarded as
beings of an inferior order, and altogether unfit to associate
with the white race, either in social or political relations; and
so far inferior that they had no rights which the white man
was bound to respect."

And now we ask: was Congress authorized to pass the Missouri Compromise Act "under any of the powers granted to it
by the Constitution?" The Louisiana territory "was acquired
by the general government, as the representative and trustee
of the people of the United States, and it must therefore be
held in that character for their common and equal benefit. . . .
It seems, however, to be supposed that there is a difference between property in a slave and other property, and that different rules may be applied to it in expounding the Constitution
of the United States." But "the right of property in a slave
is distinctly and expressly affirmed in the Constitution." It is
the opinion of the Court, therefore, that the Missouri Compromise Act "is not warranted by the Constitution, and is therefore void."

This opinion was received in the North with a tremendous
burst of anger. It is founded on false historical statements,
said the Republican press, it is bad law, it is a partisan judgment, it makes the Constitution the bulwark of inhumanity
and oppression. The Court has descended from its high position and has dragged its sacred garments in the mire of proslavery politics. "The Supreme Court of the United States
attempts to command the people of the United States to accept the principle that one man can own another man," said
Seward in the Senate, "and that they must guarantee the in-
violability of that false and pernicious property. The people
of the United States never can, and they never will, accept
principles so unconstitutional and abhorrent. . . . We shall

reorganize the Court, and then reform its political sentiments and practices, and bring them into harmony with the Constitution and the laws of nature."

The South grasped at the Dred Scott decision as a drowning man grasps at a straw. "At last we have found a means of protecting ourselves against the Northern majority," they said. "Nullification failed us, the efforts to extend slave territory have been inadequate, compromises have worked to the advantage of the North, but now that the Supreme Court has come to our defense all will be well." Ill founded though these hopes were, the Dred Scott decision became at once in the South hardly less sacred than the Constitution. Perhaps it was inevitable that the Southern leaders, as their cause became more hopeless, should have taken ground more and more advanced in regard to slavery in the Territories. From the principles of the Missouri Compromise they had changed to "squatter sovereignty," and from "squatter sovereignty" they now moved on to the position that Congress had no authority to legislate slavery from the Territories. They were surprised when they found that practically no one in the North, not even the most loyal of northern Democrats, would accompany them in the last of these important changes.

The gulf between the Northern and Southern Democrats was made obvious by the Lincoln-Douglas debates. Douglas's term in the Senate was to expire in 1859, and in 1858 the Illinois Democrats nominated him for another term. The Republicans named Abraham Lincoln. Between the two candidates a series of joint debates was arranged, which defined the issues and convinced many Southerners that slavery could be protected only by secession.

On the afternoon of August 27, 1858, Lincoln stepped out of the Brewster House, at Freeport, Illinois, and took his seat in a high, old-fashioned wagon, beside a dozen plainly dressed farmers. As they moved off, they were greeted with cheers. A few minutes later Douglas also came out of the hotel and followed them on foot. Reaching Mechanic Street both men ascended a small platform built beneath two trees, and awaited the signal to begin their debate. Although the sky was overcast and the air was chilly, 10,000 people had gathered around the stand. A strange contrast they presented, these two rivals. Douglas was short and stout, his round face confident. He was attired in a dark-blue coat with shiny buttons and ruffled shirt. Lincoln was an emaciated man, with a homely, sorrowful face, wearing an old stovepipe hat, coat with sleeves far too short, and baggy trousers over rough boots.

Lincoln began by answering seven questions which Douglas had propounded on a previous occasion. Then he proceeded to ask several questions of his own, among them the following: "Can the people of a United States Territory, in any lawful way, against the wish of any citizen of the United States, exclude slavery from its limits prior to the formation of a State constitution?"

"I answer emphatically," said Douglas in reply, "as Mr. Lincoln has heard me answer a hundred times from every stump in Illinois, that in my opinion the people of a Territory can, by lawful means, exclude slavery from their limits prior to the formation of a State constitution. . . . It matters not what way the Supreme Court may hereafter decide as to the abstract question, whether slavery may or may not go into a Territory under the Constitution; the people have the lawful means to introduce it or exclude it as they please, for the reason that slavery cannot exist a day or an hour anywhere, unless it is supported by local police regulations. Those police regulations can only be established by the local Legislature; and if the people are opposed to slavery, they will elect representatives to that body who will by unfriendly legislation effectually prevent the introduction of it in their midst."

Hardly had Douglas completed this answer when the thousands of Democrats in the crowd burst into tremendous applause, which continued so long that Douglas had to request them to stop so that he could continue his address. The Republicans were silent. It seemed that Douglas had earned a new triumph. Democratic papers all over Illinois applauded the answer. The Democrats carried the State Legislature, and Douglas returned to the Senate the most prominent leader in the party.

But hardly had Congress reassembled when the true result of Lincoln's searching question became apparent. The Southern Democrats demanded full compliance with the spirit as well as the letter of the Dred Scott decision. "I give you warning now," said Senator Brown, of Mississippi, "that if Kansas legislates in a spirit of hostility to slavery, the Southern people will come to Congress and demand that you annul their laws." "Yes," added Senator Jefferson Davis, "in the eyes of the South, the Freeport doctrine is a dangerous heresy, destructive of every hope of concord and peace." To these challenges Douglas could only reply: "I tell you, gentlemen of the South, in all candor, I do not believe a Democratic candidate can ever carry one State of the North on the platform that it is the duty of the Federal Government to force the people of a Territory to have slavery when they do not want it." Lincoln had driven a wedge between the Northern and the Southern wing of the Democratic party.

And now the long-continued strife had developed a spirit of aggravated hostility between the two sections which augured ill for the immediate future. Forgotten were the days when men from North and South fought side by side for independence, forgotten the mutual sufferings and sacrifices of Valley Forge, forgotten the triumphs of Saratoga and Yorktown. The publication of *Uncle Tom's Cabin*, by Harriet Beecher Stowe, tended to crystallize sentiment in the North against slavery and the slaveholders. The North pictured the typical Southerner as a quixotic, aristocratic fire-eater; the South looked upon the Northerner as a cold, hypocritical person, noted for pious phrases and sharp practice in business. It was the last stage in the long preparation for civil war.

While the country was in this state of tension, John Brown, of Pottawattamie fame, conceived the wild idea of establishing camps in the Appalachians, whence he could raid the neighboring plantations and incite the slaves to desert their masters. On the night of October 16, 1859, Brown's band of nineteen men seized the Baltimore and Ohio bridge over the Potomac, at Harper's Ferry, cut the telegraph wires, and occupied the United States arsenal. The next morning the citizens of Harper's Ferry seized their arms. Brown and his followers took refuge in an engine-house, where they were besieged. Later Colonel Robert E. Lee came up with a band of marines, battered down the doors, and captured Brown, severely wounded, with four of his band. Four others had escaped and ten had been killed. Brown was tried in Virginia, found guilty of treason, and promptly hanged.

During his trial he manifested the utmost composure. The invasion of Virginia, like his killings in Kansas, he regarded as "the Lord's work." His willingness to die in "a sacred cause" excited the sympathy of thousands in the North who did not approve of his methods. Governor Wise, of Virginia, was bombarded with petitions asking for his pardon, while Emerson, Theodore Parker, and others glorified him as a martyr. This created in the South the impression that Northern sentiment now favored inciting the slaves to rebellion, and swelled the ranks of the secessionists. Thus the escapade of a misguided fanatic exerted a powerful influence in hastening the crisis.

In the Democratic convention of 1860, which met in Institute Hall at Charleston, South Carolina, William L. Yancey, of Alabama, was the champion of the Southern extremists. Tall, slender, with his long, black hair, his loose-fitting clothes, and graceful manners, he seemed typically Southern. As he rose and advanced to the platform, he was greeted by a deafening burst of applause, the Southern delegates springing to their feet, while gaily dressed ladies in the galleries waved their handkerchiefs.

"Mr. Chairman," he said, "the growth of the Northwest has reduced the South to a minority section. Therefore, we take the rights and the position of the minority. What is it we claim? We claim the benefit of the Constitution that was made for the protection of minorities. Your refusal to accept the principle that slavery must be protected in the Territories will bankrupt the South. We blame you greatly, you Democrats of the North, for not combating the abolitionist agitation. You have gone down before the enemy. You tell us that if you take a definite stand to protect slavery in Territories where a majority of the people oppose it the Democratic party will not carry one Northern State. But is it not better to suffer defeat upon clear principles, than gain a victory by fooling the people with ambiguous issues?"

Yancey spoke for an hour and a half. From time to time he was interrupted by thunderous applause which left no doubt that he expressed the sentiments of a majority of the Southern people. Before he closed evening came on, and the flickering gas-lights added a touch of weirdness to the impressive scene. The strained, white faces of the delegates showed only too clearly that many grasped the significance of this prologue to secession and civil war.

Several days of bitter contention followed, and then began the balloting on the party platform. The Northern Democrats favored the nomination of Douglas. They did not dare insert the Freeport doctrine in the platform, but they accomplished the same end by indorsing both "squatter sovereignty" and the Dred Scott decision. This the Southerners considered entirely illogical. If you accept one, they said, you cannot indorse the other. The Dred Scott decision superseded and nullified "squatter sovereignty." To insert "squatter sovereignty" in the Democratic platform can mean only that the party sanctions unconstitutional methods of excluding slavery from the Territories.

The Douglas men would yield nothing. They knew that to accept the Southern contention would mean death to the Democratic party in the North. Having a majority in the convention they forced through their own platform. The effect was instantaneous. When the final vote had been taken a member of the Alabama delegation rose and made his way to the clerk's desk. As he came forward, a rustle of excitement passed over the audience, a shudder of apprehension as it were, followed by silence. "I have been instructed to announce," he said, "that the Alabama delegates will at once withdraw from the convention." After he had given, in a few words, the reasons for this step, the delegates arose from their seats and retired to the back of the hall. Then other Southern delegations went out in quick succession—Mississippi, Louisiana, South Carolina, Florida, Texas, Arkansas, Georgia. At last the Democratic party, which long had been the greatest cementing force between North and South, was split asunder.

After balloting in vain three days for a candidate, the remnant of the convention adjourned to meet again in Baltimore. When it reassembled, a new secession followed, the Virginians and most of the delegates from North Carolina, Tennessee, Kentucky, and Maryland withdrawing. The Northern Democrats then nominated Douglas. The Baltimore seceders, joined by most of the seceders from the Charleston convention, met in the Maryland Institute Hall, in Baltimore, and nominated John C. Breckinridge.

The Republican convention assembled in the Chicago "wigwam," which has been described as a small edition of the New York Crystal Palace, built of boards and capable of holding 10,000 persons. It was widely believed that William H. Seward would be nominated on the first ballot. He was the representative man of the party; he had the enthusiastic support of New York with its seventy delegates; his candidacy was in the hands of the astutest politicians in America. The New Yorkers were exultant. At their headquarters champagne flowed freely, while their bands went the rounds serenading the different delegations whose support they expected.

But while they rejoiced their opponents worked. Scores spent the night passing from one caucus room to another, pleading against the nomination of Seward. He was unpopular in Pennsylvania, they said; he was an extremist whom it would be impossible to elect; he had injured himself and the party by his talk about "irrepressible conflict." Why not unite on "old Abe Lincoln," they asked, the man of the people, the rail-splitter, to whom no such objections could be urged? The next morning the Lincoln men entered the convention hall, pale and haggard but hopeful.

On the first ballot Seward received 173½ votes, Lincoln 102, and all other candidates 189½. Two hundred and thirty-three were necessary for nomination. On the next vote several States swung to Lincoln, and the count stood: Seward, 184½; Lincoln, 181; other candidates, 99½. The third ballot blasted Seward's hopes, for it gave Lincoln 231½ votes, only 1½ less

than the necessary number for nomination. Before the count
was announced D. K. Cartter, of Ohio, mounted his chair
and said: "I rise, Mr. Chairman, to announce the change of
4 votes of Ohio from Mr. Chase to Mr. Lincoln." For a moment there was silence. Then pandemonium broke forth. So
tremendous was the shouting that the report of the cannon
placed on the roof of the "wigwam" to announce the nomination could hardly be heard by those within.

Despite the disruption of the Democratic party few thought
that Lincoln could secure a majority in the electoral college.
The remnants of the Whig party, in conjunction with the
Know-Nothings, put in nomination John Bell, of Tennessee,
and calling themselves the only truly national party, appealed
to the voters to save the Union by rebuking radicalism and
sectionalism. The Republicans laughed at the threat of the
South that Lincoln's election would be followed by secession.
"The old Mumbo-Jumbo is occasionally paraded in the North,"
said Lowell, "but, however many old women may be frightened, the pulse of the stock market remains provokingly
calm." "For ten, aye for twenty years, these threats have
been renewed," said Seward. "Who's afraid? Nobody's
afraid."

These assurances allayed the fears of the mass of voters,
and Lincoln swept the North, carrying every free State. He
secured, in all, 180 electoral votes to 72 for Breckinridge, 39
for Bell, and 12 for Douglas. Lincoln's popular vote was
1,857,610, to 1,291,574 for Douglas, 850,082 for Breckinridge,
and 646,124 for Bell. At last the North had made use of its
superior numbers to send to the White House a man who was
open in his hostility to slavery. The forty-years political conflict between the sections was over. It remained now to be
seen whether the South would acquiesce in the verdict; whether
it would remain in the Union, accepting the position of a
minority section, submitting to the measures of the majority,
and perhaps looking forward to gradual emancipation; or
whether it would withdraw, running the desperate hazard of
war, or the hardly less desperate hazard of an independent
career as a Southern Confederacy.

The people of the border States hesitated, but the cotton States were not long in making their choice. A few days after the election of Lincoln, the country was startled by the news that the South Carolina Legislature had called for the election of delegates to a convention to consider the question of secession. This convention met December 17, and three days later passed a formal "Ordinance dissolving the union between the State of South Carolina and the other States united with her under the compact entitled 'The Constitution of the United States of America.'"

The Gulf States followed South Carolina out of the Union —Mississippi, Florida, Alabama, Georgia, Louisiana, and Texas. Delegates from these States assembled at Montgomery, Alabama, February 4, 1861, and in a few days adopted a constitution for the Confederate States of America. Jefferson Davis was chosen the first President, and hasty preparations were made to put the new Confederacy in a posture of defense. The South had acted, it now remained to be seen what Lincoln and the Northern States would do about it.

CHAPTER XX

CIVIL WAR

SHORTLY after one o'clock, March 4, 1861, Abraham Lincoln stepped out on the eastern portico of the Capitol to read his inaugural. His tall, gaunt figure stooped, while his worn, colorless face was weary and anxious. Beside him stood two men who had played each a fateful part in hastening the crisis which now confronted the President-elect—Stephen A. Douglas, sponsor of popular sovereignty, and Roger B. Taney, author of the Dred Scott decision. As Lincoln seemed not to know what to do with his tall hat and gold-knobbed cane, Douglas took them from him and held them throughout the address.

"Fellow citizens," said the President-elect, in a firm, clear voice, "I enter upon my duties under great and peculiar difficulties. A disruption of the Federal Union, heretofore only menaced, is now formidably attempted. I hold that in the contemplation of universal law and of the Constitution, the union of these States is perpetual. No State, upon its own motion, can lawfully get out of the Union, and resolves and ordinances to that effect are legally void. I shall take care, as the Constitution itself expressly enjoins upon me, that the laws of the Union be faithfully executed in all the States. I trust this will not be regarded as a menace, but only as the declared purpose of the Union that it will constitutionally defend and maintain itself. The power confided to me will be used to hold, occupy, and possess the property and places belonging to the government, and to collect duties and imposts.

"In all important questions, not specially provided for by the Constitution, the majority must decide. If a minority in such a case will secede rather than acquiesce, they make a precedent, which, in turn, will divide and ruin them, for a minority of their own will secede from them whenever a majority refuses to be controlled by such minority. For instance, why may not any portion of the new Confederacy, a year or two hence, arbitrarily secede again, precisely as portions of the present Union now claim to secede from it? Plainly the central idea of secession is the essence of anarchy. In your hands, my dissatisfied fellow countrymen, and not in mine, is the momentous issue of civil war. The government will not assail you. You have no oath registered in heaven to destroy the government, while I shall have the most solemn one to 'preserve, protect, and defend it.' We must not be enemies. The mystic cords of memory, stretching from every battle-field and patriot grave to every living heart and hearthstone all over this broad land, will yet swell the chorus of the Union, when again touched, as surely they will be, by the better angels of our nature."

In this memorable address Lincoln thus contented himself with intimating that the Union would be preserved; he did not touch upon the underlying causes of disunion. Yet Lincoln understood these causes clearly. Not even the astute intellect of Calhoun had grasped more firmly the meaning of the long train of events from the Missouri Compromise to secession. Three years before, in an address at Springfield, he had declared: "A house divided against itself cannot stand; I believe this government cannot endure permanently half slave and half free." But now, with disunion at hand, Lincoln could not talk thus boldly. Eight slaveholding States remained in the Union; to declare war on slavery might drive them into the Confederacy. Yet Lincoln was determined to preserve the Union, and he knew that slavery was the cause of disunion. He must have realized the folly of staving off disruption, perhaps at the cost of civil war, only to leave the cause of disruption untouched. Many sincere men in the North reproved him bitterly for "temporizing with the slavery iniquity," but could they have read his thoughts they would have seen there the determination to restore permanently the "divided house" by destroying the social and economic structure of the South.

Just before dawn on April 12, 1861, the watchers in Fort Sumter looked anxiously out over Charleston harbor. The night was misty and dark, but the low-lying promontories of

Sullivan's Island and Cumming's Point could be distinguished to north and south, while the distant lights of the city twinkled in the water. Suddenly there appeared from the direction of Fort Johnson a flash of light, followed by the roar of a mortar, and a shell mounted high, curved through the air, and fell with a crash within the fort. There it burst. Batteries on all sides now opened. Civil war, the war which Clay, Webster, and Calhoun had labored so long to avert, had begun.

Early in March Confederate agents had come to Washington to negotiate a treaty between the embryo republic and the United States, securing the delivery of forts, arsenals, and lighthouses within the limits of the Confederacy, dividing the public property and apportioning the public debt. Lincoln refused to see them, but Seward exchanged opinions with them, and gave them to understand that Fort Sumter would be evacuated. In this matter he acted upon his own responsibility. Lincoln, it seems, knew nothing of his promises. April 8, the President notified the Governor of South Carolina that an attempt would be made to supply Fort Sumter with provisions, and the same day relief ships sailed from New York. The President was determined to force the issue before the Confederacy became strongly established, and while union sentiment in the North was at white heat. In this sense the Civil War was Lincoln's war, and the preservation of the Union Lincoln's act.

In firing upon Sumter the Confederates were playing into Lincoln's hands. He had promised that the government would not assail them. Had they withheld their hands, it is possible that the war might have been averted. But they would not tolerate a Federal fort within the limits of the Confederacy, commanding as it did the approach to one of their principal ports. So the order was issued to fire the first gun. The bombardment lasted thirty-four hours. The garrison held out until fire was raging within and supplies were almost exhausted. It was almost a bloodless battle, for not a man was killed on either side. On the 14th, after the men in blue had run up and saluted the Stars and Stripes, the Confederates conveyed them down the harbor to the United States fleet outside. The next day Lincoln called for 75,000 volunteers, and the mass of the Northern people, forgetting party distinctions, answered with an outburst of loyalty. Every town became gay with bunting; crowds paraded cheering for the Union, war sermons were preached, village greens were converted into mustering grounds.

The crisis in the wavering border slave States now became acute. The time had come when they must fight either for or against the Confederacy. After serious deliberation four seceded—Virginia, April 17; Arkansas, May 6; North Carolina, May 20; and Tennessee, June 8. For many weeks Maryland, Kentucky, and Missouri hung in the balance, but the strong Union sentiment existing in these States, together with Lincoln's tact, eventually saved them for the Union. But the border slaveholders felt that the cause of the Confederacy was their cause, and thousands of Marylanders, Kentuckians, and Missourians fought throughout the war under the Stars and Bars.

The Southern people entered the war with confidence. They failed to estimate aright the various factors which made their task almost hopeless from the first. It seems strange that a people dependent in large measure for their existence upon ocean traffic, yet possessing no adequate means of defending that traffic, could have hoped for success in a war of attrition. The South was by no means a self-sufficient economic unit. Its energies were devoted to raising staple crops—cotton, tobacco, rice, sugar—which it shipped either to the North or across the Atlantic in exchange for fabricated goods. Lacking industrial centres, it was incapable of producing many essential articles—cloth, steel, rolling-stock, household utensils, shoes, farm implements. The weakness of the Southern industrial system, which had brought defeat to the South in the struggle for political supremacy in the Union, now brought disaster upon the field of battle.

On April 19, 1861, President Lincoln declared a blockade of the Confederacy, and before many months hundreds of Federal war-ships were hovering off the coasts. The grip upon Southern commerce grew tighter and tighter. Soon salt, coffee, medicines, clothing, were hardly to be had at any price. The Confederate Government had difficulty in smuggling in the paper with which to print its currency. It had to improvise factories for the manufacture of arms and ammunition, and train unskilled hands to do the work. To replace railway material as it wore out was almost impossible. The deterioration of rails, cars, and locomotives, which made transportation more and more difficult, played an important part in the collapse of the Confederacy. Southern soldiers had to rely partly upon the raiding of a base or the capture of a supply-train to meet the need for clothing and food. "Come out of them clothes, Yank! Take off them boots! We want them blankets," were the cries often heard as the ragged men in gray closed in on their prey.

The South had the advantage of fighting upon interior lines, but this was more than offset by other geographic conditions. The Appalachian barrier, which extended from Virginia to Georgia, made communication difficult between the Eastern States and the Mississippi valley. Not only were there few railways crossing the mountains, but the poor whites who inhabited the region were unionist in sentiment. In the West the Mississippi River, which by July, 1863, had been cleared of Confederate batteries, cut through the body of the South, isolating the great food-producing States of Louisiana, Arkansas, and Texas.

In man-power the North was vastly superior. The population of the non-seceding States in 1860 was 22,350,000; that of the Confederacy 9,099,000, of whom 3,500,000 were slaves and 500,000 hostile mountaineers. It is probable that the reservoir of men capable of bearing arms upon which the Confederacy could draw, even with the recruits from Maryland, Kentucky, and Missouri, amounted to not more than 1,000,000. On the other hand, not only did the fact that slaves performed most of the manual labor in the South release thousands of whites for service at the front, but negroes often served as teamsters, laborers, cooks, and servants in the army.

In the matter of trained officers, the advantage remained with the Confederacy. Many of the ablest soldiers in the old army, men who had received their education at West Point and their seasoning at Buena Vista or Chapultepec, were natives of the South. As their States went out of the Union, they handed in their resignations and took new commissions under the Confederacy. The loss of these men greatly handicapped the Federal Government in building up an effective military machine.

Throughout the war the State-rights doctrine, which the South had espoused in the long political controversy with the North, remained to hinder the administration at Richmond. Governors of States resisted the conscription of men, the impressment of food, the suspension of the writ of habeas corpus, the regulation of exports and imports. Governor Joseph Brown, of Georgia, declared that he was ready to fight both the Union and the Confederacy if they did not stop invading the sovereign rights of Georgia. Governor Vance, of North Carolina, ignored orders from Richmond, freed military prisoners, and threatened to resist in arms the acts of President Davis.

Whereas in the North President Lincoln exercised almost despotic war powers, the government at Richmond was hampered by inconvenient constitutional limitations. The Confederacy never made its paper money legal tender, it never created a national banking system, as did the North, it never organized a Supreme Court. One Virginia newspaper, realizing that the administration must have a free hand if the Confederacy was to survive, pleaded with the opposition to stop complaining of imaginary violations of the Constitution and devote their efforts to winning independence.

In financing the war the Confederacy was equally handicapped. The South had little fluid capital, and so found it difficult to float loans. Its wealth was in cotton and tobacco, and its inability to market these crops brought disaster to its fiscal policy. The government early became committed to the issue of Treasury notes. It is estimated that the total volume of Confederate paper was not less than a billion dollars. Depreciation set in at once, and in February, 1864, the paper dollar was worth only six cents. Some months later one of Lee's officers spent an entire month's salary for a plug of tobacco.

The North, too, depended in part upon paper money, and

issued about $450,000,000 of greenbacks, or non-interest bearing Treasury notes. The greenbacks fluctuated with the varying fortunes of the Union. At one time they were worth little more than one-third of their face value. The sale of government bonds proved a more certain source of revenue, while an income tax, heavy internal duties, and a high tariff raised large sums. Toward the close of the war taxation was bringing in half a billion a year. In 1863 Congress passed a law establishing a national banking system, which aided in stabilizing the currency and opened an eager market for the sale of government bonds.

One cause of optimism in the South at the opening of the war was the expectation of English sympathy and perhaps aid. English spinners depended largely upon Southern cotton, and with the ports of the Confederacy blockaded thousands would be thrown out of work. But the South failed to foresee that the English workers themselves would sympathize with the North, because they felt that the North was fighting for free labor. Although the governing British aristocracy favored the South, the sentiment of the nation was unfavorable to intervention.

None the less, more than once the two nations were upon the verge of war. In 1861 the Confederacy appointed James Mason and John Slidell commissioners to England and France to secure recognition and alliance. They ran the blockade to Havana, and took passage on the British mail-steamer *Trent*. Captain Charles Wilkes, of the United States war-vessel *Jacinto*, overhauled the *Trent*, took off the commissioners, and carried them prisoners to Boston. England was greatly incensed and began preparations for war. After some delay Lincoln surrendered the prisoners with the statement that Captain Wilkes had acted without authority from the government.

Having escaped this danger, the Federal Government soon found itself in a new controversy with England. British shipyards, with the knowledge of their government, built several cruisers for the Confederacy, which did great damage to American commerce. The most famous of these was the *Alabama*. More serious still was the barely defeated project of the South to build two ironclad rams in England. These vessels were nearly ready for sea when Charles Francis Adams, the United States Minister, wrote protesting to Lord Russell. "It would be superfluous for me to point out to your lordship that this is war," he said. Russell had already awakened to the seriousness of the matter, and had just given orders to seize the rams. So Lincoln's government escaped the peril of foreign interference, and the South was forced to fight single-handed. Foreign aid was the Confederacy's one real hope of success, and when this failed defeat was but a matter of time.

After the surrender of Fort Sumter the Federal Government pressed vigorously its military preparations. By July 1, 30,000 raw troops had been collected at Washington under General Scott, while another force was stationed at Harper's Ferry. The Northern press clamored for an advance on Richmond. Scott protested that the troops were not ready, but finally yielded and ordered General Irvin McDowell to begin the invasion of Virginia. So the undisciplined troops, straggling by the way to pick berries or take naps under the trees, marched south to the vicinity of Manassas Junction. Here they encountered a force of Confederates under General Beauregard.

As the armies confronted each other across Bull Run, McDowell sent the larger part of his men in a long turning movement, on the night of July 20, to fall on the enemy's left. This manoeuvre at first was successful. General Beauregard was taken by surprise, and had it not been for the gallantry of small detachments of Confederates, who checked the Federal divisions until reinforcements could be rushed up from the right, would have been defeated.

The early part of the battle was clearly visible from the Confederate position at the Robinson house, on the north slope of a hill west of Bull Run. To the north the ground receded to Young's Branch, winding through fields, beyond were hills dotted with pine woods, while in the far distance, pencilled against the summer's sky, was the Blue Ridge. Over the hills came the Federal troops, with colors flying and bayonets set, while to the left the guns flashed through the dust clouds. Before them streamed a dozen broken Confederate regiments. As they waded through Young's Branch and pressed up the slope, the Confederate commander, General Bee, a handsome man with long hair, mustache, and goatee, turned his eyes to a bit of pine woods in his rear. There he saw a long line of Confederate infantry. "Look!" he shouted to his men. "Look, there stands Jackson like a stone wall. Rally behind the Virginians." The troops took up the cry, the flight was halted, and a new line formed to Jackson's rear and right.

Still the Federals continued their advance. They came swarming over the hill at the Robinson house—volunteer regiments in gray jackets and trousers, regulars in blue, Zouaves in blue shirts, loose red pantaloons, fez caps, and white turbans. Back and forth the battle surged. At one time the Federals were thrown down the hill toward Young's branch, at another they swept forward and threatened to break completely the rapidly thinning ranks of the Confederates. But the end was at hand. Beauregard had received reinforcements from the valley of Virginia, fresh regiments came up from the right, and the preponderance in numbers passed to his hands.

At three in the afternoon the Federals made one last charge over the plateau. A surprise awaited them. Suddenly a long gray line sprang from the ground in their very faces, fired one pointblank volley, and, giving the rebel yell, charged. The Federal troops hesitated, and then fell back in disorder down the slope and over Young's Branch. At this moment Kirby Smith's valley brigade charged their flank, and the repulse became a rout. Detachments of regulars fought to stem the tide, but the inexperienced volunteer regiments could not be reformed. The various units merged into a mob, rushing back to Washington. McDowell's defeat was complete.

In the afternoon messages came one after another to the White House announcing a Federal victory. President Lincoln, convinced that all was well, ordered his carriage and started on his usual drive. At six o'clock Secretary Seward rushed in, pale and haggard. "Have you any late news?" he asked of the President's secretaries. When they read him the telegrams announcing the victory, he told them that the report was false. "The battle is lost," he said. "McDowell is in full retreat, and calls on General Scott to save the capital." Returning from his drive a half-hour later, Lincoln heard the news of the disaster. He listened in silence without change of expression, and then set to work ordering up fresh troops and putting Washington in a posture of defense.

Beauregard did not pursue his victory. At the moment of triumph he received word that the enemy were attacking his right, and drew back his regiments to meet them. So the Federals were not molested in their flight, and most of them reached the lines at Washington. Beauregard might have captured the city had he moved forward the next day, but he held back and the opportunity passed. Both sides now prepared for a long war.

Three lines of attack were indicated to the Federal Government by the geographic and economic situation. The army of the Potomac must try to capture Richmond, the capital of the Confederacy. West of the Alleghanies the Federal armies must secure Kentucky, clear the Tennessee and Cumberland rivers, and sweep on to Chattanooga, the key to the newly developed industrial centre of the South. From Chattanooga ran the railway line to Atlanta, Macon, and Selma, where the Confederates had their gun-foundries and rolling-mills. The Confederacy would not long survive this loss. Thirdly, to sever Texas, Arkansas, and Louisiana from the main body of the Confederacy it was necessary to work down the Mississippi with land-forces and gunboats, and up by way of New Orleans and Port Hudson.

The first of these tasks proved the most difficult, and was accomplished only when the completion of the other two had riddled the Confederacy and made it impossible for the Southerners to supply their armies in Virginia. None the less, after the disaster of Bull Run, President Lincoln and Secretary Stanton began the creation of a new army for the capture of Richmond. The call for more volunteers met with a ready response in the North, and throughout the fall and winter of 1861–1862 Washington was the scene of constant drilling. General George B. McClellan was placed in command.

There were two ways to approach the Confederate capital: by water down the Potomac and up the York or James, or by land through Manassas and Fredericksburg. The former had the advantage of placing the Federal armies within a few miles of Richmond before the enemy could offer effective resistance, but it exposed Washington to attack from the valley of Virginia, and Washington would have been a poor exchange for Richmond. The other plan was less perilous, but more difficult, for it necessitated the crossing of the Rappahannock or its tributaries, the Pamunkey, the Mattapony, and the Chickahominy, all of them formidable obstacles.

After protracted delays the water route was selected, and in April McClellan landed 100,000 men on the Peninsula, and pushed slowly up past Yorktown and Williamsburg to the Chickahominy, where the spires of Richmond were in plain view. The Southern cause now seemed desperate. At Fredericksburg was General McDowell with 30,000 Federal troops, in the valley of Virginia General Banks had 20,000, while in West Virginia Frémont commanded 15,000 more. To oppose these forces the Confederates had 63,000 men before Richmond under General Joseph E. Johnston, and 17,000 in the valley under "Stonewall" Jackson.

Fortunately for the Confederacy the conduct of its military affairs was intrusted to a genius of the first order. In those anxious days, during the spring of 1862, could be seen in frequent consultation with President Davis, a man of fifty-five, with white beard, white hair brushed back from a lofty forehead, keen eyes, well-moulded features bearing an expression of seriousness, attired in a spotless gray uniform, with the waistcoat partly unbuttoned. It was Robert E. Lee, military adviser to the President. Lee was a graduate of West Point, who had made an enviable record in the Mexican War. At the outbreak of the Civil War the command of the Federal armies had been offered him, but, though he opposed secession, he would take no part in the invasion of the Southern States.

He saw that the only way to save Richmond was to prevent McDowell, Banks, and Frémont from closing in upon the city, by playing upon the fears of the Federal Government for the safety of Washington. So he sent reinforcements to Jackson, and directed that astute leader to make a movement down the valley. Jackson carried out the plan in masterly style. By leading his men over the Blue Ridge through mud-choked roads to Mechum's River, he convinced Stanton that he was on his way to join Johnston, and so tricked him into weakening Banks to reinforce McDowell. Then, to the surprise even of his own men, he turned west instead of east, drove the Union troops back from the passes through the Alleghanies, and descended upon Banks at Strasburg. Dodging through a pass in the Massanutton range, he got on the line of retreat of the Federal commander, forced him to retire in haste, struck him a stunning blow at Winchester, and drove his shattered regiments over the Potomac at Williamsport. Then he advanced along the road to Washington until he had planted the Confederate flag upon the hills overlooking Harper's Ferry.

The effect was electric. Newspapers in the North displayed headlines stating that Jackson was already approaching Washington. In alarm Lincoln and Stanton sent out a call for the militia to come to the defense of the capital. Frémont was ordered up from West Virginia to fall on Jackson's rear, and the various detachments of McDowell's corps—Shields, Ord, Bayard, King—were hurriedly turned toward the valley. Jackson hastened back, just managing to elude his pursuers, repulsed Frémont at Cross Keys, defeated Shields at Port Republic, and then, with his entire force, passed over the Blue Ridge and came to the assistance of the Confederate army at Richmond. With 17,000 men he had succeeded in keeping away from the critical point in the campaign 70,000 Federal troops. These 70,000 men, who should have aided McClellan in capturing Richmond, were far away when the crisis came. While Frémont, Shields, Banks, Ord, Bayard, King were scattered about along the Potomac, in the valley or in northern Virginia, Jackson's entire force was descending upon McClellan's exposed right flank, on the Chickahominy.

At three o'clock on the afternoon of June 23, 1862, five Southern generals met in a Virginia homestead, on the outskirts of Richmond. Robert E. Lee was the central figure, and around him were grouped Jackson, his clothes frayed by weeks of rough campaigning, his weariness betraying the fact that he had ridden hard to reach the rendezvous; A. P. Hill, distinguished by his long hair, ill-kempt beard, and mild eyes; the burly Longstreet; and the quiet, unobtrusive D. H. Hill. Lee explained his plan of attack to his four trusted major-generals, and then, retiring from the room, left them to arrange the details.

The disposition of the Union forces before Richmond invited attack. North of the Chickahominy and the swampy ground which extended along its northern bank was the isolated corps of Porter, numbering about 25,000 men. Against this force Lee decided to hurl the bulk of the Confederate army, leaving but a small force to hold the lines south of the Chickahominy against the other four Federal corps. June 26 regiment after regiment of gray uniformed men crossed the stream west of the Union lines, while Jackson's veterans came down from the north. Fifty-seven thousand Confederates were closing in on one Federal corps. Porter called for reinforcements, drew his forces into strong positions near Gaines' Mill, and prepared for battle.

At two o'clock on the 27th the Confederate columns came in sight. Deploying in a great semicircle, they moved to the attack. A withering fire greeted them. Dashing across the plain before the Union works, floundering in the swamps, struggling against the brushwood, brigade after brigade seemed to melt away. Others pressed on, as brave as their predecessors. Above the din of battle rose the piercing rebel yell. Reinforcements came to Porter's hard-pressed regiments, and the line held. At 6.30 the Confederates once more attacked all along the line, and broke through in two places. Slowly and in good order the Federals retired from the field, and crossed to the south bank of the Chickahominy.

McClellan had already decided to withdraw to the James River, and he now set his columns in motion southward over the mud-choked Virginia roads. June 30, Lee struck them at Frazier's Farm, south of the White Oak swamp, and for hours the Union army was in imminent peril. Desperate fighting saved the day, and that night the weary divisions bivouacked in safety upon the slopes of Malvern Hill. When the Confederates, the next day, assaulted this position, they were thrown back in bloody defeat. Lee had lost the one opportunity which presented itself to him during the war of annihilating a great Federal army. Yet he had saved Richmond.

In the meanwhile, the armies of Frémont, Banks, and McDowell were concentrated under the command of General John Pope, and sent forward to Culpeper. Had McClellan now attacked Richmond vigorously from his base at Harrison's Landing, the situation would have been serious for the Confederates. But he was ordered to embark for Aquia Creek, north of Fredericksburg, and while his troops were en route, Lee and Jackson disposed of Pope. Jackson's "foot-cavalry" swung swiftly around the Federal right and destroyed the base at Manassas. Pope concentrated for an attack on the battlefield of Bull Run; but the rest of Lee's army came up, and Pope's regiments, despite all their determination and gallantry, were disastrously defeated.

Lee now led his victorious battalions over the Potomac in the hope of winning Maryland, isolating Washington, and perhaps gaining recognition of the Confederacy by some of the European powers. The gray columns came through Frederick singing "Maryland, My Maryland." But they found the shops closed, the blinds of residences shut, and the people hostile. Western Maryland was loyal to the Union. McClellan, learning of Lee's plans from a captured despatch, hastened north and fell upon him in overwhelming force at Sharpsburg, on Antietam Creek. Here, September 17, 1862, with the Potomac at their backs, the Confederates beat off repeated assaults, until night put an end to the fighting. Lee had saved his army, but he was forced to give up his invasion of the North, and two days later retired to Virginia.

Still the tide of victory had not yet turned. In December General Ambrose E. Burnside, who had taken over the command, was pressing south in a new attempt to capture Richmond. McClellan had been overcautious; Burnside proved too rash. At the picturesque old town of Fredericksburg, on the banks of the Rappahannock, he threw his regiments against the enemy's intrenched lines, and was defeated with severe losses.

Fighting Joe Hooker next took command, and mapped out an excellent plan for trapping Lee's inferior forces at Chancellorsville. At the critical moment he hesitated long enough to permit the Confederates not only to extricate themselves but to strike him a terrific blow. While Lee feinted at the Federal front, Jackson swung far around to the south, and falling upon Hooker's right flank, drove home a death thrust. The Confederate victory cost them dear. As the approach of twilight brought a suspension of fighting, Jackson rode past his sentinels to reconnoitre in the enemy's rear. Half an hour later, when he came back, shots were heard in the darkness, and Jackson fell from his horse. A company of Confederates who had just come up, and did not know that their commander was between the lines, had fired upon him by mistake.

The wounded general was borne to the rear, and in a rough field-hospital his left arm was amputated. Later he was removed to a private residence where, despite the skill of able and watchful surgeons, despite the attentions of wife and friends, he sank rapidly. Pneumonia developed, accompanied by pleurisy. At 3.15 on a Sabbath afternoon the wounded chieftain raised himself on his pillow. "Order A. P. Hill to prepare for action!" he called out. "Pass the infantry to the front rapidly! Tell Major Hawks . . ." There he stopped, his brow relaxed, and he sank back murmuring: "No, no; let us cross over the river, and rest under the shade of the trees." And with these words he died.

On September 22, 1862, Lincoln summoned his Cabinet for an important announcement. As the members came in they found the President immersed in a humorous book, and when they had taken seats he continued, reading aloud to the end of the chapter. It was a strange picture—the President, with his thin figure, long arms and legs, rugged hands, narrow chest, furrowed face, dark hair, high forehead, dreamy eyes sunk beneath bushy eyebrows, bristly beard, large nose, and close-set mouth; the diminutive Seward, his hands and feet small and delicate, hair snow-white, eyes gray, face clean-shaven

and colorless; the portly Chase, pleasant and smiling as usual;
Welles, looking like an elderly farmer, in his long, white beard
and great wig; Stanton, the combative; Blair, Smith, and
Bates. As the President read he rubbed his hand up and down
his leg with an habitual motion, while his face lit up with kindly
humor.

After completing his reading Lincoln assumed a graver tone:
"Gentlemen, I have, as you are aware, thought a great deal
about the relation of this war to slavery; and you all remember
that several weeks ago I read to you an order I had prepared
upon the subject, which, on account of objections made by
some of you, was not issued. I think that the time for acting
has now come, and I have got you together to hear what I
have written down." The President then began the reading
of his emancipation proclamation. "I, Abraham Lincoln,
President of the United States of America, do proclaim that
on the first day of January, 1863, all persons held as slaves
within any State, or designated part of a State, the people
whereof shall then be in rebellion against the United States,
shall then be, thenceforward and forever, free; and the executive Government of the United States, including the military
and naval authorities thereof, will recognize and maintain the
freedom of such persons, and will do no act, or acts, to repress
such persons, or any of them, in any efforts they may make
for their actual freedom."

The doom of slavery had sounded. Although the proclamation, for the moment, did not free a single slave, since it
was a war measure applicable only to the parts of the South
still in Confederate hands, from the day it was issued the war
became not only a war to save the Union, but to abolish
slavery. As the Federal armies advanced it did bring freedom
to millions. The effect upon the border slaveholding States
was bad, but in the North the abolitionists, who were becoming bitter in their criticisms of the President, now rallied enthusiastically to his support. The proclamation also put an
end to the fear of foreign intervention, for in a war between
freedom and slavery, no nation dared espouse the cause of
bondage. Englishmen had little interest in the attempt of

some of their own seceded colonists to coerce others who wished, in turn, to secede from them, but a crusade against slavery elicited their sympathy.

Lincoln's proclamation did not apply to non-seceding slave States—Maryland, Delaware, West Virginia, Kentucky, and Missouri; nor did it apply to Tennessee and to those parts of Virginia and Louisiana occupied by Federal troops. But slavery in these States could not long survive. West Virginia freed her slaves in 1863, Maryland in 1864, Tennessee and Missouri in 1865. Finally the Thirteenth Amendment put an end to all slavery in the United States.

The military failures in Virginia might have discouraged the North had they not been offset by important successes in the West. If Richmond was the head of the Confederacy, the region embracing Chattanooga, Atlanta, Macon, and Selma was its heart. While the masterly operations of Lee and Jackson were warding off the strokes aimed at the capital, the Federal armies west of the Alleghanies were advancing south and east through Tennessee into Alabama and Georgia.

Early in the war the Federal Government began the creation of a fleet of gunboats for operation on the Mississippi and its tributaries. Three river-steamers were bought at Cincinnati, their frames lengthened, their engines lowered, their decks protected and fitted with guns. This nucleus of the river-flotilla soon had possession of the upper Mississippi and the Ohio, and proved more valuable to the Union cause than many regiments. On October 12, 1861, the *De Kalb*, an iron-clad gunboat, was launched near St. Louis, while the *Cincinnati*, *Carondelet*, *Louisville*, *Mound City*, *Cairo*, *Pittsburg*, *Benton*, and *Essex* followed in succession.

From the point of juncture of the Mississippi and the Ohio at Cairo, ran four great pathways into the Confederacy—the Mississippi River, the railway to Jackson and Mobile, the Tennessee River, and the Cumberland River. The Confederates had protected the rivers by a series of fortifications, the Mississippi at Island No. 10, the Tennessee with Fort Henry, and the Cumberland with Fort Donelson. Upon these posts the Union armies now centred their attention.

The Confederates surrendered Fort Henry after exchanging shots with the river-boats, and concentrated their forces at Fort Donelson. A Federal army, under General Ulysses S. Grant threw its lines about this place, while the flotilla under Flag-Officer Foote invested it from the river. The enemy decided not to remain to be starved into submission, and on a cold February day, they tried to break through the Federal right and escape to Nashville. Grant was taken by surprise. The gray lines crushed McClernand's division, and the way of escape was open. The Confederate commander, Pillow, imagining that he had Grant at his mercy, abandoned the plan to escape and entered upon a general engagement.

At this moment General Grant came galloping up, almost unattended. When told that his right wing had been routed, his face flushed slightly and with a sudden grip he crumpled up some papers which he held in his hand. In a quiet voice he said: "Gentlemen, the position on the right must be retaken." McClernand's troops were reformed, reinforcements rushed up to the danger-point, the Confederates were driven back, and the gap in the line was closed. The next day Fort Donelson surrendered. All eastern Tennessee fell into the hands of the Federal armies, and the way was opened into Mississippi and Alabama.

Grant followed up his victory by moving up the Tennessee River and taking position at Shiloh, a few miles from the Mississippi border. Here he was fiercely assailed by the Confederates under General Albert Sidney Johnston. The gray line advanced, pushing home the attack through a labyrinth of creeks, ravines, woods, fields, and swamps. The Federals were taken by surprise. They fought bravely, but superior numbers pressed them back toward the river, where escape was impossible. Disaster seemed imminent. But fate intervened. At a critical point in the battle General Johnston rode out in front of his line on his horse "Fire-eater," crying: "Men, they are stubborn; we must use the bayonet. I will lead you!" With a shout the Confederates charged and gained their objective. It was a costly triumph, for their gallant commander was wounded, and bled to death before medical assistance could be had. Beauregard, who succeeded to the command, failed to press the attack. The next day Grant rushed up reinforcements and the Confederates retired.

The Federal forces, moving slowly southward, now captured Corinth, Mississippi, and cut the trunk line railway from Memphis to Chattanooga. Their career of victory was interrupted by a Confederate invasion of Kentucky under General Bragg. General Buell headed him off, attacked him at Perryville, and forced him to retire into Tennessee. Here at Murfreesboro he fought a bloody but indecisive battle with General W. S. Rosecrans. Bragg did not succeed in regaining Kentucky and eastern Tennessee, but his operations served an important purpose in delaying the advance of the Federal armies down the Mississippi River.

Now began one of the most brilliant campaigns of the war. After the Confederates had been driven from New Orleans, on the lower Mississippi, and from Island No. 10, Fort Pillow, and Memphis above, Vicksburg was almost their only remaining stronghold on the river. If this city could be taken, not only would the Mississippi "flow unvexed to the sea," but the western States of the Confederacy, with their stores of cattle and grain, would be completely isolated. But Vicksburg was exceedingly hard to take. To the north was a wilderness, destitute of roads, intersected with unfordable rivers, and covered with dense forests, while to attack from the south it would be necessary to run the supply-boats past the Confederate batteries.

Grant did not hesitate. His army marched south through Louisiana, crossed the river at Grand Gulf, defeated the Confederates at Port Gibson, and then, cutting loose from its base of supplies, moved northeast toward the city of Jackson. In Vicksburg was General Pemberton, with 40,000 men; at Jackson, General Joseph E. Johnston, with 15,000. Grant moved in between them, captured Jackson, defeated Pemberton at Champion Hill, and again at the bridge over the Big Black River, and then laid siege to Vicksburg. In nineteen days the army had crossed a great river and penetrated far into the enemy's territory, marching 180 miles by day and night, through rain and mud, without tents, and on meagre rations; had fought five distinct battles, inflicting severe loss on the Confederates and capturing many field-pieces; had taken the capital of Mississippi and destroyed its important mills and arsenals; had divided the forces of the enemy and invested a great fortified city.

The troops now began siege operations. Day after day the men labored with spade and axe, and the Union works drew nearer the enemy's lines. The bombardment, both from the siege-guns and the mortars of the fleet became deadly. The inhabitants took to caves and cellars. Before long the bluff on which the place stands was honeycombed with subterranean vaults and passages. The city's food-supply was cut off. Mule meat was in great demand; flour and bacon sold at unheard-of prices. At the close of June it was obvious that the end was near at hand.

There had been much good-natured bantering between the pickets on either side. "Well, Yank, when are you coming into town?" the Confederates often called out. "We propose to celebrate the Fourth of July there," was the usual reply. Great was the rejoicing in the Union army when, on July 3, several white flags appeared on various parts of the enemy's works. Pemberton had decided to take advantage of this sentiment to secure lenient terms. The next day the news flashed over the country that Vicksburg had surrendered, and the national holiday was celebrated with an enthusiasm born of a new conviction that the Union would be preserved.

In June, 1863, Lee led his veterans across the Potomac for a second invasion of the North. He wished to divert Federal forces from the siege of Vicksburg, encourage the Northern peace party, threaten the industrial centres, and perhaps isolate Washington. A few weeks later his divisions were approaching Harrisburg, and Ewell's cavalry reached the Susquehanna opposite the town. But now the Federal army, under General George Meade, was hastening north to intercept the invaders, and the Confederates concentrated at Gettysburg.

On July 1 the advance detachments clashed north and west of the village. After severe fighting the Federals fell back upon a semicircular ridge, dominated at one end by Culp's hill and at the other by Round Top and Little Round Top. Lee ordered Longstreet to move against Little Round Top at dawn on July 2. But this general, who was opposed to forcing the battle, delayed the attack until the afternoon. By that time the Federals held the position in force and he was repulsed. Later in the day Ewell attacked Culp's hill, and was carrying all before him when darkness stopped the fighting.

The two days' struggle had been decidedly favorable to the Confederates. Unless their assaults were stemmed on the third, the Union positions would have to be abandoned. That night Meade held a council of war, in which it was decided to fight the battle to a finish. To General Gibbon, whose men were stationed in the centre, Meade remarked: "Your turn will come to-morrow. To-day he has struck the flanks. Next it will be the centre."

This forecast proved correct. July 3 found the Federal regiments on Cemetery Ridge waiting expectantly. Before them was a gentle depression covered with farmhouses, wheat-fields, groves, orchards, meadows, winding roads, and picket fences. Beyond, to the right, was a low ridge of hills, and in the far distance an azure mountain range.

Suddenly came the report of two signal-guns in quick succession, and then a burst of fire along the line of hills and in the plain. Lee was opening upon the Federal position with 20 batteries of 140 guns. The smoke which covered the Confederate line was lit up by the constant flashes. The Federal guns replied promptly, and for many minutes the artillery duel continued. Then the Federal fire slackened and stopped.

As the watchers on the hill scanned the plain below, a line of skirmishers appeared three-fourths of a mile away. They dashed forward, little puffs of smoke issuing from their ranks. Then from the woods emerged regiment after regiment, brigade after brigade of men in gray, deploying with the steadiness of dress parade. The waiting Federal troops could not repress a cry of admiration. The first line was followed by a second, the second by a third.

As they came on, the Federal artillery opened with deadly

effect, and great gaps soon appeared in those splendid regiments. The blue infantrymen stirred a little as they lay in waiting, and the officers warned them: "Steady, men, steady! Don't fire yet!" For a moment the Confederates were lost to view in an undulation in the ground, and then, without warning, they seemed to rise out of the very earth, the tense expression of their faces plainly visible. The Federals delivered one telling volley. Still the gray battalions came on until they broke over the breastwork. All order was now lost. Men fought singly or in little groups. For a moment the Stars and Bars waved over the Federal position. Then the shattered remnant of the Confederates gave way and fell back down the slope, while every gun and every rifle upon the eminence mowed them down. Thus ended Pickett's charge, and with it the battle of Gettysburg.

This attack was Lee's last hope. When he saw the broken remnants of his divisions fall back across the plain, he knew that the day was lost. Withdrawing under cover of night, he escaped over the Potomac, and once more took up his position in Virginia.

So far as military operations are concerned, it is a mistake to regard Gettysburg as the turning-point in the war. There was no turning-point in the war. Gettysburg put an end to the Confederate invasion of the North, but it did not shatter the Confederate resistance in the East. The Civil War was won in the West; and in the West the tide of victory ran with the Federal armies from the first. Fort Donelson led to Shiloh, Shiloh was the forerunner of Vicksburg and the opening of the Mississippi, Vicksburg was followed by Chattanooga, and Chattanooga opened the way to the conquest of Georgia and South Carolina. In the summer of 1864 Grant was no nearer Richmond than McClellan had been in 1862, but Federal success in the West and South was then fast making Lee's position untenable. It was in vain that he kept shut the front door of the Confederacy when the back of the house had been blown away.

In September, 1863, General Rosecrans moved on to Chattanooga with 58,000 men. This city was the most important position held by the Confederates, not excepting Richmond, for it was the key to Georgia and western Alabama. Rosecrans succeeded in getting control of the place, but he was later attacked by General Bragg with 66,000 troops at Chickamauga and defeated. This disaster would have been overwhelming had it not been for the courage of General George H. Thomas, who commanded the Union right. Although surrounded on three sides, he repelled charge after charge, until nightfall made it possible for him to withdraw in safety. This gallant resistance gained for him the title of "The Rock of Chickamauga."

The Confederates now fortified themselves on Missionary Ridge and Lookout Mountain, overlooking Chattanooga, and tried to cut off the Union army from its supplies. For weeks the situation was grave. But Grant and Sherman came up with reinforcements, and the combined Union armies attacked Bragg in his mountain stronghold. The Confederates were defeated and driven back. The way to the lower South now lay open.

In May, 1864, Sherman, with 100,000 veterans, advanced on Atlanta. His path lay through the hilly country of north Georgia, and before him was a Confederate army under the able Joseph E. Johnston. Progress was slow. Johnston refused to fight in the open, and Sherman was too cautious to waste men in attacking breastworks. But by making use of his superior numbers to outflank the enemy he gradually drove them back to the Chattahoochee River, six miles from Atlanta. At this moment the government at Richmond committed a fatal blunder. Disappointed with Johnston's Fabian tactics, they replaced him by General J. B. Hood. Hood at once took the offensive. In a desperate attempt to break Sherman's hold on Atlanta, he fought three battles in eleven days. His attacks were all beaten back, and when the Union army moved around to cut his communications, he was compelled to evacuate the city.

Sherman burned the machine-shops at Atlanta, and, abandoning his base, set out on his march to the sea. There was no army before him. The expedition was undertaken primarily for the purpose of destroying all kinds of property of military use to the Confederates. So, cutting a swath of desolation sixty miles wide all the way to Savannah, he rooted up rails, destroyed roads and bridges, cut down crops and burned houses and barns. "I estimate the damage done to the State of Georgia and its military resources at $100,000,000," Sherman reported to Secretary Stanton, "at least $20,000,000 of which has inured to our advantage, and the remainder is simply waste and destruction." This was terrible, but it was effective. Lee's army in Virginia, struggling against heavy odds before Richmond, found itself deprived of the means of sustenance and gradually melted away.

With the opening of 1864 the Federal Government determined to make one supreme effort to crush the Confederate army in Virginia. General Grant was brought from the West, honored with the rank of lieutenant-general, and provided with men and munitions to the limit of the nation's resources. At Vicksburg Grant had shown himself a brilliant strategist, but he now felt it advisable to wear down Lee's army by frontal attacks in overwhelming numbers. In the Wilderness, at Spottsylvania, and at Cold Harbor he hurled his regiments against the Confederate lines, only to be thrown back with staggering losses. "I propose to fight it out on this line, if it takes all summer," he had written Lincoln; but after 55,000 men had fallen he came to the realization that Richmond could not be taken from the north.

On June 14 Grant crossed the James at City Point, and extended his lines to the south of the Confederate capital. Throughout the autumn and winter the Union army worked steadily with pick and spade, so that when spring came it was in a position to seize one of the two railways by which supplies were carried into Richmond. By April 1 the attenuated Confederate lines showed signs of giving way. Thereupon General Grant ordered an assault. For the moment Lee warded off the attacks, but on April 3 he evacuated Richmond and set out for Danville in the hope of uniting with Joseph E. Johnston. Grant was soon hot on his trail. On April 8, Federal forces were on his line of retreat, and the next day he surrendered.

The two commanding officers presented a strange contrast when they met at Appomattox, in the McLean house, to arrange the terms of surrender. Grant sat at a marble-top table in the centre of the room, attired in single-breasted coat, unbuttoned in front, his trousers inside his mud-splashed boots, his nut-brown hair and beard without a trace of gray. Lee, who sat near the window, erect and dignified, his arm resting on a small oval table, wore a new uniform buttoned up at the throat. Around the room were other generals, some seated on a sofa, others standing.

"I suppose, General Grant, that the object of our present meeting is fully understood," said Lee. "I asked to see you in order to ascertain on what terms you would receive the surrender of my army." Grant replied that the officers and men were to be paroled and disqualified from taking arms again, and all arms, ammunition, and supplies were to be given up. Lee nodded assent, and presently suggested that the Union commander commit the terms to writing. Before he had reached the end of his sheet, Grant's eye happened to fall on Lee's handsome sword. After a pause he added the sentence: "This will not embrace the side-arms of the officers, nor their private horses or baggage." When Lee, in reading over the terms, came to this proviso, he flushed slightly, evidently touched by the act of generosity. In reply to Grant's question whether he had any suggestions to make, Lee said that the mounted Confederates, unlike the Federals, always owned their horses. "I take it that most of the men in the ranks are small farmers," replied Grant, "and as the country has been so raided by the two armies, it is doubtful whether they will be able to put in a crop to carry themselves and their families through the next winter without the aid of their horses. Therefore I will see to it that the men be allowed to take their horses and mules." Again Lee flushed. "This will have the best possible effect on the men," he said. "It will be very gratifying and do much toward conciliating our people."

A few minutes later Lee mounted his horse and, saluting a group of Union officers in the front yard who stood respectfully hat in hand, rode back to his army. The men greeted him with a shout of welcome. Then suddenly they recalled the mission from which he was returning, and a hush fell over the tattered veterans. As their commander rode along the lines many a weather-beaten, bearded face was wet with tears. Officers and privates alike pressed forward to take his hand, or touch his coat or stroke his fine gray horse. With bare head and tears flowing freely, Lee said good-by to his army, bidding them return to their homes as worthy and loyal citizens of the reunited country.

CHAPTER XXI

RECONSTRUCTION

FORD'S THEATRE, in Washington, was crowded on the evening of April 14, 1865. Laura Keene, in "Our American Cousin," was ending her season, and the manager had announced that President Lincoln and the "hero of Appomattox" would be present. As the audience came in, they saw that a box overlooking the stage had been decorated for the distinguished party. The rail and the two side columns had been draped with regimental flags, while at the foot of the centre column was an engraving of Washington. Some time after the play had begun, the President, accompanied, not by General Grant, but by Mrs. Lincoln and two young guests, Major Rathbone and his fiancée Miss Harris, was seen making his way behind the seats to his box. The orchestra broke into "Hail to the Chief," the play was halted, while the people rose, cheering and waving hats and handkerchiefs. The party entered the box, and the play went on.

During the second scene of the third act John Wilkes Booth, a well-known actor, came into the theatre and approached the box. No one interfered, for he was a privileged person in the theatre. Entering, he closed and bolted the door. Then stepping quickly up to Mr. Lincoln, he placed a pistol at the back of his head and fired. The President's head fell quietly forward, his arms relaxed, upon his lips was still a smile. At the sound of the shot Major Rathbone sprang to his feet and grappled with Booth. The assassin struck at him with a dagger, wounding him in the arm, and then sprang from the box to the stage below. Now occurred a strange incident. The flag, the symbol of the Union which Lincoln had preserved, caught in his assailant's spur, and brought him with a crash to the floor. Though the fall had broken his leg, he sprang to his feet, brandishing his knife, and shouting: "Sic semper tyrannis." Then, despite the cries of "Stop him! Stop him! He has shot the President!" he rushed from the stage, mounted a waiting horse, and made good his escape. The wounded President was borne from the theatre to a residence near by, and there, surrounded by relatives and friends, he died without regaining consciousness. Ten days later Booth was discovered in a barn near Bowling Green, Virginia, and when he refused to surrender was shot to death.

The untimely death of Lincoln was disastrous for the South. On the day of the murder he had said to his Cabinet: "I hope there will be no persecution, no bloody work after the war is over. . . . We must extinguish our resentments if we expect harmony and union." There was need for the sympathetic heart, the far-seeing intellect, and the firm hand of the great statesman. The South was in chaos. Everywhere cities were in ruins, farm lands wasted, highways in disrepair, railways wrecked, the negroes bewildered and disorderly, the whites poverty-stricken, the schools closed, the States without legal government. The task which confronted the Federal authorities was to bind up the wounds of war by restoring the prosperity of the South, and bringing it once more into its proper relations to the Union. The old South was gone, the South of Calhoun and Yancey, the South founded on slave labor, with interests so distinct that it felt itself to be a nation within a nation. Upon its ruins must be erected the new South, with free labor, factories, mines, intensive agriculture; a South which rejoiced in its place as a part of the reunited people. Fate had put at the head of the government the man best qualified for this work, and now the assassin's bullet had cut him down.

On April 15 Vice-President Johnson entered upon the duties of the Presidency. Andrew Johnson was a Southern unionist. Born of humble parentage, a tailor, self-educated, he became through native ability a leader among the antislavery men of eastern Tennessee. He was stubborn, prejudiced, tactless—a man unsuited for the delicate task before him. "Johnson is a man of few ideas, but they are right and true," said one who knew him well. "He is honest, right-minded, and narrow-minded; he has no tact, and even lacks discretion and forecast."

Lincoln had already pointed out the right road to reconstruction. Holding that the Southern States had not legally left the Union, and that their relations to it had merely been interrupted by the acts of rebellious individuals, he had sought to set up loyal governments wherever Federal authority was firmly established. December 8, 1863, he issued a proclamation pardoning, with certain exceptions, all Southerners who would take the oath of allegiance, and promising to recognize any government established by such persons, whenever the voters should equal one-tenth of the number enrolled in 1860. Despite bitter opposition from the extremists in Congress, led by Benjamin Wade, Charles Sumner, and Henry Winter Davis, reconstructed governments were put into operation with Lincoln's sanction in Arkansas, Louisiana, and Tennessee.

When Johnson took office it was assumed that he would reverse this mild policy. So vehement had he been in declaring that "treason must be made odious," that the radicals regarded him as one of themselves, and actually expressed satisfaction at the turn of fate which threw him into power. Disappointment was in store. As a Southern mountaineer Johnson hated slavery and the slaveholding aristocracy. But as a white man he did not wish to place the negroes in power, nor accord them social and political equality with the whites. When he discovered that this was what Sumner, Wade, and Thaddeus Stevens contemplated, he turned upon them fiercely.

Congress was not in session when Lincoln was assassinated, and Johnson made his first mistake in not calling it. It would have been easier to gain the consent of Congress in the spring of 1865 to a rational plan of reconstruction, than in December, when the regular session began. Johnson went ahead on his own responsibility, in the path marked out by Lincoln, setting up new governments in North Carolina, South Carolina, Georgia, Florida, Alabama, Mississippi, and Texas. They drew up new constitutions, ratified the Thirteenth Amendment, rescinded secession, elected governors and legislatures, and all except South Carolina repudiated the debts contracted to aid the Confederacy.

When the news spread throughout the South that Lee had

surrendered, many a white-haired planter summoned his slaves to the "big house" to tell them of their freedom. They came always respectfully, hat in hand, crowding around the front portico, old men bent with rheumatism, burly field-hands with sinuous black limbs and good-natured faces; buxom women, half-naked boys and girls. "I have called you together to tell you that you are now free," said the master. "You may go, if you please, or if you wish you may stay with me and work for a share of the crops." "Yes, master; yes, master," was the reply, "we want to stay right here with you."

None the less, many left. Freedom for these simple souls meant release from work, and soon the roads were full of negroes, on their way to the Freedman's Bureau, or to the nearest Federal garrison. They had been told that rations were handed out there, and many believed that each negro would receive forty acres and a mule. Thousands of idle men and women were concentrated in camps, or wandered over the country, living on the bounty of the government, or raiding barns or chicken-coops. Freed from restraint they became demoralized. Lawlessness, idleness, immorality, sickness, and suffering were common, while many farms were uncultivated for lack of workers. The Freedman's Bureau did much to care for the negroes, and to secure labor contracts at fair wages, but so great a problem could be handled only by the government.

When the new Legislatures convened in the summer of 1865 they at once took up this pressing question. They met the situation in a practical way, but a way which proved unwise because it was misunderstood in the North. Since the old slave codes were obsolete, they had to enact new laws, fixing the status of the negro and ending vagrancy and lawlessness. Intermarriage between the races was prohibited in several States; the negro had to have a license to carry weapons, to preach, or to engage in trade; in Mississippi he could own no land outside the limits of a town. For trespass, for rioting, for seditious speeches, for vagrancy, he was subject to fine. If he could not pay the fine, he might be handed over to a white man and forced to work. Negro children whose parents refused to pro-

vide for them were to be apprenticed to employers, prefer-
ably their former masters, who must feed and clothe them,
teach them to read and write, and keep them employed.

When these black codes were published in the North they
aroused indignant protest. "Are we going to permit the South
to re-establish slavery under a different name?" men asked each
other. "The war was a conflict between freedom and slavery.
Freedom finally won, but at a terrible cost. Can we now permit slavery to come back under the guise of laws for vagrants
and apprentices?" This feeling of distrust increased when it
became known that the reconstructed States had elected to
Congress many former Confederate leaders. Should these men
renew the old alliance with the Northern Democrats, the Republican party might lose control of the government and disunion once more become a possibility.

On December 18, 1865, Thaddeus Stevens launched an attack
in the House upon the new Southern governments, and outlined his own plan of reconstruction. A tall man, with ruddy
complexion, massive head, high forehead, bold features, projecting brows, cavernous eyes, and firm mouth, he made a
striking figure. "Mr. President," he said, "the Fourth Article
of the Constitution says: 'New States may be admitted by the
Congress into the Union.' In my opinion, this is the provision
which covers the case of the Southern States. Unless the law
of nations is a dead letter, the late war between two acknowledged belligerents broke all the ties which bound them together. The future condition of the conquered power depends
on the will of the conqueror. They must come in as new
States or remain as conquered provinces. Congress is the only
power that can act in this matter.

"The seceding States should not be readmitted until the
perpetual ascendancy of the party of union has been assured.
We must change the basis of representation in the South.
The seceding States have seventy Congressmen, fifty-one of
whom represent freemen, and nineteen represent slaves under
the three-fifths provision of the Constitution. If the slaves
are now free, this will add for the other two-fifths thirteen more,
or eighty-three in all. These eighty-three Southern members,

with the Democrats elected from the North, will always be able to control Congress. I need not depict the ruin that would follow their first victory—the assumption of the Confederate debt, the repudiation of the Federal debt, the re-establishment of slavery.

"The recent ratification of the Thirteenth Amendment by the South is a trick to delude the people and accustom Congress to hear the names of the extinct States. Congress must assert its sovereignty in this matter, and assume the dignity of a Roman Senate."

Thus did Stevens serve notice upon President Johnson that the radical Republicans would not sanction presidential reconstruction. So great was their influence that Congress refused to seat the Senators and Representatives elected under the new Southern constitutions. In January they introduced a Freedman's Bureau bill, authorizing the President to protect the former slaves of the South by overriding the black codes. The large majorities by which this measure passed both Houses should have warned Johnson that some concession to the radicals was necessary. But opposition merely aroused his combative spirit, and he vetoed the bill. Thereupon Congress drew up a Civil Rights bill, guaranteeing equal rights to all citizens, and, when Johnson rejected it, promptly passed it over his veto.

The battle was now on. The radical leaders thundered against the President; Johnson replied by heaping invectives upon the radical leaders. In June, 1866, the principles of the Civil Rights bill were embodied in an amendment to the Constitution, which, after some delay, secured the necessary two-thirds vote in both Houses of Congress. It forbade any State to abridge the rights of citizens or deprive them of life, liberty, or property without due process of law. If a State denied the suffrage to any of its citizens, its representation in Congress might be correspondingly reduced. It disqualified from office many leading Southerners. The last provision was enough to block ratification in the South, for the members of the reconstructed Legislatures refused to consent to their own political degradation. Thereupon the radicals refused to admit representatives from any reconstructed State, until it had ratified the amendment, and took their case before the people of the North in the election of 1866.

President Johnson accepted the challenge. In September he visited New York, Cleveland, Chicago, and St. Louis, speaking before great crowds in an attempt to discredit the radical programme. Unfortunately, his undignified bearing in this "swing around the circle," his violent language and abuse of his opponents, cost him the support of thousands. On the evening of September 3 the Kennard House, at Cleveland, was gaily decorated in honor of the President's visit. Various colored lanterns flickered in every window, bathed the portico in light, and hung in lines over the street. In front of the building stood a gay throng, listening impatiently to a brass band and demanding to see the President. Johnson was at dinner, but to appease their clamor he arose and stepped out on the portico. The crowd saw a man of medium height, with broad chest, stout neck, elastic step, and erect carriage.

"But a short time since you had a ticket before you for the Presidency," he said. "I was placed upon that ticket with a distinguished fellow citizen who is now no more. I know there are some who complain. [A voice—"unfortunately."] Yes, unfortunately for some that God rules on high and deals in right. [Cheers.] Yes, unfortunately the ways of Providence are mysterious and incomprehensibly controlling all who exclaim 'unfortunate.' ["Bully for you!"] I was going to say, my countrymen, a short time since I was placed upon the ticket and elected. There was a platform proclaimed and adopted by those who placed me upon it. Notwithstanding the subsidized gang of hirelings and traducers, I have discharged all my duties and fulfilled all my pledges, and I say here to-night that if my predecessor had lived, the vials of wrath would have been poured out upon him. [Cries of "Never." "Three cheers for the Congress of the United States."] I came here as I was passing along, and have been called upon for the purpose of exchanging views and of ascertaining, if we could, who was wrong. [Cries of "It's you!" A voice—"Hang Jeff Davis!"] 'Hang Jeff Davis!' he says. [A voice—"Hang Thad Stevens and Wendell Phillips!"] Hang Jeff Davis? Why don't you hang him? [Cries of "Give us the opportunity!"] Have you not got the court? Have you not got the Attorney-General? . . . I called upon your Congress that is trying to break up the government. [Cries of "You be d——d!" and cheers mingled with hisses. Great confusion. "Don't get mad, Andy!"] Well, I will tell you who is mad. 'Whom the gods wish to destroy they first make mad.' . . . I would ask you why not hang Thad Stevens and Wendell Phillips? I tell you, my countrymen, I have been fighting the South, and they have been whipped and crushed and they acknowledge their defeat and accept the terms of the Constitution; and now, as I go round the circle, having fought traitors at the South, I am prepared to fight traitors at the North. [Cheers!] God willing, with your help we will do it. [Cries of "We won't!"] . . . I do not come here as the Chief Magistrate of twenty-five States out of thirty-six. [Cheers.] I come here to-night with the flag of my country and the Constitution of the thirty-six States untarnished. Are you now for dividing the country? [Cries of "No!"] Then I am President and I am President of the whole United States." [Cheers.]

The country was greatly shocked by Johnson's conduct during the speaking tour. Many persons felt that in sinking "the Presidency to the level of a grog-house," he had shown himself incapable of leadership and unworthy of confidence. This sentiment, together with the growing anger in the North at the refusal of the Southern States to ratify the Fourteenth Amendment, made defeat certain. Many believed that the South was determined to nullify the results of the war. If the negro is denied his rights, it was said, the soldier will have died in vain. In the fall elections the voters by an overwhelming majority sustained Congress in their opposition to presidential reconstruction. It was the knell of the new Southern governments.

When Congress reassembled in December, the radicals proceeded with their own plan of reconstruction. "Our offer to receive the Southern States into the Union with no other restriction than the Fourteenth Amendment has been flung back into our faces," said Garfield; "it is now our turn to act. They would not co-operate with us in rebuilding what they destroyed. We must remove the rubbish and rebuild from the bottom." In February, 1867, Congress, under the leadership of Sumner and Stevens, passed a Reconstruction Act, and on March 2, after the inevitable veto message came, re-enacted it with the necessary two-thirds vote.

A drastic measure it was. The Johnson and Lincoln governments were swept aside, and all the territory embraced in the Confederacy except Tennessee divided into five military districts, each under the command of a Federal general. This officer was instructed to draw up a list of voters in each State, admitting all male negroes over twenty-one and excluding large numbers of whites, after which he was to hold an election for a constitutional convention. The government created by this body must ratify the Fifteenth Amendment, disfranchise the leading white men, and admit the negroes, before Congress would seat its representatives.

Radicalism had triumphed. Most of the men who voted for this measure did not wish to rend unnecessarily the prostrate South. But the enactment of the black codes, the election to office of prominent ex-Confederates, the increased Southern representation which followed emancipation, the fear that the Democratic party might be restored to power, and the distrust of President Johnson combined to swing the North into line with the radical leaders.

The result was disastrous. In February, 1873, James S. Pike, former Minister to Holland, stood gazing at the imposing front of the unfinished State-house, at Columbia, South Carolina. He noted that over the door in bas-relief were engraved in marble George McDuffie and Robert Y. Hayne, both typical leaders of ante-bellum South Carolina. As he looked, the door opened and from it issued a crowd of negroes, some coal-black, some light yellow; some typical of the house-servant or the coachman, some from the cotton-fields; some in second-hand black frock coats, glossy and threadbare, some in stovepipe hats of departed styles, others in dirty brogans, torn trousers, slouch hats, and coarse shoes. Among them, here and there, was a handful of white men. The strange procession moved out into the littered grounds and disappeared through the wooden embrasure. Such was the Legislature which Congressional reconstruction gave South Carolina. "Ah!" thought Pike, "what if McDuffie and Hayne could see this. Would they not writhe in their graves?"

Later, when the Legislature reassembles, the visitor enters the Hall of Representatives, and, leaning over the rail of the balcony, looks down upon the strange spectacle. Of the 124 members, 94 are negroes. "The Speaker is black, the clerk is black, the doorkeepers are black, the little pages are black, the chairman of the ways and means is black, the chaplain is coal-black." To these simple folk, so lately freed from slavery, this is their day of jubilee. Lounging in the costly chairs, munching peanuts, voting on important bills, making speeches in the half-singing tone of the camp-meeting, they revel in their newly acquired importance. No one is allowed to talk five minutes without interruption. "Forty questions of privilege will be raised in a day." The Speaker's hammer plays a perpetual tattoo. He orders a member to take his seat. The member obeys, but an instant later is up again. When the Speaker threatens to call the "gemman" to order, there is a general guffaw.

In the midst of this burlesque, the white men, most of them from the hill country, sit grim and silent. "They feel themselves to be in some sort martyrs, bound stoically to suffer in behalf of that still great element in the State whose prostrate fortunes are becoming the sport of an unpitying fate. They stolidly survey the noisy riot that goes on in the great black Left and Centre, where the business and debates of the House are conducted, where sit the strange and extraordinary guides of the fortune of a once proud and haughty State." Beside Mr. Pike sits a low-country planter clad in homespun. "My God! look at this!" he exclaims. "I knew the negro, and I predicted much that has happened, but I never thought it would come to this. Let me go."

The negroes themselves were in no way to blame. Back of all this strange scene lay the mistaken zeal of the radical Congress, and back of the radicalism in Congress lay the assassination of Lincoln. Had the nation not been deprived of the wise leadership of the great President, the attempt to heal the wounds of disunion and war by placing the Southern whites under the dominion of their former slaves would never have been made. Ignorant and untutored, the negroes fell under the influence of unscrupulous white leaders, some of them native Southerners known as "scalawags," others recent immigrants from the North, the so-called "carpetbaggers," and became the unwitting instruments of an orgy of misgovernment.

During the years of Republican supremacy in the South taxation quadrupled, State debts mounted, land values sank, frauds were rife. There were frauds in the purchase of land for the freedmen, frauds in underwriting railway construction, frauds in redeeming depreciated bank-notes, frauds in appropriating the public funds. In Louisiana the running expenses of the government were increased 500 per cent, in Arkansas 1,500 per cent; the Alabama State taxes mounted 400 per cent, those of Louisiana 800 per cent, those of Mississippi 1,400 per cent; the North Carolina State debt was run up from $16,000,-000 to $32,000,000, that of South Carolina from $7,000,000 to $29,000,000, that of Alabama from $7,000,000 to $32,000,000, that of Louisiana from $14,000,000 to $48,000,000. County and city debts kept step with these huge increases. Unscrupulous politicians filled their pockets at the public expense, while the taxpayers found it impossible to meet the demands upon their meagre incomes. In Mississippi alone 6,000,000 acres were sold to cover unpaid taxes.

Thus were the wounds of the prostrate South torn open afresh. The prosperity which should have followed the release from slavery—the opening of mines, the building of factories, intensive cultivation of the soil—was postponed two decades.

The whites tried to regain control of the governments by organizing themselves into secret societies, to intimidate the negroes, carpetbaggers, and scalawags. At any time in 1868 or 1869 one might have seen clattering at nightfall along some lonely road a band of weird horsemen. Their 'white robes, ornamented with golden stars and pictures of animals, and their white, masklike helmets, the eye, mouth, and nose holes edged with red braid, made them seem a company of ghosts. Some had horns on each side of the head, some painted beards, some were of gigantic stature. With a jolt they draw up before a log cabin and a voice calls out: "Mose, come out!" The door opens and a trembling negro man emerges. "Mose," says a rider, seven feet high, "bring me some water." The negro brings a gourd of water, but this is struck from his hand with the demand: "Bring me a bucket of water." The horseman grasps the bucket and drains it to the bottom. "That's good," he says. "It's the first drink I've had since I was killed at Shiloh." "Mose," adds the horseman, as the strange cavalcade turns to go, "if you ever vote the Republican ticket again, we are coming back to take you with us to the other world."

The band clatters on in quest of more serious work. Stopping before a frame house, several men dismount, enter, and after some minutes reappear, bringing with them a white man in his night-clothes. Silently the horsemen gather around the prisoner, while the spokesman begins in sepulchral tones. "This man is charged with associating with negroes and persuading them to vote the Republican ticket." "Guilty!" the ghostly ring answers. "He is charged with being instrumental in removing an honored fellow citizen from the office of justice of peace in this county, and placing a negro in his stead." "Guilty!" echoes the crowd. Turning to the prisoner, the speaker addresses him. "It is a rule of the order never to give a man more than three days to leave the county, but considering the size of your carpetbag, we will extend the time to five days. We hope you will leave without forcing us to harsh measures, but we are determined to purify this State of carpetbaggers and scalawags." With this the horsemen wheel into line and vanish in the darkness.

By such means the supremacy of the whites was gradually restored in the reconstructed States. Open rebellion against the corrupt rule of carpetbaggers and scalawags was impossible so long as it was upheld by Federal bayonets, so the people resorted to intimidation, threats, floggings, and hangings. Congress made desperate efforts to protect the negro and force bills were passed to foil the Ku-Klux Klan and the Knights of the White Camelia. These efforts proved futile. The Republican party in the South became the black man's party, and all classes of whites—ante-bellum Whigs, ex-Confederates, poor planters —united to oppose it. One State after another was redeemed— North Carolina, Georgia, and Tennessee in 1870; Alabama, Texas, and Arkansas in 1874; Mississippi in 1875. When the voters of the country went to the polls in 1876 to elect a new President, Florida, South Carolina, and Louisiana were the only States still under negro rule.

In the meanwhile, President Johnson's troubles had multi-plied. On March 2, 1867, Congress passed over his veto a ten-ure-of-office bill, designed to take out of his hands the power of dismissing members of the Cabinet. In February, 1868, John-son tested the constitutionality of this act by removing Secre-tary Stanton, and placing the War Department under the charge of General Lorenzo Thomas. Thereupon the House of Representatives impeached the President, the Senate sitting as the court with Chief Justice Chase in the chair. The indict-ment charged him with "high crimes and misdemeanors" in defying the Tenure-of-Office act, vilifying members of Con-gress, and declaring certain laws unconstitutional. The radi-cal leaders felt sure that their arch-enemy had now been deliv-ered into their hands. But as the trial proceeded it became obvious that the nation did not sanction the removal of a President for political reasons, for Johnson, however tactless and violent, had administered his office with scrupulous fidelity to law. In the end several Republican Senators, despite the threats of the party leaders, united with the twelve Democrats and prevented conviction.

In May, 1868, the Republican party nominated General Grant for the Presidency. Grant was not a politician, his early sympathies had been Democratic, and he struck a popular chord when he said in his speech of acceptance, "Let us have peace." In the election he carried 26 States with 214 electoral votes, while Horatio Seymour, the Democratic candidate, car-ried only 8 States with 80 votes. Yet Grant's popular majority was only 300,000. This was a slender margin, indeed, when it is considered that the total included 700,000 negro votes. In alarm the Republicans framed the Fifteenth Amendment, designed to perpetuate the black vote in the South and to extend the franchise to 200,000 negroes in the other States.

Many Southerners hoped that the rigors of carpetbag government would be relaxed under the administration of the kindly Grant. They were sure that the victor of Appomattox would not permit them to be trampled by greedy politicians. But the new President felt that he could not undo the work of the men who elected him to office. Throughout his two terms he kept the Federal troops in the South, turned a deaf ear to the Southern whites, and upheld the carpetbag governments. It was then that the Southerners resorted to the acts of intimidation and violence which succeeded before the end of Grant's second administration in restoring white control in every State save Florida, South Carolina, and Louisiana.

With the approach of the election of 1876, it became obvious that relief was at hand even in these States. Rutherford B. Hayes, the Republican candidate for the Presidency, was opposed to severe measures in the South, while Samuel J. Tilden, whom the Democrats put in nomination, was an ardent advocate of white supremacy. In the election Tilden carried New York, Connecticut, Indiana, and other doubtful States, and at first even Republican papers conceded his election. But South Carolina, Florida, and Louisiana sent in double sets of electoral votes, while one vote from Oregon was disputed. This left the decision in doubt. Tilden had 184 undisputed votes, and needed but one more to secure the election; if Hayes were accorded every doubtful vote he would have 185 to Tilden's 184.

A violent controversy ensued. Nothing in the Constitution covered the case. The Republicans declared that the decision should rest with the President of the Senate, the Democrats demanded a settlement by a joint vote of both Houses of Congress. Finally it was decided to appoint a commission consisting of five Congressmen, five Senators, and five members of the Supreme Court, to pass on the votes of each disputed State. This body, comprising eight Republicans and seven Democrats, met February 4, 1877, in secret session in the Supreme Court chamber, while the country waited in expectation. It was known that they would debate first whether they had the power to "go behind the returns," and upon this point the whole matter would probably hinge. Should the Commission inquire into the circumstances under which the votes for electors were cast, it was felt that Tilden would be the final victor; if they refused to do so, Hayes would have an excellent chance of success.

As the afternoon wore on, the corridors adjacent to the Supreme Court chamber filled up with Senators, Representatives, lawyers, and newspaper correspondents, all waiting for the decision. At four o'clock the door opened and the commission filed out. As they passed along the corridors, they ignored the expectant crowd. Senator Edmunds came first. Hurrying to the Senate stairway, he disappeared without being accosted. Judge Hoar, who followed, also passed without giving out information. Then came Senator Morton. Morton was an invalid, and usually was carried about the Capitol in a chair. Now he came out supported on either side. As he limped along an old gentleman bent forward and asked in an undertone: "What is the decision, Senator?" "Eight to seven," was the reply. "But, for God's sake, on which side are the eight?" "Against going back of the returns," said Morton, wearily passing on. Within a few minutes this announcement was repeated from lip to lip, and sent out over the telegraph wires.

As the days passed and Hayes won point after point, always by a strictly partisan vote of 8 to 7, the Democrats began a filibuster. But the most prominent Southern leaders took no part in this. They were reconciled to the election of Hayes, because they had received assurance that he favored local self-government in the South and would withdraw the Federal troops. A few days later the Commission awarded the last of the doubtful States to Hayes, and on March 4 he was inaugurated. In April the Federal troops were withdrawn from the State-houses of South Carolina and Louisiana. The carpetbag governments collapsed, and the period of Southern reconstruction was at an end.

It was unfortunate that the transition from the old system

in the South to the new should have required civil war, with its accompaniment of suffering, devastation, economic ruin, and political corruption. The New England revolution had cost hardly one drop of blood; but the Southern revolution produced a convulsion from which the section was slow to recover. Yet it was a wholesome revolution, and the suffering and sacrifices were perhaps not too great a price to pay for it. In freeing the slaves Lincoln had also freed the South from slavery. With slavery gone, the South could begin the erection of its new economic system. In a very real sense Lincoln is the founder of the New South.

Yet it was a stupendous task to erect the great, prosperous South of to-day from the ruins of the ante-bellum South. The Confederate soldier who trudged wearily home from Appomattox was greeted on all sides by scenes of ruin—devastated fields, burned dwellings and barns, chimneys standing without houses, houses standing without roofs, wrecked bridges, twisted rails, roads overgrown with weeds, uncultivated fields, ruined villages, cities a series of blackened walls. Upon reaching his own plantation the prospect was not less discouraging. His dwelling had fallen into disrepair, the furniture was marred and broken, dishes held together with cement, window-panes replaced by thin boards; the work-horses were gone, cattle and hogs slaughtered or driven away, farm implements out of repair, slave cabins empty.

How great is the contrast of the South of to-day with its modern cities with paved streets, towering office-buildings, beautiful parks, high schools; its manufacturing centres, where thousands labor amid the clash of machinery and the whir of spindles; its busy seaports, with great wharves where ocean steamers take on cargoes of cotton and tobacco, or coal and pig-iron! Everywhere there are excellent highways, double-tracked railways, prosperous farms, neat villages, and well-built schools. Freed from the curse of slavery, the South at last has come into its own.

CHAPTER XXII

THE CHANGING ORDER

THE night of July 21, 1877, found the city of Pittsburg in the grip of a mob of striking railway workers. The militia had been ordered out, but the local companies had refused to fight, while those from a distance were outnumbered and had taken refuge in the roundhouse of the Pennsylvania yards. Here they defended themselves throughout the night. The strikers got possession of a cannon which they brought up to batter down the walls of this improvised fortress. But the militia picked off the amateur artillerymen until they forced them to give up the attempt. Farther up the yards there were long lines of loaded freight-cars. To these the mob applied the torch, and columns of black smoke rolled up, followed by flames. The machine-shops between Twenty-fifth and Twenty-sixth Streets caught fire. The soldiers now found themselves ringed about with flames, and the heat became so intense that they were compelled to leave their stations at the windows.

Worse was to come. The strikers seized a freight-car filled with coke, which they ran from the Alleghany Railway to the Pennsylvania yards. Here they brought up quantities of oil, and, pouring it over the coke, set it on fire. Instantly the car became a mass of flames. Thereupon the mob, with a shout, rolled it against the wall of the roundhouse. As the roof caught, the soldiers came out in compact formation, a Gatling-gun in front. The mob drew back, firing in desultory fashion, while the company passed down Twenty-fifth Street, into Liberty Street to the United States arsenal. Thirty-four killed and one hundred wounded, strikers and soldiers, was the record in Pittsburg for that day's fighting.

This affair, which had echoes in Baltimore, Chicago, St. Louis, and other cities, came as the result of an attempt to lower the wages of the railway workers. Throughout the country it created great alarm. "Are we on the verge of another civil war?" men asked each other. "Shall armed mobs be permitted to burn and murder at will?" There were few who evaluated the strikes correctly, not as symptoms of decay, but as indications of a changing order; as growing pains of the American industrial giant.

The period following the Civil War was marked by the development of big business. The time when the manufacturer built up his business by individual ability, owned the entire plant, and at the approach of old age installed his son as his successor, was passing away. Consolidation was becoming the order of the day. The economies effected by large-scale production were so great that those who could not keep pace with the new development were soon outdistanced. The large concerns found it possible to install the latest machinery, purchase on advantageous terms, employ highly trained managers, prevent duplication, reduce the cost of competitive advertising, utilize waste material for by-products. It was the beginning of a new industrial revolution, destined to transform American industry and life.

In 1855 John D. Rockefeller, then a boy of sixteen, obtained his first job, and started work as a clerk in a produce commission office on a dock in Cleveland. We may picture him perched upon a high stool, his face hidden in the account-books, earning his employer's respect by his industry and talent for business. His appearance was unusual, even in youth, the high cheek-bones, the Roman nose, the long, thin upper lip, the broad forehead, the piercing eyes giving the impression of nervous energy and power. Here was the embryo genius ready to take the lead in the momentous changes of the next half-century.

At the age of twenty-three Rockefeller entered the petroleum business. So great was his success that he soon deliberately set out to gain complete mastery of this rapidly growing industry. "In another decade," we can hear him saying, "millions in America, in Europe, in Asia, and Africa will need petroleum every day in their lives. When that time comes this industry, all of it, will be mine." He determined to become what none before him had been, a captain of industry, controlling a vast monopoly compared to which the business of an Astor or a Vanderbilt was insignificant.

Rockefeller's success was startling. In 1870 he and his partners, Samuel Andrews and H. M. Flagler, joined hands with certain large capitalists to form the Standard Oil Company of Ohio. Having secured from the railways rebates so heavy that other companies could not compete with them, they offered their rivals the alternative of selling out to them or of facing ruin. There were about twenty-five independent refineries operating in Cleveland, and in two years the Standard Oil had absorbed all save five. Having conquered the largest refining centre in the United States, this Napoleon of business turned his attention to other fields. By 1874 he had gained control of the principal refineries of New York and Philadelphia, those of Baltimore and Pittsburg succumbed before the end of 1875, while four years later he had swept over the Titusville district in western Pennsylvania, where the oil business had its origin. The country suddenly became aware that one of its most important industries had fallen under the control of a single giant company, which in turn was directed by one business genius.

Equally dramatic was the success with which Rockefeller acquired, one after the other, the oil pipe-lines. At first these lines had run only from the wells to near-by railway centres, but later great underground mains were constructed from the oil region to the city refineries. When it was first announced that a design was on foot to pump oil over the Alleghany Mountains, many were incredulous, but the undertaking was carried through successfully. In 1879 an independent concern, the Tidewater Company, had completed a line to Williamsport and began pumping. Crowds of interested spectators gathered at the stations—newspaper reporters, Standard Oil men, railway men, country people. Would the experiment prove successful? Slowly the oil began its long journey, travelling as fast as a man can walk, out to the Alleghanies and then up the steepest inclines. Seven days after the pumps had been started the oil began to flow into the big receiving tank at Williamsport. A new era had come to the oil business. The Standard Oil Company struggled bitterly to strangle this new concern. Refineries upon which it depended to take its output were bought up, railway rates were lowered, lawsuits were instituted. At last, when these efforts had failed, the Standard entered into a working agreement with the Tidewater Company, which practically placed the first great seaboard pipe-line in its hands.

By the year 1882 the Standard Oil Company owned fourteen separate companies outright and held a controlling interest in the stock of twenty-six others. In order to harmonize the operation of these plants, a scheme was devised whereby each confided its stock to a board of trustees, and in return received trust certificates entitling it to a proper share of the earnings of the combined Standard Oil Trust. Thus was created the first great business leviathan.

In the meanwhile a little group of men, headed by Andrew Carnegie were working to make Pittsburg the steel centre of the world. The Bessemer process, the use of coke in smelting, the discovery of ore-beds on the shores of Lake Superior, the presence of skilled workmen, the expanding demand for steel in the United States, and the protective tariff combined to give the American manufacturers an advantage over all competitors, of which these men availed themselves fully. Carnegie prided himself upon selecting able lieutenants. "Here lies the man who knew how to get around him men who were cleverer than himself," he once suggested for his epitaph. Certainly Captain "Bill" Jones, a practical genius at steel-making; Henry Phipps, with his eye for microscopic details; Henry C. Frick, the first American to see the possibilities of coke in the manufacture of steel; Charles M. Schwab, a genius at handling workmen, constituted a remarkable group. They soon made the Carnegie Steel Works the greatest plant of its kind in the world. By 1900 they had piled up profits of $40,000,000 and there seemed no limit to the growth of their business.

At this juncture Carnegie decided to retire. Believing that no man should die rich, he wished to devote himself to philanthropy. Before he could dispose of his interests, however, his fighting spirit was aroused by the attempt of certain great financiers to get control of the steel business. Carnegie had no interest in Wall Street, he distrusted J. Pierpont Morgan and his associates, and he determined now to block their plans. Purchasing a tract at Conneaut, he began the construction of a plant for the manufacture of steel tubes. Should this enterprise be pushed to completion, it would ruin the National Tube Company, one of Morgan's creations, for the new plant with more modern equipment would operate at a far lower figure. While the Wall Street men were staggering from this blow, Carnegie struck them again by aiding George J. Gould to extend his railway system to Pittsburg. As the "Little Giant" himself controlled the larger part of the freight which made the city a railway centre, this move created the greatest alarm.

Morgan was forced to capitulate. All one night he talked the matter over with Charles M. Schwab and John W. Gates. There is but one solution, they told him; you must buy out Carnegie, even though you have to pay the top price. Morgan resisted long, but as the light of day was just creeping in at the windows he gave in. "Go and ask him what he will sell for," he said to Schwab. Schwab returned with Carnegie's price. In round figures it was half a billion dollars. The man who had started life in a cotton-mill at $1.20 a week, retired from business with wealth beyond the dreams of Croesus. As he went, there arose the United States Steel Corporation, including 70 per cent of all the steel plants in the country, with a capitalization of $1,404,000,000.

The tendency to combinations was by no means confined to the oil and steel industries. Hundreds of railways were merged into a few trunk lines linking distant sections of the country. There were formed in rapid succession the so-called Whiskey Trust, the Sugar Trust, the Western Union Telegraph Company, the Tobacco Trust, and many others. The age of individual effort in American industry had given way to the age of big business.

This development was attended by many abuses. The trusts warred upon their smaller competitors by every means in their power, foul or fair. They spied upon their officers, attacked them in the courts, ruined them by cutting prices. The railways aided in the overthrow of the small producers by granting rebates on freight to the large shippers. The American people looked on with disgust at these high-handed practices, but they were so steeped in the doctrine of individualism, that it was long before they could bring themselves to ask for governmental interference. "The public be damned," had said W. H. Vanderbilt, and many of the builders of big business acted upon that principle with impunity.

In time, however, men began to ask each other whether the trusts would not overthrow American democracy. In the good old days, they said, when the bulk of the people were farmers, and every farmer owned his land and homestead, the people enjoyed real liberty. Then one man was as good as another, and each man had as much influence in the government as his neighbor. Now that vast industries have organized themselves into trusts, the average citizen is at the mercy of a small group of capitalists. These men are crushing individual enterprise, oppressing the laboring classes, corrupting our representatives in Congress, and gaining control of the government. Unless something is done to curb them, this will become the land of oppression and slavery.

Some thought the remedy lay in a socialistic régime, in which the government would take over the trusts and run them in the interest of the people; others, considering this too radical, looked to government regulation as the proper remedy; still others believed that the great fortunes should be taxed out of existence; while some looked to the democratization of capital by the multiplication of small stockholders. As for the laboring men, they sought to protect their own interests by the organization of trade-unions.

In the days when Rockefeller was building up the Standard Oil Company, a small, stockily built man might have been seen at work in a little office in New York. The room was about ten feet by eight, with a brick floor and one window. It was hot in summer and cold in winter. The furniture consisted of a kitchen table, a child's writing-desk nailed to the wall and supported by make-shift legs, and a number of tomato-boxes, some of which served as chairs, others as files for papers and letters. The occupant of this humble office was an unimposing man of about thirty-six, with long hair, heavy mustache, round

face, big mouth, prominent nose, and small eyes. Such was
Samuel Gompers in the days when he first undertook the task
of organizing the American Federation of Labor.

From small beginnings Gompers built up this body until it
became a powerful factor in the industrial life of the country.
In 1886 the membership was but 150,000, in 1890 it had become 200,000, in 1900 it had mounted to 550,000, and in 1925
to more than 3,000,000. A man of executive skill, conserva-
tism, and fearlessness, Gompers remained at the head of the
Federation for four decades, shaping its policies and extending
its influence. Under his leadership the labor-unions demanded
higher wages, shorter hours, and better working conditions.

Many were the battles to attain these ends. Approximately
24,000 strikes and lockouts took place in the twenty years
from 1881 to 1901, involving 128,000 business concerns and
costing half a billion dollars. As the labor organizations grew
in strength, they resorted less to coercion and violence and
more to arbitration and agreements. In the end they won
success beyond the dreams of the early leaders. To-day the
American union laborer has the coveted eight-hour day, he is
protected from accident at his work, he receives excellent wages
and enjoys opportunities for recreation and mental improvement.

Though the American Federation of Labor succeeded in protecting the working man, it did not solve the problem for the
public. On the contrary, the formation of this gigantic organization tended still further to curtail the rights of the people,
and many thought that they would be crushed between the
forces of capital and labor. In this dilemma the American
citizen insisted that the government curb big business and take
a hand in industrial disputes.

This sentiment found expression in the Sherman Antitrust
Law. On December 4, 1889, John Sherman introduced a bill in
the Senate to declare unlawful all combinations in restraint of
trade, and on March 21, 1890, he rose to defend it. The figure
of the veteran legislator, with his tall, angular body, white hair
and beard, wrinkled face, high brow, and piercing eyes, had
long been familiar in the Senate. Seldom did he speak without

commanding the attention of his colleagues. This day especially there was a hush of expectation as he began.

"Mr. President," he said, "associated enterprise and capital
are not satisfied with partnerships and corporations competing with each other, and have invented a new form of combination commonly called trusts, that seeks to avoid competition. . . . If the concentrated powers of this combination are
intrusted to a single man, it is a kingly prerogative, inconsistent with our form of government, and should be subject to
the strong resistance of the State and national authorities. If
anything is wrong this is wrong. If we will not endure a king
as a political power we should not endure a king over the production, transportation, and sale of any of the necessities of
life. . . .

"I admit that it is difficult to define in legal language the
precise line between lawful and unlawful combinations. This
must be left for the courts to determine in each particular case.
All that we, as lawmakers, can do is to declare general principles, and we can be assured that the courts will apply them
so as to carry out the meaning of the law. . . .

"The popular mind is agitated with problems that may disturb the social order, and among them all none is more threatening than the inequality of condition, of wealth and opportunity, that has grown within a single generation out of the
concentration of capital into vast combinations to control production and trade, and to break down competition. These
combinations already defy or control powerful transportation
corporations and reach State authorities. They reach out their
Briarean arms to every part of our country. . . . Congress
alone can deal with them, and if we are unwilling or unable,
there will soon be a trust for every production, and a master
to fix the price for every necessity of life."

So the act was passed, declaring the trusts illegal. It succeeded neither in putting an end to big business, nor in "un-
scrambling" the trusts. The courts displayed a great tender-
ness for private interests, while the corporations evaded the
law by substituting holding companies and "communities of
interest." Of eight cases which were tried under the Sherman

Act during Harrison's administration, the courts decided against the government in seven. McKinley made no effort to enforce the law. In the decade from 1890 to 1900 no less than 157 new combinations were formed, with a total nominal capital of $3,150,000,000. The great captains of industry were rapidly coming to feel that they constituted a privileged class, beyond the reach of restraint.

They had a rude awakening. The morning newspapers of February 20, 1902, made the announcement that President Roosevelt had directed the Attorney-General, Philander C. Knox, to institute proceedings in the Federal court against the Northern Securities Company. The financial world was amazed. The Northern Securities Company, formed a short time before Roosevelt became President, was a merger of practically the entire railway system of the Northwest. Its leading spirits were J. Pierpont Morgan and James J. Hill.

Mr. Morgan went to Washington to discuss the matter with the President and Mr. Knox. An interesting trio they were: Mr. Roosevelt, courteous, urbane, forceful, his thick-set figure, iron mouth, small eyes gazing out fixedly from behind glasses, broad forehead, ruddy cheeks, giving the impression of radiant energy and vitality; Mr. Morgan, the personification of restrained power, with large frame, massive head, heavy jaws, and drooping mustaches; Attorney-General Knox, an exceptionally small man, but standing erect with chest expanded, as though to keep balanced the huge head he carried on his solid shoulders, a Napoleon head, broad and deep, with high forehead, bulging crown almost denuded of hair, smooth-shaven face without wrinkles, drooping eyelids, prominent nose, lips thin and tightly compressed.

Mr. Morgan was evidently in bad humor, and reproached the President for not letting him know in advance of his purpose to attack the merger. "That is just what we did not want to do," replied Mr. Roosevelt. "If we have done anything wrong," said Morgan, "send your man (meaning the Attorney-General) to my man (naming one of his lawyers) and they can fix it up." "That can't be done," said the President. "We don't want to fix it up," added Knox, "we want to stop it." Then Mr. Morgan asked: "Are you going to attack my other interests, the Steel Trust and the others?" "Certainly not," was the reply, "unless we find out that in any case they have done something that we regard as wrong." As the figure of Mr. Morgan retired, the President turned to Knox, saying: "That is the most illuminating illustration of the Wall Street point of view. Mr. Morgan could not help regarding me as a big rival operator, who either intended to ruin all his interests or else could be induced to come to an agreement to ruin none."

Although the Northern Securities Company fought bitterly, the United States Circuit Court at St. Paul decided in favor of the government. Mr. Morgan and his associates then appealed to the Supreme Court, but this body, March 14, 1904, by the narrow margin of 5 to 4, decided that the merger had been formed in violation of the Sherman Law. The people hailed the result with joy. At last the government was coming to their aid; at last a President had been found honest enough and fearless enough to fight the battles of the plain citizen against the power of capital. As the people of England and France in the fifteenth century looked to their kings to protect them against the lawless barons, so the people of the United States now looked to Roosevelt to protect them against these modern barons of industry and finance.

The President had no intention of turning back the hands of the clock, of destroying big business and returning to the days of free competition. To make such an attempt would not only be futile but might bring disaster. It was his purpose to control rather than to ruin. "In dealing with the big corporations which we call trusts, we must resolutely purpose to proceed by evolution and not revolution . . .," he said in an address at Cincinnati. "The evils attendant upon overcapitalization alone are, in my judgment, sufficient to warrant a far closer supervision and control than now exists over the great corporations. . . . We do not wish to destroy corporations, but we do wish to make them subserve the public good. All individuals, rich and poor, private or corporate, must be subject to the law of the land; and the government will hold them to a rigid obedience. . . . The rich man who does not see that this is in his interest is, indeed, short-sighted. When we make him obey the law, we insure for him the absolute protection of the law."

This policy found expression in the Hepburn Act of June 29, 1906. Nineteen years before, during Cleveland's first administration, an Interstate Commerce Commission had been created, to investigate the activities of the railways and prosecute offenders. Although this body had labored diligently, its powers were so limited that it had accomplished little. Rebating was as persistent as ever. Now President Roosevelt, in his message of December, 1904, asked Congress to put an end to this practice by giving the Commission the power to fix rates. This brought angry protests from the conservatives. It is time to stop meddling with business, they said. Reasonable regulation is well enough, but no good can come of persecuting men merely because they possess greater ability or greater wealth than their fellows. Even Lodge and Knox, the President's warmest friends, were opposed to the measure, while the Republican leader of the Senate, Nelson W. Aldrich, did everything within his power to block it.

Mr. Roosevelt knew that public opinion demanded a stringent rate bill and stood resolutely by his guns. On June 21, 1905, Representative W. P. Hepburn introduced a bill embodying all his recommendations. The conservatives succeeded in blocking this measure before the session adjourned, but it was brought up again in 1906. This time the House of Representatives passed it, 346 to 7. Even the most uncompromising "stand-patter" in the Senate now saw the handwriting on the wall. Senator Stephen B. Elkins, chairman of the Interstate Commerce Committee, had fought the bill bitterly. One day, at a meeting of the conservative members of the committee, he announced that he had reversed his position. "I am going to vote for the bill," he said. "What!" the others shouted. "Yes," said Elkins, "when a team is going to run away I prefer to be on the wagon rather than in front of it."

The enemies of the measure had one last card to play. When the committee reported the bill, they placed it in charge of

Senator Benjamin R. Tillman, of South Carolina, a Democrat and a bitter enemy of Roosevelt. Four years before, on Washington's Birthday, Tillman had indulged in a fisticuff on the floor of the Senate with his colleague from South Carolina, John L. McLaurin. Shocked at this undignified performance, Roosevelt had recalled an invitation to Tillman to a dinner at the White House in honor of Prince Henry of Prussia. "Pitchfork Ben," as he was called, never forgave that slight. The conservatives hoped that with Roosevelt's pet measure in charge of his implacable enemy, co-operation would be impossible and failure would result. They were doomed to disappointment. Roosevelt immediately sent for Tillman and began discussing with him the best means of pushing the measure through the Senate. "I don't care a rap who has charge of the bill," he told his friends; "what I am after is its passage." The Senate passed the measure 71 to 3, and on June 29, 1906, it became law.

The Hepburn Act increased the membership of the Interstate Commerce Commission from five to seven; extended its authority over express companies, sleeping-car companies, and pipe-lines; and gave it the authority to reduce unreasonable rates on complaint, subject to court review. Excellent results followed. "The Interstate Commerce Law has rather amusingly falsified the predictions, both of those who asserted that it would ruin the railroads and those who asserted that it did not go far enough and would accomplish nothing," said the President in his message of December 3, 1906. "During the last five months the railroads have shown increased earnings and some of them unusual dividends; while during the same period the mere taking effect of the law has produced an unprecedented, a hitherto unheard-of number of voluntary reductions in freight and fares by the railroads."

The experience gained from the Hepburn Act tended to crystallize opinion in favor of trust regulation rather than "trust busting." Roosevelt expressed the opinion that all efforts to restore the old competitive system would fail. "Business cannot be successfully conducted in accordance with the practices and theories of sixty years ago," he said, "unless we abolish steam, electricity, big cities, and, in short, not only all modern business and modern industrial conditions, but all the modern conditions of our civilization. The effort to restore competition as it was sixty years ago, and to trust for justice solely to this proposed restoration of competition, is just as foolish as if we should go back to the flintlocks of Washington's Continentals as a substitute for modern weapons of precision. . . . Our purpose should be, not to strangle business as an incident of strangling combinations, but to regulate big corporations in thoroughgoing and effective manner, so as to help legitimate business as an incident to thoroughly and completely safeguarding the interests of the people as a whole."

During the past two decades the dread of money-kings has gradually subsided. Some large fortunes have been divided up, some have been dissipated by incompetent heirs. Many wealthy men, notably Rockefeller, Carnegie, and Frick, have given away princely sums to charity, health work, and education. The Federal and State governments have cut deep into large fortunes by means of taxation. Although this has been denounced as confiscation by the conservatives, it has had an appreciable effect in making the distribution of wealth more uniform.

Far more promising, because it strikes at the root of the trouble, is the recent tendency toward democratizing capital. Many of the great corporations are endeavoring to place their stocks in the hands of small holders. Some require their employees to purchase stock; others have adopted various profit-sharing schemes. The American Telephone and Telegraph Company, the United States Steel Corporation, and other great companies now number their shareholders by the hundreds of thousands. Should the day come when every hard-working thrifty American citizen has tucked away in his safety-box a few securities, attesting that he is a partner in the nation's great industries, the problem of reconciling big business with democratic institutions will in large measure be solved.

The story of the United States during the past sixty years is the story of an amazing transformation. The life of the average American of to-day is as unlike that of his grandfather as the life of his grandfather was unlike that of Sir William Berkeley or of Cotton Mather. It is easy to picture the farmer of the Civil War period, drawing water from his well in a bucket, or breaking the ground with a crude plough, or jolting in his wagon over uneven dirt roads, or riding the farm-horse post-haste for the doctor; we can see his wife preparing the children to go to the one-room school a half-mile away, or "putting up" preserves, or dipping the candles or churning butter; we can see the city dweller as he passes down his unpaved and unsewered streets, or enters a little horse-car to go to business, or reads his paper by the flickering gaslight. To-day the farmer lights his house with his private electric system, his bathroom he supplies with running water by means of his gasoline-engine pump, in case of sickness he telephones the doctor, whose automobile appears at the door in ten minutes, he sends his child fifteen miles to school in the motor-coach over concrete roads, and takes his wife ten miles in his Ford car to buy groceries or to see the moving-picture show; the modern city dweller lives in an apartment-house with its electric lights, gas-stove, refrigeration, vacuum cleaners, and elevators; he goes to business in the subway train and takes his family to the shore for the week-ends in his automobile.

Big business is largely responsible for these startling changes. The mining of coal in vast quantities, the transportation of oil by pipe-lines, the standardization of output, production in mass, efficient organization, and masterly management have combined to place within the reach of the average citizen luxuries hitherto undreamed of. Without the genius of Henry Ford and the efficiency of his business organization, the automobile would not to-day be the servant of so many millions. Big business has become necessary to our civilization.

CHAPTER XXIII

A NATION MOVING WEST

BACK in the fourth decade of the nineteenth century the Delaware or Pawnee gazed with wonder at the immigrant trains which passed slowly along the banks of the Missouri toward the Rockies. In the lead was the guide, in blanket coat, moccasins, broad felt hat, and deerskin trousers with fringes along the seams. His knife was stuck in his belt, his rifle rested on the pommel of the saddle, his powder-horn hung at his side. Behind him was a long line of wagons drawn by oxen, jolting over the rough ground. From beneath the canvas covers dirty-faced children peeped out, while on the seat buxom girls and thin-faced, careworn women knitted industriously. The opening in the rear permitted a sight of guns, bundles, clothing, provisions, cooking-utensils, saddles, now and then a bit of furniture. The proprietor walked beside the wagon. Behind all came a drove of cattle, with half a dozen tanned men on horseback keeping them in line. Thus did the adventurous move west in those early days.

A third of a century later, in a level, circular valley, just north of Salt Lake, a group of about 500 men assembled—railway officials, public officers, contractors, surveyors, laborers, among them Chinese, Mexicans, and negroes. They stood around two little locomotives which faced each other on a single track. There were a few brief addresses. Then two men brought up a tie of California laurel, bearing a silver plate inscribed with the words: "The last tie laid on the completion of the Pacific Railroad, May 10, 1869." As they placed this beam under the rails, all hats came off and a minister offered prayer. Several men stepped up, one at a time, and presented four spikes, two of gold, two of silver. Governor Stanford, of California, and Vice-president Durant, of the Union Pacific, put the spikes in place and drove them in with silver hammers. The gathering gave a great cheer, the locomotives moved up until they touched each other, and a bottle of champagne was poured on the rails. The last step had been taken in linking the East with the West, and trains could now run from New York to San Francisco.

Some of the men who had crossed plains and mountains with the wagon cavalcades of 1846 came all the way from California to witness this scene. As their train dashed eastward over canyons, now "poised in mid-air, now flying through the tree-tops, and now circling like an eagle the beetling cliffs," now crossing the desert, their minds went back to that other journey of long ago. They grouped together in their comfortable car, these veterans of the West, to point out, as they sped along, the spots where they had abandoned their wagons, or where their oxen had perished, or where some loved one had been buried.

After the completion of the first railway to the Pacific, the Far West developed rapidly. Other lines were laid down, to Santa Fe, Tucson, and Los Angeles in the south, and to Helena and Portland in the north. Settlers poured in, some from the Eastern States, others from Europe. The task of cultivating the prairies was made easier by improvements in farm machinery, which enabled men to plough, cultivate, and reap with a small labor force. The famous McCormick reaper; the self-binder, which cut the grain and bound it into bundles; the steam-driven thresher; and finally the combined reaper and thresher, came into use on the wheat-farms of Nebraska and the Dakotas. In addition manure-spreaders, corn-planters, potato-planters, and hay-stackers made it possible to produce harvests undreamed of in the days of hand-implements. In 1860 the population of the region north of Texas and west of Missouri was 760,000; twenty years later it had mounted to 3,351,000.

In the decades following the Civil War the prosperity of the West was threatened by the fluctuations of the greenback, at that time the national standard of value. When Lee's veterans laid down their arms, there were in circulation half a billion dollars of Treasury notes, and a third of a billion of national-bank notes. The business of the country was transacted chiefly in this debased paper, which the government refused to redeem at face value in gold. At this juncture the agricultural lands of the West were filling up, and new farms opened by the thousands. To build barns and fences and purchase live stock and machinery, the settlers often had to mortgage their property. Therefore, any move to bring the greenbacks to a parity with gold would be a threat at their prosperity. When Congress passed an act in 1875 providing that on and after January 1, 1879, the government must accept greenback dollars as the equivalent of gold dollars, the Western papers protested violently. "Is this wise?" they asked. "Is it just? The Western farmer mortgages his farm and receives, let us say, $1,000 in greenbacks, worth $500 in gold. Now his government runs up the value of the greenbacks, and he has to pay back the equivalent of $1,000 in gold, or double what he borrowed. By the tricks of currency he has been robbed of $500, and perhaps forced to sell his farm."

In May, 1875, the enemies of the Resumption Act organized the National Greenback Party, which came out for "fiat money" as a permanent policy, and nominated a candidate for the Presidency. The party reached its zenith two years later, when it polled a million votes. In the East the grievances of the Westerners were not well understood. The people, regarding the resumption of gold payments as heralding the beginning of an epoch of "sound money," denounced the advocates of cheap money as fanatics bent on ruining the credit of the nation. The Westerners had to smother their resentment, and fall back upon the hope that time would right their wrongs.

But time seemed to increase rather than diminish the causes for dissatisfaction. In the election of 1880 the Greenbackers were hopelessly outdistanced by the two older parties. To the Westerner the campaign seemed a sordid struggle between the ins and the outs, with one old party as bad as the other. A feature of the electioneering was the pressure put upon office-holders for contributions to the Republican campaign funds. The public service, with its 200,000 office-holders, was converted into a party machine. The Democrats, unable to demand aid from Federal officials, had to content themselves with extracting contributions from office-holders in those States where their party was in power. Out of this struggle the Republicans emerged victorious, electing James A. Garfield by a vote of 214 to 155.

During the next four years dissatisfaction with the Republican party increased. The growth of big business and the crushing of independent dealers, the monopolizing of the best Western lands by the railways, the belief that the tariff was responsible for high prices, and the low level of public morals convinced many that a change would be advisable. When the Republicans nominated James G. Blaine in 1884, there was a large defection from the party. Blaine had been accused of complicity in the notorious Crédit Mobilier scandal, and many felt that to elect him would be to place the stamp of public approval upon official misconduct. The reformers were christened "Mugwumps," and in their ranks were included such lifelong Republicans as Carl Schurz, Henry Ward Beecher, William Everett, and George Ticknor Curtis. "They are noisy but not numerous," declared Blaine, "pharisaical but not practical, ambitious but not wise, pretentious but not powerful." None the less, they played an important part in the approaching defeat of the Republican party.

At half-past ten on the morning of October 29, 1884, a crowd of nearly a thousand men, most of them ministers in black coats with white ties, thronged into the grand hallway of the Fifth Avenue hotel, in New York, to listen to Blaine. They filled the hall and overflowed into the corridors. There was a sudden hush, and Blaine was seen descending the stairs, leaning upon the arm of Doctor James King, attired in clerical black with a polka-dot tie. He stopped on the fourth or fifth step from the floor, where an elderly minister with a benign face, set off with sideburns, joined him and made an address of welcome. "We are your friends, Mr. Blaine," he said, taking him by the hand. "We believe that you have the capacity to lead and govern 55,000,000 people. We honor your name, and we are here to give you the assurance that the voice of calumny cannot hurt you. . . . We expect to vote for you next Tuesday. We have a higher expectation, which is that you will be the President of the United States, and that you will do honor to your name, to the United States, and to the high office you will occupy. We are Republicans, and we do not propose to leave our party and identify ourselves with the party of Rum, Romanism, and Rebellion."

At these last words, so blazingly indiscreet when publicly addressed to a candidate who hoped to carry New York with the aid of Catholic votes, Blaine stood motionless and apparently attentive. But he was either not listening, or the significance of what was said escaped him. Other ministers made eulogistic addresses, Blaine replied in a few well-chosen words, the throng pressed up to shake his hand, and the meeting came to an end. In less than twenty-four hours every Democratic paper in the country had spread before its readers the fatal alliteration, every Catholic voter in the State knew that the Republican candidate had permitted a slur against his religion to go unrebuked. In the few days which remained before the election, Blaine made desperate efforts to explain and apologize, but "Rum, Romanism, and Rebellion" rolled on to his undoing. The Democratic candidate, Grover Cleveland, carried New York State by 1,149 votes, and New York gave him the Presidency by the electoral vote of 219 to 182.

The inauguration of the first Democratic President since Buchanan was favored by smiling skies and balmy spring air. A stand in front of the Capitol was crowded with Senators, Representatives, members of the Supreme Court, foreign diplomats, and other distinguished guests. The throng which faced this platform spread out over the Capitol grounds into the surrounding streets and avenues, while various military organizations, resting on their arms, added to the brilliancy of the scene. The trees were filled with onlookers, and the roofs of near-by houses were crowded. At half-past twelve the procession emerged from the Capitol, headed by President Arthur, President-elect Cleveland, Chief Justice Waite, and the Sergeant-at-Arms. As they advanced to the front of the stand and took their seats a shout went up, and a few minutes later Cleveland began his inaugural address. The crowd saw a large man dressed in black, with Prince Albert coat, high standing collar, and black tie. His massive head, firm mouth, high forehead, and steady blue eyes gave the impression of fearlessness, strength, and honesty. As he spoke, he kept his left hand behind him, and gesticulated with his right. He had no manuscript, but from time to time he consulted a small slip of paper upon which he had jotted down brief notes.

He touched upon various topics of interest, upon harmony within the Union, upon the need of civil-service reform, upon economy, upon non-intervention in Europe, upon the national domain, upon the treatment of the former slaves. But other matters which were agitating the nation—big business, the tariff, and the currency—he failed to mention. The radical elements, especially in the West, were deeply dissatisfied. There is no hope in either of the old parties, they reiterated. Both are controlled by the money power, and dare not take any measures for the relief of the people. We must organize a new party, pledged to overthrow the gold standard, to lower the tariff, and to destroy the trusts, so that we can sweep out of power both Republicans and Democrats.

As it turned out, Cleveland soon became the champion of one of the pet measures of the West. The high tariff level established during the Civil War was still maintained, because the manufacturers had insisted that lower customs would mean foreign competition, with reduced wages and non-employment. But the farmers had long protested. They contended that the protective tariff raised the price of manufactured goods, stimulated the creation of great corporations, and made the rich richer and the poor poorer; that it was a burdensome tax on the people for the benefit of a small group of manufacturers. Their hearts warmed to Cleveland when he came out openly for lower rates.

The President in his messages several times mentioned the need of tariff reform. But the industrial interests fought the measure, and Congress would do nothing. In December, 1887, Cleveland decided to devote an entire message to this one subject. His advisers warned him that he was signing his own political death-warrant, but he held to his purpose. He called the attention of Congress to the fact that "while comparatively few use imported articles, millions purchase and use things of the same kind made in this country, and pay therefor nearly or quite the same enhanced price which the duty adds to the imported article. Those who pay the imposts pay the duty charged thereon into the public treasury, but the great majority of our citizens, who buy domestic articles of the same class, pay . . . to the home manufacturer."

This message made the tariff the leading issue in the campaign of 1888. The Republicans denounced Cleveland as a "free trader," an enemy of American industry, and a friend of the British manufacturers. The Democrats rallied to his support, but the country was not yet ripe for radical tariff reduction, and the Republican candidate, Benjamin Harrison, was elected. The protective principle was saved, and in 1890 the Republicans put through the McKinley tariff bill, with rates above even the war level.

The McKinley Act was an extremely radical measure. The framers of earlier bills had been careful not to lay imposts on articles used in every household, but this act taxed clothing, tools, carpets, table linen, shoes, everything. Although the Republicans boasted that it was "protective in every paragraph, and American in every line and word," some of them had a premonition that things had been carried too far. It proved a boomerang. Even before it became law, but when its passage was a certainty, there was a perceptible rise in the cost of living. A few months later prices jumped, and every household learned that the family income had been reduced, and that the dinner-basket held less than before. At the same time, wages remained stationary, while the farmers were grieved to see a fall in the price of grain. From all sides came protests, and the McKinley tariff was denounced as "the culminating atrocity of class legislation." The elections for Congress in 1890 proved a landslide for the Democrats.

It was almost universally believed that Harrison's election had ended forever Grover Cleveland's political career. His insistence upon forcing an unpopular issue upon his party on the eve of a presidential election elicited the contempt of the professional politicians. So they relegated him to what they considered a well-deserved obscurity. "Cleveland in New York reminds one of a stone thrown into a river," said Henry Watterson. "There is a 'plunk,' a splash, and then silence." The politicians did not reckon on the reaction against the McKinley tariff. When it became obvious that the issue which had brought defeat to the Democrats in 1888 would bring them victory in 1892, the party could not pass over the man who had forced that issue to the fore. In the national convention the machine politicians made a strenuous effort to prevent Cleveland's nomination, but from the first the tide ran his way. "I can't keep the votes back," said William C. Whitney, who had charge of his campaign. "They tumble in at the windows as well as at the doors." On the first ballot Cleveland received 617 votes, 10 more than the two-thirds necessary for nomination. The Republicans named President Harrison for a second term, but his warmest supporters realized that his chances of re-election were small. Cleveland carried New York, Connecticut, Indiana, and other pivotal States, and received 277 votes to 145 for his opponent.

But disappointment was in store. When a tariff bill was introduced providing for free raw materials, for an appreciable reduction on factory-made articles, for increased duties on liquors, and for an income tax, it was found impossible to hold some of the Democratic Senators in line. A London fish-dealer once remarked: "I am in favor of free trade in everything but herring." The Senators from Maryland, West Virginia, and Alabama refused to give up the protection on coal and iron; the Senators from Louisiana would not sacrifice the sugar-planters. In the end the various interests had so transformed the bill that Cleveland bluntly declared it a sad memorial of "party perfidy and party dishonor." But he felt that it was preferable to the McKinley Act, and permitted it to become a law without his signature.

Even before the passage of this unsatisfactory measure, thousands of Western farmers had turned against Cleveland and the Democratic party. They felt that his policies offered them no hope of relief. And the West was in desperate need of relief at this moment, for the price of agricultural products had fallen to new depths. Wheat was selling at less than fifty cents a bushel, corn was so cheap that in places it was burned for fuel. A long series of droughts had parched the fields, withered the growing grain, and brought despair to the farmers. The annual corn production of Kansas and Nebraska fell from 287,816,000 bushels in 1885 to 110,579,000 bushels in 1889. Unable to make ends meet, the farmers borrowed heavily from Eastern bankers and capitalists. The Topeka *Advocate*, which conducted an investigation of the situation in Kansas, found that of 3,000 farms, 1,727 were burdened with mortgages amounting to nearly a million and a half dollars.

"The virgin soil of the West is rapidly ceasing to be the home and possession of the sturdy American freeman," declared a writer in the *Forum*. "He is but a tenant at will, or dependent upon the tender mercies of corporations and absentee landlords. We have abolished monarchy and primogeniture and church establishments supported by the state, yet the universal curse of humanity, the monopoly of the earth by the wealthy few, remains." A wave of despair passed over the West, and the farmers turned for relief to direct political action.

During the administrations of Garfield and Arthur local associations of farmers had sprung up in the West and South, which soon began to merge, first into State bodies and later into a national federation known as the Farmers' Alliance. Into this great society rushed many fanatics, loud in their complaints of calamity and insistent upon radical remedies. Typical were Mrs. Mary E. Lease, of Kansas, who went about exhorting the farmers to "raise less corn and more hell," and Governor Waite, of Colorado, who warned the Eastern capitalists that he was prepared to ride in blood up to his bridles. In 1892 the Farmers' Alliance joined hands with the Knights of Labor to create the Peoples' Party, or Populists. At a mammoth convention in Omaha, on July 2, this movement was launched amid scenes of intense excitement. The adoption of the platform was greeted by "cheers and yells which rose like a tornado . . . and raged without cessation for thirty-four minutes, during which women shrieked and wept, men em-

braced . . . and leaped upon tables and chairs in the ecstasy
of delight." The new party nominated James B. Weaver, of
Iowa, for the Presidency, and demanded a graduated income
tax, government ownership of railways and telegraphs, a
shorter work-day, the direct election of United States Senators,
and the free coinage of silver at the ratio of sixteen ounces of
silver to one of gold.

Around the last of these issues was destined to rage in the
next four years one of the fiercest political battles in the nation's history. Prior to 1873 every citizen was permitted by
law to take gold or silver bullion to any of the United States
mints, and have it coined into standard dollars at the ratio of
sixteen to one. Since, under this arrangement, silver bullion
was undervalued, silver dollars had long ago passed out of circulation. No one would pay debts in silver dollars worth $1.02
when he could do so with gold dollars worth 100 cents. There
was no protest when, in 1873, an act was passed quietly re-
scinding the free coinage of silver. Since that date, however,
the opening of great mines in Nevada, Utah, Colorado, and
Montana had deluged the country with silver, and the price
of the metal dropped rapidly. In 1872 the content of the old
silver dollar was $1.02; in 1875 it was 96 cents; in 1885 only 82
cents. This changed the situation. It dawned upon the advocates of cheap money that, had it not been for the act of 1873,
the silver dollars would have driven gold out of circulation, and
the country would have been upon a silver basis. Prices would
then have gone up, and the hard-pressed Western farmers could
have lifted the mortgages on their property. The radical leaders denounced bitterly what they called the "crime of 1873,"
asserting that corrupt capitalists had smuggled it through Congress by stealth. For this charge there was no basis. In one of
the later debates, when Senator Stewart, of Nevada, was thun-
dering against the "crime," Senator Sherman put him to rout
by showing from the record that Stewart himself had spoken
and voted for it. None the less, thousands of men in the West
and South now turned to the restoration of the free coinage of
gold and silver at the ratio of sixteen to one as their one hope
of salvation.

They found in Richard P. Bland, of Missouri, a leader so enthusiastic that to all the country he became known as "Silver Dollar Dick." In 1877 Bland pushed through the House of Representatives a bill providing for free silver, but in the Senate the measure was blocked. He was forced to accept a compromise, offered by W. B. Allison, by which the Treasury Department was directed to purchase from two to four million dollars' worth of silver bullion each month and coin it into dollars. In 1890 this law was superseded by the Sherman Silver Purchase Act, which required the government to buy each month 4,500,000 ounces of silver bullion, paying for it in new Treasury notes redeemable in either gold or silver at the option of the government.

The Sherman Act created great satisfaction in the West, for it added $50,000,000 a year to the substitute money in circulation, and gave promise that the country would soon be upon a silver basis. The government's meagre gold reserve had to support not only $346,681,016 in greenbacks, but the accumulating mass of Treasury notes. In the last months of Harrison's administration the reserve began to wane. This led to something like a run upon the Treasury, and from all sides the notes poured in for redemption in gold. President Cleveland, who had already announced his intention of maintaining the gold standard, a few months after his inauguration called an extra session of Congress to consider the condition of the currency. Despite the frantic opposition of the silver men, the Sherman Act was repealed.

Yet the situation remained critical. The leak in the financial dike had been stopped, but the flood of money which swamped the country had not been drained off. The reserve continued to sink, and finally Secretary Carlisle began selling bonds to prevent its complete exhaustion. This proved a discouraging operation. Of $58,660,917 in gold coin which the first bond issue yielded, $24,396,459 had been obtained beforehand from the Treasury by presenting legal tender for redemption. "What was poured in through the funnel was first drawn out through the bunghole." March 6, 1894, the reserve had been restored to $107,000,000; but by August 7 it had fallen to $52,000,000

and in February, 1895, despite a fresh bond issue, to $41,000,-
000. This was a slender store, indeed, with which to secure
the half-billion dollars of notes still in circulation.

President Cleveland was perplexed. The inadequate results
obtained from the bond issues had been in part the result of
restrictions imposed by the Resumption Act of 1875 upon the
rate of interest and the length of time they should run. To
resort to the old expedient seemed a matter of doubtful wisdom. Moreover, both Mr. Cleveland and Secretary Carlisle
had scruples against selling bonds without the authorization of
the existing Congress. But when, after much delay, the President asked for an issue of fifty-year bonds at a low rate of interest, the silver majority blocked him. For the moment it
seemed that the gold standard was doomed.

On February 7, 1895, J. Pierpont Morgan, accompanied by
Robert Bacon, walked hurriedly across Lafayette Square, in
Washington, to the White House. There they were greeted,
rather formally, by President Cleveland, Secretary Carlisle,
and Attorney-General Olney. As Morgan took a seat, he noticed that the President was not smoking, and so, out of
courtesy, refrained from lighting the cigar which he held in his
hand. The President explained that he had decided to offer
bonds for popular subscription, and wished Mr. Morgan's assistance in bolstering up the reserve until the gold had begun
to come in. He then began discussing the situation with Carlisle and Olney, while Morgan and Bacon listened.

At last a message came in stating that there were but $9,000,-
000 of gold left in the New York Subtreasury. "Mr. President," said Morgan, "the Secretary of the Treasury knows of
one check outstanding for $12,000,000. If this is presented it
is all over." Deeply moved at the imminence of the crisis,
Cleveland turned to the financier and said: "Have you anything to suggest?" Thereupon Morgan replied that during
the Civil War a law had been passed authorizing the Secretary of the Treasury to purchase coin upon such terms as he
deemed wise, and that if it had not been repealed it would relieve him of his embarrassment. Olney stepped out of the
room and in a moment returned with the book of Revised

Statutes. Cleveland took the book, and with deep concentration read the act, while every one in the room sat in suspense. At last the President laid the book slowly on his desk, saying: "Mr. Morgan, I think the act is ample for our needs, and that it will solve the situation."

The tension was broken. Cleveland entered into a contract with Morgan and his associates, by which the bankers agreed to furnish the Treasury with 3,500,000 ounces of gold coin, to be paid for in 4-per-cent bonds, running thirty years. When this had been decided, Cleveland's face once more became grave. "How about this drain of gold abroad?" he asked. "Suppose the government does purchase this gold from the bankers, and it is immediately withdrawn from the Treasury and sent abroad. Can you guarantee that such a thing will not happen?" Morgan did not hesitate. "Mr. President, I will so guarantee," he said. As Morgan rose to go, some one noticed a brown powder on his clothes and on the floor around his chair. It proved to be the cigar he had held in his hand, which in the tenseness of the situation he had ground to pieces.

The President's eleventh-hour move in purchasing gold saved the day. Confidence was restored, gold exports were checked, and not until January 6, 1896, was it necessary to make another bond issue. Eventually expanding trade, with its new demands for currency, brought the drain upon the gold reserve to an end. The free-silver men were frantic with anger. Here is the President, who set himself up as the enemy of privilege and the friend of the people, they said, and what does he do? Why, instead of redeeming Treasury notes in silver, as the law allows, he buys gold from a syndicate at usurious rates and adds millions to the national debt. All through the West astonishment and disgust were wide-spread, and as Cleveland's following melted away Populism rose on a new high tide.

It became increasingly evident that Populism was on the verge of gaining control of the Democratic party. The South had joined hands with the West in demanding free silver, and the conventions of thirty States had passed resolutions condemning the gold standard. When the Democratic convention assembled in the Coliseum at Chicago on July 7, 1896, the radical element, men desirous of shaking off the domination of the East, found themselves in the ascendancy. As they marched, shouted, and sang, unheedful of the sweltering summer's heat, it was obvious that many of them were determined to "smash things." The conservative members from the East, David B. Hill, Roswell P. Flower, Arthur P. Gorman, and others, looked on with amazement and disgust, but they were powerless to stem the tide.

The Committee on Resolutions reported a platform devoted chiefly to the money question. "We demand the free and unlimited coinage of both silver and gold at the present legal ratio of sixteen to one," they said, "without waiting for the aid or consent of any other nation. We demand that the standard silver dollar shall be a full legal tender, equally with gold, for all debts, public and private." The conservative leaders pleaded against this surrender of the Democratic party to the cheap-money group, but their words were lost in the howling and stamping of 15,000 men and women. After David B. Hill, W. F. Vilas, and W. E. Russell had spoken, William Jennings Bryan, of Nebraska, was seen to approach the platform, and, ascending two steps at a time, take his stand before the audience. His appearance was striking. The smooth-shaven, almost boyish face, the heavy head with its wavy black hair, the square chin, wide mouth, large, lustrous dark eyes, aquiline nose, square shoulders gave the impression of earnestness, dignity, and power.

"Mr. Chairman and gentlemen of the convention," he began in a melodious, ringing voice, which penetrated to the most distant corners of the vast Coliseum, "I should be presumptuous, indeed, to present myself against the distinguished gentlemen to whom you have listened, if this were a mere measuring of abilities; but this is not a contest between persons. The humblest citizen of the land, when clad in the armor of a righteous cause, is stronger than all the hosts of error. I come to speak to you in defense of a cause as holy as the cause of liberty—the cause of humanity." Turning to the gold delegates, he continued: "When you come before us and tell us that we are about to disturb your business interests, we reply that you have disturbed our business interests by your course. We say to you that you have made the definition of a business man too limited in its application.

"The man who is employed for wages is as much a business man as his employer. The attorney in a country town is as much a business man as the corporation counsel in a great monopoly. The merchant at the crossroads store is as much a business man as the merchant of New York. The farmer who goes forth in the morning and toils all day—who begins in the spring and toils all summer—and who, by the application of brain and muscle to the natural resources of the country, creates wealth, is as much a business man as the man who goes upon the board of trade and bets upon the price of grain. . . .

"We do not come as aggressors. Our war is not a war of conquest; we are fighting in defense of our homes, our families, and property. We have petitioned, and our petitions have been scorned. We have entreated, and our entreaties have been disregarded. We have begged, and they have mocked when our calamity came. We beg no longer; we entreat no more; we petition no more. We defy them. . . .

"We care not upon what lines the battle is fought. If they say bimetallism is good, but that we cannot have it until other nations help us, we reply that, instead of having a gold standard because England has, we will restore bimetallism, and then let England have bimetallism because the United States has it. If they dare to come out into the open field and defend the gold standard as a good thing, we will fight them to the uttermost. Having behind us the producing masses of the nation and the world, the laboring interests, and the toilers everywhere, we will answer their demand for a gold standard by saying to them: You shall not press down upon the brow of labor this crown of thorns—you shall not crucify mankind upon a cross of gold."

At the conclusion of this address ensued a scene of the wildest enthusiasm. Delegation after delegation rose, shouting and waving hats, handkerchiefs, flags, canes, umbrellas. The spectators joined in the demonstration. A Texas delegate started a procession of the silver men, and for many minutes they marched around the floor, holding up their State banners, stamping, dancing, shouting, and singing. It was obvious that the Democratic party had found its leader, and the next day Bryan was nominated for the Presidency. The West was elated, but the disgust of the East knew no bounds. "Lunacy having dictated the platform, it was perhaps natural that hysteria should evolve the candidate," was the comment of the New York *World*.

The campaign was full of excitement and of bitterness. The Republicans had reaffirmed their allegiance to the gold standard and had nominated William McKinley, of Ohio. McKinley was a man of winning personality. But his association with Marcus A. Hanna and other wealthy business men cost him the support of many to whom the trusts in politics were still the leading issue. Bryan fought a good battle. Travelling all over the country, he harangued multitudes, everywhere dwelling on the iniquity of the gold standard, extolling the virtues of the working man, and pleading for free silver. The Republican press answered with bitter personal attacks. "Rattle-headed idiot," "lunatic," "demagogue," "anarchist" were some of the epithets hurled at Mr. Bryan.

As the summer drew to an end, a feeling akin to terror passed over the East. Contracts were made contingent upon the election of McKinley; employees were notified that they need not return to work in the event of Democratic success; vast quantities of "literature" were distributed describing the ruin which would follow the abandonment of the gold standard; contributions from business men poured in upon the Republican headquarters. The Saturday before the election 150,000 New Yorkers—lawyers, doctors, clergymen, bankers, merchants, clerks—marched up Broadway, waving flags and cheering for McKinley and sound money. In the end the Republicans won the day. Confronted with the choice between the triumph of big business in politics and the overthrow of the gold standard, the American voters chose the former. McKinley won by a vote of 271 to 176 in the electoral college, and a popular vote of 7,111,607 to 6,509,052.

Though the inflationists lost at the polls, in the end victory came to them through natural causes. New gold-mines were opened in the frozen wastes of the Klondike, new processes of treating the ore were put into practice, and the precious metal in vast quantities began to pour upon the world market. Under the weight of this golden flood the value of the dollar sank and commodity prices rose. With wheat selling for $1.50, and with the Western farmers rapidly paying off their mortgages, the cry of free silver lost much of its charm. The agrarian West to this day has its grievances, still complains of the oppression of Wall Street, but the demand for cheap money has almost ceased.

The building up of the Far West is an event of great importance in American history. This region, so recently a wilderness, is now full of thriving communities. Where once were deserts are now alfalfa-fields or apple orchards; in place of empty prairies are prosperous farms where the proprietor tends his wheat, corn, cotton, or rice; the great river is now but a tiny rivulet, for its waters have been diverted through irrigation ditches to field and orchard; the lonely trails have given way to concrete roads, crowded with automobiles; along the shores are cities with modern hotels, wharves, mills, factories, and paved streets.

The growth of the West, especially of the Far West, had its roots in the soil. It was in large part in response to the reclamation of arid land through irrigation works, fostered and aided by the Federal Government, that prosperity came to this region. In California, Idaho, Oregon, Washington, Montana, and Wyoming waste places have been made to bloom. In Arizona the great Roosevelt dam, which was completed in 1911, straddles the Salt River and creates a lake 240 feet deep, containing 400,000,000,000 gallons of water. The Arrowrock dam, in Idaho, is even larger, being 354 feet high; the Sun River dam, in Montana, is 329 feet high; the Elephant Butte dam, in New Mexico, 318 feet high; the Shoshone dam, in Wyoming, 328 feet high.

These projects have drawn to the West thousands of enterprising settlers. In the decade from 1900 to 1910 the population of the Far West increased 66.8 per cent. Washington and Idaho more than doubled; California, Oregon, and Arizona increased 60 per cent; while the cities of Los Angeles, Seattle, Spokane, Portland, Tacoma, and Oakland enjoyed phenomenal growth. In the years from 1910 to 1920, although the rate of increase was less rapid, the Far West gained a full 30 per cent, while the country as a whole gained only 14.9.

For many decades the Far West bore to the East the relation of a colony to the mother country. It sent across the continent its food and its raw material, and received in return the manufactured goods essential to its economic life. But in recent years it has been rapidly shaking off this dependency by developing great industrial plants of its own. To-day thousands of skilled workmen are employed in the shipyards of the Pacific coast; mills for the manufacture of motors, tractors, and trucks are flourishing; there are large tire-factories in California and Denver; San Francisco and Portland are developing soap-factories; while in various places are furniture-plants, cotton-mills, shoe-factories, and paper-mills.

Nothing more clearly shows the prosperity of the Far West than the rapid increase in the number of automobiles. In 1915 the number of cars in the three coast States of Washington, Oregon, and California was 169,701; in 1919 it had increased to 414,685; in 1921 to 847,682, and in 1925 to 1,427,471. To-day California alone has a population of 4,000,000. Its wealth is estimated at $15,000,000,000, its railway mileage is 8,282, there are 29,365,667 acres of cultivated land, of which 4,219,040 acres are irrigated. In 1920 its crops were valued at $589,757,000, its dairy products at $276,424,000, its petroleum output was 263,729,000 barrels, while its factories turned out goods to the value of $1,901,204,701.

The rapid development of the West has eliminated the frontier with its distinctive life and influence; has added enormously to the agricultural output of the country, and saved it from dependence upon foreign lands for a large part of its food-supply; has made it possible to absorb the stream of immigrants which for decades poured unchecked upon our shores; increased many times over our trade in the Pacific; involved the nation in the problems of the Far East; added millions to the population, hundreds of millions to the annual output, and billions to the national wealth.

CHAPTER XXIV

DOMINION OVER PALM AND PINE

IT did not occur to the founders of the Republic that the day would come when the United States would seek to acquire distant possessions. With the West inviting settlement, in the early days there was little temptation for expansion overseas. Why search for crumbs, with a splendid banquet spread at home? But a century later, when the last frontier was disappearing, and when American production was outstripping domestic needs, the United States began to reach out, first for world trade and then for foreign possessions.

This movement coincided with the wave of imperialism which swept over Europe in the last two decades of the century, caused by the desire of the great powers to open new markets, secure investment opportunities, and extend their influence. Though the United States took no part in the partition of Africa, nor in the dividing of Turkey and China into spheres of influence, it did seek to enhance and protect its growing commerce by acquiring a limited number of dependencies.

Its efforts to maintain the Monroe Doctrine forced it, half reluctantly, to acquire also a position of dominance in Central America and the West Indies. While holding off the hungry European powers with one hand, with the other it compelled its turbulent Latin-American neighbors to respect its interests, economic and political. The State which failed to keep order or pay its obligations, which confiscated alien property, or put itself in pawn to foreign powers, soon felt the correcting hand of the United States. Thus, in two separate parts of the world, in Latin America and the Far East, American diplomacy became increasingly absorbed in the problems of commerce and of a group of dependencies.

Far out in the south Pacific lies the group of volcanic islands known as Samoa. Despite the insignificance of their size, they have commercial and naval value because of their situation in the track of vessels plying between San Francisco and Australia, and between Cape Horn and the ports of China. Upon the principal island a number of Americans, Germans, and English had settled in the years from 1830 to 1885, traders and missionaries most of them, and the United States, Germany, and Great Britain all had made treaties with the natives. By 1888 it had become evident that Germany, under the leadership of Bismarck, was determined to get complete control of the islands. Finding that the native King, Malietoa, was favorable to the Americans and English, the Germans seized him, and set up a creature of their own named Tamasese. Civil war followed, with the natives playing the part of pawns, one side directed by the German consul, Herr Becker, and the other by the American consul, Harold M. Sewall.

When the German corvette *Adler* was ordered to shell a native village, the United States gunboat *Adams* prevented, by placing itself in the line of fire; when a battalion of German marines landed to attack the native camp, it was an American named Klein who took the lead in driving them back. This resistance to their plans aroused the Germans to fury. "Germans swear vengeance," cabled Vice-Consul Blacklock. "Shelling and burning indiscriminately, regardless of American property. Protest unheeded. Natives exasperated. Foreigners' lives and property in greatest danger. Germans respect no neutral territory. Americans in boats flying. American flag seized in Apia harbor by armed German boats, but released. Admiral with squadron necessary immediately."

The squadron was not long in coming. Soon the *Nipsic*, the *Vandalia*, and the old sea-fighter *Trenton* were lying beside the *Adams* in Apia harbor. They found there the British cruiser *Calliope*, and a German squadron consisting of the *Adler*, the *Eber*, and the *Olga*. The decks of all the vessels were cleared for action, and so tense was the situation that a single rash act might have provoked a war. As it turned out, the assembling of the war-vessels did lead to a terrible disaster, but it was a disaster caused by the hand of nature, not by man.

The harbor of Apia is formed by a circular chain of coral

reefs about a mile in circumference, having but one narrow outlet. Into this small space were crowded the seven men-of-war, a merchant ship, and numerous smaller vessels, all anchored in dangerous proximity to each other. About four o'clock on the afternoon of March 15, 1889, a storm broke over the harbor which grew in violence throughout the night, until with the approach of dawn it had become a hurricane. The water, lashed by the wind, swept over the ships, threatening to engulf them or to tear them loose from their anchors and hurl them upon each other or upon the beach. The sailors worked heroically to avert disaster. Here and there one could distinguish through the murky atmosphere the dim outline of vessels, tossing and rolling. The little gunboat *Eber* was the first to succumb. She was dashed against the reef with terrific force and was seen no more. The *Nipsic* ran ashore in a comparatively safe position, whence most of the crew escaped over hawsers fastened by the natives to trees. The *Adler* was lifted by a gigantic wave and thrown on its side high upon the reef; the *Vandalia* was beached broadside to the sea, where for hours she was pounded by the waves; the *Trenton* went aground upon a projecting ledge of coral.

When the hurricane was at its height, the crew of the *Trenton*, which then was drifting helplessly, saw looming up through the gloom the hull and spars of the *Calliope*. "My anchors are gone," shouted Captain Kane, "and I am going to try to force my way out to sea." With every pound of steam crowded on and with boilers red hot, the British cruiser fought its way forward in the face of the wind. As they passed, the 400 American tars on the *Trenton* swarmed up into the rigging to send after them a cheer of "Godspeed." With almost certain death staring them in the face, these men were generous enough to rejoice in the better fortune of others. "When we saw the noble conduct of the *Trenton's* crew," Captain Kane afterward reported, "and heard them, in the face of a fate even more certain than our own, cheer us on in our perilous path, all traces of listlessness and insubordination vanished, and I knew that the *Calliope* was safe."

The news of this disaster dispelled all thought of war. On

April 29, 1889, a joint commission of the three powers concerned met in Berlin to devise means for a peaceful solution of the Samoan problem. Bismarck did his best to frighten the English and American delegates into recognizing Germany's political predominance in the islands, but in vain. He was compelled to sign an agreement under which Malietoa was restored to his throne, and an equal protectorate of the three powers established. The Samoan incident marks the beginning of a new epoch in American diplomatic history. It was the first assertion by the United States, as John Bassett Moore has said, "not merely of a willingness, but even a right, to take part in determining the fate of a remote and semibarbarous people, whose possessions lay far outside the traditional sphere of American political interests."

A few years later, then, when the Government took steps leading to the annexation of Hawaii, the people accepted it as the continuation of the new policy. The Hawaiian Islands, situated midway between San Francisco and the Philippines, for many decades had enjoyed good government under a line of wise native rulers. But when King Kalakaua, who came to the throne in 1873, reversed the policy of his ancestors and gave himself up to wastefulness and vice, many leading citizens, both white and native, combined to force upon him a liberal constitution. In 1891 Kalakaua was succeeded by his sister, Liliuokalani. The new queen was a woman of regal bearing and broad education, but she was bent on ruling as a despot. In less than two years she had driven the people into rebellion.

Early in 1893 the best elements of the community deposed the Queen, formed a provisional government headed by Sanford B. Dole, and appealed to the American minister, John L. Stevens, for aid in preserving order. At Stevens's request a battalion of soldiers and marines, coming ashore from the United States cruiser *Boston*, encamped before the government building. "I must yield," said Liliuokalani, "because I cannot resist the superior forces of the United States of America." A few weeks later a delegation from the new government appeared before President Harrison to ask that the United States take over the islands. A treaty of annexation was hastily drawn up, signed by the President, and submitted to the Senate for ratification.

"The restoration of Queen Liliuokalani to her throne is undesirable, if not impossible," said Mr. Harrison in his message to the Senate, "and unless actively supported by the United States, would be accompanied by serious disaster and the disorganization of all business interests. . . . It is essential that none of the great powers shall secure these islands. Such a possession would not consist with our safety and with the peace of the world." Yet serious opposition arose to annexation and the Senate thought it best to let the matter rest until President Cleveland entered the White House. As it turned out, Cleveland condemned the whole programme, and advised the restoration of the Queen. But Congress refused to sanction the use of American soldiers and sailors in overthrowing the government of President Dole, voting May 31, 1894, not to interfere further in Hawaii. The republic continued to govern the islands until 1898, when, with the Republican party once more in power at Washington, a resolution of annexation passed the House of Representatives 209 to 91, and the Senate 42 to 21. In 1900 the islands were organized as a Territory, and its citizens made citizens of the United States.

While the Hawaiian affair was still hanging fire, an incident occurred which was destined to exert a far-reaching influence upon the foreign policy of the United States. When, on the evening of December 17, 1895, the people of England went to their accustomed rest, there was not one person in a hundred thousand who did not suppose that the most amicable relations existed between Great Britain and the United States. The next morning, when they read their newspapers, they were amazed to learn that a crisis existed which might well lead the two nations into war. "What is the Venezuelan question?" the average Britisher asked himself, rubbing his eyes. "What is the Schomburgk line? Why is the United States so interested in the matter? Why has the British Government permitted an insignificant question to bring us to the verge of catastrophe?"

For a full half-century Venezuela and British Guiana had engaged in a boundary dispute. In 1841 Great Britain had made claims to a large expanse of territory regarded by the Venezuelans as their own, and had employed a surveyor named Schomburgk to run the boundary line. The Government of Venezeula protested vigorously. They were especially concerned because the Schomburgk line ran to the mouth of the Orinoco River, the control of which was essential to the safety of their republic. Repeated offers to submit the matter to arbitration were rejected by Great Britain. Later, when gold was discovered west of the Schomburgk line, England extended her claim to include the region containing the mines. Finally, in despair, Venezuela appealed to the United States.

Protracted negotiations ensued between Washington and London, in which the American Secretaries of State earnestly requested Great Britain to accept arbitration. It was obvious, so they reasoned, that any encroachment upon the territory of an American country under pretense of fixing a boundary endangered the Monroe Doctrine. The crisis came in Cleveland's second administration. On July 20, 1895, Secretary Olney sent a long despatch to London, tracing the history of the Monroe Doctrine, explaining how it applied to the Venezuelan question, and once more urging arbitration. Unless there was a satisfactory settlement, he said, it would "greatly embarrass the future relations between this country and Great Britain."

Strangely enough, Lord Salisbury, the British Foreign Minister, seems not to have recognized the serious purport of these words. He delayed his reply for four months, and then delivered Olney a lecture upon international law and diplomatic usage. The Monroe Doctrine, he explained, had nothing to do with the dispute. "The dangers which were apprehended by President Monroe have no relation to the state of things in which we live at the present day." Therefore the Venezuelan affair in no way concerned the United States. As for arbitration, it was a procedure open to many objections. "The claim of a third nation which is unaffected by the controversy to impose this particular procedure on either of the two others cannot be reasonably justified, and has no foundation in the law of nations."

Cleveland was greatly angered, both by the condescending tone of this reply and by its blunt refusal to recognize the rights of the United States. He decided upon heroic measures. All through the night of December 16, 1895, he sat at his desk working upon a message, which the next day was read before Congress. It was a stirring paper. The President asked for an adequate appropriation for the expenses of a commission to determine, after careful investigation, "the true boundary line between the Republic of Venezuela and British Guiana," and expressed the opinion that, when the line had been ascertained, it would be the duty of the United States to uphold it "by every means in its power." "In making these recommendations," he said, "I am fully aware of the responsibility incurred and keenly realize all the consequences that may follow. . . . There is no calamity which a great nation can invite which equals that which follows a supine submission to wrong and injustice."

Although this message took the American people by surprise, they did not hesitate. Congress voted $100,000 for the expenses of the commission, the press rang with patriotic utterances, the governors of many States voiced approval and promised support. In England the people were at first inclined to look upon the message as an unprovoked insult. The London *Times* denounced jingoism in the White House, declaring that the whole affair was a bit of unparalleled insolence. To yield would be unthinkable, it declared.

None the less, yield England did. On New Year's Day 354 members of the House of Commons sent a memorial to the President and Congress asking that, in the future, differences between the United States and Great Britain be referred to arbitration. As this was just what Mr. Cleveland was contending for, it augured well for a peaceful solution. In the end public opinion in England veered around to the conclusion that the game was not worth the candle. Lord Salisbury was severely condemned for permitting an inconsequential dispute in far-off South America to drift into a *casus belli* with England's natural friend and best customer. Forced to recede from their original position, the government consented with what grace they could to submit the points in dispute to a tribunal of arbitration, and the Venezuelan affair was ended.

It would be difficult to exaggerate the importance of this victory. "It has established the Monroe Doctrine on lasting foundations before the eyes of the world," wrote Mr. Cleveland himself; "it has given us a better place in the respect and consideration of the people of all nations, and especially of Great Britain; it has confirmed our confidence in the overwhelming prevalence among our citizens of disinterested devotion to American honor."

As the sky was clearing and peace with England was assured, another war-cloud made its appearance on the horizon. Directly south of Florida, basking under semitropical skies, beautiful with its many-colored cities, its fields of sugar-cane and rich tobacco plantations, is the island of Cuba. The Pearl of the Antilles it is called. This charming place was for centuries a prey to misgovernment and oppressions. Proud Spanish officials monopolized every post of honor, robbed the natives, and subjected them to indignities. The island was frequently torn with rebellion. Guerilla bands would raid the plantations of the ruling class, and, after spreading destruction, retire to the mountains or the jungle.

In 1896 the Queen Regent of Spain sent General Valeriano Weyler to Cuba. Unable to distinguish the loyal natives from the rebels, this officer attempted to keep the entire population of the disaffected districts under watch by herding them together in the vicinity of the fortified towns. Here the unhappy "reconcentrados," penned in like cattle, with foul air, foul water, and foul food, perished by the thousand. Their condition excited pity and indignation in the United States.

The American people had long been interested in Cuba. "It lies so near to us as to be hardly separated from our territory," President Cleveland pointed out. "Our actual pecuniary interest in it is second only to that of the people and government of Spain. It is reasonably estimated that at least from $30,-000,000 to $50,000,000 of American capital are invested in plantations and in railroad, mining, and other business enterprises on the island. The volume of trade between the United States and Cuba, which in 1889 amounted to about $64,000,-000, rose in 1893 to about $103,000,000." Obviously we could not be indifferent to unending turmoil produced by Spanish inefficiency.

On June 27, 1897, Secretary of State Sherman sent a note to the government at Madrid, protesting against Weyler's inhuman conduct. For his pains he received a reply from the Spanish Foreign Minister, intimating that Weyler had acted with no greater severity than General Sherman, the Secretary's own brother, in his famous march to the sea during the American Civil War. None the less, Weyler was recalled, and a grant of autonomy for Cuba published. It seemed that war would be avoided. But the Cuban insurgents insisted upon unqualified independence, while the ruling class was furious at the sacrifice of their old privileges. Mobs paraded through the streets of Havana, cheering for Weyler and cursing President McKinley and the United States. At this juncture General Fitzhugh Lee, our consul-general at Havana, advised the government that the presence of a war-ship in Cuban waters was necessary for the protection of American interests. On January 25, the second-class battleship *Maine* steamed into Havana harbor past the battlements of Morro Castle, and was conducted to her anchorage next to the Spanish cruiser *Alfonso XII*.

At twenty minutes of ten on the evening of February 15, 1898, all was still aboard the *Maine*. The small boats had been hoisted, most of the crew had turned in, and the anchor watch was dispersed about the deck. A sentry paced back and forth, gazing at the twinkling lights of the harbor and the dim outlines of the old castle. Suddenly there came a blinding flash of light, accompanied by a roar as though the bottom of the ship were groaning in agony. Fragments could be seen flying through the air—pieces of cement, blocks of wood, steel railings, bits of grating—and then a cloud of black smoke. From the forward part of the ship, where the crew were quartered, came groans, shrieks, and cries for help. There followed a trembling and lurching motion, then a heavy list to port, and the vessel began to sink. Captain Sigsbee, cool and collected, directed the lowering of the boats, and then, at the last moment, gave the order: "Abandon ship." He was the last to leave. The next morning, as the sun rose over Havana harbor, a twisted mass of blackened steel was all that was visible of the once proud battleship.

A cry of anger and horror went up from the people of the United States. Who is responsible for this disaster? they asked. Can it be that the Spaniards anchored the *Maine* over a mine with the purpose of destroying her? Have they taken this means of diminishing the naval power of the United States on the eve of war? When a board of naval experts examined the hull and reported that the condition of the armorplates indicated that the explosion had been external, indignation rose to fever-heat. War was inevitable.

Although President McKinley still hung back, he was pushed into hostilities by Congress and the nation. "Every Congressman has two or three newspapers in his district, most of them printed in red ink and shouting for blood," declared Mr. Boutelle, of Maine, on March 30. Twelve days later the President sent a message to Congress advocating forcible interference as the only means of bringing peace to Cuba. "In the name of humanity," he said, "in the name of civilization, in behalf of endangered American interests, which give us the right and the duty to speak and act, the war in Cuba must stop." On April 19, the anniversary of Lexington, Congress passed a series of resolutions virtually declaring war on Spain, and hostilities began.

The first blow was struck not in the West Indies, but on the opposite side of the world. At Hong-Kong was Commodore George Dewey, in command of a squadron of cruisers—the *Olympia*, the *Boston*, the *Raleigh*, the *Concord*, and the *Petrel*. On April 22 he was joined by the cruiser *Baltimore*, and soon after he received orders to proceed to the Philippine Islands to destroy the Spanish fleet there. On April 27 he set sail for the Island of Luzon, 628 miles away. Three days later low-lying hills covered with tropical verdure were sighted, and while the last preparations were being made for battle, the squadron turned toward Manila Bay.

On the evening of April 30 Dewey approached the entrance to the bay, and with all lights out sailed boldly in. During the early morning hours he moved to a position opposite the sea walls of Manila, and then, making a great loop, steamed past the arsenal of Cavite. Here Admiral Montojo awaited the attack with his squadron of seven vessels. As the gray American fighters approached, two submarine mines were exploded just ahead of the *Olympia*. They hurled water high in the air, but did no harm. Dewey did not falter. The guns at Cavite and on the Spanish fleet opened fire, and shells began to burst over the Americans and in the water around them.

On board the *Olympia* all was silence save the whir of the blowers and the throb of the engines. The men stood at their posts in the intense heat, stripped to the waist. Then suddenly arose the cry: "Remember the *Maine!*" Dewey saw that the moment for action had come. "You may fire when you are ready, Gridley," he said to the captain of the *Olympia*. An eight-inch gun in the forward turret roared forth, followed by barks from the *Baltimore* and the *Boston*. At 4,000 yards came the order, "Open all guns!" and a storm of shells began to fall upon the doomed Spanish vessels.

Five times the American cruisers moved past Cavite, each time drawing closer, each time dealing greater havoc among the enemy. Flames burst from some of the Spanish cruisers. The *Reina Cristina* keeled over until her bulwarks were awash. The *Don Antonio de Ulloa* was still making a gallant fight, but the American vessels now concentrated their fire upon her, and in a few moments she too went down. At half-past twelve the red-and-yellow flag of Spain was lowered from the staff over Cavite and Dewey was master of Manila Bay. This victory had been won without serious injury to any of the American ships, with not a man killed and with but seven wounded.

The world was astonished. The Spaniards were at first incredulous; the American people were jubilant. The Germans, who resented the intrusion of the United States in the Far East, hinted broadly at intervention. Admiral Von Diedericks, who commanded the German Asiatic squadron, sailed into Manila Bay, and did all in his power to annoy Dewey and encourage the Spaniards. Not until 15,000 American soldiers had arrived, and the Stars and Stripes had been raised over the plaza at Manila, could Dewey be sure that Von Diedericks would not attack him.

In the meanwhile, four great war-vessels, the pride of the Spanish navy, were steaming across the Atlantic for the West Indies. The government at Madrid realized that Spain must stake all upon a naval engagement, for without control of the water Cuba would fall an easy prey to the American land forces. But prudence dictated that this battle should be fought only after the fleet had arrived at one of the West Indian ports, and had been overhauled. For the Americans the obvious policy was to strike at once, while Admiral Cervera was at the end of his long journey. Admiral Sampson, with the *New York*, the *Iowa*, and the *Indiana*, watched off the coast of Porto Rico, while Admiral Schley, with the *Brooklyn*, the *Massachusetts*, and the *Texas*, guarded the southern ports of Cuba. But Cervera gave them both the slip, and on May 19 entered the harbor of Santiago unobserved by the Americans. A few days later the lead-colored war-vessels of Schley and Sampson appeared off the harbor's mouth, and the Spaniards were bottled up.

With the way cleared for the landing of troops, regiment after regiment was despatched to Tampa, there to take transport for Cuba. There was much delay, much red tape, much confusion, not a little inefficiency. Heavy woollen clothes were provided for this campaign in the tropics, the transports were jammed to suffocation, a general was selected who was incapacitated for active work in the field by ill health and corpulency. These handicaps were offset by the gallantry of the soldiers themselves. When once they had set foot on Cuban soil, they went forward rapidly, through jungles, past tangled wire, over fortified posts, until they had planted the Stars and Stripes on the hills above Santiago. Cervera had to run the gauntlet of Sampson's fleet, or be battered to pieces by the guns of the American army.

Sunday, July 3, 1898, found the American fleet grouped

around the entrance to Santiago harbor, patiently waiting
for the enemy to come out. The day was unusually clear, and
the men in the watch-towers could easily distinguish the Spanish blockhouses in the distant blue mountains. Suddenly their
attention was caught by several columns of black smoke arising over the Moro promontory, and a moment later the *Maria
Teresa* came into view, followed by the *Vizcaya*, the *Cristobal
Colon*, the *Oquenda*, and two destroyers. The great cruisers
swept majestically out of the harbor, their red and yellow en-
signs standing out against the dark-green background of the
Cuban hills, their black prows piling up the white waves on
either side.

On board the American vessels the alarm gongs sounded,
the signal for action was hoisted, and the cry went up: "There
they come! There they come!" A terrific fire was concentrated
on the leading Spanish ships. As they turned westward along
the coast, shells burst around them. Then a panoply of smoke
settled over each of the ships, through which the flashes of the
guns glared red. When the breeze blew the smoke away, the
Maria Teresa was heading for shore, smoke and flames pouring
from her upper works. A few minutes later this proud vessel,
Cervera's flagship, was aground on the Cuban shore, a hopeless wreck.

The *Oregon*, the *Texas*, and the *Indiana* now turned their
attention to the *Oquenda*, and this cruiser, after turning in
shore, blew up, scattering a shower of steel splinters around
her. The *Vizcaya* labored on for another forty minutes, but
in the end she too made for the beach, her decks a mass of
flames. The *Colon* was now tearing along six miles ahead, and
for a while it seemed that she would escape. But the *Brooklyn*,
the *Oregon*, and the *Texas* gave chase. Inch by inch they overhauled her. At fifteen minutes past one the *Colon* lowered her
colors, and the battle of Santiago was over. The Spanish fleet
had been annihilated. More than 350 Spaniards were killed
or drowned in the tangled wreckage, 160 were wounded, and
1,750 taken.

As the *Texas*, the *Oregon*, and the *Brooklyn* lay with engines
stopped, off Rio Tarquino, in a semicircle around the *Colon*,

cheers went up from the American crews and came echoing back from the mountains. From the *Oregon* could be heard the strains of "The Star-Spangled Banner." The *Brooklyn* cheered the *Texas*, the *Texas* cheered the *Brooklyn*, and both cheered for the *Oregon*. On board the *Texas* the officers, with but one exception, were jubilant and hilarious. That exception was Captain John W. Philip. It had been noticed that he seemed unusually reserved and silent. Suddenly he turned to his executive officer, saying: "Call all hands aft." Then 500 men, many stripped to the waist, some blackened with smoke and powder, trooped to the quarter-deck, and stood facing their gallant commander. "I want all of you," he said, "officers and crew, unless there be those who have conscientious scruples against so doing, to lift your hats and in your hearts to offer silent thanks to God." For a moment every man stood reverently, with bowed head, many with moistened eyes, and then three hearty cheers went up for Captain Philip.

The Spanish cause was now hopeless. With Sampson's warships in command of the sea, Spain could neither reinforce her armies in Cuba nor prevent the landing of American troops. On July 22 Madrid asked for terms, and a few weeks later a cessation of hostilities was proclaimed. The treaty of peace was signed December 10, 1898. Spain relinquished sovereignty over Cuba and ceded to the United States the Philippines, Porto Rico, and Guam, while the United States paid $20,000,-000 for the Philippines, and assumed the claims of her citizens for damages inflicted during the Cuban insurrection.

Thus, as the imperial experiment of Spain in America came to a close, an experiment which had lasted four centuries, the great republic of the West began an imperial experiment of its own. We acquired nearly a million subjects of Spanish and negro blood in Porto Rico, and became responsible for 7,500,-000 people in the Philippines, ranging from the cultured Tagalogs of Manila to the head-hunting Igorrotes. There were many who doubted the wisdom of this step. Was it not contrary to the traditional policy of the nation? they asked. Could the American people retain their own liberties while holding other peoples in subjection? Our democratic institutions were threatened by the trusts; now the war with Spain was to bring the still greater menace of imperialism. The Democratic party, in the election of 1900, made opposition to the new colonial policy the chief plank in their platform.

Whether or not these fears were groundless, imperialism brought the United States athwart the colonial ambitions of certain European powers, and increased the risk of international complications. Germany especially looked with a jealous eye at the spread of American influence in the Far East and in the West Indies. Her hostility to the Monroe Doctrine, long nourished in secret, became more outspoken. The rule which Uncle Sam lays down for others he will not follow himself, complained the German leaders. While excluding European powers from American soil, he does not scruple to assume sovereignty over Latin-American territory. The Kaiser made up his mind that at the first opportunity he would get a foothold in the Western Hemisphere.

This opportunity was not long in coming. At the opening of the new century the finances of Venezuela became so involved that the republic could no longer meet its obligations to foreign powers. This gave the Kaiser a pretext for interfering, and in 1902 he induced Great Britain and Italy to join him in a "pacific blockade" of the Venezuelan coast. The United States took no notice of this step until President Roosevelt discovered "that Germany intended to seize some Venezuelan harbor and turn it into a strongly fortified place of arms, on the model of Kiao-chau, with a view to exercising some control over the future isthmian canal, and over South American affairs generally." He at once urged Germany to settle her difficulties by arbitration. But the Kaiser would neither arbitrate nor give a satisfactory guarantee not to seize Venezuelan territory.

Thereupon Roosevelt assembled the American battle fleet at Culebra, Porto Rico, and ordered Admiral Dewey to put the vessels in fighting trim, ready to sail at an hour's notice. He then sent for Herr von Holleben, the German Ambassador, and asked him to inform his government that, if no notification for arbitration came within ten days, he would order Dewey's fleet to Venezuela to prevent the seizure of territory. Von Holleben thought the President was bluffing, and apparently so advised the Kaiser. A week later he called again at the White House, but failed even to mention Venezuela. As he arose to go, Roosevelt asked him whether he had received an answer to his request for arbitration. The Ambassador said he had had no news on that subject. "In that event," said the President, "it is useless to wait so long as I had intended, and I shall order Dewey to sail twenty-four hours in advance of the date originally set."

Not a little alarmed, von Holleben consulted Doctor Buenz, the German consul-general at New York, a man thoroughly acquainted with the United States and a personal friend of the President. Buenz convinced him that Roosevelt meant what he said, and a few minutes later a message was on its way over the wires to Berlin that Germany must back down or fight the United States. Within thirty-six hours word came from the German embassy to the President that Kaiser Wilhelm was willing to arbitrate. It was a bitter humiliation for the proud Hohenzollern. Von Holleben at once left for Germany in such disgrace with his master that not a member of the German diplomatic corps dared to see him off. Roosevelt, with an ironic touch of humor, publicly complimented the Kaiser on being a stanch advocate of arbitration, and not until years afterward did the people of the United States know that the Venezuelan affair had so nearly involved them in war.

The Spanish-American War and the resulting acquisition of far-flung possessions aroused the country to the necessity of constructing a canal through Panama or Nicaragua. With the main body of the fleet stationed in the Atlantic, an attack upon the Philippines might succeed before the ships could steam 14,000 miles around Cape Horn to Hawaii, and then 4,800 more to Manila. During the war the battleship *Oregon* had made the voyage from San Francisco to the West Indies to join Sampson's squadron, but this feat only emphasized the gulf which lay between the Atlantic and Pacific fleets. The canal, so long dreamed of, had now become a necessity. It would cut down the sea voyage from New York to San Fran-

cisco to 5,219 miles, and make it possible for the fleets to concentrate in less than two weeks, off either the eastern or the
western coast. The commercial advantages would also be great.
It would multiply the traffic from the Atlantic and Gulf ports,
not only to our own Pacific Coast region, but to Peru and
Chile.

President Roosevelt entered into the project with zeal, and in
November, 1901, the chief international difficulty was removed
by the Hay-Pauncefote Treaty. Under its provisions Great
Britain renounced her claims to control jointly with the United
States any isthmian canal which might be constructed, and
gave us the right, on our own initiative, to dig, manage, and
fortify it. Seven months later Congress passed an act empowering the President to purchase the unfinished De Lesseps
Canal at Panama for not more than $40,000,000, and to acquire
from the Republic of Colombia a strip of land across the isthmus. Accordingly Secretary Hay negotiated a treaty with the
Colombian *chargé d'affaires* at Washington which granted the
United States a ninety-nine year lease of a canal zone, in return for $10,000,000 in cash and an annual rental of $250,000.
Unfortunately, the Congress of Colombia, by a unanimous
vote, refused to sanction the agreement.

President Roosevelt was angered at this unexpected repulse.
He believed that Colombia meant to postpone final action until
the original Panama Company's concession expired, and then
claim the $40,000,000 which the United States had offered for
the French rights. He favored going ahead, "without further
dealing with the foolish and homicidal corruptionists at Bo-
gota." The way was prepared by a revolution in Panama.
The people of the isthmus felt that Colombia, which had long
ruled them despotically, was now sacrificing their most vital
interests. On November 3, 1903, under the leadership of Señor
Arango and Doctor Amador, they rose in revolt, organized a
provisional government, and proclaimed the independence of
the Republic of Panama. A small body of Colombian troops
at Colon made several ineffectual efforts to reach the town of
Panama, where the insurrection was in progress, and then
sailed away, leaving the rebels in possession of the country.

The United States promptly recognized the new republic, and on November 18 concluded with it a new canal treaty. Panama granted for our perpetual use a zone of land ten miles wide, receiving in return a guarantee of independence, $10,000,000, and after nine years an annual payment of $250,000.

Work was begun at once. In November, 1906, when President Roosevelt visited Panama, he found the digging going on vigorously. Mr. Roosevelt saw the drills pounding away at the rock; the great steam-shovels devouring the masses of stone and earth; gangs of Jamaican negroes singing at their work or shouting excitedly as a cliff gave way before a mighty blast; he visited the neat little villages built for the workmen; inspected hospitals, commissary stores, bath-houses, cook-sheds, machine-shops; marvelled at the progress made in eliminating the mosquito and freeing the zone of malaria and yellow fever; praised the engineers for securing a supply of excellent drinking-water; listened to the plans for huge dams and locks.

Eight years later the *Ancon*, a 10,000-ton steamer, entered the towering Gatun locks. The electric locomotives deftly moved her into place, and the great gates, weighing hundreds of tons, swung behind her, their ends meeting with the exactness of a micrometer. Then up the vessel went, eighty-five feet through the triple locks, until she floated out upon Gatun Lake. A beautiful body of water it was, this great artificial lake, dotted with charming little islands and framed by the restful green hills. The ship went on past the tops of dying trees, to where the lake narrowed into the Chagres River, into the hand-made gorge of Culebra, where Gold Hill and her sister peak towered hundreds of feet above the canal, past the dangerous Cucaracha slide, out into the charming little Miraflores Lake, set in rolling hills covered with tropical verdure, then through the Pedro Miguel and Miraflores locks, out into the waters of the Pacific. It was the first voyage through the Panama Canal from ocean to ocean. The dream of Balboa for a water passage between the Atlantic and Pacific had at last been realized.

CHAPTER XXV

THE NEW FREEDOM

WHILE the attention of the nation was still fixed upon foreign affairs and the acquisition of colonies, a strong movement had begun for internal reform. Many thoughtful men lamented the fact that in practice democracy did not mean literally the rule of the people. "We have long rested comfortably in this country upon the assumption that because our form of government was democratic, it was therefore automatically producing democratic results," said Robert M. La Follette. So there arose a demand for a more direct democracy, for the rule of the people without the intervention of political "middlemen."

The ideals of Jefferson have by no means been attained, it was said. The conventions which nominate our public officers are controlled by corrupt politicians, our legislatures have fallen under the power of big business, our cities are run by unscrupulous bosses. Let us shake off the incubus of machine politics, so that our institutions can serve the purpose for which they were created. If the old machinery of government does not function properly, we must devise new machinery which will serve the needs of the people.

In this spirit the people of many States adopted a device for direct government known as the initiative and referendum. The initiative authorized a certain per cent of the voters to place a measure upon the ballot to be voted upon either by the legislature or by the public. The referendum made it obligatory for the legislature, upon the petition of a group of voters, to submit any of its laws to the people for their veto or their sanction. Hand in hand with these radical reforms went the demand for the recall by popular vote of public officers, for the election of Senators by direct popular vote, for nominations by primaries, for the short ballot, and for the commission government of cities.

The reform movement received impetus from the renewed

outcry against big business and the unequal distribution of wealth. The Socialists denounced the control of industry, transportation, land, and credit by great aggregations of capital, and demanded government ownership of railways, mines, mills, banks, and public utilities. More conservative groups believed that the extremely high tariff was chiefly responsible for the evils of the day, and insisted upon downward revision. Some thought that much could be accomplished by more stringent laws for the control of the trusts.

Thus on all sides there was unrest, on all sides a demand for reform. The magazines and daily papers teemed with articles exposing the corruption and incompetence of public officials. Everywhere people said that democracy was once more on trial, everywhere the question was asked: "Shall the people rule?"

At this moment fate placed in the Presidency a man constitutionally unfitted to take the lead in radical reform. William H. Taft, whom the Republicans nominated and elected in 1908, was an able administrator, a jurist of distinction, and a man of winning personality. But he was too conservative to satisfy the demands for radical changes. He feared to apply the knife for fear of cutting sound tissue. His term was by no means devoid of progressive measures, for he was sponsor for the prosecution of trusts, for railway regulation, for the extension of the civil service, for the establishing of postal savings-banks, the parcel post, a commerce court, and an expert tariff board. But he moved too slowly and soon found himself out of step with the reformers.

The outstanding "crime" of the Taft administration was the passage of the Payne-Aldrich Tariff Act. The Republican platform of 1908 had promised a "genuine and honest revision" of the tariff. When Congress convened in March, 1909, in extra session, Sereno E. Payne, of New York, introduced a bill extending the free list, and making many substantial reductions. But when it came to the Senate Finance Committee, that body, under the leadership of Nelson W. Aldrich, mutilated the measure by making wholesale increases. The House protested against this breach of the party pledge, but in the end it was forced to yield. President Taft affixed his signature August 5.

A burst of indignation followed. Once more our representatives have betrayed us, it was said. Once more the corrupt alliance of big business and the politicians has defeated the people's will. It is "the most outrageous assault of privileged interests on the people in tariff history," said one progressive Senator. A humorous writer on public affairs ridiculed it for placing on the free list such "necessities of life" as "curling-stones, sea moss, nux vomica, and canary-bird seed." When Taft defended the law as "the best tariff ever passed by the Republican party," the reformers turned against him as a hopeless reactionary. There is no hope for the country, they said, so long as this "stand-patter" remains in the White House.

A group of progressive Republicans, led by La Follette, believing that they had come to the parting of the ways, called a meeting in Washington for January 21, 1911, to form a National Progressive Republican League. They adopted a declaration of principles, which lamented that "popular government in America has been thwarted and progressive legislation strangled by the special interests, which control caucuses, delegates, conventions, and party organizations, and through this control of the machinery of government dictate nominations and platforms." It declared in favor of direct election of Senators, direct primaries, and the initiative, referendum, and recall. The League disclaimed any intention of seceding from the Republican party, but its very existence testified to a division of sentiment which at any moment might become an open breach.

The crisis came with the Republican convention of 1912. Roosevelt was the choice of the progressive wing of the party; the conservatives remained faithful to Taft. Thirteen States had adopted the system of preferential primaries and in each of these now was fought a hot pre-convention fight for delegates. The result was a great victory for Roosevelt. Of the 382 delegates named by these primaries, he received 278.

But in those States where delegates were chosen by the convention method, Taft was still strong. Moreover, the national committee, which was authorized to make up the temporary roll of the convention, was filled with his partisans. "We can't elect Taft," one of the members stated, "but we are going to hold onto this organization, and when we get back four years from now we will have it, and not those damn insurgents." Of 254 disputed seats which came before the committee, 235 were awarded to Taft men. Before they had completed the list, Roosevelt announced that he was "through," and his supporters either left the hall or refrained from further participation. On the first ballot Taft received 561 votes, and was declared the nominee.

Three days after the Republican convention had adjourned, the Democrats met at Baltimore. Their hopes were high, for the dissensions of the Republicans made victory reasonably certain. But in their ranks, too, there was a sharp line of cleavage between progressives and conservatives. When the bosses nominated Judge Alton B. Parker for the temporary chairmanship, they encountered the powerful opposition of William J. Bryan. Bryan, who was still regarded by thousands as the champion of the plain people, appealed to the leading candidates to oppose this choice. When Woodrow Wilson alone frankly and cordially acceded, he at once became the candidate of Bryan and the progressives.

Bryan next startled the country by offering a resolution declaring the convention opposed to any candidate "who is the representative of or under obligations to J. Pierpont Morgan, Thomas F. Ryan, August Belmont, or any other member of the privilege-hunting and favor-seeking class." In the debate which followed he said: "Extraordinary conditions need extraordinary remedies. . . . There is not a delegate who does not know that an effort is being made right now to sell the Democratic party into bondage to the predatory interests of the country. It is the most brazen, the most impudent attempt that has been made in the history of American politics to dominate a convention, stifle the honest sentiment of a people, and make the nominee the bond-slave of the men who exploit this country."

There were 1,088 delegates in the convention, and under the two-thirds rule 726 votes were necessary to a choice. On the first ballot Champ Clark, of Missouri, received 440½, Wilson

324, and all other candidates 323½. On the tenth ballot the New York delegation went over to Clark, and it seemed that his nomination was inevitable. But Bryan transferred the Nebraska delegation to Wilson, while his henchmen in all parts of the country sent telegrams, threatening, urging, imploring their representatives to support the new champion of the people's rights. Slowly Wilson crept ahead, until, on the forty-sixth ballot, he was nominated. The progressive element, which was defeated in the Republican convention, had conquered in the Democratic.

The meeting of the Progressives, at Chicago, on August 5, was more like "a family reunion or a great religious revival meeting than a political convention." As the two thousand delegates shouted and stamped, or sang the "Battle Hymn of the Republic" they seemed to be fired with the crusader's zeal. When Roosevelt appeared he was greeted by a tremendous ovation. At the conclusion of a stirring address, in which he called upon the delegates to gird themselves "for this great fight in the never-ending warfare for the good of mankind," he was nominated by acclamation. The party platform declared that behind the ostensible government sat an invisible government, owing no allegiance and alleging no responsibility to the people. "To destroy this invisible government, to dissolve the unholy alliance between corrupt business and corrupt politics, is the first task of the statesmanship of the day."

In the election Wilson won a sweeping victory, carrying forty States, with a total of 435 votes. Roosevelt won in six States, with 88 votes, and Taft in two States, with 8 votes. Wilson's popular vote was 6,286,214, as compared with 4,126,020 for Roosevelt, and 3,483,922 for Taft. The Democrats secured control of both branches of Congress, the Senate by the narrow margin of 6 seats, and the House by the majority of 291 to 144.

Woodrow Wilson approached the Presidency in the spirit of the reformer. "This is not a day of triumph," he said in his inaugural address, "it is a day of dedication. Here muster not the forces of party, but the forces of humanity. Men's hearts wait upon us, men's lives hang in the balance, men's hopes call upon us to say what we will do. Who shall live up to the great trust? Who dares fail to try? I summon all honest men, all patriotic, all forward-looking men to my side. God helping me, I will not fail them if they will but counsel and sustain me."

Congress met in extra session on April 7, 1913, and proceeded without delay to the consideration of tariff revision. Oscar Underwood introduced a bill which called for the removing of duties on foodstuffs and raw materials, for a reduction on metals, cottons, and woollens, for the heavy taxation of luxuries, and for a graduated income tax. It passed the House promptly, by a vote of 281 to 139. But when it came to the Senate it encountered the opposition of certain threatened interests—the sugar-growers of Louisiana, the iron manufacturers of Alabama, the cotton manufacturers of Georgia. Some of the Southern Senators yielded to this pressure, and it seemed that the bill would suffer the fate of the tariff of 1894. The nation looked on anxiously, wondering whether Wilson could close the breach in the party ranks. It had not long to wait. The President issued a startling statement, warning Congress against the numerous industrious and insidious lobby which was trying to mutilate the bill. This vigorous action drove some of the wavering Senators back into line, and the bill, essentially unchanged, passed 44 to 37. The battle which had been opened by Cleveland in 1887 now, after the lapse of a quarter of a century, had been brought to a victorious conclusion.

On June 23, 1913, the President came before Congress to urge the necessity of a new banking and currency system. "We must have a currency not rigid as now," he said, "but readily, elastically responsive to credit. . . . Our banking laws must mobilize reserves, must not permit the concentration anywhere in a few hands of the monetary resources of the country. . . . And the control of the new system of banking must be vested in the government itself, so that the banks may be the instruments, not the masters, of business."

A monetary committee had been at work since 1908 studying the banking and currency systems. Its findings, published in thirty-eight volumes, cleared the way for vital changes. A bank bill, shaped by the President, Secretary McAdoo, Senator

Owen, and Representative Glass, in consultation with Paul M. Warburg, was introduced in Congress on June 26, 1913. It called for a Federal Reserve Bank system, which divided the country into twelve districts, with a central bank in each. Private banks might enter the system on terms prescribed by the bill. At the head of the system was to be a Federal Reserve Board, consisting of the Secretary of the Treasury, the Comptroller of the Currency, and five other members. The struggle over this far-reaching measure was long and bitter, but in the end Wilson's masterful leadership beat down the opposition, and in December it became law.

The conclusion of the first year of Wilson's administration found the President victorious, exulting in his accomplishment, confident of the future. He had fulfilled his pledge to the American people, he had delivered powerful blows at "intrenched privilege," and had made the "new freedom" a reality. In twelve months he had carried through liberal legislation which the people for years had demanded in vain. A new era of prosperity and progress seemed to open before the nation. But at this juncture an event occurred in Europe which was to divert the attention of the people from internal affairs and involve the country in hitherto undreamed-of problems and perils. This event was the outbreak of the World War.

CHAPTER XXVI

THE EUROPEAN MAELSTROM

EUROPE, in the early years of the twentieth century, was ripe for war. On all sides were hatred and fear, conflicting claims for territory, commercial rivalries, racial antipathies, and long-nurtured ambitions. Italy, Serbia, and Rumania wished to "redeem" their lost nationals; France waited for an opportunity to regain Alsace-Lorraine; Russia guarded jealously her influence in the Balkans; Germany dreamed of conquering her "place in the sun"; Austria-Hungary looked with suspicion upon the national ambitions of her smaller neighbors. Every frontier bristled with forts; the people staggered under the burden of military and naval armaments. Peace depended upon the precarious "balance of power," in which Germany, Austria-Hungary, and Italy were aligned on one side, and Russia, France, and Great Britain on the other. Although many leading statesmen spoke hopefully of peace, and boasted of international good-will, of "frankness and fair concession," it was obvious that war clouds were gathering over Europe.

On June 28, 1914, the Archduke Francis Ferdinand, heir presumptive to the Hapsburg realm, paid a visit to Sarajevo, capital of Bosnia. The little city presented a picturesque appearance, with its stately buildings, oriental bazaar, mosques, slender minarets, attractive streets, many bridges, its interesting blending of Eastern and Western civilizations. After a celebration in the town hall, the Archduke, with his wife, the Countess of Hohenberg, entered an automobile and drove along Appel Quay. At the corner of the Franz-Josefsgasse, where the street narrows, a man rushed forward and fired at the royal guests. Without a word the Duchess fell across her husband's knee, and a moment later the Archduke collapsed over his wife's form. The automobile sped on to the palace, where both victims expired without regaining consciousness. Thus did Gavrilo Prinzip ignite the mine which set the world on fire.

For some weeks there was an ominous calm. Then came an ultimatum from Austria-Hungary to Serbia, practically indicting the Serbian nation for complicity in the murder, making demands which could be acceded to only by compromising Serbian honor and independence, and requiring an answer within forty-eight hours. This imperilled Russian interests in the Near East, and threatened to involve the Triple Entente in war with the Triple Alliance. For two weeks Sir Edward Grey and other statesmen made frantic but vain efforts to ward off the impending catastrophe. Soon Europe was resounding to the tread of countless hosts. The World War had begun.

On these unexpected happenings the American people looked with amazement. They regarded themselves as distant spectators of a terrible phenomenon. That their own country would be drawn into the struggle at first occurred to no one. It had been our traditional policy to keep out of European entanglements, a policy outlined by Washington, strengthened by the Monroe Doctrine and crystallized by time. Seven days after Austria-Hungary had declared war on Serbia, President Wilson issued a proclamation of American neutrality. On August 18 he appealed to the people for a spirit of impartiality to all belligerents. "I venture . . . to speak a solemn word of warning to you," he said, "against that deepest, most subtle, most essential breach of neutrality which may spring out of passionately taking sides."

This appeal proved futile. The action of Germany in invading Belgium in order to strike an unprotected part of the French frontier, the belief that the Central Powers had been the aggressors, together with a feeling of kinship with Great Britain and France, conspired to create sympathy with the Entente Allies. Moreover, Americans were concerned at the possibility that, in place of the time-honored balance of power, there might arise in Europe a vast military empire under the leadership of the Kaiser. This would endanger not only the Monroe Doctrine, but the liberal institutions and perhaps the very existence of the United States. This feeling of suspicion grew into anger when German submarines began endangering the lives of neutrals by sinking merchant vessels on the high seas.

On the afternoon of May 7, 1915, the great ocean liner *Lusitania* was steaming off the south coast of Ireland through placid sunlit seas. Many of the passengers were at luncheon, expecting an early termination of their journey and apprehensive of no imminent danger. Suddenly came a muffled drum-like explosion, followed by a shivering or trembling of the vessel. Instantly the word went round that a German torpedo had found its mark. There was no panic. The passengers quietly assembled on deck, while the crew attempted to lower the lifeboats. But the liner was already listing sharply to starboard, and in twenty minutes she gently dipped her bow and began to sink. From her crowded decks came one long, despairing, mournful cry, and a moment later she had disappeared under the water.

The fishing-boats and tugs which hastened to the spot found many survivors clinging to life-belts and bits of wreckage, some desperately injured, all chilled and exhausted. They were taken ashore and tenderly cared for. The hearts of the kindly Irish people were torn at the scenes enacted around them—of distraught mothers seeking their children, wives looking for husbands, children for their parents. When word arrived that a little boy or girl had been taken to this house or that, now and then some mother would rush up, asking: "Is it my boy?" or "Is it my little girl?"

Over 1,500 persons perished on the *Lusitania*, among them 114 Americans. A cry of horror went up from the United States. Are we to sit with folded hands, it was asked, while the Germans send unoffending Americans to their death? Enormous pressure was brought to bear upon the President to demand prompt reparation. Mr. Wilson, like Thomas Jefferson after the *Chesapeake-Leopard* affair, for the moment held in his hand the option of peace or war. But, like Jefferson, he was unwilling to permit one incident, no matter how outrageous, to divert the country from its policy of peace.

A long interchange of notes followed between Washington and Berlin, in which the President tried to wring from the

German Government a promise not to sink ocean liners without giving crews and passengers an opportunity to escape. "The Government of the United States is contending for something much greater than mere rights of property or privileges of commerce," wrote Secretary Lansing. "It is contending for nothing less high and sacred than the rights of humanity." Germany parried, but in a note of July 21, 1915, President Wilson made it obvious that evasion of the main issue would no longer be tolerated. If the commanders of German naval vessels continued to contravene the rights of American citizens, he said, the Government of the United States would regard their action as deliberately unfriendly.

On September 1 Ambassador von Bernstorff sent Secretary Lansing a note promising that "liners will not be sunk by our submarines without warning and without safety to the lives of non-combatants, provided the liners do not try to escape or offer resistance." The favorable impression created in America by this promise was largely nullified by secret acts of hostility on the part of the German Government. The German embassy at Washington employed agents to foment strikes, to blow up bridges and munition factories, and to place bombs in the holds of vessels bound for England or France.

The climax of this hostile intrigue was reached in January, 1917, when a German plot to embroil the United States in war with Mexico and Japan was detected and made public. Foreign Minister Zimmerman sent instructions to the Minister at Mexico City to propose to the Mexican Government an alliance on the following basis: "That we shall make war together and together make peace. We shall give general financial support, and it is understood that Mexico is to reconquer the lost territory of New Mexico, Texas, and Arizona." The Minister was also to suggest that the President of Mexico propose an alliance with Japan and offer to mediate between Japan and Germany.

While the country was still ringing with this affair, news came that the German Government had given notice of its intention to resume the unrestricted submarine campaign. The Kaiser and his advisers had convinced themselves that by an intensive campaign against Allied shipping they could, in six months' time, starve Great Britain into submission. The withdrawal of Great Britain would give Germany undisputed supremacy over the remaining Allies both on land and sea, and force them to make peace on Germany's terms. It was hoped that the United States would still remain neutral, but should she enter the war the German leaders were confident that all would be over before she could make her weight felt. Therefore they notified President Wilson that after February 1, 1917, they would prevent all navigation in a zone around Great Britain, France, and Italy, by sinking merchant vessels without warning, and without safeguarding the lives of passengers and crews. Two days later the President announced to Congress that diplomatic relations with Germany had been severed. War followed two months later, after news had reached the Government that submarines had sunk the *City of Memphis*, the *Vigilancia*, the *Illinois*, and several other American merchant ships.

On the evening of April 2 a notable assemblage gathered in the Hall of Representatives. Directly in front of the Speaker's desk sat the members of the Supreme Court, at one side were many foreign diplomats, behind on the floor were Senators and Congressmen, while the gallery was crowded with distinguished guests. At half-past eight the Speaker rose, announcing simply: "The President of the United States." As Mr. Wilson entered and took his place on the Speaker's platform, the assemblage sprang to their feet and burst into prolonged cheering. When Speaker Clark had rapped for order, the President advanced to the clerk's desk, and, resting both arms on the green baize, began to read in a quiet, even voice.

"I have called the Congress into extraordinary session, because there are serious, very serious choices of policy to be made, and made immediately. . . . The new [German] policy has swept every restriction aside. Vessels of every kind, whatever their flag, their character, their cargo, their destination, their errand, have been ruthlessly sent to the bottom without warning and without thought of help or mercy for those on board. . . . American ships have been sunk, American lives taken, in ways which it has stirred us very deeply to learn of, but the ships and people of other neutral and friendly nations have been sunk and overwhelmed in the waters in the same way. There has been no discrimination. The challenge is to all mankind. Each nation must decide for itself how it will meet it. . . . (But) there is one choice we cannot make, we are incapable of making; we will not choose the path of submission. . . ." Before the President could finish, the venerable Chief Justice White dropped his big soft hat, and, springing to his feet, raised his hands and brought them together with a bang. It was the signal for a tremendous demonstration. The cheers were not the wild cheers of a national convention nor the triumphant cheers of a victorious army, but the deep, intense cheers of men who were fired with unswerving determination.

When all had resumed their seats, the President continued. "We will not choose the path of submission and suffer the most sacred rights of our nation and our people to be ignored or violated. . . . With a profound sense of the solemn and even tragical character of the step I am taking and of the grave responsibilities which it involves, but in unhesitating obedience to what I deem my constitutional duty, I advise that the Congress declare the recent course of the Imperial German Government to be in fact nothing less than war against the Government and people of the United States; that it formally accept the status of belligerent which has thus been thrust upon it; and that it take immediate steps not only to put the country in a more thorough state of defense, but also to exert all its power and employ all its resources to bring the Government of the German Empire to terms and end the war." Four days later, on April 6, 1917, Congress passed a resolution declaring that war existed between Germany and the United States.

The German leaders blundered badly when they provoked the American people to war. The unrestricted submarine campaign, while inflicting severe losses upon the Allies, did not force Great Britain to sue for peace. At the same time, in 1917, Russia fell into the hands of the Bolsheviki, who signed a treaty of peace with Germany at Brest-Litovsk, thus eliminating the great eastern front. With large masses of troops released for service in the west, the Germans might have crushed the British and French armies, had it not been for the timely aid of the United States.

In the closing days of April a war council met at Washington, in which Arthur J. Balfour, M. Viviani, Marshal Joffre, and other British and French leaders pointed out to the American Government how best it could make its weight felt in the war. "Our most pressing need is for money," they said, "for it is increasingly difficult to meet the financial drain of the war; next in order let us have food, especially sugar, wheat, and fats, else a lack of proper nourishment may lower the efficiency of our fighters and our workers; then we would have you aid in combating the submarines, not only by sending your navy to European waters, but by building merchant vessels; and, lastly, you must brace the morale of our forces, by sending some troops to the western front."

It was a gigantic task to mobilize this great peace-loving nation for the purposes of war. But the government entered upon the task with an energy which boded ill for Germany and her allies. Under the leadership of Herbert C. Hoover, the production of foodstuffs was stimulated, consumption and waste cut down, and the exports of breadstuffs, meats, fats, and sugar to our Allies increased; the Shipping Board drew up plans for a new merchant fleet to offset the depredations of the submarines; the navy was set to work patrolling the North Sea, chasing submarines, and conveying merchant vessels to and from Europe; capital and labor were diverted from peaceful channels into the manufacture of shells, rifles, guns, military airplanes, tanks, and other war material; billions of dollars' worth of bonds were sold, so that credit could be extended to Great Britain, France, Italy, and Belgium; an army numbering eventually 4,000,000 was put in the field.

The American people responded nobly to the call of their leaders. Thousands of small gardens were planted, special efforts were made to preserve food by canning, and millions of households voluntarily cut down their consumption of sugar and fats. "Food will win the war" became a national slogan.

Congress passed an act placing the entire manhood of the nation at the disposal of the government. Those who were best fitted for the army were selected for the firing line; those who were engaged in essential industries, or were otherwise responding to the needs of the war, were exempted from active service. "The whole nation must be a team," said President Wilson, "in which each man shall play the part for which he is best fitted." On June 5, 1917, 9,700,000 men between the ages of twenty-one and thirty years inclusive, from every community in the country, came to their nearest voting-places and registered. From these, during the next month, the first draft of about 685,000 was made.

Soon after the United States entered the war General John J. Pershing was appointed commander-in-chief of the American forces in Europe, and on May 28 he sailed for France with a staff of fifty-three officers. Sixteen days later he landed at Boulogne. It was a bright, sunny day, and the scene at the harbor was one of striking beauty. War-vessels and merchant craft alike were gay with bunting, crowds of citizens and soldiers lined the quays, while from every housetop floated the Stars and Stripes. As the steamer neared the landing, Pershing's figure stood out prominently from the centre of his staff. A martial figure it was, which reflected force, energy, determination. To the eager throngs it seemed to personify the spirit of America. As they raised their voices in one mighty shout they saw, in the person of this unassuming general, the future American army, millions strong, which was coming to carry the war on to victory.

Pershing stepped ashore and was greeted by General Dumas, commander of the northern region. "I salute the United States of America," he said, "which has now become united to the United States of Europe." It was the first time in history that a soldier wearing the American uniform had landed on the continent of Europe for the purpose of engaging in war. Drawn up on the quay was a detachment of French infantry in battle uniform, middle-aged men most of them, just from the trenches. As the American general strode past and they came to salute with bodies erect, their faces betrayed their eager joy. Forgotten was the submarine menace, the long years of bitter struggle, the suffering and hardship. Here was America to help them, and soon all would be well.

As the months passed it became evident that the Allies could not win without the aid of a great American army. In July, 1917, General Pershing wrote that "plans should contemplate sending over at least 1,000,000 men by next May," while he advised for the future the creation of a force of not less than 3,000,000. It was a stupendous task to create a vast army, transport it across the Atlantic, and maintain it in France. When war was declared, the total forces of the United States, including regular army, national guard, and reserves, amounted to hardly more than 300,000 officers and men. From a military point of view the country was ranked below Belgium.

But the task was faced with characteristic energy. The General Staff was enlarged and its functions expanded; schools were opened both in the United States and France to train officers; the regular army was increased and organized into divisions; the national guard was made the nucleus for a great federalized army; a national army was created from the drafted men; provisions were made for feeding, arming, and caring for millions of men. In France the service of supply built great docks for the transports, repaired and maintained thousands of miles of roads, laid down 1,035 miles of railway; constructed warehouses covering storage space of 500 acres, remount depots adequate for 39,000 animals, veterinary hospitals for 23,000 animals, mechanical bakeries capable of producing half a million pounds of bread a day, and 81 sawmills which turned out 218,000,000 feet of lumber, 4,000,000 railway ties, and vast quantities of fuel wood. The medical service, comprising 16,407 physicians, 8,593 nurses, and 126,231 soldiers, maintained 153 base hospitals, 66 camp hospitals, and 12 convalescent camps —in all capable of caring for half a million patients.

General Pershing chose as the American sector the region around Verdun and the St. Mihiel salient. This selection was determined by questions of communication and supply. The channel ports of France were crowded with shipping and supplies for the British army, while throughout the zone around

Paris every railway and highway was taxed to serve the armies of France. The Americans were compelled not only to bring their men and supplies over the Atlantic Ocean, but to transport them several hundred miles from Bordeaux, La Pallice, and St. Nazaire to the region of Chaumont and Bar-le-Duc. The sector chosen by Pershing was a difficult field for offensive operations, for the ground was covered with forests and hills, and the German lines were many and powerful. But a successful advance here would cut the Coblenz-Trier-Mézières railway, without which the German armies could not be maintained in France.

General Pershing insisted upon training the American troops for open warfare. All through the winter of 1917–1918 he kept his regiments marching and drilling amid the snows and rains of northeastern France. Some of the Allied officers regarded these activities with good-humored condescension. Do the Americans not know that open warfare is a matter of the past? they said. Let them train for the trenches, and there will be no need for exhausting manœuvres of this kind. But Pershing was wiser than they. If ever we are going to drive the Germans out of France, he argued, must we not first force them into the open? It is for that day that the Americans are preparing. A few months later, when the lines which had been rigid for three years suddenly began to give way, every officer in the Allied armies paid tribute to the foresight of the American general.

In 1917 the Germans remained largely upon the defensive on the western front. They would not hazard their men in assaults upon the Allied lines, when they were confident that the submarines would bring the war to an end. But with the opening of 1918 it became obvious that the submarines had failed. The Allied countries were increasing their output of merchant vessels, the ocean channels were kept open, each month a larger number of submarines was sent to the bottom, and Great Britain was as far as ever from suing for peace. On the other hand, the Bolshevik revolution and the withdrawal of Russia from the war released many divisions for work in France. With a definite preponderance in the west, Marshal von Hindenburg now resolved to launch a major offensive to destroy the British and French armies before the Americans could come to their aid.

Late in March he hurled against the British forty divisions on a front of forty miles. Favored by a heavy mist, the Germans broke the line and threatened to separate the British army from the French, capture the Channel ports, and drive the British out of France. When this offensive had been brought to a halt, a few miles east of Amiens, von Hindenburg launched another, equally fierce and unexpected, against the French between Soissons and Rheims. The French were swept from the famous Chemin des Dames, and before they could make a stand, a great salient had been made in the Allied line from the Aisne to the Marne. The outlook for France and her Allies seemed dark indeed.

All eyes now turned anxiously upon the American troops. By the end of May there were eleven combat divisions in France, numbering about 300,000 men, while the transports were bringing in new detachments at the rate of nine divisions a month. Can the Americans fight? was the question all Europe asked. With their imperfect training and their lack of experience, is it possible that they can hold their own against the veteran troops of Germany? If so, the millions of men already in France or training in the United States will soon give Marshal Foch a great preponderance in numbers.

The answer came from Cantigny. This little village, situated at the extreme tip of the Amiens salient, was selected as the place for testing the Americans. The First Division, commanded by General Robert L. Bullard, was brought to the sector and prepared for battle. On May 28, at 6.45 in the morning, after an hour's artillery preparation which annihilated the village, the men delivered a perfectly executed attack. Amid the roar of guns, the glare of flame-projectors, and the rumble of tanks, the men in khaki went forward and took the coveted positions. The Germans were deeply chagrined. The next day they counter-attacked, determined to teach the Americans a lesson. But they attacked in vain. Bullard's men repulsed every assault. The effect of this little battle was electric. On the streets of the cities of France and England, in secluded villages, up and down the Allied trenches, weary and discouraged men discussed the news from Cantigny with new hope. The Americans can fight, they said. The Americans are ready to take their place in the line.

It was none too soon. At this very time the Germans were sweeping south from the Aisne to the Vesle, and from the Vesle to the Ourcq and the Marne. Before them fled the terror-stricken refugees. The roads to Paris were choked with men, women, and children, some walking, some riding on trucks, some driving carts piled high with household belongings. Here was a wan mother wheeling her child in a babycarriage, here a peasant driving a flock of sheep, here an old woman leading a goat. Everywhere one saw the sick and infirm resting beside roads or lying in the fields. Suddenly the refugees heard the rumble of trucks coming from the opposite direction, and, stepping aside to let them pass, their faces lit with hope when they saw that they were filled, not with French troops, but with Americans. Ah, they said, the Americans are on their way to stop the German drive.

Pershing's soldiers did their work nobly. The Third Division reached the Marne May 31, amid the cheers of the French soldiers. By heroic fighting in the streets of Château-Thierry and at the Jaulgonne bend, they drove the Germans back and so played an important part in fixing the Marne River as the southern limit of the drive. At the same time the Second Division took position at Meaux, athwart the road to Paris. Here, despite the desperate efforts of the enemy to dislodge them, they not only held their own, but strengthened their position by driving the enemy from Belleau Wood and Vaux. The whole world rang with the deeds of these two inexperienced divisions. They had proved themselves more than a match for the best German troops.

The two great German drives—the drive of March 21 against the British and the drive of May 27 against the French—completely changed the configuration of the western front. For four years the line had made a great right angle, with the apex pointing at Paris. This had favored the Germans, for it made one reservoir of reserves, placed back of the apex, sufficient for all needs. But now, since the spring drives had created the Amiens salient to the west and the Marne salient on the south, the point of the angle was reversed and pointed no longer at but away from Paris. This made it possible for Marshal Foch in his turn to mass his reserves in one place—in the region northeast of the capital.

Von Hindenburg was not discouraged, for he believed that the situation offered an opportunity for a drive in Champagne. By thrusting southward east of Rheims and southeastward from the Marne salient, he hoped to pocket Rheims, force the evacuation of Verdun, cut the French army in half, and fold the dislocated left wing back on Paris. All this was to be done before Foch could bring his reserves around the Marne salient to the point of danger. He overlooked the fact that, should the Allied line hold, all these reserves would be in position for a counter-offensive against the exposed western side of the Marne salient.

On the night of July 14 the Germans opened with an artillery preparation of great intensity, and the next morning the masses of gray infantry advanced to the attack. East of Rheims they met unexpected resistance from the French, aided by the Forty-second American, the famous Rainbow Division. The Allied artillery mowed them down, so that by noon of the 16th the operations in this sector were abandoned. The attack along the eastern side of the Marne salient was more successful. Here the French were pushed back over the Marne, and for a day or two Rheims was in danger. At the Jaulgonne bend the Third American Division again fought gallantly. At one point, where the enemy had gained the south bank of the river, General Dickman decided to drive them back at the point of the bayonet. The French corps commander under whom he was operating advised against this move, but Dickman was firm. "We regret being unable on this occasion to follow the counsel of our preceptors, the French," he replied, "but the American flag has been forced to retire. This is unendurable. . . . We are going to counter-attack." The counter-attack was so well executed that the general could report that "there were no

Germans left in the foreground of the Third Division sector except the dead."

While the Germans were still going forward, Marshal Foch prepared for his great counter-offensive. The Marne salient offered an inviting field for attack, not only because the enemy were massed on its eastern side, but because the only railway line entering the salient passed through Soissons, which was dangerously close to the western boundary. Foch planned to attack just south of Soissons, cut these lines, and so force the Germans to retire from the salient. A spearhead thrust was to be made by three divisions, the American First on the left, the American Second on the right, 54,000 men in all, with the First Moroccans, 13,000 strong, in the centre. The jump-off was set for 4.35 on the morning of July 18, and the night of the 17th was spent in bringing the men up through wheat-fields and forests. It was a delicate operation, for, should they fail to arrive in time, they would miss the protection of the artillery barrage and the offensive would be a failure.

Those seven hours of darkness were full of anxiety for the Americans. It rained hard; the roads were muddy, the night inky black. Down the centre of one small highway came artillery, caissons, tanks, motor-trucks, staff-cars, motor-cycles, ambulances, little one-mule machine-gun carts, combat wagons; at one side, through the muddy ditches, moved the never-ending column of infantry. Every now and then, as the men struggled forward, making desperate efforts to keep their places, villages would emerge from the darkness. Here the road usually narrowed to twenty feet or less, and through these openings the whole traffic had to jam its way. The infantry, in single file, would flatten themselves against the walls, as tanks and trucks and cannon thundered past. Captains shouted commands in the hope of keeping their companies together, lieutenants struggled to hold even their platoons. At times the officers became desperate. Could they reach the line in time for the jump-off? As the night wore on, the regiments, one by one, got to their designated places, until all were ready save parts of the Fifth Marines and the Ninth Infantry. Finally, as the roar of the barrage announced that the zero hour had come, and the forest was lit up by the glare of guns, these detachments came up on the double-quick. They reached their places in the line, straightened themselves out, and, amid cheers, advanced to the attack.

The offensive was a brilliant success. The surprised Germans resisted feebly, and the assaulting columns swept over their lines and on toward the all-important highway to the south. When evening came the Stars and Stripes had been planted on the plateau overlooking the valley of the Crise, and thousands of German prisoners, many wounded, all with a look of perplexity on their faces, were streaming back to the rear. Then came the cry: "Forward the guns!" It was the old cry of open warfare, the sure sign of victory. The next day the advance continued until the artillery of the Second Division played a devil's tattoo upon the road to Château-Thierry, and the Marne salient had become untenable. In those two days Marshal Foch had wrested the initiative from von Hindenburg, to hold it until Germany and her allies had been beaten to their knees.

As the Germans retired, fighting bitterly, from the Marne to the Vesle, and from the Vesle to the Aisne, General Pershing gathered his divisions together into a great American army for an attack upon the St. Mihiel salient. In the first months of the war the Germans had extended their line over the heights of the Meuse at the city of St. Mihiel, and there they had remained for four years. The salient cut important Allied lines of communication, threatened Verdun, and protected Metz and the Briey iron-mines. The task which Pershing chose, therefore, as the first great operation of the new American army, was of the very first importance. On September 12 he attacked the salient with 216,000 Americans and 48,000 French in line, and 190,000 Americans in reserve. The men advanced with precision, and early on the morning of the 13th detachments of the First Division coming from the south, and detachments of the Twenty-sixth from the west, met at Hattonchattel, east of the heights, and the St. Mihiel salient was no more.

A thrill of joy swept over the Allied nations at the news of this remarkable victory. In their editorial utterances the English and French papers vied with each other in praise of Pershing and his men. At last a powerful American army has taken its place in the line, they said, has instantly attained a great triumph, has shown the German staff that a new and all-important factor has arisen in the war. More has been destroyed at St. Mihiel than a German salient—General Pershing has shattered the belief that the United States could not raise, equip, and transport to the front an army capable of holding its own against von Hindenburg's veterans. The end cannot now be distant.

The Americans next undertook a task beset with untold difficulties and dangers. Twenty-five miles north of the Allied line was the city of Sedan, through which ran the vital Coblenz-Mézières railway. Pershing decided, with the consent of Foch, to fight his way over these twenty-five miles, through the dense Argonne forest, over several successive highly developed lines of trenches, up river valleys dominated by wooded heights, across sharp ravines, through woods strewn with machine-gun nests, until he had cut the railway and made it impossible for Germany to maintain her armies in France.

At eleven o'clock on the night of September 25, the American line from the Meuse to the western edge of the Argonne forest burst into flame, as 3,928 guns opened upon the German positions. For six and a half hours the bombardment continued, and when, the next morning, the infantry charged, they found only shattered wire, ruined trenches, shell-holes, and villages levelled with the ground. Nine American divisions went forward, up the valley of the Meuse, through the Bois de Cheppy, over the ruined town of Vauquois, up the Aire beneath the heights of the Argonne. Before evening called a halt they had captured 7,000 prisoners and had carried the front four miles over the Hindenburg line to the famous Volker-Stellung.

Thereafter the advance was not so rapid. It was necessary to bring up guns, ambulances, kitchens, and supplies, and this was no easy matter over roads pounded to fragments. The Germans rushed fresh divisions to the points of danger and delivered fierce counter-attacks. But Pershing would not be denied. As this division or that wilted before the unceasing fire, it was withdrawn for another with full ranks and rested men. There was work enough for all in the weeks of bitter fighting which followed. The Metropolitan division won distinction in the Argonne forest, the First in the Gesne valley, the Fourth before Brieulles, the Fifth at the Ardon creek, the Second at Landres et St. Georges. Slowly the line moved forward, through the Volker-Stellung, through the Argonne forest, to Grand Pré, past Brieulles, past Aincreville, through the Kriemhilde-Stellung, out into the open. Then, on November 1, with one last smashing attack, the Americans swept away resistance and pushed on rapidly toward their final goal. On November 7 a part of the First Division reached the outskirts of Wadelincourt, and looked out over the mills and clustered houses of Sedan. Here they halted to permit a French detachment, in which were many natives of Sedan, to have the honor of taking the town.

The end was now at hand. General Pershing's penetration of the Kriemhilde-Stellung had dislocated the entire German system of defense in France, while the cutting of the Mézières railway had made withdrawal difficult, if not impossible. With the British, French, and American armies pounding the reeling German divisions ceaselessly, von Hindenburg's army faced supreme disaster. Nor was this all. An Allied drive in the Balkans had ended resistance in that region; Allenby had conquered Syria, the Italians had overwhelmed the Austrian army on the Piave, and Turkey, Bulgaria, and Austria had been forced to lay down their arms. The war was really over. On November 9 Kaiser Wilhelm II abdicated, and two days later German envoys signed an armistice which was in effect an unconditional surrender.

In the early weeks of 1919 Secretary Pichon's study, in the Quai d'Orsay, at Paris, presented an interesting picture. The room itself was charming, with its rich Gobelin tapestries, rare carpet of gray sprinkled with roses, and high French windows opening on the Foreign Office gardens. Behind an empire desk sat the squat Clemenceau, the "Tiger," as he was called, his gray face, high cheek-bones, drooping mustaches, and clasped hands giving an impression of strange immobility. On his right was President Woodrow Wilson, immaculately attired, his intellectual face lit up with expectation. With them was Lloyd George, eager, electric, alert, always on the edge of his chair; "Balfour with his long legs outstretched, his head on the back of his chair, eyes not infrequently closed, philosophic in attitude"; the stern Sonnino, with prominent nose, sharp features, and iron jaw; the eloquent Orlando; the sphinx-like Japanese. It was the Peace Conference, called to impose terms upon the defeated Central Powers and reconstruct the shattered world.

The delegates of the various smaller nationalities stood or sat before Clemenceau's desk, pleading for an extended boundary line, the control of an important river, or the possession of a port. Of especial interest were the black-bearded Bratiano, of Rumania, moody, resentful of opposition; the smiling young Foreign Minister of Czecho-Slovakia, Edward Benes; Dmowski, the Pole, clear of logic and powerful in satire; Pachitch, the Serb, a patriarch with flowing white beard; the smooth-spoken Vesnitch. While the leading statesmen listened to the conflicting claims, starvation was spreading over Europe and the spectre of Bolshevism was everywhere raising its head. "We had to . . . work long and late," said Lloyd George, "because, while we were trying to build, we saw in many lands the foundations of society crumbling into dust. . . . [We worked] with stones crackling on the roof and crashing through the windows, and sometimes wild men screaming through the keyholes."

To President Wilson the Peace Conference seemed the one great opportunity of the ages to make over a misshapen world, to correct old injustices, eliminate occasions for future wars, do away with rivalries, jealousies, and hatreds. While not minimizing the difficulty of the task, he set about it with enthusiastic confidence. In the smaller conferences in Wilson's residence one might have seen him on all fours "kneeling on a gigantic map spread upon the floor, and tracing with his finger a proposed boundary, other plenipotentiaries grouped around him, also on all fours."

The peace terms were severe. Germany lost her foreign dependencies and colonies, had to surrender 50,000 square miles of her empire in Europe, was forced to reduce her army to

100,000 men, surrender her warships, demolish her fortifications, and pay a tremendous bill of damages. The Austro-Hungarian Empire was annihilated. The Entente Allies profited in various degrees from the treaty. England secured control over huge expanses of territory in Africa and Asia; France recovered Alsace-Lorraine and rounded out her African empire; Italy advanced her frontiers to the north and east; Rumania received Transylvania; Serbia expanded into Jugo-Slavia; Poland regained her independence. The United States secured no territory, its part of the indemnity was insignificant, and all that it asked was a treaty which would make it impossible for the events of 1914–1918 to happen again.

President Wilson felt that he was carrying out the wishes of the American people when he insisted upon incorporating in the treaty provisions for a League of Nations. The main object of this organization was to "achieve international peace and security by the acceptance of obligations not to resort to war." The Constitution, or Covenant, of the League made provisions for reducing national armaments, for settling disputes by peaceful methods, and for abolishing secret treaties. When the details of the treaty and of the League had been completed, Wilson, elated at his success, returned to the United States. Two days after landing he entertained the members of the Senate and House Committees on Foreign Affairs at dinner in the White House, where he pleaded earnestly for a prompt acceptance of the League.

But he met with determined opposition. A storm of controversy arose over the League, both in the Senate and in the country at large. There was a sincere feeling of hesitation on the part of many Americans at what seemed a radical departure from the traditional policy of abstention from European entanglements. Wilson was deeply chagrined. He contended that the obligations and the purposes of the League were misunderstood, and with characteristic zeal started upon a long speaking tour to explain them to the people. His strength had already been undermined by years of incessant labor, and while in Colorado he suffered a paralytic stroke which confined him to the sick-room for most of the remainder of his Presidency.

The deadlock between President and Senate made it inevitable that the League of Nations should become the paramount issue in the election of 1920. The Republicans nominated Senator Warren G. Harding, of Ohio, and Calvin Coolidge, of Massachusetts, both opposed to unqualified ratification. The platform pledged the party to "such agreements with the other nations . . . as shall meet the full duty of America to civilization and humanity . . . without surrendering the right of the American people to exercise its judgment and its power in favor of justice and peace." The Democrats named Governor James M. Cox, of Ohio, as their candidate, defended the Wilson policies, domestic and foreign, and declared for an immediate ratification of the peace treaty, including the League of Nations.

The Republicans swept the country. The vote in the electoral college stood 404 to 127 in favor of Harding; while his popular plurality was nearly 7,000,000. Even the solid South was shaken, and Tennessee for the first time since 1868 cast its vote for the Republican ticket. Mr. Harding felt that he had received a mandate from the American people. "Confident of our ability to work out our own destiny and jealously guarding our right to do so, we seek no part in the destinies of the Old World," he said in his inaugural address. "We do not mean to be entangled. We accept no responsibility except as our own conscience and judgment may determine." In accordance with this policy the League of Nations was repudiated, and, on July 2, 1921, peace with Germany was declared by a joint resolution of both Houses of Congress.

The Harding administration did not forget its pledge that the United States should do its part in lifting the heavy burdens from the shoulders of humanity. To many it seemed that the whole world was facing bankruptcy. The great European powers, exhausted by the war, overwhelmed with debts, were laying out millions for military and naval defenses. Even the United States was spending nine-tenths of its national revenues in paying for past wars or in preparing for the wars of the future. Accordingly, in the summer of 1921, President Harding invited the leading powers to a conference at Washington to consider a limitation of armaments.

This conference met on November 12, in the main hall of the beautiful Pan-American Building. It was a brilliant scene.

The white marble room, 200 feet square, with a great cluster of flags hanging from the ceiling, with its galaxy of State emblems bathed in the light of the chandeliers, with its low-hung galleries filled with distinguished guests, was a worthy meeting-place for so notable a gathering. Among the delegates were: Hughes, Root, Lodge, Underwood; Balfour and Geddes; the British colonials—Borden, of Canada, Pearce, of Australia, Salmond, of New Zealand; the doughty Briand, his massive head crowned with a mane of shaggy black hair; Jusserand and Viviani; Scrinivisa, the brown-faced native of India, distinctive in his black frock coat and white turban; Prince Takugawa, of Japan; the blond-headed Schanzer, of Italy; and the trim, bespectacled Chinaman, Alfred Sze.

At 10.45 A. M. members of Congress, seated in the gallery, began to applaud, and immediately the assemblage rose as the President of the United States entered. Mr. Harding shook hands with Hughes and Balfour, waited reverently while the meeting was opened with prayer, and then delivered a brief address of welcome. After he had left the room Secretary Hughes rose, and with a directness which startled the foreign diplomats, proceeded to suggest a radical cut in the navies of the great powers. "The world looks to this conference to relieve humanity of the crushing burden created by competition in armament," he said; "and it is the view of the American Government that we should meet that expectation without any unnecessary delay.

"Hundreds of millions are devoted to acquiring terrible engines of destruction, which, though to-day regarded as the last word of science, are destined to-morrow to lose all value in consequence of some fresh discovery in the same field. National culture, economic progress, and the production of wealth are either paralyzed or checked in their development. . . . The economic crises, due in great part to the system of armaments *à l'outrance* and to the continual danger which lies in this massing of war material, are transforming the armed peace of our days to a crushing burden, which the peoples have more and more difficulty in bearing."

Mr. Hughes then proposed that a large number of capital

ath, left an indelible mark
the Monroe Doctrine from
rld safe for democracy" by
military despotism in Eu-
country to a new sense of
ion was capable of mobiliz-

...tes to...
...cretary Hughes...
sig... ...y treaties and international agr... ...ith... ...the past
three years," and declared emphatically that "whoever says
America stands aloof and withholds her support from a stricken
world is guilty of a reckless slander." The dominating principle of our foreign policy, now as in the past, he said, is helpful
co-operation for the promotion of international arbitration and
peace.

It was in accordance with this policy that Mr. Hughes himself suggested to France and Great Britain so early as December, 1922, that a commission of experts be appointed to determine Germany's capacity to pay reparations. Late in 1923
France gave a tardy consent to this plan, and the United States
agreed to designate American experts for the work. In due
time the commission, headed by Charles G. Dawes, later Vice-
President of the United States, submitted a plan by which
Germany might recover her former industrial and financial
vitality, and at the same time pay a maximum indemnity.
This scheme, which was accepted by all concerned, has already
accomplished much for the restoration of prosperity and lasting peace in Europe.

The World War, with its afterm
upon the United States. It relieved
a serious menace; it made the "wo
destroying the chief strongholds of
rope; it awakened the people of th
nationalism; it showed that the nat
ing its giant strength.

CHAPTER XXVII

PROBLEMS—SOLVED AND UNSOLVED

IT has often been predicted that modern civilization will break down of its own weight. The increasing complexity of life—the growth of populations, the development of big business, the expansion of governmental activities, the extension of international trade—are ever presenting new problems. Will not these problems accumulate, it is asked, until it becomes impossible for human insight to solve them? Although the future alone can answer, Americans believe that they will solve each perplexing question as it arises. For a people who have attained unity from diverse racial and geographical elements, have won their liberty in the face of untold difficulties, and have erected in the wilderness the richest and most powerful nation on earth, the future seems to hold out only new triumphs.

No question of recent times has aroused more discussion than the proper place for women in modern life. Even in the colonial period women at times ventured to complain of their subordinate position. "I long to hear that you have declared an independency," Mrs. John Adams wrote her husband in March, 1776, "and, by the way, in the new code of laws which I suppose it will be necessary for you to make, I desire you would remember the ladies and be more generous and favorable to them than were your ancestors. Do not put such unlimited power into the hands of husbands. Remember all men would be tyrants if they could."

Sixty-five years after Mrs. Adams made this appeal, Ernestine L. Rose, Elizabeth Cady Stanton, Paulina Wright Davis, and Lydia Mott were trying to arouse the American people to the seriousness of the question. In 1848 several of these far-sighted women called at Seneca Falls, New York, a convention which issued a Declaration of Sentiments, modelled upon the Declaration of Independence. It complained that men had monopolized all profitable employments, closed the colleges to women, denied them civil rights if married, taxed them to support a government in which they were unrepresented, had taken from them all rights in property even to the wages they earned, and had tried to destroy their confidence in their own powers, so that they would be willing to lead a dependent life.

Gradually the movement for women's rights expanded. In 1869 two organizations were formed to further the cause—the National Woman Suffrage Association and the American Woman Suffrage Association. Later these bodies were merged into one society. Under the able leadership of Susan B. Anthony and Carrie Chapman Catt, the women's rights cause won victory after victory. In 1869 Wyoming Territory granted the suffrage to its women, and the next year Utah followed suit. Colorado fell into line in 1893 and Idaho in 1896. By 1916 seven more States—Oregon, Washington, California, Arizona, Nevada, Montana, and Kansas—had conferred full suffrage rights upon women. In 1917 the great State of New York joined the procession, and it became evident that the cause of women's rights was upon the eve of a national triumph.

The suffrage leaders used every legitimate means of bringing their case to the attention of the American people, by combating old prejudices and answering adverse arguments. In 1913, the day before the first inauguration of Woodrow Wilson, they held in Washington a great parade and pageant. Seven thousand women marched up Pennsylvania Avenue, from the Capitol to the Treasury Building. At their head was Mrs. Richard Coke Burleson, mounted on a fine bay horse and wearing a green band over her shoulder. Next came Miss Inez Milholland in herald's costume in advance of a float bearing the words: "We demand an amendment of the United States Constitution enfranchising the women of the country." Mrs. Catt led the first foot division, followed by groups of young women carrying floats representing Norway, Finland, New Zealand, Australia, and other countries which had granted the suffrage. The second division bore floats showing the changed attitude of the world to women's rights, while the third had representations of women at work in various pursuits—as farmers, home-makers, teachers, nurses, physicians, lawyers. As the marchers passed by, 250,000 persons lined the avenue. There were some evidences of hostility. On the other hand, the applause which greeted them all along the line was so vigorous as to testify to the growing popularity of their cause.

Nation-wide enfranchisement of women was near at hand. In 1919 an amendment to the Constitution was proposed in Congress, forbidding any State to deny or abridge the rights of citizens to vote on account of sex. The resolution passed the House of Representatives 304 to 89, and the Senate 56 to 25. The first State to ratify was Wisconsin, but Michigan, Kansas, New York, Ohio, Illinois, Pennsylvania, Massachusetts, and Texas followed in rapid succession. By August, 1920, 35 States had assented, and one more only was needed to make the amendment effective. The final battle was fought in Tennessee.

On August 18, 1920, the Hall of Representatives at Nashville witnessed a scene of tense excitement. Of the 99 members of the House, 96 were in their seats, while the floor and galleries were crowded to suffocation with interested spectators. The suffragists, who were present in large numbers, wore yellow flowers, while the anti-suffragists were distinguished by red roses. The Senate had voted for ratification, and the House was now debating a motion to concur. Suddenly Speaker Walker resigned the chair to a fellow Representative, and, taking the floor, said: "I move that this measure go where it belongs, to the table." Instantly the room was in an uproar, several suffragists clamoring for recognition, while their opponents were shouting in chorus: "Second the motion."

The acting chairman refused to recognize any one, and ordered the roll-call. The tally showed a vote of 48 to 48. Again pandemonium broke loose, the members crowding around the Speaker's desk and endeavoring to make themselves heard. A second roll-call was ordered, and the vote stood once more 48 to 48. It was evident that the motion to table the resolution could not be carried. But the enemies of suffrage were by no means discouraged. They now demanded an immediate vote on the resolution itself, realizing that if the tie continued and it failed to pass, ratification would be lost.

Once more the roll was called. There was no change in the vote until the name of Harry T. Burn, of McMinn County, was called. This young man, from the mountains of east Tennessee, had formerly voted with the anti-suffragists, but now, to the surprise of all, he changed his alignment and came out with a clear "Ay." Ratification had won. When the voting was over there was an uproarious demonstration. Women threw their arms around each other's necks and danced, hundreds of banners waved, while from the gallery came a shower of yellow flowers. The century-long battle, to all intents and purposes, was over, and 27,000,000 American women had the right to vote.

Hardly less important than women's rights is the question of immigration. The United States is a land of immigrants. Captain John Smith, John Winthrop, William Bradford were immigrants. For three hundred years the stream of newcomers poured across the Atlantic. In the seventeenth century came the workers for the tobacco-fields of Virginia and Maryland, the Puritans to New England, the Dutch to New Amsterdam, and the Quakers to Pennsylvania; in the eighteenth century came Germans and Scotch-Irish; in the nineteenth and twentieth centuries came Irish, Germans, Poles, Scandinavians, Italians, Greeks, and Russians. It is estimated that since the founding of Jamestown 25,000,000 foreigners have settled in this country. Thus the New World long served as an outlet for the overflow population of the Old.

The newcomers have been welcomed in the past. The unexploited resources of America—her rich agricultural lands and stores of priceless minerals—called always for labor and ever more labor. There was room for all, work for all to do, and still the demand for labor was not satisfied. At first the immigrant contented himself with the humbler tasks—with work in the fields or mills. But gradually he pushed his way up, accumulating capital, acquiring an education, accepting American ideals, learning his duties as a citizen. He made of himself and his children law-abiding, industrious, useful citizens.

The influx of foreigners was greatly accelerated in the years just preceding the World War. In 1898 only 229,299 came in, but from that figure the number increased to 648,743 in 1902, to 857,046 in 1903, to 812,870 in 1904, to 1,026,499 in 1905, to 1,100,735 in 1906, and 1,285,349 in 1907. In the decade from 1904 to 1914 over 10,000,000 foreigners entered the United States. This situation was fraught with danger. In 1920 the number of foreign-born in the country was 13,920,692, or 13 per cent of the entire population, while there were 36,398,958 persons having one or both parents of foreign stock. Of the foreign-born whites over ten years of age, 1,763,740 were illiterate. Millions could not speak the English language. The aliens were coming faster than they could be assimilated. Many were hostile to the United States Constitution, and proclaimed their intention of setting up a communist government modelled upon that of Russia. More than 1,000 newspapers printed in foreign languages were in circulation.

Moreover, the day had passed when the country could absorb new workers in unlimited numbers. The most fertile spaces had been filled up, the frontier had disappeared, factories and mines were no longer undermanned. Waves of economic depression brought unemployment, and the labor-unions were trying to check the flood of cheap European workers. Their efforts were seconded by many who feared that overpopulation might lower the average standard of living. It was realized that the country was capable of supporting a larger number of people, but only by the more intensive application of labor. They saw no reason why the government, by its policy of unrestricted immigration, should hasten the approach of the saturation-point. Many noted with apprehension that some of the newcomers were inferior, mentally and physically, to the immigrants of earlier days.

The conclusion of the World War brought matters to a crisis. It was evident that the terrible plight of many of the nations of Europe would create a great wave of migration unless steps were taken to check it. "The world is preparing to move to America," said Commissioner of Immigration Wallis. Labor-unions and patriotic societies forced the matter upon the attention of Congress, and in 1921 a law was passed limiting the quota of immigrants which any country could send to the United States to 3 per cent of its people already living here according to the census of 1910. Under the provisions of this law only 357,000 aliens were permitted to land annually. Even this restricted number seemed too large, and it was cut down to 161,990 by the Johnson-Lodge Bill of 1924. The new law allotted to each country 2 per cent of the number of its people residing in the United States in 1890. This greatly reduced the quotas of the countries from which immigration had increased rapidly in recent years. It cut down Italy's quota from 42,000 to 3,889, Poland's from 30,000 to 8,872, and Russia's from 24,000 to 1,792. On the other hand, Great Britain's quota was reduced from 77,000 only to 62,000, and Germany's from 67,-000 to 50,000.

The new immigration laws mark an epoch in American history. This reversal of a policy adhered to for three centuries cannot fail to affect profoundly the life of the nation. It will gradually reduce the number of foreign-born and so diminish European influence in press and government. It will retard the growth of population. It will make it easier to solve the problems of illiteracy, overcrowding, corruption in politics, and the spread of radicalism. Apparently the nation has accepted for the future as its slogan, "America for the Americans."

In education, especially in elementary and secondary education, a development hardly less revolutionary is now in progress. The one-room rural school is being eliminated. The "little red schoolhouse" has been a picturesque element in our life—the tiny wooden structure, the bell which called the children to classes, the ill-ventilated schoolroom, the wooden blackboard, the water-bucket and dipper, the rows of desks each carved with initials, the teacher striving faithfully to impart the principles of arithmetic or spelling.

To-day those who visit the spot find perhaps a striking change. The little schoolhouse is gone, and in its place is a handsome building of stone or brick. Instead of 1 room there are 6; instead of 1 teacher, 8; instead of 20 children, 150; in place of the unsightly blackboard and desks, the latest school equipment. This change has been brought about by the hard-surfaced road and the automobile. Formerly the district served by one country school was limited by the distance children could travel to and from school on foot or in the family carriage. To-day pupils are brought to school, often ten or fifteen miles, in the motor-coach. The consolidation of rural schools has gone on apace. In Randolph County, Indiana, 131 one-room schools have been replaced by 21 consolidated schools, 5 of which have both graded and high-school departments. This case is exceptional, for in 1918 there were still but 10,500 consolidated schools in the United States, but it is significant of the development which is taking place. A new epoch is opening for the 12,000,000 school-children in the rural districts.

This movement in the lower schools is matched by the recent expansion of the high-school system. A few years ago an insignificant proportion of the school-children continued their work after reaching the age of fifteen; at present of the 3,828,131 children aged sixteen or seventeen, 1,644,061, or 42.9 per cent, remain at school. In all, there are 14,000 high schools in the United States, and the number is increasing rapidly.

The colleges, too, are experiencing a period of rapid growth. Since the World War young men and women have thronged to the leading universities in such numbers that many have been forced to limit their enrolment. In 1922 the number of matriculates at the University of California was 14,367, at the University of Chicago 11,385, at the City College of New York 13,744, at Columbia 8,193, at Harvard 6,073, at the University of Illinois 9,009, at the University of Michigan 9,803, at New York University 12,254, at the University of Pennsylvania 10,193. Many colleges suffered severely from the inflation of the war period. Fortunately the decline in the value of their invested funds in most cases has been offset by successful campaigns for larger endowments. To-day the American college is playing a larger part in the life of the nation than ever before.

The progress which is being made in education is a matter of great importance. Democracy requires a high level of enlightenment. In a despotism the despot and a restricted group of advisers alone need understand the art of governing; but in a republic the people must know how to conduct the affairs of the nation. It is this which makes despotism the easiest form of government to conduct and democracy the most difficult. "Enlighten the people generally, and tyranny and oppressions . . . will vanish like evil spirits at the dawn of day," said Thomas Jefferson.

But as old problems are solved, new problems, not less perplexing, force themselves upon the attention of the American people. There is the ever-present problem of preserving our democracy in the face of a changing civilization; the problem of conserving our natural resources—preventing forest-fires, eliminating waste in mining and using coal, guarding our stores of oil, restoring the fertility to exhausted soil; the problem of Americanizing the millions of foreign-born who live within our borders; the problem of eradicating illiteracy; the problem of purifying our political life; the problem of protecting our interests and rights abroad without doing injustice to other nations; the problem of reconciling capital and labor in such a way that equal justice will be done to workers, owners, and public; the problem of stabilizing the currency so as to eliminate the recurring periods of rising and declining values, with their inevitable trail of suffering and bitterness.

As the American of to-day looks back over the history of his country, he marvels at the changes which time has wrought. He sees the settler of the seventeenth century as he goes about the work of empire-building; he sees him making his clearing in the forest, erecting his cabin, breaking the ground with his hoe and putting out his little crop, defending his family from the Indians, creeping through the woods in pursuit of wild game, riding over narrow trails to church or a meeting of the Assembly; in short, battling day by day to conquer the wilderness and erect a civilized state in the New World. He thinks of the little colonies hugging the Atlantic coast, disunited, weak, dreading the Indian, the French, and the Spaniard, dependent upon Europe for existence.

Then he turns his vision to the America of to-day, the great nation stretching from the Atlantic to the Pacific, with its millions of people, its cities, its great agricultural lands, its smoke-covered industrial centres, its network of concrete roads and railway lines, its automobiles, subways, irrigation systems. He contemplates the nation's wealth, its resources, power, and unity, its leading position in the family of nations, and realizes that his ancestors built wisely and well. So long as it is faithful to the ideals of those noble men, he tells himself, so long as it emulates their courage, their faith, their love of justice, their loyalty to democratic institutions, its leadership, material and spiritual, will be unquestioned.

INDEX

Abolitionists, combat annexation of Texas, 299; support Lincoln, 355.

Abraham, Plains of, battle on, 47.

Adams, at Samoa, 416.

Adams, Charles Francis, minister to England, 347.

Adams, John, negotiates Treaty of 1783, 94; at Court of St. James's, 102–103; asks trade concessions, 103; 114; 151; bares X-Y-Z insult, 153; secures peace with France, 154; elected President, 155; quarrels with Cabinet, 158–159; breach with Hamilton, 159; defeated for Presidency, 160; 162.

Adams, Mrs. John, describes Washington, 66; 463.

Adams, John Quincy, 188; at Ghent, 212–213; 248; negotiates purchase of Florida, 252–254; shapes Monroe Doctrine, 255–260; 261; presidential candidate, 263–268; elected, 268–269; 302.

Adams, Samuel, organizes committees of correspondence, 59; 114; advises ratification of Constitution, 130.

Adet, Pierre Auguste, interferes in American politics, 151.

Alabama, 336; secedes, 339; 356; 368; 376; 378.

Alamo, capture of, by Mexicans, 295–296; 297.

Albany, fur trade of, 37; Congress at, 38–41; description of, 39.

Aldrich, Nelson W., 392; 434.

Alexander, Tzar, letter to, 256–258.

Algonquins, allied with French, 38.

Alien and Sedition Acts, 156.

Allison, W. B., 406.

Almonte, demands passports, 303.

Amador, Dr., 431.

Ambrose, sails for Massachusetts, 11.

Amendments, Thirteenth, 368; Fourteenth, 373; Fifteenth, 374; 379; Nineteenth, 465–466.

American Federation of Labor, 388.

Ames, Fisher, 129; 221; 227.

Amherst, Sir Jeffrey, made commander-in-chief in America, 45; attacks Montreal, 48.

Ancon, 432.

André, Major, conference with Arnold, 88; captured and executed, 89–90.

Andrews, Samuel, 384.

Andros, Sir Edmund, Governor-General of northern colonies, 32; expelled from Massachusetts, 33.

Anglican Church, 7.

Annapolis, convention at, 112–113.

Anthony, Susan B., 464.

Antietam, battle of, 353.

Anti-Federalists, defend Articles of Confederation, 104–105; ignore Constitutional Convention, 124; combat Constitution in Congress, 126; in Pennsylvania, 126–127; in Massachusetts, 128–130; in Virginia, 130–132.

Apia, hurricane at, 417.

Appomattox, surrender at, 364–365.

Aranda, Count, plan for Mississippi valley, 93–94.

Arango, Señor, 431.

Arbella, sails for Massachusetts, 11.

Argonne-Meuse offensive, 455–456.

Arista, Mariano, attacks Taylor, 305; defeated at Palo Alto, 305–306; defeated on Rio Grande, 306–307.

Arkansas, 336; secedes, 343; 349; 368; 378.

Arnold, Anthony, trial of, 30.

Arnold, Benedict, 69; in Saratoga expedition, 79–80; treason of, 87–89; invades Virginia, 90.

Arthur, President, 400.

Assumption bill, 139–140.

Atlanta, 356; captured, 362.

Austin, Stephen A., founds Texas, 292–293; imprisoned, 294.

Bacon, Nathaniel, leads rebellion in Virginia, 29–30.

Balfour, A. J., 446; at peace conference, 457–458; 460.

Baltimore and Ohio Railroad, construction of, 237–238; 239.

Baltimore, Democratic convention of 1860, 337; Democratic convention of 1912, 436–437.

Baltimore, Lord, visits America, 13.

Bank, Federal, Hamilton proposes, 141–142; first, expires, 198; Jackson attacks second, 282–286.

Banks, General, in valley of Virginia, 350–351.

Barbour, P. P., address on Missouri question, 245.

Barney, Joshua, at battle of Bladensburg, 204–206.

Barré, Colonel Isaac, opposes Stamp Act, 52; toasted by Virginia Burgesses, 57.

Barron, Commodore, 184–185.

Beauregard, General, at Bull Run, 347–349; 358.

Bedford, Gunning, opposes Virginia plea, 116–117.
Bee, General, at Bull Run, 348.
Beecher, Henry Ward, 399.
Bell, John, 338.
Bellamy, M., 153.
Belleau Wood, 451.
Belmont, August, 436.
Benes, Edward, 457.
Benton, Thomas, 287; 289.
Berkeley, Sir William, 22; defies Parliament, 28; despotism of, 28; captured by Bacon, 29–30; condemns Anthony Arnold, 30.
Biddle, Nicholas, 283–285.
Bienville, Céleron de, claims Ohio region, 40.
Big business, changes wrought by, 395.
Birney, James G., 303.
Bishop, Abraham, 223.
Bismarck, Count, 418.
Black codes, 369–370; 374.
Blacklock, Vice-Consul, report on Samoa, 416.
Bladensburg, battle of, 204–206.
Blaine, James G., defeated for Presidency, 399–400.
Bland, Richard P., 406.
Bland-Allison Act, 406.
Blennerhassett, Herman, 177–179.
Board of Trade, tightens control over colonies, 21–22.
Boone, Daniel, leads settlers to Kentucky, 105.
Booth, John Wilkes, murders Lincoln, 366–367.
Boston, at Manila Bay, 424–425.
Boston, founded, 11; expels Andros, 32–33; tea destroyed at, 59–60; harbor closed, 60; siege of, 64–66; British evacuate, 66; ratifying convention at, 128–130.
Boston Massacre, 58.
Botetot, Governor, dissolves Virginia Assembly, 56.
Braddock, Colonel Edward, expedition of, 42–44.
Bradstreet, John, captures Fort Frontenac, 45.
Bragg, General, in Kentucky, 358; at Chickamauga, 362.
Bratiano, 457.
Brearly, David, opposes Virginia plan, 115–116.
Breckinridge, John C., Southern Democrats nominate, 337; defeated, 338.
Breed's Hill, battle on, 64–65.
British colonial system, defects of, 24; its failure, 24.
Brooklyn, at Santiago, 426–428.
Brooklyn Heights, battle of, 73–74.

Brown, John, murders of, in Kansas, 328; Harper's Ferry raid, 334–335.
Brown, Governor Joseph, 345.
Bryan, William Jennings, cross of gold speech, 409–410; defeated for Presidency, 411–412; in convention of 1912, 436–437.
Buchanan, James, 296; elected President, 329.
Buell, General, 358.
Buena Vista, battle of, 308–309.
Buenz, Dr., 430.
Bull Run, battle of, 347–349.
Bullard, Robert L., at Cantigny, 450.
Bunker Hill, battle near, 64–65.
Burgoyne, General John, invades New York, 78–80.
Burke, Edmund, explains American Revolution, 62.
Burn, Harry T., 466.
Burnside, Ambrose E., defeated at Fredericksburg, 353.
Burr, Aaron, tied for Presidency, 160–161; defeated for Presidency, 161; 163; kills Hamilton, 176; plot of, 176–177; trial, 178–179.
Butler, Pierce, opposes duty on ships, 136.

Cabinet, President's, evolution of, 137.
Cabot, George, 208; 221–222.
Cabot, John, voyage of, 4.
Cadwalader, General, 76.
Calhoun, John C., demands war on England, 195; shapes Monroe Doctrine, 254–260; 263; South Carolina Exposition, 276; 279; nullification, 280–282; 286; protests against expunging, 288; last address of, 320–322; death of, 323; 341.
California, 304–305; acquisition of, 312; discovery of gold in, 314–315; rapid growth of, 315; excludes slavery, 316; Compromise of 1850, 317–325; irrigation in, 412; development of, 412–413.
Calliope, escape of, at Apia, 417.
Calvert, Cecilius, founds Maryland, 13–14.
Cambrian, 182.
Cambridge agreement, 11.
Camden, battle of, 86.
Canada, French settle, 36; sparseness of population, 39; invaded by English, 45–48; proposed conquest of, 193; invasion of, 204.
Canning, George, repudiates Erskine agreement, 191; proposals of, 255.
Cantigny, battle of, 450–451.
Cape Cod, Pilgrims reach, 9; English raid, 204.
Carlisle, Secretary, purchases gold, 406–408.

Carmathen, Secretary, refuses trade concessions, 103.

Carnegie, Andrew, steel business of, 385–386.

"Carpetbaggers," 376; 377.

Cartier, Jacques, explores the St. Lawrence, 36.

Catholics, found Maryland, 13–14.

Catt, Carrie C., 464.

Cerro Gordo, battle of, 310.

Cervera, Admiral, defeat of, 426–428.

Chads Ford, battle at, 81.

Champlain, Lake, French secure, 44.

Champlain, Samuel, founds Quebec, 36; aids Algonquins, 38.

Chancellorsville, battle of, 354.

Chapultepec, storming of, 311–312.

Charles II, grants Carolina patent, 14; quarrels with Massachusetts, 31; Louis XIV pensions, 31; despotism of, 31–32.

Charleston, S. C., British capture, 85; convention of 1860 at, 335–337; 341–343.

Charlestown, Mass., founded, 11; burnt, 65.

Chase, Salmon P., denounces Kansas-Nebraska bill, 325; address of, 326–327; 378.

Château-Thierry, battle at, 451.

Chattanooga, 349; 356; battles around, 361–362.

Chesapeake, encounter with Leopard, 183–185; 198; captured, 203.

Cheves, Langdon, 195.

Chickahominy, battles on, 352.

Chickamauga, battle of, 362.

Churubusco, battle at, 311.

Cincinnati, description of, 231.

City of Memphis, 444.

Civil Rights bill, 371.

Clark, Champ, 436–437.

Clark, George Rogers, takes Kaskaskia and Vincennes, 83–84; 149; 168.

Clark, William, expedition of, 174–175.

Clay, Henry, demands war, 193; 195; 196; at Ghent, 212–213; on admission of Maine, 247; 250; opposes Florida Treaty, 253–254; presidential candidate, 263–265; President-maker, 265–268; "bargain and corruption," 267–268; appeal of, for tariff of 1824, 274–275; manages tariff bill of 1833, 281; defends United States Bank, 283–285; election of 1832, 285; denounces removal of deposits, 286; address on expunging, 288; nomination of, blocked in 1840; 299–300; nominated in 1844, 302; defeated, 303; address of Feb. 5, 1850, 318–320; 324.

Clayton, Thomas, 280.

Clemenceau, Georges, at peace conference, 456–458.

Cleveland, city, oil industry of, 384.

Cleveland, Grover, 392; elected President, 400; inaugural address, 400–401; tariff message of, 401–402; election of, in 1892; denounces Wilson tariff, 403–404; purchases gold, 406–408; opposes annexation of Hawaii, 419; Venezuelan message, 420–422; on Cuba, 422–423.

Clinton, DeWitt, pleads for Erie Canal, 234–235; 236.

Clinton, George, 104.

Clinton, Sir Henry, at battle of Long Island, 72–74; at battle of Monmouth Court House, 82; captures Charleston, 85; sends troops to Virginia, 90.

Clymer, George, 126; wants duty on steel, 136; 140.

Cockburn, Admiral, ravages of, 204; captures Washington, 204–206.

Cold Harbor, battle of, 363.

Colleges, 469.

Colombia, refuses to lease canal zone, 431.

Colon, at Santiago, 427.

Columbus, discovers America, 2–3.

Compromise of 1850, 317–325.

Concord, at Manila Bay, 424–425.

Concord, expedition to, 63–64.

Confederacy, 338; created, 339; weakness of, 343–345; plans to invade, 349; war with, 349–365; collapse of, 364.

Confederation, Articles of, inefficiency of, 96; sentiment demands change of, 104; anti-Federalists defend, 104–105; Maryland refuses to ratify, 107.

Congress, Continental, recommends boycott, 60; assumes powers, 65–67; weakness of, 66–68; declares independence, 70–71.

Congress, under Articles of Confederation, 96; in Shays' Rebellion, 100–101; organizes Northwest, 107–108; sanctions Constitutional Convention, 113.

Connecticut, charter of, 27; trade laws of, 103; Western claims, 106; factories of, 216; political revolution in, 220–224; 225.

Constellation, victories of, 154; 198; 203.

Constitution, 198; defeats Guerrière, 201–202; 203.

Constitution, drawn up, 114–125; Pennsylvania ratifies, 126–128; Massachusetts ratifies, 128–130; Virginia ratifies, 130–132; adopted, 132; New York ratifies, 133.

Constitutional Convention, called, 112; meets, 114; discusses Virginia plan, 115–118; status of West, 119–120; slave representation, 121–122; slave-trade and Federal control of commerce, 122–

123; shapes frame of government, 124–125.

Contreras, battle at, 311.

Corinth, capture of, 358.

Cornstalk, defeated at Point Pleasant, 82–83.

Cornwallis, Lord, at battle of Long Island, 72–74; faces Washington at Trenton, 76; retires to north New Jersey, 78; invades Virginia, 90; besieged at Yorktown, 90–93.

Coureurs de bois, fur trade of, 37.

Cox, James M., defeated for Presidency, 459.

Crawford, William H., presidential candidate, 262–270.

Crédit Mobilier, 399.

Crime of 1873, 405.

Crisis of 1837, 289–291.

Cross Keys, battle of, 351.

Cuba, revolution in, 422; interest of United States in, 422–423; war in, 426–428; independent, 428.

Culpeper, Lord Thomas, secures revenue bill in Virginia, 32.

Curtis, G. T., 399.

Darlington, William, on Missouri question, 246.

Dartmouth, cargo of tea destroyed, 59–60.

Davis, Henry Winter, 368.

Davis, Jefferson, at Buena Vista, 309; 334; President of Confederacy, 339; 345; 372; 373.

Dawes, Charles G., reconstruction plan of, 461.

Day, Luke, in Shays' Rebellion, 100.

Debts, dispute over English, 143–144.

Declaration of Independence adopted, 71.

Democratic-Republican party, friendly to France, 150–151; organized, 154–155; wins in 1800, 160–162; disintegration of, 260–262.

Dewey, George, victory of Manila Bay, 424–426.

Dickinson, John, 114.

Dickman, General, at Jaulgonne bend, 452–453.

Dinwiddie, Robert, quarrels with Virginia Assembly, 40; sends Washington to warn French, 41.

Discovery, reaches Virginia, 6.

Dole, Sanford B., 418–419.

Don Antonio de Ulloa, 425.

Don Carlos IV, cedes Louisiana to France, 169.

Donelson, Fort, 356; captured, 357; 361.

Dorchester Heights, American fortify, 66.

Douglas, Stephen A., reports Kansas-Nebraska bill, 325; address of, 326; 329; debates with Lincoln, 332–334; returned to Senate, 333; Southern Democrats oppose, 334; Northern Democrats nominate, 337; defeated, 338; 340.

Dred Scott decision, 329–332; South on, 334, 336.

Duane, W. J., 285.

Dudley, Thomas, at Sempringham, 9–11.

Dunbar, Colonel, retreats to Philadelphia, 44.

Duquesne, Fort, French construct, 41; Braddock's expedition against, 42–44; taken by English, 45.

Dutch, settle on Hudson, 13; surrender New Amsterdam, 14.

Dwight, President, 225.

Eaton, J. H., 273.

Education, recent progress of, 468–470.

Electoral Commission, 379–381.

Elkins, Stephen D., 392–393.

Ellsworth, Oliver, 114; 156.

Embargo, passed, 187–188; repealed, 189.

Emigrant Aid Society, 327.

England, desires colonies, 4–5; Baltic trade, 5; 16; seeks economic independence, 16–17; "rotten boroughs," 51; colonies revolt from, 63–95; sues for peace, 80; treaty of peace, 94; disputes over treaty, 143–144; holds Northwest posts, 144–145; Jay's treaty, 147–148; American trade alarms, 181; seizures of, 182; orders in council, 186–187; War of 1812, 195–213; Treaty of Ghent, 212–213; "dumping" in American market, 217–218; Latin-American policy, 255; applauds Monroe Doctrine, 259–260; interferes in Texas, 302; Oregon settlement, 304; during Civil War, 346–347; Venezuela controversy, 419–422.

English colonies, 24; liberty in, 34–35; lack of unity, 40; independent spirit, 51; Stamp Act, 52–55; Townshend acts, 56; independent governments, 60; causes of revolt of, 62.

Erie Canal, 234–236.

Erskine, D. M., 190.

Essex, decision concerning, 185.

Eustis, William, 197.

Eutaw Springs, battle of, 87.

Everett, William, 399.

Ewell, General, at Gettysburg, 360.

Expunging the Senate record, 287–289.

Far West, migration to, 396; railway to, 396–397; growth, 412–413.

Farmers' Alliance, 404.

Fauquier, Governor, 55.

Federal capital, located on Potomac, 140–141.

Federal ratio, 121–122.

Federal Reserve Act, 438–439.

Federalist party, enact Alien and Sedition Laws, 156–157; defeated in election of 1800, 159–160; scheme of, to defeat Jefferson, 160–161; causes of downfall of, 161–162.

Ferguson, Colonel Patrick, defeated at King's Mountain, 86.

Fifth Division on Meuse, 456.

Fillmore, Millard, President, 324; 325.

Finances, of Revolution, 68; of War of 1812, 198–199; of Confederacy, 345–346; of Union, 345–346; of World War, 446.

First Division, at Cantigny, 450; in Marne counter-offensive, 453–454; in Argonne-Meuse, 456.

Fish, value of, to New England, 17.

Flagler, H. M., 384.

Florida, importance of, 172; purchase of, 251–254; 336; secedes, 339; 368; 379.

Flower, R. P., 409.

Foch, Marshal, strategy of, 450–453; counter-offensive of, 453–454.

Foote, Flag-Officer, 357.

Forbes, John, takes Fort Duquesne, 45.

Force Bill of 1833, 281.

Forty-niners, in California, 315.

Fourth Division, on Meuse, 456.

Fox, Charles, rejoices at success of American arms, 61.

France, occupies Ohio region, 40; troops of, at Duquesne, 41; successes in America, 43–44; reverses of, 45; loses American colonies, 48–49; loans to United States, 68; alliance with, 81; sympathy with, 148; wars of, 149–151; Jay's treaty angers, 151; X-Y-Z affair, 152–154; sea battles with, 154; acquires Louisiana, 168–169; sells Louisiana, 171–172; trade decrees, 187; American army in, 448; reverses of, 450–451; peace treaty, 458.

Francis Ferdinand, murder of, 440.

Franklin, Benjamin, at Albany Congress, 38–40; expects submission to Stamp Act, 53; deplores misrepresentation of Americans, 61–62; negotiates Treaty of 1783, 94; 114; in Constitutional Convention, 117; 125.

Frazier's Farm, battle of, 352.

Fredericksburg, 350; 353; battle of, 353.

Free Silver, controversy over, 405–412; Democrats demand, 409–412.

Freedman's Bureau, 369; bill for, 371.

Freeport heresy, 332–333.

Frémont, John C., defeated for Presidency in 1856, 329; 350; at Cross Keys, 351.

French and Indian War, 41–49; effect of, on English colonies, 49.

Frick, Henry C., 385.

Frontenac, Fort, 44; English capture, 45.

Fry, Colonel Joshua, 41.

Fuller, Timothy, on Missouri question, 246.

Fur trade, Dutch carry on, 13; French and English rivals for, 37.

Gage, General, sends force to Concord, 63; attacks Breed's Hill, 64–65.

Gaines' Mill, battle of, 352.

Gallatin, Albert, Secretary of Treasury, 164; demands retrenchment, 165; opposes embargo, 187–188; at Ghent, 212–213.

Gardoqui, offers Spanish treaty, 110.

Garfield, James A., 373; elected President, 399.

Garrison, William Lloyd, 299.

Gates, General, at Saratoga, 79–80; defeated at Camden, 85–86.

Genêt, Citizen, violates American neutrality, 148–151; censures Washington, 149; recalled, 151; 168.

George III, accession of, 51; coerces colonies, 61; 79; receives Adams, 103.

Georgia, British invade, 85; vote of, on Virginia plan, 118; secedes, 339; 356; 361; Sherman devastates, 363; 368; 378.

Germantown, battle at, 81.

Germany, in Samoa, 416–418; interferes in Philippines, 425–426; Venezuela; 429–430; invades Belgium, 441; plots against United States, 443; unrestricted submarine warfare, 443–444; war against, 445; forces defeated, 453–456; armistice, 456.

Gerry, Elbridge, 114; reports compromise in convention, 118–119; fears West, 119–120; fears democracy, 124; in X-Y-Z affair, 152–154.

Gettysburg, battle of, 359–361.

Ghent, treaty of, 212–213.

Glass, Carter, 439.

Glorious Revolution, 33–34.

Gompers, Samuel, builds up labor federation, 387–388.

Gonzales, engagement at, 294.

Goodspeed, reaches Virginia, 6.

Gorham, Nathaniel, 129.

Gorman, A. P., 409.

Gould, George J., 386.

Grant, Ulysses S., western campaign of, 357–359; captures Vicksburg, 358–359; 362; campaign in Virginia, 363–364; Lee surrenders to, 364–365; 366; elected President, 378; reconstruction policy of, 379.

Grasse, Count de, sails for America, 90–91; at Yorktown, 92–93.

Great Lakes, fur trade of, 37; English cut

off from, 44; battle on, 203–204; canal to, 234–236.

Great Meadows, battle at, 41–42.

Greenback party, 398.

Greenbacks, controversy over, 397–399.

Greene, Nathanael, at Breed's Hill, 65; Long Island, 73; southern campaigns of, 86–87.

Grenville, George, secures Stamp Act, 52.

Griswold, George, 221.

Griswold, Roger, 175.

Guadalupe Hidalgo, treaty of, 312.

Guam, ceded to United States, 428.

Guerrière, 194; defeated by *Constitution*, 201–202.

Guilford Court House, battle of, 87.

Hakluyt, Edmund, points out need for colonies, 4–5.

Halifax, Earl of, administers colonial affairs, 51.

Half Moon, in Hudson River, 13.

Hamilton, Alexander, 114; 117; opposes republican government, 124; political creed of, 137–138; active force in government, 139; plans for restoring credit, 139–141; bargain of, on assumption, 140–141; proposes Federal bank, 141; advises suppression of Whiskey Rebellion, 143; 154; 156; influence in Adams's Cabinet, 158–159; breach of, with Adams, 159; 160; opposes Burr for Presidency, 161; shot by Burr, 176.

Hamilton, Colonel Henry, 83; surrenders Vincennes, 83–84.

Hamilton, J. H., 273.

Hamilton, Paul, Secretary of Navy, 197.

Hancock, Governor, 130.

Hanna, Marcus A., 411.

Hardin, Benjamin, on Missouri question, 244.

Harding, Warren G., elected President, 459; at Washington Conference, 460.

Harper's Ferry, John Brown at, 334–335; 347; 351.

Harriot, Thomas, 4.

Harrison, Benjamin, 390; elected President, 402; defeated in 1892, 403; on Hawaii, 418–419.

Harrison, W. H., at Tippecanoe, 194–195; victory on Thames, 203–204; 287; nominated, 300; death, 301.

Hartford Convention, 208–209.

Hauteval, M., 153.

Hawaii, revolution in, 418–419; annexation of, 419.

Hay, Anthony, 57.

Hay-Pauncefote Treaty, 431.

Hayes, Rutherford B., election disputed, 379–381.

Hayne, Robert Y., debate with Webster, 276–277; 374–375.

Henry, Fort, 356; captured, 357.

Henry, Patrick, resolutions on Stamp Act, 53–54; 56; 83; 114; 130; in Virginia convention, 130–132.

Hepburn, W. P., 392.

Hepburn Act, 392–394.

Herrara, President, 305.

Hessians, use of, 70; at Long Island, 72–74; at Trenton, 75–76; at Saratoga, 79–80.

High schools, 469.

Hill, A. P., 352.

Hill, David B., 409.

Hill, D. H., 352.

Hindenburg line, Americans break, 455.

Hobkirk's Hill, battle of, 87.

Holleben, Herr von, 429–430.

Holy Alliance, interferes in America, 255–260.

Hood, General J. B., defeated at Atlanta, 362.

Hooker, "Fighting Joe," defeated at Chancellorsville, 354.

Hoover, Herbert C., 446.

Horizon, 186.

Hottinguer, M., 153.

Houston, Sam, 295; at San Jacinto, 296–297.

Howe, General William, invades New York, 72–75; at Long Island, 73–74; captures Fort Washington, 75; goes into winter quarters, 75; 78; 79; captures Philadelphia, 81.

Hudson, Henry, explores Hudson River, 13.

Hudson River, explored, 13; campaign on, 78; Arnold's plot to open, 88–89.

Hughes, C. E., address at Washington Conference, 460; address of April 15, 1924, 461.

Hull, Captain Isaac, 201–202; 203.

Hull, William, 198; defeated, 199.

Humphrey, Captain, 184–185.

Humphrey, John, at Sempringham, 9–11.

Hutchinson, Thomas, at Albany Congress, 39–41.

Idaho, development of, 412–413.

Illinois, conquered by Clark, 83–84; settled, 232.

Immigration, to New England, 226–228; laws restricting, 466–467.

Indiana, at Santiago, 426–428.

Indiana, 229.

Indians, life of, 1–2; attack Jamestown, 6–7; allied with whites, 37; used in war, 38; at Braddock's defeat, 42–44; raid frontiers, 44; at Fort William Henry, 44; British use in Revolution, 70; with

Burgoyne, 79–80; at Point Pleasant, 82–83; aid British in West, 83–84; defeat St. Clair, 145–146; defeated by Wayne, 146; at Tippecanoe, 194–195.

Initiative and referendum, 433.

Interstate commerce, under Confederation, 101–102.

Interstate Commerce Commission, 392–393.

Iowa, at Santiago, 426–428.

Iroquois, allies of English, 37–38.

Irrigation, 412–413.

Island No. 10, 356.

Jacinto, 346.

Jackson, Andrew, at New Orleans, 209–212; invades Florida, 252; candidate for Presidency, 262–269; elected in 1828, 272; inauguration, 272–273; Cabinet, 273; "Union" toast, 279; opposes nullification, 281–282; United States bank, 282–286; elected in 1832, 285; defies Senate, 287; dinner to expungers, 289; retires, 290–291; 296.

Jackson, F. G., insults Madison, 191.

Jackson, "Stonewall," at Bull Run, 348; 350; Valley campaign, 350–351; Gaines' Mill, 352; Second Manassas, 353; death, 354.

Jackson, Miss., 356; captured, 358.

James I, persecutes Puritans, 7–8; sets up despotism in Virginia, 25; revokes London Co. charter, 26.

James II, despotism of, 33.

Jamestown, founded, 6; harsh rule at, 25; Bacon captures, 29–30; 69.

Jay, John, Treaty of 1783, 94; 114; Jay treaty, 147–148; 160.

Jefferson, Thomas, 56; 69; Declaration of Independence, 71; plan for Northwest territory, 108; 114; political creed, 137–138; influence of, 139; location of capital, 140–141; opposes bank, 142; Genêt annoys, 150; 151; organizes Democratic-Republican party, 154–155; defeated for Presidency, 155; Virginia and Kentucky resolutions, 157; States-rights, 158; tied with Burr, 160–161; elected President, 161; inaugurated, 163; Cabinet, 164; policies, 165–166; attacks judiciary, 167; Louisiana, 167–172; 173; Lewis and Clark expedition, 174–175; prosecutes Burr, 177–179; peaceful coercion, 183; prevents war in 1807, 185; Non-Importation, 186; Embargo, 187; retires, 189–190; gunboats of, 192; 196; advocates manufactures, 216; principles of, in New England, 223–224; 228; Missouri question alarms, 241–242; 250; 256; 266; 270; 470.

Jewel, sails for Massachusetts, 11.

Joffre, Marshal, 446.

Johnson, Andrew, becomes President, 367; reconstruction policy of, 368; struggle of, with radicals, 371–374; swing around circle, 372–373; impeached, 378.

Johnson, Isaac, at Sempringham, 9–11.

Johnson, William, at Albany Congress, 39–41.

Johnson-Lodge bill, 468.

Johnston, Albert Sidney, at Shiloh, 357.

Johnston, Joseph E., 350; at Jackson, 358; defends Atlanta, 362.

Kansas, struggle for, 327–329; 404.

Kansas-Nebraska bill, 325–327.

Kaskaskia, 83.

Kent, Chancellor, 235.

Kentucky, 82; 84; demands open Mississippi, 110; 229; 275; 349; 356; 358.

King, Rufus, 113; 114; 129; fears South, 242; 243; on Missouri question, 248–249.

King's Mountain, battle of, 86.

Kinsey, Charles, 249.

Knox, General Henry, 137.

Knox, Philander C., prosecutes trusts, 390–391.

Ku Klux Klan, 376–378.

Lafayette, Marquis, at Yorktown, 90–93.

La Follette, Robert M., 433; 435.

Laud, Archbishop, persecutes Puritans, 9.

Lawrence, 203–204.

Lawrence, John, 136.

League of Nations, United States rejects, 458–459.

Leander, 182.

Lease, Mary E., 404.

Leclerc, General, in San Domingo, 170.

Lee, General Charles, treachery of, 82; warns Gates, 85–86.

Lee, Fitzhugh, 423.

Lee, Richard Henry, introduces resolution of independence, 71; 96.

Lee, Robert E., captures John Brown, 335; description of, 350; seven days' fighting, 351–353; invades Maryland, 353; at Chancellorsville, 354; Gettysburg campaign, 359–361; campaign of 1864, 363; surrenders, 364–365.

Leopard, attacks *Chesapeake*, 183–185.

Leslie, General, invades Virginia, 90.

Lewis, Meriwether, expedition of, 174–175.

Lexington, battle of, 63–64.

Liliuokalani, Queen, 418–419.

Lincoln, Abraham, Douglas debates, 332–334; nominated in 1860, 337–338; elected, 338; inaugural address, 340–341; forces issue of war, 342; declares blockade, 343; despotic powers, 345; 348; 349; Emancipation Proclamation, 354; 356; murder of, 366–367; reconstruction policy, 367–368; 375; 376; 381.

Lincoln, General, at Saratoga, 79; at Charleston, 85; Shays' Rebellion, 100.

Lincoln-Douglas debates, 332–334.

Little Sarah, 150.

Livingston, R. R., Louisiana Purchase, 171–172.

Livingston, William, combats inflation, 98; 101.

Lloyd George, David, at peace conference, 457–458.

Lodge, H. C., 460.

Long Island, battle of, 72–74.

Longstreet, General, 352; at Gettysburg, 360.

Lookout Mountain, battle of, 362.

Loudoun, Earl of, replaced, 45.

Louis XIV, pensions Charles II, 31.

Louis XVI, and American Revolution, 70.

Louisburg, English capture, 45.

Louisiana, Spain acquires, 49; 167; 168; France acquires, 171; United States buys, 171–172; Burr's plot, 176–178; 336; secedes, 339; 356; reconstruction of, 376; 379; 380.

L'Ouverture, Toussaint, dictator of San Domingo, 170.

Lowell, James Russell, 299.

Lowell, John, 217.

Loyalists, in American Revolution, 69–70; treatment of, 144.

Ludwell, Philip, 32.

Lundy, Benjamin, 298.

Lusitania, sinking of, 442.

Lyon, Matthew, 156.

Macedonian, 203.

Macon, G., 356.

Macon Bill No. 2, 192.

Madison, James, address in Virginia Assembly, 111; efforts for closer union, 111–112; 114; appearance, 117; address in convention, 118, 120; 130; argues for ratification, 130–132; revenue bill, 135–136; 157; Secretary of State, 164; 165; annexes West Florida, 173–174; President, 189–190; negotiations with England, 190–193; war message, 195–196; war measures, 197; illness, 199; flight from Bladensburg, 206; 212; 213.

Maine, destroyed in Havana harbor, 423–424.

Maine, applies for statehood, 247–249; 275.

Malietoa, King, 416–418.

Malvern Hill, battle of, 353.

Manassas, first battle, 347–349; second battle, 353.

Marbois, Barbé, negotiates sale of Louisiana, 172.

Maria Teresa, at Santiago, 427.

Marion, Francis, 85.

Marne, Americans defend, 451–453; retreat from, 454.

Marne salient, formation of, 450–451; reduction of, 453–454; counter-offensive, 453–454.

Marshall, James W., 314.

Marshall, John, 130; in X-Y-Z affair, 152–154; 163; 167; Burr decision, 178–179; 189; 273.

Martin, Luther, 114; 178.

Maryland, founded, 13–14; tobacco staple of, 18–19; trade of, 23; 28; proposes national domain, 107; suggests national convention, 112; ratifies Constitution, 130; Lee invades, 353; 356.

Mason, George, Virginia bill of rights, 71; 114; 120; opposes Federal control of commerce, 122; denounces slavery, 123; 124; 130.

Mason, James M., reads Calhoun's address, 320–322.

Mason, John, Confederate commissioner, 346.

Massachusetts, settlement of, 11; second Stuart despotism in, 32; expels Andros, 32–33; charter of 1691, 34; charter annulled, 60; Shays' Rebellion, 99–100; Western claims, 106; 113; ratifies Constitution, 128–130; factories of, 216; 220; 225; 275; 426–428.

Massachusetts Bay Company, charter of, 10–11.

Mawhood, Colonel Charles, defeated at Princeton, 77–78.

Mayflower, voyage, 8–9.

McAdoo, Secretary, 438.

McClellan, George B., organizes army of Potomac, 349; peninsula campaign of, 350–352; at Antietam, 353.

McClernand, General, 357.

McCormick reaper, 397.

McDowell, Irvin, at Bull Run, 347–349; 350; 351.

McDuffie, George, 374–375.

McHenry, James, 159.

McKinley, William, 390; tariff of, 402–403; elected President, 411–412; war message of, 424.

McKinley tariff, 402–403.

McLane, Louis, 285.

Meade, General George, at Gettysburg, 359–361.

Mercer, General Hugh, at battle of Princeton, 77.

Merry, Anthony, 177.

Metropolitan Division, in Argonne, 456.

Mexico, Cortez conquers, 3; Burr plans to conquer, 178; admits settlers to Texas, 292–293; invades Texas, 296–298; forces war on United States, 303–304; Palo Alto, 305–306; Taylor invades, 307–309; Scott invades, 309–312; peace with, 312.

Mexico City, captured, 312.

Missionary Ridge, battle of, 362.

Mississippi, secedes, 339; invasion of, 359; 368; reconstruction in, 376; 378.

Mississippi River, French forts on, 40; 143; 167; opened, 168; 171; 173; Burr expedition on, 178; 229; 344; 349; operations on, 356–359, 361.

Missouri, slavery question in, 241–250; 275; 356.

Missouri Compromise, 241–250; repeal of, 326–327; declared unconstitutional, 331.

Mohawk River, fur trade follows, 37.

Molina, at Jamestown, 25.

Molino del Rey, battle of, 311.

Monmouth Court House, battle at, 82.

Monroe, James, Minister to France, 151; 171; 172; inauguration, 251–252; Monroe Doctrine, 254–260.

Monroe Doctrine, development of, 255–260; influence of, 259–260; 415; Venezuelan controversy, 420–422.

Montcalm, Marquis de, commands French armies in America, 44; defeated before Quebec, 47–48; death of, 48.

Monterey, siege of, 307–308.

Montmorency, battle on, 46.

Montreal, fur trade of, 37; captured by English, 48.

Morgan, J. Pierpont, defeat of, by Carnegie, 385–386; interview with Roosevelt, 390–391; interview with Cleveland, 408; 436.

Morris, Gouverneur, opposes equality for West, 120; opposes representation for slaves, 121; 167.

Morris, Robert, 114; 136.

Morton, Senator, 380.

Mt. Vernon, conference at, 111.

"Mugwumps," 399.

Murfreesboro, battle of, 358.

Napoleon, acquires Louisiana, 169; attacks San Domingo, 170; sells Louisiana, 171–172; trade decrees of, 187; repeals decrees, 192–193.

Navigation Acts, provisions of, 22.

Necessity, Fort, 40; defeat of Washington at, 41–42.

Neptune, voyage of, 180.

Newcastle, Duke of, sends troops to America, 41.

New England, fisheries, 17; ship-building, 18; trade, 18; free labor, 18; semi-independence, 27; second Stuart despotism, 32; resists Stamp Act, 54–55; Sugar Act of 1764, 57; war in, 64; British raid, 70; commercial policy, 102–104; asks Spanish treaty, 110; Federal control of commerce, 122–123; secession sentiment, 175–176; carrying trade, 180–181; embargo, 188–189; 196; War of 1812, 199–201; discontent of, 207; ultimatum of, 208–209; industrial revolution, 214–220; political revolution, 220–222; change in population, 224–228; 276.

New Jersey, British occupy, 75; paper money of, 97–98; taxed by neighbors, 101–102.

New Mexico Territory, acquisition of, 312; in Compromise of 1850, 317–325.

New Netherlands, founded, 13; conquered, 14.

New Orleans, battle of, 209–212.

Newport, Captain Christopher, reaches Virginia, 6.

New York, at Santiago, 426–428.

New York, Indians of, 37; Assembly suspended, 56; British invade, 72–75; triple invasion of, 78–80; claims in West, 106; ratifies Constitution, 133; Erie Canal, 234–236; 275.

New York City, British capture, 74; Congress at, 134; during embargo, 189; celebrates opening of Erie Canal, 236.

Niagara, in battle of Lake Erie, 204.

Nicholson, Sir Francis, 34.

Nicolls, Richard, conquers New Netherlands, 14.

Nipsic, at Samoa, 416–417.

Non-Importation, Act of 1806, 186; 191.

North, Lord, 93.

North Carolina, founded, 14; enters Union, 133; secedes, 343; 368; 376; 378.

Northern Securities Company, 390–391.

Northwest, British hold posts in, 144–145; Indian war in, 145–146.

Northwest Territory, organized, 107–108.

Nullification, South Carolina, 280–282.

Olympia, at Manila Bay, 424–425.

Onis, Don Luis de, 252–254.

Oquenda, at Santiago, 427.

Oregon, voyage of, 430.

Oregon, 379; development of, 412–413; boundary settlement, 304.

Orlando, Vittorio, at peace conference, 457–458.

Oswego, captured by French, 44.

Otis, H. G., 208; 209; mission of, 212.

Paine, Thomas, 107.

Pakenham, General, defeated at New Orleans, 209–212.

Palo Alto, battle of, 305–306.
Panama Canal, 430–432.
Paredes, Mariano, 305.
Parker, Alton B., 436.
Parker, Captain John, at Lexington, 63–64.
Parker, Theodore, 335.
Paterson, William, 114; opposes Virginia plan, 116; opposes representation for slaves, 121.
Patronage, Federal, Jefferson's policy, 166.
Payne, Sereno E., 434.
Payne-Aldrich tariff, 434–435.
Pemberton, General, at Vicksburg, 358–359.
Peninsula campaign, 350–352.
Penn, William, 14.
Pennsylvania, founded, 14; 44; taxes New Jersey, 101; ratifies Constitution, 126–128; 264; 276; oil industry of, 384–385.
Percy, Captain George, describes Virginia sickness, 7.
Perry, Captain O. H., victory on Lake Erie, 203–204.
Pershing, General J. J., plans great army, 447–448; trains army for open fighting, 449; reduces St. Mihiel salient, 454–455; in Argonne-Meuse offensive, 455–456.
Philadelphia, British occupy, 81; British evacuate, 82; convention at, 114; celebrates, 128; 132; welcomes Genêt, 149.
Philip, John W., 428.
Philippine Islands, United States conquers, 424–426; ceded to United States, 428.
Phipps, Henry, 385.
Pickens, Andrew, 85.
Pickering, Timothy, 175; 207; 209; 221.
Pickett's charge, 360–361.
Pierce, Franklin, elected President, 325.
Pike, James S., on reconstruction, 374–375.
Pilgrims, sail, 8; at Plymouth, 9.
Pillow, Fort, 358.
Pillow, General, 357.
Pinckney, C. C., 114; 123; France refuses to receive, 152; in X-Y-Z affair, 152–154; Hamilton supports, for Presidency, 159.
Pinckney, Charles, address of, at Trenton, 102, 114; in convention, 121.
Pindall, James, address of, on Missouri question, 245.
Pinkney, William, address of, on Missouri question, 247–248.
Pitt, William, Secretary of State, 45.

Pitt, William, the younger, denounces war against Americans, 61; refuses trade concessions, 103.
Pittsburg, 143; 230–231; riot at, 382; 384.
Plymouth, England, Pilgrims leave, 8.
Plymouth, New England, Pilgrims found, 9.
Polk, James K., President, 302–303; desires California, 304; war message, 305; signs Mexican Treaty, 312.
Pope, General John, at second Manassas, 353.
Populist party, formation of, 404–405.
Port Republic, battle of, 351.
Porter, General, at Gaines' Mill, 352.
Porto Rico, ceded to United States, 428.
President, defeats Little Belt, 194; 198; captured, 203.
Preston, Levi, 50.
Princeton, battle of, 77–78.
Prinzip, Gavrilo, 439.
Progressive party, nominates Roosevelt, 437.
Progressive Republican League, 435.
Pueblo Indians, customs of, 2.
Puritans, groups of, 7; 9; exodus of, 11; 17.
Putnam, General Israel, at battle of Long Island, 73–74; settles Ohio, 109.

Quakers, 12; found Pennsylvania, 14.
Quebec, founded, 36; fur trade of, 37; taken by English, 46–48.
Quebec Act, passed, 60.

Rainbow Division, 452.
Raleigh, at Manila Bay, 424–425.
Rall, Colonel, defeated at Trenton, 75–76.
Randolph, Edmund, 114; presents Virginia plan, 115; 124; 130; advises Virginia to ratify, 132; 137; 178.
Randolph, John, 178; 186; mocks unpreparedness in 1812, 198–199; opposes Missouri Compromise, 250; 268; 275.
Rankin, Christopher, 245.
Reconstruction of Southern States, 367–381.
Reina Cristina, at Manila Bay, 425.
Revere, Paul, ride of, 63.
Rheims, 450; effort to pocket, 452–453.
Rhode Island, charter of, 27; inflation, 98; ignores convention, 113; enters Union, 133.
Richmond, 349; defense of, in 1862, 350–353; captured by Grant, 363.
Riedesel, Baroness, at Saratoga, 80.
Robinson, John, 8.
Rochambeau, General, Yorktown campaign, 90–93.
Rockefeller, John D., monopolizes oil business, 383–385.

Rockingham, Lord, becomes Premier in 1782, 93.

Rolfe, John, cures Indian tobacco, 19.

Roosevelt, Theodore, prosecutes trusts, 390–391; on trust regulation, 391–394; threatens Germany with war, 429–430; construction of Panama Canal, 431–432; defeated for Republican nomination in 1912, 435–436; Progressives nominate, 437.

Root, Elihu, 460.

Rose, George, 190.

Rosecrans, W. S., 358; at Chickamauga, 361–362.

Ross, General Robert, invades Maryland, 204; at battle of Bladensburg, 205; captures Washington, 205–206.

Rotch, Francis, his tea destroyed, 59–60.

"Rum, Romanism, and Rebellion," 399–400.

Rush, Richard, 255.

Rutledge, John, 114.

Ryan, Thomas F., 436.

St. Clair, General Arthur, defeated, 145–146.

St. Lawrence River, Cartier explores, 36; shapes destiny of Canada, 37; English fleet enters, 45.

St. Leger, Colonel, invades New York, 78–80.

St. Mihiel salient, reduction of, 454–455.

Salisbury, Lord, Venezuelan note, 420–421.

Samoa, contest over, 415–418.

Sampson, Admiral, at battle of Santiago, 426–428.

San Domingo, defies Napoleon, 170.

San Francisco, 397; 413.

San Ildefonso, treaty of, 169.

San Jacinto, battle of, 296–297.

Sandy Hook, light on, taxed by New Jersey, 102.

Sandys, Sir Edwin, 8; 25–26.

Santa Anna, President of Mexico, 293–294; invades Texas, 294–297; captured, 297–298; regains power, 308; defeated at Buena Vista, 308–309; in Mexico City campaign, 311–312.

Santiago, siege of, 426; battle of, 427–428.

Sarah Constant, reaches Virginia, 6.

Saratoga, surrender of Burgoyne at, 80.

Saunders, Admiral, 45.

Savannah, British capture, 85.

"Scalawags," 376; 377.

Schley, Admiral, at battle of Santiago, 426–428.

Schomburgk line, 419–420.

Schurz, Carl, 399.

Schuyler, General, in Saratoga campaign, 79.

Schwab, Charles M., 385; 386.

Scotch-Irish, in South Carolina, 85; in West, 105.

Scott, Sir William, *Essex* decision of, 185.

Scott, Winfield, captures Vera Cruz, 309–310; at Cerro Gordo, 310; captures Mexico City, 311–312; 347; 348.

Secession, West threatens, 110; New England threatens, 175–176; of cotton States, 339; 341; of second group, 343.

Second Division at Belleau Wood, 451; in Marne counter-offensive, 453–454; in Argonne-Meuse fighting, 456.

Sedan, capture of, 456.

Selma, 356.

Sempringham, conference at, 9.

Servants, indentured, in Virginia and Maryland, 20.

Seward, W. H., opposes Toombs bill, 329; loses Republican nomination, 337; promises to Southern commissioners, 342; 348; 354.

Seymour, Horatio, 378.

Shannon, 203.

Shattuck, Job, 99.

Shays, Daniel, leads rebellion, 100.

Shays' Rebellion, 99–100.

Shepard, General, defeats Shays, 100.

Sherman, John, Antitrust Law, 388–390; 406; Cuban note, 423.

Sherman, Roger, 114; 118; 120; 124.

Sherman, General W. T., 309; captures Atlanta, 362; march to sea, 362–363.

Sherman Antitrust Law, 388–390; enforcement of, 390–391.

Sherman Silver Purchase Act, 406.

Shields, General, at Port Republic, 351.

Shiloh, battle of, 357; 361.

Shippen, Margaret, 87.

Sigsbee, Captain, 424.

Slater, Samuel, 214.

Slave-trade, 122–123.

Slavery, use of, in New England, 18; thrives in Virginia, 20; in South Carolina, 21; in West, 108; dispute in convention, 121–123; Mason denounces, 123; in Missouri, 241–250; in Texas, 298–302; in California and New Mexico, 312–325; in Kansas, 327–329; Dred Scott decision on, 329–332; Emancipation Proclamation, 354–356; end of, in South, 368–369; Thirteenth Amendment, 368.

Slidell, John, Mexican envoy, 304–305; Confederate commissioner, 346.

Smith, Captain John, 16; on New England fisheries, 17.

Smith, Robert, 188.

Snow, Isaac, 129.

Soissons, 450; 453.

Somers, Sir George, 4–5.
Sonnino, Baron Sidney, at peace conference, 457–458.
Sons of Liberty, 54.
South Carolina, founded, 14; British invade, 85; Greene's campaigns in, 86–87; ratifies Constitution, 130; fights tariff, 276–282; nullification, 276–282; 336; secedes, 339; 342; 361; 368; reconstruction, 374–376; 379; 380.
South Carolina Exposition, 276.
Spain, colonies, 3–4; war on England, 90; closes Mississippi, 110; treaty of 1795, 168; cedes Louisiana to France 168–169; sells Florida, 252–254; war with United States, 424–428; peace with, 428.
Spanish Armada, defeated, 4.
Specie circular, 290.
Speedwell, 8.
Spottsylvania, battle of, 363.
Squatter sovereignty, 327.
Stamp Act, passed, 52; opposition to, 52–55; repealed, 55.
Stamp Act Congress, 54–55.
Standard Oil Company, 384–385.
Stanton, Secretary, 355.
Stark, General John, at Bennington, 79.
States-rights, Jefferson defends, 138; Hamilton opposes, 142; 158; New England espouses, 206–209; South returns to, 244–245; Hayne advocates, 276–277; nullification tests, 281–282; weakens Confederacy, 345.
Stevens, Thaddeus, 368; address on reconstruction, 370–371; 372.
Stewart, Senator, 405.
Stirling, Lord, at battle of Long Island, 73–74.
Stowe, Harriet Beecher, 334.
Sugar Act of 1764, New England resents, 57; hastens Revolution, 57–58.
Sullivan, General, 73.
Sumner, Charles, denounces Kansas-Nebraska bill, 325; 368.
Sumter, Fort, 341–343.
Sumter, Thomas, 85.
Sutter, John A., 314.

Taft, William H., President, 434; defends Payne-Aldrich tariff, 435; nominated in 1912, 435–436; defeated, 437.
Talbot, 11.
Talleyrand, X-Y-Z affair, 152–154; 169; Louisiana, 171–173.
Tallmadge, James, Jr., his amendment, 241; address of, 242; 245.
Taney, Roger B., removes deposits, 285–286; Dred Scott decision, 329–332; 340.
Tariff, of 1816, 218–219; of 1824, 274–275; of 1828, 275–276; of 1832, 280; of 1833,

281; Cleveland's message, 401–402; McKinley, 402–403; Wilson, 403–404; Payne-Aldrich, 434–435; Underwood, 438.
Taylor, John W., 243.
Taylor, Zachary, at Palo Alto, 305–306; drives Mexicans over Rio Grande, 306–307; captures Monterey, 307–308; at Buena Vista, 308–309; President, 317; death of, 324.
Tea, duty on, 59; destroyed in Boston harbor, 59–60.
Tennessee, settled, 105–106; 229; 230; 275; secedes, 343; 349; 358; 368; 374; 378; ratifies Nineteenth Amendment, 465–466.
Tenure-of-Office Act, 378.
Teran, Manuel de Mier, invades Texas, 293.
Texas, claim to, surrendered, 253–254; settlement of, 292–293; Teran occupies, 293–294; Santa Anna invades, 294–298; expels Mexicans, 296–298; asks annexation, 298; annexation postponed, 299; English interference with, 302; annexed, 303; 312; 336; secedes, 339; 349; 368; 378; 426–428; 443.
Thayer, Eli, Emigrant Aid Society, 327.
Theocracy, in Massachusetts, 12; in New England, 220–224.
Third Division, at Château-Thierry, 451; at Jaulgonne Bend, 452.
Thomas, George H., at Chickamauga, 362.
Thomas, Jesse B., 249.
Thomas, Lorenzo, 378.
Thompson, General, 129.
Thornton, Colonel, at New Orleans, 211–212.
Thurston, Charles, 104.
Ticonderoga, English failure at, 45; British take, 79.
Tidewater Co., 384–385.
Tilden, S. J., election disputed, 379–381.
Tillman, Benjamin R., 393.
Tippecanoe, battle of, 195.
Tobacco, 18–20.
Tobacco trade, Navigation Acts injure, 22–23.
Tom Thumb, locomotive, 238.
Toombs bill, 329.
Topeka constitution, 328.
Tories, in Revolution, 69–70; at King's Mountain, 86; in Treaty of 1783; 94, 143, 144.
Townshend, Charles, on Stamp Act, 52; secures act taxing colonies, 56.
Townshend Acts, passed, 56; repealed, 58–59.
Travis, W. B., defends Alamo, 295–296.
Treaty of 1783, 94; disputed, 143–144.

Trent, 346.
Trenton, at Samoa, 416–417.
Trenton, battle of, 75–76.
Trist, N. P., Mexican treaty, 312.
Trusts, 385–387; prosecutions of, 390–391; regulation of, 391–393.
Tucker, Dean Josiah, prophecy of, 96.
Tuyl, Baron, 256.
Tyler, John, Vice-President, 300; President, 301; annexes Texas, 301–303.

Uncle Tom's Cabin, 334.
Underwood, Oscar, tariff bill, 438; 460.
Union Pacific R. R., 396–397.
United States, 198; captures *Macedonian,* 203.
United States Steel Corporation, 386; 394.
Upshur, Abel P., 301.

Valley Forge, American camp at, 81–82.
Van Buren, Martin, 273; 286; President, 287; 299; 302.
Vandalia, at Samoa, 416–417.
Vanderbilt, W. H., 387.
Van Rensselaer, General, defeated, 199.
Van Rensselaer, Stephen, 268.
Venezuela, controversy with England, 419–422; German threat to, 429–430.
Vera Cruz, 303; siege of, 309–310.
Vergennes, 93–94.
Vicksburg, capture of, 358–359; 361; 363.
Vigilancia, 444.
Vincennes, George Rogers Clark takes, 83–84.
Virginia, settled, 6; resources, 16; tobacco, 18–19; servants, 20; slavery, 20–21; Navigation Acts, 22–23; Assembly of, 26; Parliament conquers, 28; Bacon's Rebellion, 29–30; second Stuart despotism, 31–32; Townshend Acts, 56–57; committee of correspondence, 59; proposes independence, 71; invaded, 90–93; claims in West, 106; Annapolis convention, 111–112; ratifies Constitution, 130–132; opposes assumption, 140; 155; Western migration from, 230; 275; secedes, 343; 356.
Virginia and Kentucky resolutions, 157.
Virginia Company of London, 5, 6, 7, 25.
Virginia Magna Charta, 26.
Virginia plan, 115–118.
Viviani, M., 446.
Vizcaya, at Santiago, 427.
von Bernstorff, 443.
von Hindenburg, offensives of 450–451; offensive of July 15, 1918, 452–453; defeated, 453–454; faces disaster, 456.
von Steuben, Baron, at Valley Forge, 82; in Virginia, 90.
Vulture, 88–89.

Wade, Benjamin F., denounces Kansas-Nebraska bill; 325; 368.
Waite, Governor, 404.
War of 1812, declared, 195–196; early defeats, 199; naval battles, 201–204; conclusion, 212–213.
Washington, city, captured, 206; 349; 351; 353.
Washington Conference, 459–461.
Washington, Fort, Howe captures, 75.
Washington, George, 40; journey to Ohio, 41; Fort Necessity, 41–42; Braddock's expedition, 42; 56; described, 65–66; at Boston, 65–66; difficulties of, 67; at New York, 72–74; retreat of, 74–75; crosses Delaware, 75; at Trenton, 75–76; eludes Cornwallis, 76; Princeton, 77–78; Chads Ford and Germantown, 81; Valley Forge, 81–82; Monmouth Court House, 82; Yorktown, 90–93; Chesapeake-Ohio canal, 109–111; Constitutional Convention, 113; 114; 130; President, 134; inauguration, 135; Cabinet, 137; 142; Whiskey Rebellion, 143; St. Clair's defeat, 145–146; 147; Genêt, 149–151; 155.
Washington State, development of, 412–413.
Watauga, founded, 105.
Wayne, Anthony, 90; defeats Indians, 146.
"We the people," Madison explains, 131.
Weaver, James B., 405.
Webster, Daniel, on manufactures, 218–220; 268; 275; debate with Hayne, 277–278; 284; 286; 287; expunging, 288; 299; 301; March Seventh address, 323; 324.
West, the, war in, 82–84; settlement, 105–109; claims to, 106; restrictions on proposed, 119–120; Spain tries to strangle, 167–168; French in Louisiana, 171; explorations in, 174–175; Burr's plots, 176–178; wants war, 194; New Englanders in, 224–225; migration to, 229–232; life in, 232–234; plans for canals to, 234–237; railways to, 237–240; importance of, 239–240; asks inflation, 398–399; dissatisfaction in, 401; radicals of, 403–405; Free Silver, 406–412; 415.
West Florida, annexation of, 173–174.
West Indies, 57; 90.
West Point, plot to betray, 88–89.
West Virginia, 356.
Weyler, Valeriano, harshness of, in Cuba, 422–423.
Whiskey Rebellion, 142–143.
White, Abraham, opposes Constitution, 129.
White Camelia, 378.
Wilderness, battle of, 363.

Wilkes, Captain Charles, 346.
Wilkinson, James, plots with Burr, 177–179.
William II, of Germany, threat of, to Monroe Doctrine, 430; 441; 443; abdicates, 456.
William Henry, Fort, French capture, 44.
William of Orange, made king of England, 33.]
Wilmot Proviso, 316; 317.
Wilson, James, 114; defends Virginia plan, 116; champion of Constitution in Pennsylvania, 127.
Wilson, Woodrow, nominated, 436–437; inaugural address, 437–438; tariff lobby, 438; Federal Reserve Act, 438–439; neutrality, 441; submarine campaign, 442–443; war message, 444–445; 447; peace conference, 456–458; League of Nations, 459.
Winchester, battle of, 351.
Winder, W. H., 198· defeated at Bladensburg, 204–206.

Wingfield, Edward-Maria, 4.
Winthrop, John, 9–11.
Wirt, William, 178; 206; 254–260.
Wise, Governor, 329; 335.
Wolcott, Oliver, Jr., 223–224.
Wolfe, James, expedition of, against Quebec, 45–48; death of, 48.
Women's rights, 463–466; pageant for, 464–465.
Women's suffrage, 464; amendment grants, 465–466.
Worth, General, at Monterey, 307–308.

X-Y-Z affair, 152–154.

Yancey, William L., Charleston address of, 335–336.
Yeardley, Sir George, establishes Virginia Assembly, 26.
Yorktown, Cornwallis surrenders, 90–93.
Yrujo, Don Carlos Martinez, 173.

Zimmerman, Foreign Minister, Mexican note of, 443.